In Plain Sight

Tom Smart and Lee Benson

In Plain Sight

The Startling Truth Behind the Elizabeth Smart Investigation

CHICAGO
REVIEW
PRESS

Library of Congress Cataloging-in-Publication Data
Smart, Tom, 1953–
    In plain sight : the startling truth behind the Elizabeth Smart investigation / Tom
Smart and Lee Benson.— 1st ed.
        p.   cm.
    ISBN 1-55652-579-6
    1. Smart, Elizabeth, 1987– Kidnapping, 2002. 2. Kidnapping—Utah—Salt Lake
City—Case studies. 3. Missing children—Utah—Salt Lake City—Case studies. 4. Crim-
inal investigation—Utah—Salt Lake City—Case studies. I. Benson, Lee, 1948– II. Title.
HV6603.S63S65 2005
364.15'4'09792258—dc22   2004024519

Cover and interior design: Laura Lindgren Design

First edition
Published by Chicago Review Press, Incorporated
814 North Franklin Street
Chicago, Illinois 60610
ISBN 1-55652-579-6
Printed in the United States of America
5 4 3 2 1

To all the volunteers who unselfishly gave their time,
energy, and resources to help bring Elizabeth home

Acknowledgments

THE SEARCH

We would like to thank the thousands who helped in the search effort, especially those in the neighborhood who gave so much in the initial weeks, and the literally hundreds of business and service organizations that donated food, supplies, lodging, transportation, printing, and other services. Our family will never forget your kindness. Also the tireless efforts of the hundreds in law enforcement, including the SLCPD; FBI; Utah State Crime Lab; Utah Highway Patrol; and various sheriff, police, and governmental entities across the state of Utah, culminating with the superb work of the Sandy City Police Department. Law enforcement efforts to find Elizabeth went well beyond the call of duty. We would like to commend Rick Dinse and Cory Lyman. Although we disagreed on many points (and I suspect we still do on some), Salt Lake City and Ketchum are lucky to have two such dedicated police chiefs. Cory, in particular, has made it a point to travel around the country with David Smart, addressing police groups about lessons learned from the Elizabeth Smart investigation. A most heartfelt thank-you to Special Agent Mick Fennerty of the FBI for your indefatigable drive and determination. Thanks, too, to all those who stepped forward to identify the kidnappers and secure Elizabeth's safe return, especially Tom and Lisa Holbrook for their uncommon selflessness. And finally, thanks to the local and national media who played such an important role in raising awareness throughout the search for Elizabeth—with a special thanks to John Walsh.

THE BOOK

This book could not have been written without the help, cooperation, and assistance of many people. Foremost is my wife, Heidi, who put up with my mania, not only during the search, but also during the 18 months spent writing this book. The authors feel a great debt of gratitude to the following, who contributed their personal experiences, their expertise, and their talents. To Joan Harrison and Judy Farkas who led us to the Dystel/Goderich Literary Agency. We couldn't ask for a more professional and talented group to represent us than Jane Dystel, Miriam Goderich, and Leslie Josephs. To Chicago Review Press, particularly Cynthia Sherry, who was willing to publish this story. To editor Lisa Rosenthal, who took the time to skillfully and thoughtfully hone this story. A writer couldn't wish for a more considerate editor. To Lisa Dillman, thanks for adding your expert copyediting skill to this project. To Gerilee Hundt, managing editor, and Allison Felus, production editor, for their thoroughness and fine attention to detail. To the proofreader, David Clark, thanks for the great backup work. To Catherine Bosin, head publicist, for her time and expert attention.

Many helped review the manuscript before we had a publisher and gave helpful edits and critiques. They include: Charles and Dorotha Smart, Angela Dumke, Dee Benson, Eric Benson, Kerri Benson, Ray Grass, Dewain Campbell, Ravell Call, Elaine Jarvik, Tom Fenske, Troy Duffin, Linda Sillitoe, Emma Lou Thayne, Chris Thomas, Susan Whitney, Amy Donaldson, Lucy Dillon Kinkead, Liz Abel, Larry and Jan Rubenstein, Kathi Soper, and Jim Parkinson.

Well over a hundred interviews were conducted specifically for this book, and many others for Lee Benson's *Deseret News* columns during the search for Elizabeth. While some individuals at the *Salt Lake Tribune* and in law enforcement have asked to remain anonymous, we would like to thank the following for their contributions: Ray Adame, Phil Adams, Suann Adams, Julie Adkison, Sterling Allan, Annette Anderson, Mayor Rocky Anderson, Russell Banz, N. J. Behunin, Ryan Blake, Debbie Boede, Joyce Brooks, Dick Camp, Evelyn Camp, Sierra Smart Campbell, Karen Christensen, Dora Corbett, Vickie Cottrell, Dawn Davis, Lindsey Dawson, Randy Dryer, Paul "Bomber" Dubois, Angela Smart Dumke, Zeke Dumke III,

Pamela Een, Vincent "Bub" Farrell, Special Agent Augustus "Mick" Fennerty IV, Mike Freed, Jake Garn, Kathleen Garn, Judy Gaspers, Melinda Giffard, Mike Grass, Jamie Gutierrez, Rodger Hardy, Dusty Harrington, Harold Harris, Delaun Hendrickson, Lisa Mitchell Holbrook, Tom Holbrook, Tim Hollinger, Charlene Holmstrom, Larry Holmstrom, Sharon Johnson, Karen Jones, Peggy Kemp, Virl Kemp, Christy Kinney, Deputy Gus Kurupas, David Lamb, Don Lane, Doug Larsen, Missy Larsen, Joe Lenge, Kate Levier, sandaFer loGan, Chief Cory Lyman, Robert McDonald, Paul Mecham, Pastor Bob Mentze, Amber Merriweather, Charlie Miller (the best milkman a neighborhood could ask for), Roy Miranda, Debbie Mitchell, Irene Mitchell, Shirl Mitchell, Tim Mitchell, David Morrow, Neth Moul, Rudi Mueller, Darrell Newbold, Dalene Nielson, Debbie Norris, Dean Oliver, Rick Olsen, Bill O'Neal, Patrick Orr, Doug Owens, Cynthia Smart Owens, Brent Pack, Heidi Perry, Charles Pickett, Nancy Pomeroy, Rafe Potres, David Poulson, Captain Glen Revell, Angela Ricci, Katherine Ricci, Cody Richmond, Deputy Mark Robinson, Marcia Roundy, Clay Ruis, Roger Ruis, Laura Seitz, Mike Sibbett, Amanda Smart, Charles Smart, Chris Smart, David Smart, Dorotha Smart, Heidi Smart, Ingrid Smart, Julie Smart, Nicole Smart, Linda Sosa, Terri Sparks, Craig Sudbury, Mike Sweet, Robert Swenson, Shirley Tajedini, Chris Thomas, Derrick Thompson, Deputy Manuel Vargas, Mack Voorhees, Karl West, C. Samuel West, Dru White, Lee Willis, Kathy Wilson, Ted Wilson, Rebecca Woodridge, and Steve Wright.

Introduction

Mark Twain advised, "Write what you know." In the pages that follow I have written what I personally know about the kidnapping and rescue of my niece, Elizabeth Smart.

Much of the information comes from my own experiences during the nine months Elizabeth was missing as I stayed true to my own monomania, a family trait of dogged—sometimes blind—pursuit that the kidnapping fully awakened and this book attempts to describe. I have made every effort to portray my actions, for better or worse, in a completely unvarnished light.

A good deal more of the information comes from research by my brother, David, who exhibited the same resolute behavior in putting together the pieces of this book as he did in searching for Elizabeth. David conducted key interviews and edits with an accuracy and tenacity that would make any journalist proud. In all, we consulted hundreds of sources, from family members to law enforcement to media transcripts to eyewitnesses, to paint as complete a picture as possible of what happened and why.

From the start, David, Lee, and I shared the same goal: to let the story tell itself. A few names have been changed, as noted by an *, to protect the innocent. Otherwise, the ordeal is laid out as it happened and as we lived it.

We've made every effort to report accurately, despite the passage of time, all conversations, meetings, memorandums, law enforcement procedures, and other communications that are represented or re-created in these pages. This wasn't as difficult as we first feared. Many details of the kidnapping were so well documented that multiple sources for most information proved the rule rather than the exception. Additionally, in the final weeks before

Elizabeth's rescue, David and I recorded virtually all phone conversations. Much of the dialogue in the latter part of the book is verbatim.

The life of my coauthor, Lee Benson, has been intertwined with mine for more than twenty-five years, not just at the *Deseret Morning News* (formerly the *Deseret News*), but on a much more personal level. From the first day of the kidnapping until Elizabeth returned, Lee lived this case. As a volunteer, he was searching from the first day, and as a journalist his work was unparalleled. I'm lucky to have him as a cowriter, but even more grateful to have him as a friend.

One person who was not consulted for information was Elizabeth. Since her return, I, along with the rest of her extended family, have spent time with Elizabeth. We have ridden horses with her, visited her home, been with her at family gatherings, teased her, and been thrilled to stand back and watch her return to a normal life. But we have not personally asked her to talk about her abduction. As her father, Ed, wisely said after she returned—what happened to Elizabeth is Elizabeth's story to tell, or not to tell, as she sees fit.

We have included certain details about the kidnapping that Elizabeth felt comfortable enough to share with various members of the family, and in some cases the media. These personal insights, along with information we collected from a number of eyewitnesses who saw Elizabeth during her captivity, contributed greatly to our ability to produce a general picture of when and where she went.

The narrative charts two circuitous courses that began and ended at the same place. The first is the one traveled by all of us who were searching for Elizabeth: family, volunteers, law enforcement, the media, and everyone praying at home. The second is the one traveled by Elizabeth and her captors. To me, one of the most haunting aspects of the kidnapping is how these courses so often intertwined and yet for so long failed to collide. Elizabeth truly was hidden in plain sight.

For perspective on the "why" of the kidnapping, considerable research went into the lives of Brian David Mitchell and his wife, Wanda Barzee Mitchell. We interviewed family members, friends, coworkers, and associates of the Mitchells to better understand how they came to stray so far from the path of normalcy.

People have asked me what compelled me to write this book. I wrote it for several reasons. One reason is that it is cathartic. Another is that I wanted to give Elizabeth a glimpse into what her family and community did while she was missing to help bring her safely home. Another is that it is simply one of the most amazing stories I have ever run across as a journalist. I think it is important, and potentially beneficial, to illuminate the numerous acts of selflessness and kindness that were part of the search for Elizabeth. It can be inspiring to see how a story that began with such evil wound up producing such an enormous amount of good. I also think that throughout the story there are valuable lessons for law enforcement and the media against being too sure of any one theory and course of action, to the exclusion of all others.

For all its twists, turns, suspense, despair, hubris, pathos, dignity, and mystery, the story starts with the agony and ends with the ecstasy of a family that, to reference Winston Churchill, never, never, never gave in.

—Tom Smart

In Plain Sight

1

The tip of the knife penetrated the window screen at the right edge, near the top, and sliced straight down. A cut across the bottom came next, followed by a final incision down the left-hand side, allowing access to the handle inside that cranked open the window.

Normally, the kitchen window was shut and locked at night, but at dinnertime the evening before someone had opened it to let out cooking odors, and no one remembered to close it.

The blade of the knife moved silently and easily. The screen's light nylon mesh was meant to keep out roaches and flies, not sharpened steel. Soon a slight, narrow-shouldered man holding the knife slithered through the ten-inch opening he had made, taking care not to disturb assorted utensils, plants, and window ornaments as he dropped eight inches to the kitchen counter below.

The man moved quietly through the spacious, modern house. It was for sale. Interested buyers who called the number on the real-estate agent's sign out front discovered a list price of $1.19 million.

But the million-dollar house held no appeal for the man silently ascending the stairs beyond the kitchen. He turned down a long hallway, toward the corner room where the girls slept.

Fourteen-year-old Elizabeth Smart awakened to the sight of the man standing above her, tapping her shoulder and motioning for her to get up. As the startled girl got out of bed, her nine-year-old sister, Mary Katherine, lay motionless on the other side. The sisters had recently started sharing a queen-size bed, after giving their twin beds to the boys. Each of their four brothers had his own room. William, Edward Jr., and Andrew were just down the hall while sixteen-year-old Charles, the oldest of the Smart children, had recently taken up residence downstairs. But the girls stuck together.

The intruder had first circled the bed and paused at Mary Katherine's nightstand on the far side of the room. He tapped her on the shoulder but got no response. Instinctively, the younger girl stayed still and feigned sleep as the disturbance in the bedroom brought her to consciousness. When Mary Katherine dared to open her eyes briefly, she thought she saw that the backs of the man's hands were covered with dark hair and he had wrinkles of some sort on the side of his face. His voice was soft. When Elizabeth stubbed her toe in the dark and reflexively said "Ouch," Mary Katherine heard the man whisper for Elizabeth to be quiet, "or I'll kill you and your family." He then ordered her to get some shoes and the two walked through the adjoining bathroom into the walk-in closet, where Elizabeth had to briefly turn on the light to find her shoes. Mary Katherine heard Elizabeth ask, "Why are you taking me?" The stranger's reply was muted, but she thought she heard him answer, "For ransom or hostage."

After they left the bedroom—Elizabeth in red silk pajamas and white tennis shoes, the man holding what Mary Katherine thought was a gun— the nine-year-old waited until she thought it was safe and then got out of bed to run to her parents' room and tell them what happened.

But she was too quick. As she looked out the door of her room and down the hallway she saw the man and Elizabeth coming out of one of the boys' rooms. On the far side of the boys' bedroom there was a door to the atrium, which led to the backyard—the quickest way out of the house. But there was a sleeping boy in between. Maybe the man stealing Elizabeth didn't want to risk waking him. Fearing the kidnapper might be returning for her, Mary Katherine retreated into her room and carefully got back into bed, faking sleep again, too terrified to move. She wasn't having a nightmare. This was real. She knew it as well as she knew there was a big empty space on the side of the bed where the older sister she idolized had been only moments before. In the hall, Mary Katherine got another brief look at the man. She would describe the clothes he was wearing as light-colored;

he also had on a cap, which Mary Katherine found difficult to describe. In the dim light, she could see he was only an inch or so taller than Elizabeth, the same height as her brother Charles. He was carrying some kind of duffel bag or backpack. The man and his voice were vaguely familiar to Mary Katherine; she felt a dim connection to something too hazy to recall.

Mary Katherine stayed under the covers. She was taking no more chances. She had heard the threat: "I'll kill your family." They were all in danger. She waited. She listened to the chimes from the big clock in the living room. They rang every quarter-hour. When she heard enough of them she would run and tell her dad. It was hard waiting, but she forced herself to hear the chimes, and then hear them again, before wrapping herself in her blanket and running to the master bedroom at the far end of the hall, where she shook her dad and said, "She's gone! Elizabeth is gone!"

Edward Smart bolted up out of a deep sleep, rubbing his eyes, as his wife, Lois, aware of the commotion, also struggled to wake up. Ed thought his youngest daughter must have had a bad dream. Elizabeth sometimes slept elsewhere in the house, especially if Mary Katherine was kicking her in her sleep. She might have gone to one of the boys' rooms or to the couch downstairs.

But his anxiety mounted as he ran from room to room, not finding Elizabeth anywhere. His heart, mind, and adrenaline began to race as Mary Katherine pleaded, "You're not going to find her! A man came and took her! A man with a gun!"

Mary Katherine woke her dad at 3:58 A.M. according to his nightstand clock. The police logged Ed's subsequent 911 call three minutes later, at 4:01. "My daughter's missing! Oh my gosh! Please hurry!" On the police tape, Ed is shouting, but even more chilling are the horrified screams in the background. Lois had discovered the open window and the sliced screen inside the kitchen. In that instant, all reasonable explanations disappeared. Elizabeth was gone. It was as simple, and as complicated, as that.

The police responded in twelve minutes. At 4:13 A.M. a uniformed Salt Lake City Police Department officer, the first outsider on the scene, stood in the kitchen, staring at the screen and asking the first of what would become a torrent of mostly unanswerable questions. Outside, another officer stood guard at the bottom of the stairs leading to the front door.

After calling the police, Ed had gone into action, calling friends, neighbors, and family for help as he first searched his own house and then ran out the door and across the cul-de-sac to his neighbor's house. He knew, as did many others in the neighborhood, that Brent and Bonnie Jean Beesley's family had been victimized by a kidnapping attempt a decade earlier. "Check your kids," he begged the Beesleys because one of his was gone.

When the phone rang at our home sometime between 4:15 and 4:30 A.M. I did not look at the clock or even budge. After getting home from a late assignment and getting to sleep after midnight with the help of an Ambien sleeping pill, a quick reaction wasn't possible. My wife, Heidi, answered. Ever since our three daughters were small the phone has been on her side of the bed; she's the night watchman and mother superior at our house. A marshmallow could fall on the driveway at four in the morning and Heidi would hear it. She picked up the phone after one ring.

"Elizabeth has been kidnapped at gunpoint!" Ed told her.

"What?" said Heidi.

"Elizabeth has been kidnapped at gunpoint," he repeated, at which point Heidi handed me the phone. Fighting to wake up as Ed spoke the awful words yet again, I mumbled, "How can we help?" Ed told me to please come over, and hurry. Then he hung up.

Heidi and I just lay there as if we were paralyzed. We'd just received the proverbial phone call in the middle of the night. It was not unlike the shock of getting drenched by a bucket of cold water.

We had hardly moved when the phone rang again. It was Ed. Sensing my grogginess on the first call, he was calling back to make sure I had heard him correctly. "Haven't you left yet?" Ed said. "Please come, please hurry." The panic in his voice was now even thicker.

Within two minutes we were dressed and out the door. As we sped along the nearly deserted interstate, trying to turn the thirty-minute drive to Ed's house into thirty seconds, a small army was mobilizing and bearing down on the same coordinates. Ed comes from a large family. There are six of us Smart siblings, plus our parents. Then there's Lois's family; she's the second youngest of nine siblings. That gives Elizabeth twenty-six aunts and uncles and more than seventy first cousins. Before the sun began to rise over the Rocky Mountains, both sides of the family had been called and were racing by the dozens to Ed and Lois's home in the foothills of those mountains on the East Bench of Salt Lake City, about to join a crowd of police, neighbors, and friends.

Everyone who knew Elizabeth was thinking the same thing: "not her." Of all the children in the family, no one was less likely to be in any kind of trouble or be the center of controversy. She was the quintessential good kid. She didn't cruise the malls or surf the Internet. She wasn't the kind to sneak out at night with a boy. If she had a rebellious side to her nature, no one had ever seen it. She was beyond obedient.

Calling Elizabeth angelic was not a stretch. She was very accomplished on the harp, which only added to the image. She started taking harp lessons when she was very young and by fourteen she was performing regularly in public, to excellent reviews. Just three months earlier she had been a featured soloist at a concert for the Paralympics that followed the Salt Lake 2002 Olympic Winter Games. She was happy to let her harp do the talking. Both she and Mary Katherine were quiet girls, sometimes painfully shy, especially around strangers. Even around family, Elizabeth was never one for long conversations.

All Ed and Lois's children, with the exception of Charles, had spent the previous weekend with my parents, Charles and Dorotha Smart. Lois's father, Myron Francom, had died the previous Wednesday, and Ed and Lois were busy helping with arrangements for the viewing Sunday night and the funeral service scheduled for Monday afternoon. Myron Francom lived a healthy, robust life for virtually all of his eighty-one years, but during his final three months he had been bedridden with a brain tumor. Lois had spent part of nearly every day at her father's bedside.

Dad and Mom did their best to spoil the grandkids over the weekend. They all came by Charleston, just west of Heber City, where I was a partner in a horse property development called Winterton Farms. We had pastured several horses there for the spring and we checked on the horses, haltering and leading Ranger, our newest colt, around the pasture. Deer Creek Reservoir is only a few minutes from Winterton Farms, so after playing with the horses, my father towed his ski boat to the lake and everyone went boating. Elizabeth, the oldest girl in the family and second oldest overall; twelve-year-old Andrew; nine-year-old Mary Katherine; seven-year-old Edward; and even little William, who was three, took turns steering the boat through tight turns with wide smiles on their faces.

The kids and their grandparents then left for a family cabin located farther east in the mountains on the Weber River, where they stayed until Sunday afternoon before returning for Myron Francom's viewing that evening at Holbrook Mortuary in the Millcreek area of the Salt Lake Valley. In the foyer near the guest register, Elizabeth played the harp as hundreds of people filed in to pay their respects to her grandfather.

The funeral the next afternoon, held in a church in the Salt Lake City suburb of Holladay, was the last time I had seen Elizabeth. My father and I had spent the morning working with the horses, breaking Ranger. We arrived at the church just in time for the service. Elizabeth and Mary Katherine played their harps as part of the program. Afterward I saw Elizabeth in the parking lot. She took a moment to say hi while she was running and playing with her cousin Olivia Wright. Heidi remembered the dress Elizabeth was wearing, a high-necked Laura Ashley–type you might see on a younger girl.

I remember thinking how tall she was getting—already five-foot-seven and rail-thin. Running in that frilly dress with her cousin, her blond hair blowing behind her, Elizabeth Smart was really still a girl and not a woman. As a family friend who knew her well observed, Elizabeth was "fourteen going on eleven."

I wasn't the only Smart who had a short night. My sister Angela had been up till midnight, working on her yard. My brother David had been working in his basement until 12:30 A.M., putting in pipes for a shower. As for my parents, they had driven late into the night towing their boat to Lake Powell in southern Utah, where they planned to dock it for the summer. They had left the city late Tuesday afternoon and had been unsuccessful finding a motel reservation anywhere near Lake Powell. About an hour into their trip they pulled off the freeway in Provo to buy sleeping bags at a sporting goods store. They figured they would sleep under the stars on the sand by the lake if it came to that.

We are a close family, biologically and psychologically. All six Smart siblings were born within eleven years of each other, starting with me in 1953. Ed came next, eighteen months later, then my brother, Chris, followed by the two girls, Angela and Cynthia, and finally David in 1964. We have always spent a great deal of time together. As the family grew—by the summer of 2002 the extended Smart family numbered thirty-five—so did occasions for getting together. Something was always going on: birthdays, baby blessings, graduations, summer trips, and holidays.

But we had never gotten together for anything like this.

Ed called all his siblings within the first hour. In every instance, it took a moment for the news to register. Part of it was the early hour, but the bigger part was the shock. *"Elizabeth has been taken at gunpoint!"*

Once reality did sink in, we all went into action. My brother Chris grabbed his gun, a CZ nine-millimeter, semiautomatic—a serious handgun. Before he left his house, he put in it in the car, locked and loaded.

The phone ringing in the early morning dark hadn't initially alarmed Chris. As an engineer who buys energy for Duke Energy, he's used to fielding phone calls at odd hours. But the look on his wife Ingrid's face as she handed him the phone did alarm him. "I'll be right over," Chris had told Ed as he leaped out of bed. Ingrid wasn't as fast. "I was scared," she remembered. "If I went over (to Ed's house), it would be true and, more than anything, I didn't want it to be true. I heard Chris fiddling in the study. 'What are you doing?' I asked. 'Getting my gun,' he said. 'If I see him, I'm going to kill the son of a bitch.'" Within minutes, Chris and Ingrid left their house in Centerville, about fifteen miles from Ed and Lois's, hugging their eighteen-year-old daughter Alicia on the way out, and asking her to watch their younger kids.

My sister Angela and her husband, Zeke Dumke III, likewise left teenagers, their seventeen-year-old daughter, Elise, and sixteen-year-old son, Mitchell, in charge. Their oldest son, twenty-year-old Zeke IV, was in Bolivia waiting for the rest of the family to join him. Zeke and Angela had arranged a family trip to Bolivia to help build a well in a poverty-stricken village as a summer service project. They had their shots, their passports, and their airline tickets. They were supposed to leave the next day. Now Angela and Zeke were driving through the dark to Ed's house, flashlights beside them.

"I got the call a little after four and you could just hear the fear and the panic in Ed's voice," Angela said. "It was very palpable. I knew it wasn't something little. 'Elizabeth has been taken at gunpoint,' Ed said. 'Get up here and bring a flashlight.' I kept thinking something's not right. I knew it was Ed. I knew it was fear. There was such great angst in his voice. But it didn't make sense that someone came into their home with a gun and then Ed called me to come look for Elizabeth in the mountains. So we checked on all our kids first because I had the thought that somebody might be trying to get us out of our house. I checked all the doors. Even though Zeke and I are fanatic about locking the house, I found doors were unlocked. It was probably because I was gardening so late, but later, when I heard people criticizing Ed for the open window, I thought, nobody's perfect."

As Zeke and Angela were driving, Ed called them again to make sure that they were on their way.

My sister Cynthia didn't jump when the phone rang. Cynthia is a pediatrician; it wouldn't have been the first time a patient called her at 4:30 A.M. "I got the phone and it was obviously Ed," Cynthia remembered. "He said 'A man has taken Elizabeth.' I said, 'This is a dream, right?' He said, 'No, someone came and took Elizabeth at gunpoint.' So I said, 'She's gone?' I kept answering his statements with questions because it just didn't seem possible. We decided to have Doug [Cynthia's husband, Doug Owens] go over to help and hopefully find her. It made more sense for me to stay with the kids, at least until they woke up. The first thing Doug and I did was kneel down and pray. I was crying. Doug said, 'Do you want me to get the gun for you?' He has a magnum. I said 'Oh yeah, I'll either end up shooting myself or the kids.' I remember taking Emmeline—she was two—from her bed early that morning. We have a strict policy, the kids sleep in their own beds, but boy, I picked her up and I just held her next to me in our bed, and I thought I just couldn't handle it if it was one of my children."

My brother David answered the phone. His wife, Julie, remembered how quickly the atmosphere in their bedroom changed. "David's back was toward me when he answered the phone," Julie said. "I heard him asking questions about a *her*. I thought it was my mom he was talking about, because she's diabetic. Then he said, 'They can't find her?' and his back started moving quickly and his breathing got heavier and heavier. 'I'm going to Ed's,' he said after he hung up. 'Elizabeth has been taken at gunpoint.' And I remember thinking: our world has just changed. The unimaginable has just happened."

David quickly left his house in Draper, about twenty-five miles from Ed's, promising Julie he'd call as soon as he knew anything. They have young children, so one parent needed to stay with them.

The most jarring call came in a motel room in Ticaboo, Utah. Ticaboo is a wide-open spot in the road surrounded by sagebrush about twelve miles from Lake Powell in the extreme southeast corner of Utah. My father had pulled into the motel late Tuesday night, hoping someone hadn't showed up for a room reservation. They were in luck. A reservation had canceled. Charles and Dorotha Smart registered with the desk clerk, checked into their room, and went to sleep until the phone next to their bed rang at 5:30 in the morning.

It hadn't been easy finding them. One of Ed and Lois's neighbors, Lynn Godfrey, was among the first to their house and upon hearing Elizabeth's grandparents had gone to Lake Powell, she assumed the task to find and notify them. Lynn contacted a phone company operator in southern Utah. "Please call every motel within a thirty-mile radius of Lake Powell," she pleaded. The operator found the Smarts in Ticaboo on the ninth call.

Dad and Mom quickly packed, left their room, unhitched the trailer, and drove off, leaving the boat in the middle of the parking lot. The motel owner towed the boat to a secure place in the back.

My father tore up the rural highways of southern Utah in his Mercury Mountaineer. Between Ticaboo and Green River he drove over one hundred miles an hour. The irony was that when he finally got pulled over by the Highway Patrol, in the sixty-five-mile-per-hour zone between Green River and Price, he was only doing ninety-five.

"It was on Highway 6, there were no other cars around, just us," my mother remembered. "The patrolman said, 'Please step out of your car, sir. Do you have any idea how fast you were going?' Charles said, 'Yes, ninety-five.' Then I leaned over and said, 'What would you do if your granddaughter was kidnapped and you were told to get home as fast as you could?' He said, 'Well, you better slow down so you don't kill yourself or anyone else.' And he let us go."

As they steered again toward Salt Lake City, news reports of the disappearance of a Salt Lake teenager began airing on the radio. There was an eyewitness to the alleged abduction, the reports said. Mom and Dad had already been told on the telephone that Mary Katherine was that eyewitness. The news of their nine-year-old granddaughter witnessing the abduction was particularly sobering to them. Only they knew how close they had come to taking Mary Katherine with them to the lake. My parents are deeply religious people; as they drove, they thanked God that Mary Katherine had been home the night before and not with them. Thank God Elizabeth hadn't been in her bed alone. Thank God someone had seen what happened and could describe the kidnapper. The speedometer remained buried as they prayed.

2

There was just a hint of light in the eastern sky as Heidi and I parked on the street next to Ed's driveway around 5:00 A.M. In another half hour it would be light enough to see the countryside clearly.

There was a police officer at the bottom of the stairs that led to Ed's front door, which was surrounded by the yellow crime-scene tape all too familiar to any news journalist. Ed's house sits at the end of Kristianna Circle, a flat cul-de-sac about a quarter-mile in length that is part of a neighborhood known as Arlington Hills. There are about two hundred homes in Arlington Hills. Most of them are upscale, and all have impressive views of the Salt Lake City skyline below. Ed's house was among the most recent additions. He had purchased the lot at the end of the circle, tucked into the northeast corner. He'd acted as general contractor for the construction of the house, which was something of a six-year work-in-progress. More than sixty construction workers had worked in the house, and Ed had been careful to use only subcontractors that he had either worked with previously or who came recommended. Above Ed's house were two higher streets, Chandler and Tomahawk, and beyond those were the mountains. There was just one road leading to his driveway; any vehicle that entered Kristianna Circle had to exit the same way. Hardly a prime spot for a kidnapping.

We had hoped that by the time we arrived Ed would come running out with the news, "We've got her back." But the police officer at the stairs and all the yellow tape dashed that hope. At first the officer blocked our way. I said, "We're family," and he stepped aside and let us through.

Inside the house, every light was on. Neighbors, family, and police were everywhere. I caught a brief glimpse of Lois. She was in the living room just off the kitchen, being consoled by her mother, Jenny Francom, who had buried her husband two days earlier. I turned away and found Ed surrounded by people wanting to know how they could help and also wanting details. I could see in my brother's eyes the panic I'd heard in his voice over the telephone. But I could also see that he was not falling apart. He was fully engaged.

Ed confided in me that he was as baffled as anyone. He could make no sense of what had happened. He could not think of anyone who would want to hurt Elizabeth. He went over and over in his mind the events of the last few days. The viewing and funeral of his father-in-law had occupied everyone through Monday night. Perhaps there was a connection there, but he couldn't think what it might possibly be. He said Elizabeth had been her usual unobtrusive self during the funeral and surrounding events. No trouble at all. After taking Monday off from school for the funeral, she had returned to classes on Tuesday, the second to last day of her eighth grade year, her last year at Bryant Intermediate School. The school's awards ceremonies had been that night. Elizabeth, who was listed in the program as one of sixty-four eighth-graders in a class of two hundred and ninety-seven with grade point averages above 3.5 in both citizenship and scholarship, was supposed to play the harp but she arrived too late to perform. It had been one of those nights. Everything and everybody was running late—in Elizabeth's case, literally. She had been out jogging. The high school track coach had visited the intermediate school that day and watched the eighth-graders run. He told Elizabeth he was impressed by her long stride and encouraged her to try out for cross-country when she entered East High School in the fall. Elizabeth was too shy to look the coach in the eye, but she heard every word he said. That night she went home, borrowed her mom's tennis shoes, and went jogging through Arlington Hills.

The jogging was fine with Ed and Lois, but Lois didn't like her kids running off just anywhere. When Elizabeth went out for her run, Lois wanted to know the route. Elizabeth left the house on an approved course that went down Kristianna, then up Virginia Street to Chandler Drive, along Chandler to the cement reservoir for several laps, then back along Chandler, down a gully that accessed the house from the north, and back home. For good measure, Elizabeth took along her little sister, Mary Katherine, who would follow her anywhere.

There was one troubling incident that occurred near the end of the run. A boy Elizabeth knew from school rode past the girls while they were jogging and rolled down his car window and tried to talk to them. When the girls got home, Elizabeth told her dad about the boy, who was riding in the car with his mother, and said he made her feel uneasy. That incident was one of the first things Ed told the police, and the boy became one of the first people questioned as a possible suspect. He was also the first suspect to be dismissed.

The kitchen was easily the most congested area in the house. The cut screen and open window acted like a magnet. People were drawn there to look at the screen hanging at an unnatural angle inside the kitchen. Outside, directly below the window, a patio chair was propped up against the stucco wall. The police weren't restricting entry to the kitchen area, which even as I opened my computer on the kitchen counter to begin transmitting photographs of Elizabeth, I thought odd. I was no detective, but wasn't the kitchen a crucial piece of evidence? If the person who stood on the chair and came through the screen had left any clues, wouldn't they be here?

It was now apparent that the kidnapper had left through the kitchen as well, although not back through the assumed entry point, the screen, but out the side door just a few feet away. Ed had checked that door the night before to make sure it was locked, but he found it unlocked after Elizabeth's disappearance. That meant that sometime after Mary Katherine saw them in the hall, the man had taken Elizabeth down the corridor to the stairs, descended to the main floor, and left through the kitchen door. It also meant that he had not only managed to avoid stepping on the creaky floorboard outside Ed and Lois's room—the creaky floorboard Ed always heard when one of the kids stepped on it—but that he had also succeeded in exiting out one of just three doors not wired to the alarm system. Due to an oversight during construction, the kitchen door, one sliding door, and the door to the garage were not fitted with beepers. Going out any other door, including the door to the atrium in Andrew's bedroom, would have resulted in a loud beep resonating throughout the house.

Whoever the abductor was, he was very smart or very lucky. On a quiet summer night he had entered a locked home, with a security system, on a dead-end street, by crawling through a ten-inch window opening while wearing light-colored clothing and carrying a bag, after which he had taken a fourteen-year-old girl from her bed not three feet from her sleeping sister, and walked back out, leaving a cut screen as the only sign of his crime. As my sister Angela observed, "He walked into that house like he thought he was God himself."

It is nearly impossible to describe the urgency that sets in when a child is missing. Statistics specify the importance of the first few hours after an abduction, but when the kidnapping is in your own family, when you are personally confronted by the horror of an empty bed, statistics are unnecessary. There is a foreboding, and you sense it with every nerve ending. Everyone who rallied to Kristianna Circle the early morning of June 5, 2002, instinctively understood there wasn't a second to spare. Elizabeth needed to be found, and she needed to be found *now*.

My first thought was that we needed to alert the media. My background as a newspaper photographer—since 1972, I have worked for the Salt Lake City *Deseret News*—led me to believe that the more people who knew about this right away, the better. The public needed a description of both Elizabeth and her kidnapper. I collected recent photographs of Elizabeth from Ed and Lois and quickly loaded them onto my laptop for media distribution.

At first the police asked that the story be withheld. So although the family wanted the news out, we waited for police permission. By 5:30 A.M., Angela had already called her friend and neighbor, Kim Johnson, the morning news anchor at KSL-TV (the local NBC affiliate), and I had alerted Chuck Wing, the photo editor on duty that morning at the *Deseret News*, that I was sending him photos of Elizabeth for distribution. All they needed was a go-ahead from us. It was a long time coming. The police didn't give us the OK to go public with the story until more than three hours after the kidnapping. When the approval finally came, Chuck immediately forwarded the digital photos I had sent him to every television station in Utah as well as the Associated Press and Reuters News Service. The entire nation had Elizabeth's photo within minutes.

The police said the wait was necessary to verify that this was indeed a kidnapping and not some domestic disturbance or a teenager who'd run away or snuck out of her house for the night. But considering the content of the 911 call, the sliced window screen, and Mary Katherine as an eyewitness, the delay was inexplicable. Statistics show that when a kidnapped child is murdered, 74 percent of the time the child is dead within the first three hours.

The police were also slow to seal off the crime scene. They didn't clear Ed's house and start a visitor's log chronicling who came into the house until 6:54 A.M. And it wouldn't be until 10:30 A.M., after scores of footprints had been left by citizen searchers, that the hills and mountains behind the house were declared off-limits to all but police investigators.

The police would later suggest that part of the reason for the early morning confusion and delays was because Ed had alerted family and neighbors before calling 911 and that the home was crawling with people before police arrived. Ed's phone records, however, would verify that Ed's call to 911 was his first of the morning. The police watch log incorrectly stated that neighbors were at the home when the police arrived—the first neighbor to arrive was Suann Adams and the police were already there.

What *was* true was that the response of neighbors and family was formidable and fast. Many members of Ed and Lois's local ward, or congregation, of the Church of Jesus Christ of Latter-day Saints, got out their membership directories and started systematically calling everyone on the rolls as soon as they heard the news. By 4:30 A.M., before any family members arrived, the streets and foothills of Arlington Hills were already alive with neighbors carrying flashlights, peering over fences, and literally turning over rocks.

By then it was becoming apparent that no one had seen or heard any suspicious traffic leaving Kristianna Circle from its one entrance onto Virginia Street during the early morning hours. A resident near the front of the circle checked his security videotape that had been running all night and it showed no activity in the predawn hours until the first police car arrived just after four o'clock in the morning. It was beginning to look like the man who took Elizabeth may have departed, at least in the beginning, on foot and uphill through the backyard toward the mountains.

Chris was the first of the extended family to go out and search. Within minutes of arriving at Ed's house, he and Cynthia's husband, Doug, left to scour nearby Memory Grove and City Creek Canyon. Chris's wife, Ingrid, had a feeling that area was where a kidnapper was likely to flee and they should look there first. Chris and Doug split up and each encountered several walkers and joggers. It was after six o'clock in the morning by now, and they asked everyone if they had seen anything and to please keep a sharp lookout. Chris's gun stayed in the trunk. "I realized I probably wasn't thinking the most rationally," he said, "and it would be better to just leave the gun in the car."

David and Zeke joined Doug for another search after he returned from Memory Grove. They intended to search the old pioneer lime kilns in the foothills a half-mile above Tomahawk Circle, but they were stopped by law enforcement and asked not to search that area. The kilns date back to the nineteenth century when Brigham Young's Mormon pioneers began settling the Salt Lake Valley. They once provided limestone for the settlers, but in more recent times the pits at the bottom of the hundred-foot caverns have hosted picnics, bonfires, and untold numbers of beer parties. Doug, Zeke, and David chose another area near the kilns, but they found no evidence of Elizabeth. Later that day, the police would take a team of dogs and search the kilns. They, too, found nothing.

After the police cleared Ed's house of all non–law enforcement personnel, the Beesleys' home across the street became a kind of family-and-friends search headquarters. Dave, Doug, and Zeke, along with Larry Holmstrom, a neighbor back from his own early-morning search, taped a large map of the area to the back window of a Chevrolet Suburban that was parked in the driveway. It was agreed that every time a new area was searched, it would be checked off on the map, so people wouldn't keep searching the same place.

Inside the Beesleys' house, Heidi, Angela, and Ingrid, along with various friends, neighbors, and other family members, were designing fliers while I went to work producing a poster. Other neighbors brought over running shoes and hiking boots; still others brought food and bottled water. People just pitched in. Zeke quickly reached out to his numerous contacts in government and business, almost instantly recruiting thousands of eyes and ears. Among others, he talked to Earl Holding, owner of Sinclair Oil and the Little America Hotel chain; Salt Lake County mayor Nancy Workman; administrators at LDS church headquarters, and officers of the local hotel and restaurant associations. In no time, e-mails and phone messages were flying around the intermountain west to hotels, restaurants, truck stops, gas stations, government offices, and LDS church leaders: a Salt Lake teenager was missing and was possibly on the move with her captor.

One neighbor, Trish Bennion, recalled seeing an article in *Parade* magazine about an organization that helped set up volunteer searches for missing kids. On the Beesleys' computer, Trish, Angela, and Heidi started typing keywords such as "abducted" and "kidnapped" into the search engine. The scene was almost surreal—so many neighbors and friends going into action on what should have been an ordinary Wednesday morning. There was a palpable expectation that this would all be over soon. Every time the phone rang, everyone in the house jumped.

About 11:00 A.M., my parents arrived, maneuvering around police cruisers and news trucks. With Ed's street barricaded by police as they processed the crime scene, Mom and Dad drove around the corner to their home on Chandler Drive, the large house where they'd raised their family. Even though my parents left Utah for extended periods of time—my father had been chief of the early detection branch of the National Cancer Institute in Bethesda, Maryland, for six years, and later he and my mother spent eighteen months in Moscow, Russia, on an LDS mission—they kept their house.

It wasn't as if they could wave a magic wand and end the nightmare, but just having Mom and Dad back home had a therapeutic effect on all of us. Those family members who weren't out searching met at our parents' home just before noon. We held a short meeting to coordinate our efforts and have a family prayer. Most of us had already gravitated to the jobs where we felt we could be the most useful—and to a large extent that's where each of us would remain throughout the search for Elizabeth. There was no manual to follow, just instinct.

Dave's wife, Julie, and my sister Cynthia were the last of the family to arrive, after finding someone to watch their young children. Julie and Cynthia, along with Angela, Heidi, and others, helped care for Ed and Lois's children and gave extra comfort and compassion to Lois. The pain she was going through was debilitating. Lois's agony was the first thing Angela noticed when she arrived at Ed and Lois's house. "Lois was in the living room crying," Angela said. "But it was not crying, it was the most horrible sound I have ever heard. It was just wailing. It was so sad. I had never heard a sound like that."

When Cynthia arrived at Mom and Dad's, she saw three women on the couch, the two on either side with their arms around the one in the middle. "They were being very, very quiet so I didn't dare interrupt my mother to say hi or anything," Cynthia said. "I literally could not recognize that it was Lois in the middle. She was between Mom and her own mother, Jenny, and I recognized them but I kept looking and looking and I could not recognize Lois. Later, I remember Mom and Jenny trying to help her walk and she couldn't put one foot in front of the other. She was being almost carried on both arms." Cynthia called in a prescription sedative for Ed and Lois— although both refused to take it—and mobilized a team of therapists and psychologists to assist in providing emotional therapy.

When Julie encountered Lois, she was sitting by herself at my mother's house. "She was in the front room just sobbing uncontrollably, just kinda rocking," Julie remembered. "She kept saying, 'How could this happen? How could this happen?' She was alone. Then a neighbor called and suggested we figure out what shoes Elizabeth had been wearing. So I said I'd take Lois over to the house and we'd look through the shoes. I took her over and as we were walking up the steps inside the house, Lois started talking. 'She was probably walking right here,' she said, meaning Elizabeth. 'What was she thinking? What did she go through?' It was a tender, emotional moment, a mother in great pain trying to feel her daughter's pain. We walked into the bedroom and everything was dusted for fingerprints. We looked around the room and then she sat in the closet and started going through the shoes. The closet was messy, like a kid's would be, but she knew right away what shoes were gone. They were a pair of her own. She said, 'Oh yeah, they're my tennis shoes.' Elizabeth had taken them over. Elizabeth was getting to the age where she could wear her mother's shoes."

In an attempt to preserve potential evidence, the police asked us not to search the mountains behind Ed's home, so distributing fliers and searching door-to-door seemed like the most useful things to do. By noon there were thousands of fliers stacked on a chair outside the Beesleys' home. They went quickly as more and more people joined the effort. Almost immediately fliers with Elizabeth's picture and description began appearing on telephone poles, utility poles, and bulletin boards throughout Utah and to the Wyoming, Idaho, and Nevada borders and beyond. Hundreds of stores posted the fliers in their front windows. More fliers were faxed to areas throughout the intermountain west. Longtime Arlington Hills residents Ted Wilson, the former Salt Lake City mayor, and his wife, Kathy, were driving on the interstate outside Twin Falls, Idaho, when they heard the news on KSL-Radio. Ted had spent the last few weeks riding his motorcycle along the Canadian–Alaskan highway, and Kathy had driven their truck to Seattle to pick up Ted and his bike and then return to Utah. At a truck stop, the Wilsons phoned home and asked to have a flier faxed to them. They made several hundred copies and then Ted backed his motorcycle out of the truck and went home one way while Kathy went another, hanging fliers and handing them out to truckers all the way back to Salt Lake City.

Help came from everywhere, and much of it was completely unexpected. By mid-afternoon Wednesday, I was at the Salt Lake City & County Building with Salt Lake City mayor Rocky Anderson for a meeting to iron out details for a $250,000 reward friends and family wanted to offer. Several people were there with the mayor and the city attorney. One of them pulled out a checkbook and wrote a personal check to guarantee the full amount of the reward. That way it could be posted without delay and in advance of securing the necessary donations.

At a press conference that afternoon, Mayor Anderson announced a $10,000 reward for information leading to Elizabeth's safe return (the $250,000 privately donated amount wouldn't be announced until the next day). Rick Dinse, chief of police of the Salt Lake City Police Department, stepped to the microphone with the public assurance that everything possible was being done by his department. Then Detective Dwayne Baird, a police department public information officer (PIO), detailed what little information the police had: the suspected kidnapper was a white male between thirty and forty years old, five-foot-eight inches tall, and wearing light-colored pants, a white ball cap, and a light jacket. Based on the abductor's confusion upon exiting the home, Baird said, "He did not seem to know his way around the house." The PIO's report included the erroneous statement, as written in the police report, that Ed had called neighbors before calling the police. Another piece of misinformation was that "The suspect threatened the younger sister," which is what Ed had thought when he first called police.

There was no doubt now that the police had a kidnapping on their hands, and no making up for the time it had taken them to come to that conclusion. It hadn't been until 7:21 A.M., more than three hours after the 911 call, that the state's Rachael Alert system for missing children—a rapid transmission to all police agencies and media outlets—was activated for the first time ever. After that, things began to happen quickly. Mary Katherine had been interviewed twice—first informally by Sergeant Don Bell, the head of SLCPD's Sex Crimes Unit (with assistance from one of his interview specialists), and formally that afternoon by the same specialist at the Children's Justice Center. State helicopters went to search the mountains and more than a hundred officers from a variety of jurisdictions went to work on the case. An SLCPD bloodhound named J.J. picked up Elizabeth's scent in the gully where she had jogged the night before, and also on the other side of Ed's home leading up to Tomahawk Drive in the circle above the backyard, but then the trail apparently went cold, which led investigators to theorize that she had been taken in a car from there. All around Arlington Hills, officers on foot canvassed the neighborhood.

At the Boede home, a mile from Kristianna Circle, Debbie Boede told the patrolmen who knocked on her door, "You guys sure are being thorough." "The last thing we want is another JonBenet on our hands," one officer replied, referring to the notoriously bungled police investigation of the still-unsolved 1996 Boulder, Colorado, murder of six-year-old JonBenet Ramsey.

One success we had that first day was in locating the national organization that assists in organizing searches for missing children. While Trish Bennion, Heidi, and Angela were scanning the Internet for the name of the group, the organization itself, the Laura Recovery Center (LRC) in Friendswood, Texas, was attempting to contact the family of Elizabeth Smart. It turned out that Dawn Davis, the LRC's search coordinator, had a sister, Debbie Norris, who lived in the Salt Lake area. After Debbie awakened Wednesday morning to the news of the kidnapping, she called Dawn and told her she thought the Smarts might need help. Dawn asked Debbie to make contact with the family, explaining that while the LRC wanted to become involved as soon as possible, the organization first had to be invited by the family. Debbie in turn got in touch with Ed, who said he would welcome the help. Dawn caught the next flight out of Houston.

The Laura Recovery Center, like many groups aimed at helping kids, sprang from a tragedy. Laura Smither was just days from her thirteenth birthday when she disappeared while jogging near her Friendswood home on April 3, 1997. Six thousand people looked for seventeen days before Laura's body was found in a retention pond twenty miles from where she went missing. In the aftermath, Laura's parents, Bob and Kay Smither, sat down with a core group of volunteers who had led the search for Laura and discussed what went wrong and what went right. They listed all the right things in a manual, set up a nonprofit foundation, and made their expertise and experience available to anyone who asked.

While Dawn was en route to Utah with the LRC manual, Debbie drove to Arlington Hills to help get things started. She told us the first things we needed to do were to arrange for a search headquarters and to put out a call for volunteers beginning the following morning.

As a search center, the Beesleys' driveway, and the back window of the Suburban, would no longer do. We needed a place with enough space for a secure mapping area, an orientation room, multiple telephones, and a place for volunteers to register. We talked about the fire station a few blocks away, but then a neighbor mentioned that Shriners Hospital, located just off Virginia Street less than a mile below Ed's house, had a boardroom that might be ideal. Longtime family friend Eric Cannon and I went to the hospital, where a security guard got us in touch with one of the directors. He said there were meetings planned for the boardroom the next day, but they could meet in the closet if they had to. Without hesitation, Shriners offered us the use of the boardroom, parking lot, outside grounds, and extra offices if required. The hospital also offered to set up extra phones for us. Shriners' mission is to provide medical aid to children, and no one at the hospital balked at providing aid to a child in this unconventional way.

With a search headquarters secured, and darkness descending, Smart and Francom family members made their way to the entrance of Kristianna Circle, where the local television stations had set up their floodlights and cameras to broadcast live remotes for the 10:00 P.M. newscasts. We split up and made ourselves available for interviews, pleading for anyone eighteen or over to show up at Shriners Hospital the next morning at eight to help look for Elizabeth. After the interviews we went to Shriners to set up for the morning.

It was almost midnight when I left an empty Shriners Hospital parking lot and drove the short distance up the hill to my parents' house, where I hoped to get a few hours' sleep. On my right I passed Kristianna Circle. At the far end, I saw that Ed's house was dark. Except for an FBI agent inside who was manning the phones, the house was empty. It wasn't a home now; it was a crime scene.

Ed's family was all at Mom and Dad's. They had brought sleeping bags and were camped on the floor of the living room. I found my wife, Heidi, in the kitchen and she told me about a conversation she had overheard earlier between Elizabeth's brothers and sister. Twelve-year-old Andrew was pressing Mary Katherine for more details about the hat she said the kidnapper was wearing. "Andrew was saying, 'You say he had a hat. Was it a baseball cap?'" Heidi remembered. "Mary Katherine said 'No, no.' Then Andrew said, 'I have a baseball cap, was it like that?' Mary Katherine kept insisting it wasn't a baseball cap. She put her hands into a cup shape. 'It went like this,' she said. She couldn't describe it but she knew it wasn't a baseball cap. Andrew just wanted to know. Like we all did. But he was really grilling her, the way kids do."

Heidi and I understood the frustration the kids were going through. Their sister had been kidnapped and no one knew who did it or why. Hundreds of people had spent the day looking for clues and waiting for a ransom note or some other explanation for the abduction. But nothing had happened. At night, in the dark, with the outside world again asleep, the silence and frustration only increased.

As Heidi turned to leave and drive home to be with our girls, she told me that while I was at Shriners she had made a run to the Smith's supermarket nearby. The forecast for the next day was hot and dry and the volunteer searchers we hoped and prayed would show up in the morning would need plenty of water. She had gone to Smith's to see if she could get some donated. She talked to the night manager, who told her he had no authority to authorize donating water. He tried to call his boss, but he was out of town. He looked at Heidi, who was barely keeping it together by this point, and pulled out his credit card and personally paid for four cases of bottled water.

"Everyone has been so nice," Heidi said to me as her eyes filled with tears. She threw her arms around my neck and whispered, "Happy Anniversary." Lost in the day's madness was the memory that twenty-three years ago, on June 5, 1979, Heidi and I had gotten married.

As I went to a spare room in my parents' house, my brother David and his wife, Julie, were coming back from making the final search center arrangements at Shriners with Debbie Norris and Dawn Davis. They had thought they might sleep at the hospital but decided against it and drove back to my parents' house. They had forgotten their key so they had to knock on the door.

It was well after 1:00 A.M. by now, but as soon as they knocked they heard footsteps approaching the door. Then they detected the first note of hope they had heard in Lois's voice all day. "Elizabeth," said her mother, "is that you?"

In a house on Chandler Drive not far from the Smarts, someone else was having trouble falling asleep. Brent Pack was a former cop who now owned a video surveillance business. His company's digital video recorders, more than two thousand of them, were set up in markets, convenience stores, gas stations, and motels throughout northern Utah. As soon as he learned about the kidnapping, Brent had run a check on all of his hard drives. The kinds of places that used his service were precisely the kinds of places an abductor might show his face while on the run. Everybody needs food and gas, and Brent knew from his years on the police force that crooks aren't always the most intelligent creatures on the planet.

He had a description of the kidnapper: Caucasian, five-foot-eight, light-colored clothes, and some kind of hat. He quickly got the word out to his clients and even sent some employees to Evanston, ninety miles away on the Utah–Wyoming border. He asked them to report if anyone had seen anything.

One of his clients at a Maverik gas station and convenience store on the corner of 300 South and 500 East near downtown Salt Lake City reported something from the night before. At about 10:30 P.M., several hours before the kidnapping, the camera inside the store's walk-in beer cooler video-taped a man hoisting a twelve-pack of beer. The night clerk said the man walked out of the store without paying. The shoplifter in question was a Caucasian wearing light-colored clothing. He looked to be about five-foot-eight, and had a bag on his back.

Pack called the police. On Wednesday afternoon he had a visit from SLCPD lieutenant Cory Lyman, the man who would soon be assigned by Chief Dinse to take over as task force commander of the Elizabeth Smart investigation. Lyman studied the videotape from the Maverik. "That's not our guy," the lieutenant said to Pack, not going into any further detail. Lyman would say later that he distrusted Pack's motives; Pack was a former cop seemingly interested in furthering his new career in surveillance security.

But despite the police's dismissal, the image from the convenience store nagged at Brent Pack, a longtime neighbor and friend of Elizabeth Smart and her family. He had hunted for Elizabeth in Memory Grove and other places near his home all day long. Like so many people who knew the Smarts, he took the loss personally; he desperately wanted to find the girl. That's why he searched till dark, that's why he put out the urgent alert to all his clients, and that's why he called the police and showed them the digital video. The man in the video was the right height, he wore clothing that matched the kidnapper's description, and there was something else: the man who stole the beer was wearing a light-colored cap.

3

On a steep hillside thick with huge scrub oak trees exactly 3.6 miles from Kristianna Circle, deep within the rugged Wasatch Mountains that serve as the eastern boundary of the Salt Lake Valley, a bearded man dressed in muslin lay inside a dark tent. His given name was Brian David Mitchell, but it was a name he no longer acknowledged. In 1993 he had heard God calling him to be a prophet and instructing him to change his name. He became Immanuel David Isaiah. In the years since, he had attracted only one convert, his wife, Wanda, whom he now called Hephzibah Eladah Isaiah. As Immanuel, Mitchell preached that the world was awful and wicked, a place he and Wanda separated themselves from by dressing in robes and living a nonmaterial existence. His message was that God had set him apart and personally called him to rail against evil. Breaking into the house on Kristianna Circle in the middle of the night to take the pretty blond girl from her bed had been a directive from God. It was also God who had told Mitchell to shackle the girl's ankle to a steel cable in his camouflaged camp so she could not possibly escape.

It was daylight the previous morning when Mitchell arrived with Elizabeth. They had walked in from above the campsite, directly over the top of the mountain. Prodded by the long hunting knife in Mitchell's right hand, the same knife that had so easily sliced the kitchen screen, Elizabeth Smart had done what she was told. After leaving her house through the kitchen door, they had followed the footpath around the scrub oak in her backyard, passed the neighbor's gazebo, and then headed up a vacant lot that emptied them onto Tomahawk Circle at the top of Arlington Hills.

From there they could have turned to their right and hiked past the big block "U" on the mountain—a route that would have avoided traffic but would have meant walking dangerously close to a number of backyards. They could have walked straight ahead and up a steep embankment filled with shale rock—the quickest exit away from the city and into the mountains, but also the loudest. Or they could have turned to their left and walked north on Tomahawk Drive past ten houses, five on each side of the road, and then turned right onto the trail leading to the old pioneer lime kilns. Mitchell had chosen left. Under a sliver of light from a crescent moon, the pair quickly passed the ten houses in silence and turned at the dirt trail. Seconds later they disappeared from sight.

About a quarter-mile later, they passed the kilns as they continued up the steep narrow path to its intersection with the main thoroughfare of the foothills, the Bonneville Shoreline Trail. This is a wide dirt path that circumvents the east rim of the Salt Lake Valley and marks the shoreline of ancient Lake Bonneville, which thirty thousand years ago filled much of present-day Utah. The Shoreline Trail is a favorite of hikers, joggers, and mountain bikers, especially in the summer.

Mitchell did not linger to admire the view of the Salt Lake Valley below them. He marched them across the dusty, well-traveled trail and soon left it behind as they hiked straight up the mountain. He moved quickly, as it was already getting light.

The temperature was in the low fifties as they bushwhacked through the undergrowth and scrub oak. To their left was the north fork of Dry Creek Canyon; to their right, up and over the ridge, the canyon's south fork. Once they were out of sight of the Shoreline Trail they slowed down. The terrified teenager asked, "Why are you doing this? Why are you taking me?" and in a high-pitched voice the man carrying the knife responded that he was fulfilling the Lord's work. A faint memory crawled into Elizabeth's mind and she said, "You worked at our house once, didn't you?"

Periodically, Mitchell would stop to rest and rant, nervously alternating his comments between God and himself. Then he would abruptly stand up with the knife clutched in one hand, Elizabeth in the other, and they would set off again, each step moving the bewildered girl farther away from her home and her old life. The stylish Polo brand tennis shoes Elizabeth had taken from her closet saved her feet, but the sheer fabric of her favorite red silk pajamas could not stop the rocks and tree branches from tearing at her arms and legs.

Near the crest of the hill, after climbing nearly three thousand vertical feet, with nothing but more peaks and canyons beyond, they turned right (east), and scrambled down a steep pitch. About a quarter of a mile above the bottom of the south fork of Dry Creek Canyon, Mitchell and Elizabeth emerged into a campsite improbably perched on the severe slope. The small clearing was camouflaged on all sides by trees so thick they eclipsed the sky. From five feet away it was not visible. Mitchell's wife, Wanda, was there waiting for them. There was a tent set up on a small rectangular area that had been leveled. A cast-iron cooking pot was wedged in a tree just below the tent, and in the center of the tilted camp was a large, freshly dug cutout burrowed into the hill. A hammer, a saw, and other carpentry tools were scattered on the ground, along with stripped trunks of felled aspen trees, a few of which lay across the cut in the mountain, the beginnings of a roof.

4

I would like to say I woke up at 3:30 on Thursday morning, the day after my niece went missing, but that would not be accurate. I *got up* at 3:30 A.M. After staring at the ceiling in my father's study for the better part of two hours, I finally gave up on sleep. It was time to get moving again.

If I knew anything, I knew I would never let this go—nor would anyone in the Smart family. People would later wonder why Ed's extended family—his brothers and sisters, in particular—became so involved, so resolute, so *belligerent*, in the search for Elizabeth. She wasn't *our* daughter. Elizabeth hadn't been stolen from *our* homes. All I can say in answer is that, for better or worse, it is our family nature. It might ruin us, it might make us unpopular, it might make others question our sanity, but no one in the extended Smart family would stop until Elizabeth was found. From day one, I knew this.

We have a favorite word in our family. It comes from Herman Melville's novel *Moby Dick*. He's describing Ahab going after the white whale at the risk of everything. The word is "monomaniacal." This is a trait we all share. It comes largely from my dad, but my mom has it as well. My father is one of the brightest men I know, but more importantly he is one of the most tireless. My father would go for three or four days without sleep, then he'd need a day or so to recover. My mother isn't quite as driven as my dad, but she is an incredibly passionate woman. Whatever she's doing, she throws herself into it completely. When you mix my dad's drive and my mom's passion you end up with six kids pretty much helpless to turn out any other way. On the upside, you have people who will die before they will quit; on the downside, you have people so resolute they neglect to ask for directions.

I also knew no one in the family would approach the problem the same way. We're alike, but we're different. Chris attacks things head-on; David tends to take a more cerebral approach; Cynthia prays; and Angela looks out for everyone else. We would apply our own personalities to the task.

Me, I would try to out-think the problem. Thinking was why I couldn't sleep. During the night, while staring at the ceiling, I had been thinking specifically about a man named Bill Krebs*, a gardener who worked on a regular basis at a house nearby and who did occasional work for Ed and Lois. The gardener's name had come up as a possible suspect during a conversation I'd had the previous afternoon with John Smith*, a relative of the people Krebs worked for.

Smith had walked into the Beesleys' driveway after he'd passed two journalists on the street. "You know, in a couple of hours they'll find her in a dumpster and we'll be out of here," he overheard one reporter say to the other, and they both laughed. The remark and the laughter incensed Smith. His first reaction, he told me, was to beat the hell out of them, which he wisely reconsidered. His second reaction, he said, was to promise himself never to get so desensitized. At that moment, he committed to do whatever it took to help bring Elizabeth home.

As we stood there talking, he brought up the gardener. He said there were a number of reasons why Bill Krebs might be looked at as a possible suspect: he was mentally unstable and an alcoholic, he had had previous run-ins with law enforcement, and, most importantly, he knew Ed's children well, and had been working at Ed's house within a day or two of the kidnapping.

Smith said Krebs had already called him to ask if he should turn himself in for questioning. Krebs insisted he had nothing to do with the kidnapping; he said he loved the Smart kids and would never hurt them. But he figured, as did Smith, that he would be regarded as a suspect because of his past and his relationship to the Smart children. Krebs hadn't come near Kristianna Circle since the morning of the kidnapping and Smith said he sounded frantic over the phone, as if he were on the verge of losing control. It was all very suspicious, particularly when Smith added that the gardener often wore a white cap and he had deep crow's feet around his eyes—they could be the wrinkles Mary Katherine had described on the side of the abductor's face. Also, Mary Katherine had said the kidnapper seemed vaguely familiar, which made sense in the case of someone who visited the house only occasionally. Ed felt certain that it wasn't Krebs because Mary Katherine would have recognized him, but with no idea who could have taken Elizabeth, it seemed obvious that the gardener should be questioned as soon as possible. Within minutes of speaking with Smith, I contacted the police and told them so. Through my short night, I had spent much of it wondering what progress had been made with regard to Bill Krebs.

I took a short shower and made my way to the Sabala home on the corner of Virginia Street and Kristianna Circle, where I met David and Julie. The Sabalas, who were out of town, had agreed to turn their house into a TV studio for the morning news shows, including NBC's *Today*, ABC's *Good Morning, America*, and *CBS This Morning*. The set-ups began at 4:00 A.M. (6:00 EST), to prepare for the live feeds at 5:00. With the help of SLCPD detective Jay Rhodes, I had helped make the arrangements for the morning shows the day before. Numerous other cable TV, radio, and newspaper outlets would arrive later in the day.

As I came into the Sabalas' house I saw that Ed and Lois were about to be interviewed via satellite by NBC's Katie Couric from New York. They obviously hadn't had a bit of sleep either. Ed's face was pale, and Lois's eyes were shut tight. Even when the cameras turned on and she opened them they were barely slits. It may have seemed cruel to pull parents who had lost their child only twenty-four hours earlier into the nation's homes for breakfast. But as much as the networks wanted the interviews, Ed and Lois, no matter how they looked, wanted them more. National exposure meant national awareness. Someone, somewhere, who knew something, might tune in.

After I left the morning shows, I drove down the hill to Shriners Hospital, where I could already see the parking lot was filling up with cars. People were lined up outside the south entrance where we had set up our search center registration table the night before. The search was supposed to start at eight o'clock. I looked at my watch. It was just past 6:30.

Inside the hospital, Dawn Davis from the Laura Recovery Center, the only one among us with any experience in organizing a search, was already under siege. She had helped direct more than thirty searches since she'd volunteered to look for Laura Smither in Friendswood, Texas, in 1997—an event so profoundly moving that it inspired her to become a full-time search coordinator when Bob and Kay Smither set up the Laura Recovery Center Foundation. But none of the searches she'd been involved with had come close to starting this quickly. Word of mouth about the citywide search, along with the pleas for help from the newscasts the night before, had resulted in an overwhelming community response. June 6 was a Thursday, a regular workday, but that didn't matter. At first light, people began lining up at Shriners. A number of businesses and government agencies announced that they were either shutting down operations or allowing employees the option of searching instead of working. Ron McBride, the University of Utah football coach, sent his team over. Dozens of LDS missionaries stopped proselytizing and came to search. I could see that the line forming outside the registration office was a cross-section of society; there were young people, old people, businessmen, soccer moms, hippies, cowboys, students, you name it.

Inside the makeshift search headquarters, scores of people from the neighborhood were there to help. Heidi and others pulled a long table outside on the patio and started registering people well before 8:00, sending them into the hospital auditorium, where a doctors' meeting adjourned just in time to see dozens of people march in wearing long pants and hiking boots. The auditorium quickly transformed into the search center orientation room, where people were given a physical description of Elizabeth, shown an example of her pajamas, and told to tag, with strings of red tape, anything they found that they considered suspicious. Everyone got an orange vest and search groups of about twelve to fifteen people were organized. One person was designated as leader for each group, and given a cell phone number to call in the event of emergency.

In the map room, Doug, Zeke, and Larry Holmstrom were soon under pressure to provide designated areas for the quickly forming search groups. The core of family and friends who had come early to the hospital to handle the logistics was soon overwhelmed, and total strangers who had come to search found themselves drafted into the organization. Two sisters from Ogden, Melinda Giffard and Christy Kinney, came dressed in long pants, ready to search the mountains. The next thing they knew, someone shouted, "We need two people on phones." "My sister and I will," Christy reflexively answered. For the next two months Melinda and Christy, who became known affectionately as "The Girls," made the daily ninety-mile round trip from Ogden so they could answer phones. Melinda would skip her summer term of college to look for a girl who, until that Thursday morning, she never knew existed.

By 10:30 A.M., a line of more than two hundred volunteer searchers stretched out behind the registration table and David noticed the volunteer registration forms were running low. He alerted Dawn, who replied, "There's no way we're out of volunteer forms. I brought 450 with me." When she saw that the forms were in fact running low, she explained that in other searches, 450 volunteers would be considered a very successful day. David whited out a used registration form and started making copies on a photocopier Julie had brought from home.

By noon, dozens of searches had already been completed, both in the nearby hills and door-to-door in the city, and group reports, as well as leads to be followed, were piling up. Strands of red tape marked suspicious piles of discarded clothing, recently used campfires, and other trash and signs of activity throughout the foothills. David put in a call to Detective Jay Rhodes, asking SLCPD to send someone to start working on the leads. "Do you have any yet?" the detective asked. "Only about two hundred," said David. By noon, Sergeant David Craycroft was on the scene; he immediately called for backup. By the end of the day, three full-time detectives were at the search center processing leads.

Also about midday, four volunteers from the Abby and Jennifer Group in Grand Junction, Colorado, arrived. They brought in a number of orange vests and other supplies that the Laura Recovery Center had furnished the previous month during a search in Grand Junction for Abby and Jennifer Blagg, a mother and daughter who disappeared in November of 2001. The mother's body was found in the city dump but six-year-old Abby remained missing. In addition to the vests, the Abby and Jennifer volunteers contributed a first-rate communications center, with scanners, walkie-talkies, and telephones, which helped considerably in communications with the police and volunteers.

Hundreds of people had dropped what they were doing to help look for a kidnapped girl. This wasn't a school assignment or a church calling. No one was getting paid. Members of the family often broke down emotionally in the midst of so much unmitigated goodness and selflessness. Later, some would attribute the unprecedented numbers to the influence of the LDS church, since Ed and Lois and their family, as well as my parents, were active members of the local LDS Arlington Hills Ward. Ed was a member of the bishopric, or ward leadership, and more than half of the people in the neighborhood, as in all of Salt Lake City and throughout the state of Utah, were members of the LDS Church.

On Wednesday, only hours after Elizabeth was taken, I received a call on my cell phone from Gordon B. Hinckley, the LDS Church president, and a person I had met many times over the past twenty years while taking his photo at various times for the *Deseret News* and the *New York Times*. President Hinckley offered his personal support and said that the Church would assist in any way it could. It was a kind and gracious gesture, but he was not suggesting that the Church would lead the search. In a follow-up conversation with my brother-in-law Zeke Dumke, President Hinckley made that perfectly clear. The Church would provide as much help as possible—it would lend its networking capabilities, it would rally support—but it would be a volunteer like everyone else. "This is a community concern and it needs to be a community effort," President Hinckley told Zeke.

President Hinckley came to Ed and Lois's home at 9:30 Thursday night. The ninety-two-year-old Mormon prophet (with a bad hip that necessitated the use of a cane) paused at the base of the cement stairs leading to the front door. Then he turned to his son, Richard, and said, "Well, let's get started." After blessing the home and the family, and offering words of encouragement, the Hinckleys left. Ed and Lois stayed and spent the night in their home. Within the week, their five children, who had been staying with various relatives, would also return. While the kids would sleep on the floor of their parents' room for many nights to come and drapes would be installed throughout the house, Ed said he had no concerns about staying in the home after President Hinckley's blessing.

■   ■   ■

In addition to the volunteer searchers, the media began arriving in waves on Thursday. Satellite trucks from major networks and local affiliates lined up on the street between Shriners Hospital and the Federal Heights LDS wardhouse. It was mind-boggling how quickly the world could come together in the information age. Almost before the trucks turned off their engines, producers from the various networks began arranging for interviews. The media's capacity to reach millions made the potential impact incalculable.

Among those in the national media I met that day was Darin Mackoff, a producer for Fox News, who let me know that Fox was bringing in Marc Klaas to help Ed and Lois and the family. Klaas is the father of Polly Klaas, the twelve-year-old California girl who in December 1993 was kidnapped, raped, and murdered by a monster named Richard Allen Davis. The emotional courtroom scene of Marc Klaas going after Davis when Davis taunted him about his dead child is a standard case study in most college journalism-in-the-courtroom classes. Klaas, I learned, had gone on to help set up two foundations to fight for children's rights. Mackoff said Klaas wanted to have a chance to talk to Ed and Lois personally; the network also wanted to bring in Jeanne Boylan, the noted forensic artist who had sketched the Unabomber as well as Polly's killer. My answer was that the family was working with law enforcement and whatever law enforcement decided about Boylan was our decision as well.

In the meantime, there was still my nagging concern about the gardener. All morning I'd been asking various police officers if anyone had questioned Bill Krebs. By early afternoon, with Elizabeth's disappearance now thirty-six hours old, it was obvious from the puzzled looks and blank stares that he hadn't been located, let alone interviewed. John Smith was as frustrated as I was at the lack of action. By early afternoon we were so agitated that we decided to find and question Krebs ourselves.

We got in Smith's car to drive across town to a house where Krebs was living. For good measure, we called Smith's father-in-law, who knew Krebs well, and picked him up at his downtown office. On the way, I called Rick Dinse, the police chief, and told him what we were doing. "Don't go, wait for us," Dinse said. "No, we are already on our way," I replied and quickly hung up. There were two reasons why we wanted to go in before the police. First, Smith had told me that Krebs was afraid of the cops, but trusted Smith and Smith's father-in-law. Second, a day and a half was a long time to wait to rule someone out as a suspect. We weren't willing to wait any longer.

We pulled up to a modest bungalow with construction wheelbarrows in the front yard and drywall leaning against the building. Nobody answered the front door so we walked around the back and down the stairway to the basement and knocked on the door. We could hear movement inside and soon a bleary-eyed Bill Krebs opened the door a crack, peered through, and, recognizing Smith, let us in.

The basement had no walls, just bare studs framing the rooms. Clothes, cans, dishes, and garbage were everywhere. Krebs cleared an area around an old sofa for us to sit. He was drunk and in tears. He talked about how sweet and beautiful Elizabeth was and how he couldn't imagine anyone doing something terrible to her. He talked about all of Ed's children. As he talked, we noticed a white baseball cap lying on the shelf. I asked Krebs if I could go to the bathroom, a ruse to look around, and he pointed me to the back of the basement. I scanned for any sign of Elizabeth but saw none. Smith asked for a drink and Krebs brought him a bottle of soda, which Smith carefully kept with Krebs's fingerprints intact. Chief Dinse had indicated to me that the police had gathered evidence from the crime scene—a fact they did not want the public to know about. Comparing the gardener's prints would go a long way in clearing him—or identifying him—as a suspect.

Although our suspicions had been high, it seemed apparent after talking to him and looking around his wreck of a residence that Krebs was simply a very drunk, very paranoid person who literally had been hiding out, terrified that the police were coming to charge him with a crime he didn't commit. Smith explained that the police would indeed be coming, but just to talk and he shouldn't be afraid. On our way back to Shriners, we stopped to give the bagged soda bottle to police officers stationed at Ed's home. We also gave them Krebs's address. Within the hour the police interviewed and fingerprinted Krebs themselves—and eliminated him as a suspect.

■　■　■

By the time the search center officially stopped sending out volunteer groups at 5:00 P.M. Thursday, eighteen hundred people had filled out registration forms. Some had gone on two or more searches, while others hadn't bothered to check in officially and had searched on their own, which made calculating the exact number of volunteers only an educated guess. Many, like Elizabeth's brother Charles who hardly stopped for a break and drove himself to the point of exhaustion, set a remarkable pace. The Francom family constituted a small army of searchers all by itself. When they weren't in the foothills, they were helping Lois with her children or cleaning the house, which had been covered with fingerprinting powder. Stan Francom, Lois's brother, approached me that first day and made it a point to thank me for handling the press. "We will do anything you want," he said, "but we would rather be in the background helping, not in front of the camera." For months the Francoms would do just that, helping with everything they could, including media interviews when asked.

The minimum search age of eighteen left out Elizabeth's friends, but they flocked to the search center anyway. That day many of them elected to skip Bryant Intermediate School's year-end outing to Lagoon, a local amusement park, so they could help out with registration or food and water distribution or just lend moral support. Rod Livingston brought in big spools of light blue ribbon (which Lois said was Elizabeth's favorite color), and teenagers tied the ribbons on car antennas in the parking lot, on telephone poles up and down the street, on porches, flagpoles, mailboxes, and their wrists.

Food and supplies poured in from local businesses. There were mass donations of batteries, flashlights, and sunscreen. Entirely unbidden, the Red Cross and the Salvation Army set up assistance booths. To alleviate parking snarls, the Utah Transit Authority bused volunteers from parking lots a mile away at the University of Utah. It was as if the whole community had stopped to help Elizabeth Smart.

As the search center's first day came to a close, the big news was that a small group of volunteers had chased a man matching the kidnapper's description in Emigration Canyon, three short drainages south of Ed and Lois's home. The volunteers recounted an intense tale of a chase across the mountain and of shots being fired at dusk. Police helicopters equipped with infrared tracking monitors were circling the area. On television the local stations were interrupting regular programming with live updates of what appeared to be a promising development.

With this news in the air, I got in the car for the drive home. On the way my cell phone rang. I looked at my watch; it was not quite midnight. On the line was one of my best friends, Mike Freed. Freed and I met when we were fourteen and attending the same intermediate school Elizabeth attended. He had been searching nonstop since he first heard of the kidnapping. He had also been doing his own detective work. He knew Elizabeth spent a lot of time playing the harp, and wondered if the clue to her disappearance might be in that area of her life.

By coincidence, the business Freed runs with his wife, Suzi, Q Street Fine Arts, is located in the Avenues section of Salt Lake City only a couple of blocks from the Salt Lake Harp Center on P Street and South Temple, home of the city's most prominent harp instructor, ShruDeLi Ownbey. Freed and Suzi had bought some art from ShruDeLi, who is also an artist, and they had become acquainted. ShruDeLi taught many of the valley's most promising harpists, including Elizabeth.

Freed had called ShruDeLi to see if she could think of anything strange or unusual that may have occurred in the recent past in the harp community. ShruDeLi emphatically answered yes. She remembered a man who attended all four Olympic concerts held the previous February when the Olympic Winter Games were in Salt Lake. In an attempt to appeal to a wider audience, the concerts had been advertised, for the first time, in *The Catalyst* magazine, a publication that circulates to the offbeat, artsy population of Salt Lake City. "We wanted to attract a different group, and, boy, did we get a different group," ShruDeLi told Freed. Many people, especially parents of the harpists, remembered the man in question because of his unusual appearance. He had long hair and a missing front tooth, and he wore a beret on his head. They also remembered his habit of going down to the stage after the concerts and talking to the female harpists. ShruDeLi remembered that he seemed to particularly like Elizabeth. He talked to her directly and was very friendly.

No one knew who the man was, the harp teacher told Freed. To thicken the mystery, the guest book from the final concert had turned up missing. ShruDeLi told Freed that the police had already talked to her about the kidnapping, but at the time she had not remembered to tell them about the strange man.

"Smart," Freed said to me when he first came on the phone, "I think I know who did it. Now just hear me out."

By the time we hung up I was just buzzed. In the absence of any other leads or suspects, this fit. I was overwhelmed by the feeling that this was our man. I felt so strongly that I called Rick Dinse on my cell phone. I wanted to tell him that if the police were successful in catching the man with the gun in Emigration Canyon, he might very well turn out to be the harp man, on the run. If that were the case, a woman named ShruDeLi Ownbey could identify him.

I pulled my car over at the top of the mountains so I wouldn't lose my cell phone service. To his credit, the chief of police listened to what I had to say. He was kind and very patient. After I finished, he went into a detailed explanation of how the police were systematically going through everybody who worked in Ed's house and was familiar with it. Ed used a lot of handymen in building his house, and the police wanted to look at all of them because they would have known where the girls slept. Fixed on the harp lead, I was losing patience fast and let out a string of obscenities ending with, "Look, any idiot can see that the house is basically a fishbowl. There are no drapes on the windows and anybody could check it out from the outside and know how to get to the girls' room." As soon as I finished my outburst, I apologized. "Don't think anything of it," Dinse said, again exercising what I considered remarkable patience. "Under the circumstances, I would probably react the same way."

We hung up with the chief promising to look into the story of the man with the beret. I drove into my driveway convinced Freed had cracked the case.

When I walked into the house it was well after midnight and Heidi and our nineteen-year-old daughter, Nicole, were talking in the kitchen. Nicole was sobbing at the thought of never seeing Elizabeth again. I put my arms around her and, completely energized by what I'd just heard from Freed, exclaimed, "Nicole, I promise you, you will see your cousin again, and hold her in your arms!"

Heidi stood and listened to my vow with her arms folded tightly. She was furious. "Please don't ever do that again!" she said after Nicole went downstairs. "Don't make promises you don't know you can keep."

I looked at my beautiful wife through sleep-deprived eyes—I had been awake forty-four straight hours now—and numbly nodded that I would not do that again. In my mind, though, I thought I wouldn't have to. I was just so sure.

Lost amid the day's frenetic pace was a late-afternoon incident that involved my sister Angela. She had gone to Kinko's to pick up another batch of fliers. "Kinko's was so great," she recalled. "They first said they'd do a thousand free. Ten thousand later they finally said, 'We can't do any more free.'"

The closest Kinko's copy center was less than a mile from Shriners, straight down Virginia Street and over a block on the west side of the University of Utah campus. Under normal circumstances, Angela and her family would have been packing for the flight they'd booked to Bolivia. But these were not normal circumstances. The trip was canceled and young Zeke IV was left watching CNN updates about the kidnapping in airports while finding his way back from South America.

Angela was hurrying up the sidewalk to the copy center when a man begging for money stopped her. Behind the man was a woman. They were both dressed in robes. "They were wearing natural muslin. It's not white, its unbleached muslin," remembered Angela, who has an eye for that kind of detail. "He had kind of a backpacky thing on his back and they both had sort of hiking boots on their feet. She had big glasses and her hair pulled back and his hat was so strange. I'm a seamstress and I had a hard time describing it later when I was trying to tell everyone what it looked like. It was round like a baker's hat with sewed-up corners so it was kind of a pyramid thing at the top."

Angela said the robed man told her that he and the woman were traveling, preaching the word of Christ, and they didn't have jobs. Did she have some money for them? "I remember thinking, 'Boy, you stay clean for a homeless guy,'" reflected Angela. "Then I asked him what he needed the money for. He looked away from me, he averted his eyes, and the woman didn't say anything. It was bugging me that he wouldn't answer me so I kind of stepped in front of him and tried to make eye contact. And that's when I noticed his eyes. They were blue. Not blue-blue, but piercing blue. The best way I could describe them is they looked like Jeremy Irons's eyes. I mean they were beautiful, but they were also kinda crazy. I said to him, 'I'm not saying to you that I'm not going to give you money. I'm just trying to get some accountability for it.' But he wouldn't look at me and he wouldn't talk to me. He started walking away and I thought, I'm not going to pick a fight, but I had this horrible feeling. I kept wondering why do I have such a bad feeling about this? I went in, got the fliers, came out, and the man and woman were gone."

Back at Shriners, Angela was unnerved enough by the experience that she detailed her encounter to family and friends. "There was the weirdest guy down by Kinko's," she said. "If Jesus was traveling without purse or scrip, is that what he would look like? He gave me the weirdest feeling. Is it because I didn't give him anything?"

She turned to me and asked, "Do you think he could be the kidnapper?" Without hesitating, I told her no and explained that I knew exactly who she was talking about. While it was her first encounter with the strange bearded man who dressed in robes, the Jesus Man was a common sight downtown, an area where I spent considerably more time than Angela. I had personally seen him begging many times. I'd seen him once dressed in LDS temple clothes, standing directly across the street from the Salt Lake Temple. He was wearing the cap and apron that are supposed to be worn only during ceremonies performed inside the walls of the temple—an exceptionally shocking sight for any orthodox Mormon. In addition to the beard and robes, he sometimes had a woman with him; I guessed it was probably the same woman Angela had seen. I told my sister that I seriously doubted that whoever took Elizabeth would be with a woman.

5

The woods were full of noises that night, and not the usual ones. Helicopters buzzed overhead, so close that the searchers on the ground could see and hear the blades whirring. In the distance, human voices carried on the wind. "Elizabeth," the voices called out, "Liz!"

Wildlife abounded in this part of the forest, but human beings were infrequent visitors who rarely stayed long. Other than deer- and elk-hunting seasons, which wouldn't begin until October, there wasn't much to draw anyone to the far end of Dry Creek Canyon. There was no water to speak of—it wasn't called Dry Creek for nothing—only a faint stream fed by a small spring, its source camouflaged about a third of a mile below the campsite of Brian David Mitchell and his wife, Wanda.

In other years they had camped on flatter ground closer to the spring. In the summer of 1997, the first year they came to the canyon, Mitchell had bought an authentic teepee kit at a sporting goods store in town—thanks to a loan from his father, a loan he never repaid—and hauled the contents up the trail alongside the mostly dry streambed. He'd developed some carpentry skills, and with Wanda's help he erected the teepee, which had served its purpose until Dry Creek's harsh winters snapped the poles. Those broken poles, now littered among the aspen trees, reflected an earlier attempt at comfort—in sharp contrast to Mitchell's current camp. A dug-out clearing on a steep slope, it was a hideout more than a camp, a place no one was meant to find. The digging was a work in progress, the beginnings of a man-made lean-to that, when finished, would have a natural earthen roof piled on top of the aspen trees. Let the winter snows try to topple that. Next to the unfinished lean-to was the small level spot with the tent on it—the summer quarters.

He wasn't the first to set up residence in Dry Creek. Scattered about was evidence of other attempts to colonize the upper arm of south fork—a piece of canvas tarp here, some corrugated tin there, and in a large flat clearing nearby, a rusted-out metal stove. The most ambitious undertaking had been by a homesteader at the turn of the twentieth century who had built a cabin and planted two apple trees. The cabin was gone, with only a few stones remaining, but the apple trees were still standing. One was sweet and one was sour and they provided a regular part of the daily diet for the three full-time residents of Dry Creek Canyon—Brian and Wanda, and the girl who was now dressed, like them, in muslin. They called her Augustine.

Brian David Mitchell had grown up eating apples and plenty of other fruit. His father, Shirl Mitchell, insisted on it. Shirl was a health nut before anyone coined the term. As a kid growing up in the Salt Lake Valley in the 1950s, if Brian wanted sweets he had to get them from the neighbors on the sly, which he did whenever the opportunity arose. But now he was a devoted fruit eater.

Shirl V. Mitchell was a revolutionary preacher. Even before Brian was born, Shirl began working on his own writings of personal philosophy that ridiculed mainstream religious thought as a "troubling nightmare," and declaimed the need for "an antibody mutant maverick poetic macrocosmic thinker" to "break the logjam." And who would fit that role better than the author? Each night when he came home from his job as a social worker for the state of Utah, Shirl Mitchell shut himself off in his room and wrote. His "solipsistic" ramblings took on different titles—"The Facts of Life" in the 1950s, "The Barrier of Infinity" in the 1960s, "Jack and the Beanstalk" in the 1970s, and, finally, "Spokesman for the Infant God or Goddess" when he bound everything together and pronounced the project finished in April 1997. The result was more than a thousand pages long and fifty-three years in the making.

"Humankind need look no further than this planet and The Stellar Entities that contain and gestate them evolutionally and involutionally, if they would seek for their orientation and identity in such an astronomic milieu," Shirl wrote in a conclusion equally as bizarre as his crude but detailed drawings of human anatomy at the back of the manuscript and a recurrent dark fixation on sexuality and voyeurism throughout the text. He repeatedly cast aspersions on the claims and practices of the LDS Church, and parceled out his most vitriolic ridicule on the institution of marriage, which he predicted would be abolished following the birth of the infant deity for whom he was acting as spokesman. In the end, no one knew what to make of what was in the manuscript any more than they knew what to make of the lifetime it took to write it.

Like many longtime Utahans, Shirl Mitchell's roots, and thus his son's, extended to out-of-the-mainstream religious beginnings that had been responsible for settling the state in the first place. Shirl's great-grandfather, Benjamin T. Mitchell, was one of the earliest converts to the Church of Jesus Christ of Latter-day Saints, a religion that broke from eighteen centuries of traditional Christianity by claiming to be the modern restoration of the church Jesus Christ established during his ministry at the meridian of time. He was among the first wave of persecuted Mormon pioneers who entered the Salt Lake Valley in the late 1840s. Benjamin was a stonecutter who worked on many of the early LDS temples, the religion's sacred houses of worship where eternal ordinances are performed. He was a polygamist, with six wives and fifty-seven children. Shirl's maternal ancestors were also early Mormon converts and Utah settlers, but by the time Shirl came along, family ties with the dominant church had long since been broken. Shirl's parents were LDS but rarely attended services, and, as he wrote in "Spokesman for the Infant God or Goddess," Shirl saw himself as a "mutation from the accepted LDS Church party line. Neither a Mormon, or a Christian, for that matter, in the commonly accepted sense of either of the terms."

But as a child, Shirl had once experienced a profound Christian moment. When he was seven years old, he heard a voice call out to him, "You are Christ." He was alone when he claimed to have heard the voice, and he said he never heard it again. But as he would tell the story to friends and family—including his son Brian—it was an experience he would never forget.

For all their similarities—the same piercing eyes, the same high-pitched voice, the same antisocial tendencies, the same fanatical fixation on bringing truth to an ignorant world—the father and son spent little time together during Brian's formative years. By all accounts, theirs was a difficult relationship, exacerbated by the continual conflict between Shirl Mitchell and his wife, Brian's mother, Irene Mitchell.

Brian's parents did not get along. When Irene wasn't asking Shirl to leave the house, he was leaving of his own volition. When they were together, they argued constantly. Among their regular disputes was how Brian should be disciplined for all the trouble he got into. Irene, a meek, passive high school English teacher, opted for more time at church, gentle nurturing, and finding the right kinds of friends for the boy. Shirl was in favor of tougher love for his "very erratic" son. He did not hesitate to strike Brian when he thought he deserved it; he punished the boy harshly for youthful indiscretions, banishing him to sleep alone in the basement as early as the age of two. Shirl was an eye-for-an-eye kind of dad. When three-year-old Brian smacked a neighbor kid with a hose, Shirl smacked Brian with the same hose. When Brian was eight and showed excessive interest in sex, Shirl sat him down and made him look at a medical textbook. When Brian was ten and exhibited what Shirl considered a lack of personal discipline, Shirl drove Brian to Rose Park, a Salt Lake suburb ten miles across the valley from where the Mitchell family lived in East Millcreek, dropped him off, and told him to find his own way home. Shirl considered all this part of teaching his son to be a man.

Through the acrimony, volatility, and irreconcilability, Shirl and Irene somehow managed to conceive six children, three boys and three girls. Brian was the second son and third child overall, an unruly middle child growing up in the sixties with above-average intelligence, plenty of free time, and little attention from a meek, overworked mother and an overbearing, reclusive father. The boy's home life offered the classic formula for low self-esteem and bad behavior.

At Canyon Rim Elementary School, Brian became the playground loner. A wiry boy smaller than most of the other kids, he threw rocks at the girls at recess and regularly got into fights. At Wasatch Junior High, he stopped throwing rocks and tried other tactics to get attention. A classmate recalled the week when Brian started on Monday by wearing an all-white outfit—white pants, white shirt, white socks, white shoes, even a white hat. Then he dyed the entire outfit a different color on Tuesday, Wednesday, and Thursday, until, on Friday, everything was black.

But the attention never lasted, and it was rarely positive. He was dismissed as a weird kid, then a weird teenager. Unlike his brothers and sisters, three of whom would go on to serve two-year proselytizing missions for the LDS Church, Brian didn't find sanctuary in the local LDS congregation, the Canyon Rim Fourth Ward. He looked for acceptance in all the wrong places. He was good at getting in trouble. He stole a little, cut school a little, got into drugs and alcohol, and developed a smart mouth. Then, just as he was beginning his first year of high school, he exposed himself to a young neighborhood girl, about four years old, who wandered by the Mitchell's house. He was placed in juvenile detention after the girl's parents complained to Brian's parents. Shirl himself turned Brian in to the authorities. Following a short stint in detention, Shirl, who had written in "Spokesman for the Infant God or Goddess" of fondling young girls as a youth himself, and admitted to being a "peeping tom" as an adult, banished Brian again, not to the basement this time, but to his grandmother's house, for his "excessive disruptive behavior." Brian transferred from Skyline High School, where few knew him, to East High School, where no one knew him. He kept it that way. In 1969, East had moved into a modular schedule, a short-lived experiment designed to develop each student's individuality. Sixteen-year-old Brian decided his individuality did not include any more school. He stopped going to classes entirely, and no one noticed.

If he didn't get attention anywhere else, Brian finally got it from Heaven. By the time he reached his forties, a veritable lifetime from his wild, formative years, he was able to see that clearly. He wasn't different, he was special. Those early challenges and difficulties were God's way of shaping him and preparing him for his prophetic role. He had endured his refiner's fire, even if the world could not see him for who he really was any more than they could see the secluded camp he had dug into the hillside—or the terrified fourteen-year-old girl trapped in the middle of it.

The noises around him, the buzz of the helicopter rotors and the shouts of the people searching for the girl, were coming from the same lost souls who scoffed at him on the streets of the city when he begged. Years ago, they were those who had taunted him at recess.

They had never understood him. How could they possibly understand that he had taken the young girl to begin his kingdom? How could they know that they could search and search, but they would not find her?

When Elizabeth heard the helicopter, she moved toward the sound as far as the cable attached to her ankle would allow. She was able to peer through the leaves of the thick trees hiding the camp and see the shiny object high above, the sun's rays reflecting off its windows. Elizabeth tilted her head back toward the blue sky, making herself as visible as possible, but watched in vain as the helicopter stopped its hover, banked, and disappeared over the hill.

Later, she heard the searchers' calling her name over and over. One of the voices, she was sure, belonged to Uncle David, her mother's brother. She wanted to answer—more than anything in her life, she wanted to answer—but the bearded man threatened to kill her if she made a noise. The voices grew faint and then disappeared entirely. The only evidence that anyone had been there at all were strips of search center red ribbons tied around bits of abandoned refuse on the canyon floor, a short walk below the horrible camp.

6

I was back in front of my parents' house at 3:30 A.M., right on schedule. Set-ups for the morning shows would start around 4:00 and I planned to take Ed and Lois to the Sabalas' for a second day of all-important media appearances. I sat in the car in the dark as I checked the time on my cell phone. It was still too early to go in.

It had been another sleepless night. After hearing Heidi collapse into an exhausted sleep, I had gotten out of bed very early and called John Smith, who seemed to have about as much interest in sleep as I did. An extremely bright person who knows quite a lot about law enforcement, Smith is also very computer savvy. On Thursday, he had set up the first Web site to help find Elizabeth.

Smith reminded me of Dante's guide, Virgil, leading me through my own version of hell. As we talked, he kept focusing me on the only important goal: to find Elizabeth. "Your urgency is much greater than that of the police," he kept saying. "Don't underestimate the bureaucracy." He also warned me that the police wouldn't necessarily be the family's advocate and that it might be wise to look for outside help. He suggested one of his best friends, a forensic psychologist named Stephen Bernard*, or "Doc," as Smith called him. Smith told me that Doc was the smartest man he knew, particularly in the area of human behavior. He could be invaluable at profiling the kind of person who might kidnap a fourteen-year-old girl. He would know how such a person might act and what he might do. Smith said Doc had contacts within the police department. In the twenty years they'd been friends, he'd never known Doc to be wrong.

I felt comfortable talking to Smith. I told him about the harp lead and my inappropriate outburst to Chief Dinse. Smith said not to worry about the outburst because I now had their attention. Then, at two in the morning, we woke Doc up from a dead sleep with a conference phone call. I asked him for advice in coaching Ed and Lois on how to respond on the early television shows. How might we best appeal to the person who took Elizabeth? With harsh words or understanding? Would Ed or Lois be the best person to make the appeal? Doc told us he thought Lois was the best choice.

After this call, I tried to sleep, but it was no use. I had experienced trouble sleeping lately, largely due to financial worries. The horse property I was developing at Winterton Farms had gone into a slump after the September 11 terrorist attacks. The sleep medication that helped me get at least four hours in the past was no longer working. I got out of bed at one point to soak in the hot tub on the deck outside our bedroom. I looked up at a sky filled with countless stars but all I could focus on was Freed's beret-wearing harp fan. According to descriptions from those who had seen him at the Olympic concerts, the man wasn't very tall, and it seemed that he always wore the unconventional beret. Witnesses said the beret was red, but as any Physics 101 student knows, in a dark room, color isn't reflected, so it could have been the light-colored hat Mary Katherine was having a difficult time describing. And this guy had showed particular interest in Elizabeth. By the time I dressed and drove back down the canyon, I was more convinced than ever. It just had to be him.

At 3:45 A.M. I went inside Dad's house, only to discover that Ed and Lois were not there. "They spent the night back at their house," my father told me. He added, "They won't be doing the morning shows." He explained that Ed had been so tired the night before that two police officers had to carry him up the stairs to his bedroom. Ed needed to rest this morning.

I hurried over to the Sabalas', where I joined other early morning guests, including two expert profilers—retired law enforcement officers who were there to theorize about the type of person who had taken Elizabeth—and three young men, about eighteen or nineteen, dressed in camouflage with handcuffs and other combat gear on their belts. These Rambo types were the ones who claimed to have heard shots the evening before in Emigration Canyon. Something about their eagerness to be on television, their swagger, and their military lingo—"We called him down"—seemed a little over the top. I had this sick feeling that their story was a hoax. The networks, of course, were disappointed that Ed and Lois were not there. I explained that Elizabeth's parents were exhausted.

After the shows, I talked to the two profilers, who encouraged me to get to Ed's home because they had heard there was something going on. I went the short distance to the end of Kristianna Circle and let myself in. I found out that Lois had called my dad shortly after I left for the Sabalas' and told him Ed had collapsed from exhaustion. My father quickly made arrangements for Ed to be admitted at nearby LDS Hospital, where Dad was once chief of surgery. Ed was checked in under an alias so he would not be bothered. He hadn't gotten any sleep since the morning of the kidnapping and the physicians were going to make sure he got the rest and nourishment he needed, even if it meant doing it intravenously. Dad was now in the bedroom holding Lois's hand. The two of them were very quiet, and I instinctively walked away.

I moved to the back deck, realizing I had just mistakenly told three separate network morning shows that Ed was home in bed. A pair of FBI agents interviewed me and I tried to explain how important the harp guy seemed as a suspect. After that, Don Bell of the Salt Lake Police Department, the lead sergeant assigned to the case, interviewed me, along with another officer. Bell was in street clothes, but I knew who he was from my various assignments shooting pictures for the *Deseret News*. Bell was an SLCPD veteran. In 1983, he reportedly caught a verbal slipup while interviewing notorious pedophile Arthur Gary Bishop; Bell's catch led to Bishop's confession to the murders of five boys. Bell had also investigated the Mark Hofmann forgeries and murder and the racist killings by Joseph Paul Franklin. Bell had been in on the investigations of nearly every high-profile case in Salt Lake City in the past twenty-five years. In 1991, he was the hostage negotiator at Alta View Hospital during an eighteen-hour standoff with Richard Worthington, who was angry with the doctor who had performed a tubal ligation on his wife. The siege ended with the death of a nurse. Bell was hired as a consultant on a CBS made-for-television movie about the incident, which, not coincidentally, portrayed him as the hero. Although he was known for his huge ego, most journalists in Salt Lake City, myself included, believed Bell to be one of the smartest cops around. I was grateful to be able to talk to him.

"Look, Tom," he said apologetically after listening to a few of my comments about the harp lead, "in an investigation of this kind we have to start with the family and work out, and we can't get past the family right now until we get some answers. For starters, we don't even know what your brother does for a living."

I knew what Bell was thinking. Although there had been no indication of a ransom note, the police hadn't ruled out money as a possible motive. He wanted to know, without coming right out and asking, whether Ed might have orchestrated his own daughter's kidnapping.

I could understand Bell's confusion. Ed's business is kind of complicated. He owns real estate and mortgage companies, which he runs from his home. He sometimes buys and sells cars, and as a general contractor he builds homes to live in and then sells them for a profit. He was in the process of turning over the house on Kristianna Circle. He'd bought the building lot, served as general contractor for the house, hired all the subcontractors, supervised the whole project, and then put it up for sale. Ed had been working on the house for the better part of six years; he did much of the finish work himself. It had been on the market only about a month.

Bell had other questions and theories. He wanted to know whether we had hired a private investigator. If we had, he said, the investigator would not be given full access. I assured him we had not hired a private investigator; we were placing our faith in law enforcement.

The sergeant was candid in his questions. I gave him straightforward answers, but I was upset. Why had it taken three days for the police to find out how Ed made his money? Anyone in the family could have explained it to them, as I just had, in a couple of minutes. The insinuation that my brother could have had anything to do with his daughter's kidnapping rattled me. I said to Bell, "Look, if it's a financial thing, then you might as well put me and David on the list, because we're in a lot deeper trouble than Ed."

(David was recovering a company he owned that had recently gone out of business, and I was sitting on horse property that wasn't selling).

My rational self understood that family members are often involved in abductions and the police were only doing their job by taking a close look at all of us. But I knew my brother, and I had never seen anyone more devastated in my life. I didn't want him to go through the pain of being questioned as a suspect on top of everything else. "You don't know me at all," I told Bell. "But one thing about me is I don't often say absolutes. But one thing I am absolutely certain of is that Ed and Lois would never do anything to harm their child, and if that's not true you can put a bullet in my head."

While trying my best to answer the detective's questions in a conversation I would later come to realize was also an interrogation, my mind kept drifting to something I was sure needed to be chased down fast—the harp lead. After stressing its importance to Sergeant Bell, I drove to Shriners—where even more volunteers were showing up than the day before—and found someone who shared my sense of urgency: Mike Freed.

Since we'd talked at midnight, Freed had been busy. It happened that he personally knew the publisher of *The Catalyst*, the weekly magazine that ran the harp concert ads in February, and he managed to get a copy of the last ad. It showed two teenage girls posing, one in a tennis outfit and the other in a cheerleader outfit, alongside the information for the harp performances. It was just the right appeal, we agreed, for the wrong kind of guy.

Law enforcement, I was pleased to discover, was moving much more quickly on the harp lead than it had in finding the gardener. Freed told me that he and ShruDeLi, the harp teacher, had already been officially questioned that morning and that ShruDeLi was working with an SLCPD sketch artist. Investigators were also in the process of interviewing all the harp students and their parents.

In a case devoid of promising developments, this finally qualified as something encouraging: a suspicious, seemingly eccentric individual who dressed oddly (including the hat) and took an unusual interest in young girls who played the harp. And, perhaps of most significance, no one knew where he was. When word of the harp lead reached Ed in the hospital, he would tell me later, it had a tremendous positive effect on his state of mind.

He said it was one of the reasons he was able to walk out of the hospital on his own that afternoon—mere hours after his physical and emotional collapse. The harp lead gave Ed and Lois something they needed desperately: hope.

John Smith was anxious to continue discussing the case, as was Doc, who agreed to drive to Salt Lake City so he could talk with Smith and me in person. We arranged to meet at a local Thai restaurant. He asked me to wear a hat and sunglasses so people wouldn't recognize me. Coming in disguise seemed a bit bizarre to me, but so did everything else about this case.

At a corner table we talked nonstop for three hours. Smith impressed me with his drive and determination. He wasn't family or even particularly close to any member of the family, but he had a great deal of enthusiasm about helping to solve the case. The night before, he had personally called the CEO of America Online (AOL), the nation's largest Internet service provider, and succeeded in getting a link to the ElizabethSmart.com Web site on the front page of AOL. By Friday, every AOL customer was learning about the Elizabeth Smart kidnapping.

As for Doc, he appeared every bit as intelligent as Smith had said he was. He listened carefully and spoke with a great deal of insight about human nature and what we should be looking for in a suspect. He had a very calming way about him. I was totally open and tried to share any information I could. Smith offered to leave the table if there was anything of a privileged nature I wanted to talk to Doc about, but I insisted he stay. I assured him I had nothing to hide; all we wanted was to find the truth. By the end of our lunch, Doc made a couple of conclusions. Based on the vaguely familiar, soft-spoken manner of the kidnapper, the confused "for ransom or hostage" comment Mary Katherine had overheard, and, most importantly, the fact that he had taken Elizabeth to get her shoes, Doc believed the kidnapper had not killed Elizabeth. "I believe she is alive," Doc said. "Whoever took her cares for her. He may have some confused sexual issues, but he probably did not rape her. He may bring her back himself." When I left Smith and Doc in the parking lot, I was exhausted. I was also more confident than ever that Elizabeth was coming home.

■   ■   ■

By mid-afternoon, another two thousand searchers had signed in at Shriners and were hitting the streets, fields, and hills for a second straight day. Inside forty-eight hours, much of the Salt Lake Valley had already been covered. Air searches were also underway, coordinated by Wayne Owens, my brother-in-law Doug's father. A former Utah congressman, Wayne worked tirelessly to get a small air force of twenty-three fixed-wing aircraft into the skies, joining the police helicopters and airplanes. Volunteer pilot Jamie Gutierrez brought aerial maps to the search center, which he and Wayne divided into sectors. Wayne Owens also enlisted help from his political friends. Early Friday, Wayne handed me his cell phone. "It's Orrin Hatch," he said. "He wants to talk to you." Senator Hatch, Utah's senior U.S. senator, expressed his concern and support for our family, and he confirmed what I had already heard: the FBI was sending out a group of its specialists to aid in the investigation. Senator Hatch's reassurance strengthened our family's resolve to work with law enforcement, particularly when it came to protecting the only eyewitness, Mary Katherine, from outside influence.

The media presence continued to grow. As a family, we were holding two daily press conferences, at 11:00 A.M. and 4:00 P.M., in addition to trying to make ourselves available for individual interviews in between. Some people accused the Smarts of being publicity seekers, and all we could plead was guilty as charged. We wanted to be in front of the cameras as much as the media would let us. We desperately needed the help.

Several members of the media encouraged me to talk with John Walsh of *America's Most Wanted*. "He is the real deal," one confided. "You can trust him." I knew little about Walsh—only later would I learn the full story of the 1981 kidnapping and murder of his young son—but I welcomed his call. He told me that we were doing the right thing by getting Elizabeth's name and photograph to the media. "Just keep doing it. We will get her back," he said. Walsh had a crew in town that documented, among other things, the correct information that Mary Katherine had not been threatened by the kidnapper and that he was probably unaware that she had seen him; it was the first media organization to do so.

It was impossible to keep track of how and what people were giving. By the second day of the search, my brother David's copy machine was ready to burn up. Suddenly, two new copy machines appeared. No one knew who sent them. No one took credit.

In the Arlington Hills neighborhood, a group that called itself "We're Neighbors" assumed the task of questioning someone from every residence within a half-mile radius of Ed's home. Clark and Carolyn Jensen, Russ McSweeney, Scot Safford, and Todd Winegar worked with Art Brown to create a detailed, color-coded map of more than two hundred homes. Names and phone numbers were coded to indicate whether the residents had been interviewed and whether a second interview was needed. This group also produced a uniform questionnaire and a database to store all the material for the police. Beginning on Thursday, We're Neighbors recruited other volunteers and designated a team leader for each section of the neighborhood. Although the effort wasn't complete enough to rule out various scenarios, it resulted in dozens of leads, which would keep us busy for months.

Energized by brainstorming with Smith and Doc, I returned to Ed's house. When I emerged from my car I saw Brent and Bonnie Jean Beesley across the street. I walked over to tell them I thought I knew who did it—and to assure them that Elizabeth was coming home. They took one look at my bloodshot eyes, connected that to my slurred speech, and ordered me straight to bed. Bonnie Jean and Brent led me by the arm to one of their bedrooms. I laid down and closed my eyes. But a scruffy man wearing a beret was all I could see. After an hour of resting but not sleeping, I got back up.

Soon I was back at Shriners discussing the harp lead with my kindred spirit, Mike Freed. We could not talk at length because of what were now almost constant interruptions from the media. News of Ed's hospitalization that morning had made it into the media, making the question of the day more "How is Ed?" than "Where is Elizabeth?" But by the 10:00 evening newscasts, news of Ed's departure from the hospital that afternoon put the focus back on Elizabeth. The media was still not aware of the harp lead, but I knew that the police were quietly pursuing the beret-wearing man for questioning.

As the search center quieted down Friday night, Heidi and I, along with Freed and his wife, Suzi, left Shriners and drove the short distance to John Smith's house for more talk about the investigation.

Freed told us that he had just talked to a police officer at Shriners who worked part-time at The Bay, a downtown dance club frequented mostly by teenagers. The officer said that a few months ago the beret-wearing harp enthusiast had had to be escorted out of the dance club by security because he was making some sort of disturbance. The policeman couldn't recall the exact nature of the problem, but the idea of an older man hanging around a teenage dance club was disturbing in and of itself. The plot seemed to be thickening. This guy had to be found. I was so certain of his guilt that I told Freed, "When we catch him, you shouldn't feel bad about taking the reward." Freed just smiled and told me that getting Elizabeth back was reward enough; he wouldn't accept any money for it. I knew he would say that, but I wanted him to know I thought he deserved it.

We also discussed other leads, including one connected to the funeral of Elizabeth's grandfather. Several people who attended the funeral Monday afternoon reported seeing a person at the service no one seemed to know. This person was wearing hospital scrubs, or something similar, and came in after the funeral service had begun. Heidi remembered seeing him sitting behind her. Our imaginations now began to take over. Elizabeth performed at her grandfather's funeral. Could it have been the harp guy, following Elizabeth and her harp? I called one of Lois's sisters to find out more. She gave me the name of a Francom family friend who was one of several people who had been alarmed by the stranger at the funeral. It was well after midnight when I called the elderly woman. I could tell that I'd awakened her. I described the harp man to her, but it didn't seem to make much of an impression. I asked her if she had any idea who the mystery man at the funeral might be. She said she did not, but she must have sensed the urgency in my voice, because instead of chastising me for waking her, she thanked me for calling, and apologized for not being more helpful.

Yet another promising lead had come from Charlie Miller, a Winder Dairy deliveryman whose route included Arlington Hills. Miller reported to the police that he had seen a green vehicle in the neighborhood the morning before the disappearance. He had written down a part of the license number that he could remember: WHZ. Police, we were told, were already searching their database to identify the car.

A beret. A man wearing scrubs to a funeral. A green car that alarmed the neighborhood milkman. At two in the morning, it didn't add up to anything I could get my arms around. But there were solid, identifiable clues. And with them came the momentum to keep digging.

7

It was just before 11:00 A.M. when the little old man tapped me on the shoulder.

"Excuse me," he said, "but I'm a friend of Ira's."

Nothing stopped after that, or even slowed down, but everything changed.

The day was Saturday, June 8, 2002, seventy-two hours since Elizabeth had gone missing. Another record number of volunteers were reporting to the search center at Shriners. More than 2,200 would sign in by the end of the day. Four detectives were now on full-time duty, recording and prioritizing thousands of leads called in by search groups.

Early that morning, David had gone to Ed and Lois's home to see how they were holding up. Ed was already in the shower, but Lois was sitting in a chair in her bedroom, staring out the window at the city. "Where is she?" Lois asked absently as David entered the room. "Are we going to find her? What is happening in trying to find her?"

As David knelt beside Lois he realized Elizabeth's parents, trapped in overwhelming grief for the past three days, were not aware of the magnitude of what was going on at Shriners. "We'd all seen the incredible community support," remembered David. "The rest of the Smart and Francom families were aware of all the people who were helping in so many ways. But Ed and Lois weren't. They were really in their own vacuum."

"I'd like you to see what's happening in trying to find Elizabeth," David told Lois. "But be prepared to be overwhelmed by what you see."

Shortly afterward, when David relayed his conversation with Lois to me, I suggested that we also make Ed and Lois's visit to the search center a media opportunity. So many members of the media had arrived that it was impossible to satisfy all their requests for one-on-one interviews with Ed and Lois. This was a way to introduce Elizabeth's parents to the media—and vice versa. I set up a media pool consisting of a still photographer from the Associated Press and a cameraman, a soundman, and a reporter from CNN who would follow Ed and Lois on their visit to Shriners. Afterward, they could share their video and still photos with the rest of the media.

I brought Ed and Lois to the back door of Shriners about mid-morning. They walked through the map room, the massive communications center, the registration room, and the phone center, meeting surprised volunteers at every turn. Inside the auditorium/briefing room, more than a hundred volunteers were waiting for their orientation when Ed and Lois came in. The room grew quiet as everyone realized who had arrived. In an unscripted moment, Ed and Lois stood in front of these people who were giving up their Saturday to search for Elizabeth and, unsuccessfully fighting back tears, thanked them for what they were doing. The crowd looking back at Ed and Lois represented an amazing sea of diversity where bankers sat next to bikers; all of them were choking back emotion.

After the tour through the center, I introduced Ed and Lois to various members of the media. Elizabeth's parents went up to each media member, shook hands, and personally thanked them for being there. It gave the media a little taste of what Ed and Lois were really like. The face-to-face meetings made it easier to see that these parents were real people with a real problem—and that they were grateful for the media coverage. I think I can trace the moment when Elizabeth Smart became everybody's little girl. It was that day at Shriners when her parents met the media. After that, the story became personal.

Ed and Lois weren't the only ones to go public that Saturday morning. The police had spent a day and a half readying the sketch and description of the harp suspect, and with just minutes to go before the morning press conference, Detective Baird informed us that they would be releasing the sketch and announcing the lead to the media.

And that's when I got the tap on the shoulder.

"Excuse me, but I'm a friend of Ira's."

Seriously sleep-deprived, absorbed in the case, and about to do a press conference, few words could have brought me to a cold stop. But these did.

Even as a rebellious teenager, when I seriously challenged the goodwill and patience of my parents, I never avoided my mother's father, my grandfather, Ira B. Sharp. Ira knew when I was partying and doing stuff I shouldn't. He'd wake me up at daybreak after I'd spent a long night on the town and he'd take me out to Redwood Road where we kept our horses. There he'd put me to work shoveling oats and the like.

"How you feelin', Tom?" he'd say.

"Pretty bad, Grandpa," I'd answer.

"You know what that is, don't you?" he'd respond, thumping me on the chest. "That's nature's way of telling you you're a horse's ass."

We had a wonderful relationship. Later on, when I fell away from the LDS Church, it was especially hard for Ira. But it didn't change how we felt about each other. I would massage his feet and he would preach to me about the Church. "Tom," he'd say, "you have to return," and I would say, "You can preach all you want right now, Grandpa, but all you have to do is just come back once, when you're on the other side of the veil, and that's when I'll come back."

He would answer, "It's a wicked and adulterous generation that seeks for a sign," and we'd go back and forth like that. It became kind of a joke in our family. Would Ira come back and give me the word? Three days after Ira died, we gathered at my parents' home following the funeral. The phone rang. When I answered it, a voice said, "Collect call from Ira B. Sharp." Somebody had obviously set me up. But it put me in shock. "He's dead," I said, and hung up. I turned around and everybody was giving me a hard time but nobody confessed.

In the twenty-five years since Ira died, my mother, brothers, sisters, and cousins all joke with me about whether Ira has visited me yet.

"Excuse me, but I'm a friend of Ira's."

The elderly man who tapped me on the shoulder said his name was Brent Cook and that he had worked in the temple with Ira. He handed me a slip of paper and said, "I think we have to think about a different way of bringing her home." Literally seconds before the press conference was to begin, I opened the paper and quickly read what the old man had written. It was a note to the kidnapper:

> Sometimes we do not understand where our actions lead us. When we think about what we have done to others, in that moment, we know it is not what we want and are ready for a solution.
>
> We have that solution. The solution is to hold your feelings aside and send Elizabeth back where she feels most at home. Let her walk alone where someone can recognize her and that person will take care of the rest for you.

The words hit me like a thunderbolt, and not just because of the reference to Ira, but also because of Doc's comments at lunch the day before about his belief that Elizabeth was alive and with someone who might, in at least one sense, care for her. Because the press conference was about to begin, I said, "Brent, I can't talk to you right now." I asked him to please talk to John Smith, who was standing next to me. I turned to Smith and asked him to meet with Cook and take the note and see that it got to the family.

The impact of Cook's words was just as strong on the rest of the family as it had been on me. That note, all of five sentences long, changed the way we looked at the case. We knew the odds. We knew how critical the first few days were to getting Elizabeth back alive, and that, statistically, every additional hour increased dramatically the chances she was dead. Before the note, that had been our reality. But now, after Brent Cook's visit, we had a new reality: that Elizabeth was still alive, and if we appealed to the good will of her kidnapper—crazy as that sounded—we just might get her back.

So that became our mind-set.

The craziness of the day and the clamor for information about the harp suspect kept Smith from getting the letter to my sister Cynthia until that evening. As soon as she read the words and heard about the Ira connection, she wanted to call another press conference—and appeal to the good side of the kidnapper. But by then it was well past prime time for press announcements. We decided to wait until the next morning. Cynthia kept the letter. She wanted to deliver the message herself.

It had been a hard seventy-two hours on my youngest sister. In many ways Cynthia was the original Elizabeth—an obedient, bright, blond girl who grew up loving music and horses. Because Cynthia was away at medical school at Yale and then lived in Oregon during her residency, she hadn't spent a lot of time around Elizabeth. But when she and Doug moved back to Salt Lake, Cynthia observed a lot of herself in her teenage niece. She saw that Elizabeth was her grandfather's little buddy, helping him with the horses at the cabin and following him around his office, just as Cynthia had once been her father's little buddy. There were other similarities. Cynthia and Angela, two girls with four brothers, were especially close growing up, as were Elizabeth and Mary Katherine. Both Cynthia and Elizabeth tended to be serious-minded and spiritual by nature. They even looked alike. "I'd watch her and think, she's replaced me," said Cynthia.

Such feelings only intensified Cynthia's fears about what might have happened to her niece. "At first I worried what she was thinking, how she was doing. Was she cold? Was she terrified? How was she being treated?" Cynthia said. "Then the longer we searched, the more despair I felt. I began to think we'd find a body if we found her. It was a mixed feeling. I wanted to find her but I was terrified to find her."

Brent Cook's letter changed all that. "It rang so true to me that it completely changed my attitude about where she was and what was happening to her," Cynthia said. "It had such an incredible impact on me. It gave me a completely new sense of hope and urgency."

Everything was happening so fast—the everyday miracles that were surrounding us, the overwhelming support, the appearance of Ira's friend, Brent Cook, a cry from the other side. It all intensified a belief among us as a family that what was happening was bigger than all of us. The love and support of a community was an antidote for the pain brought on by such a dark, evil crime. I was no longer living the life of a skeptic, but was convinced there was a higher power involved in this nightmare.

I had worked as a photo editor at the *Deseret News* for more than eighteen years, yet when I needed the product of my trade most, I was at a loss. After the Saturday afternoon press conference was over and news of the harp suspect was announced, I was inundated with requests for photos of Elizabeth. I hadn't seen my cameras since Wednesday morning. Fortunately I noticed Trent Nelson, a photographer for the rival *Salt Lake Tribune*, at the press conference. He was there to lend a hand. I asked him to go to Ed's house where Lois had just received a stack of photographs of Elizabeth with her harp from photographer Joy Gough. I asked Nelson to take the photos, along with about a dozen others from family and friends, and copy them and make media-ready CDs. The timing and his help were critical, as these fresh photos would surely result in more media coverage.

But not everyone's motive was as pure as it seemed on the surface. Darin Mackoff, the producer I had met earlier from Fox News, reminded me of the meeting we had scheduled for that afternoon between Ed and Lois and Marc Klaas. I had some concern about a television network helping arrange the interview between the veteran grieving parent and the new grieving parents. I suspected Fox was flying Klaas in for the interview and paying his expenses. My concern increased when Mackoff told me Fox wanted to film the meeting.

It made no sense to me that a private meeting between parents should be filmed and made public. I talked to David and he felt the same way. We told Mackoff that if Marc Klaas, who knew how it felt to have a daughter kidnapped, wanted to give Ed and Lois personal advice and moral support it would remain private, period. No cameras allowed. But Klaas wanted the meeting filmed and we didn't want to alienate Fox, so we reached a compromise. Klaas could have ten minutes alone with Ed and Lois. At that point they would discuss things of a personal nature, after which Fox would be allowed to tape a five-minute interview, where the parents would talk in more general terms about the kidnapping.

During his off-camera talk with Ed and Lois, Klaas spent a portion of his time making the same pitch that I had rejected the day before. He felt that Fox should bring in forensic sketch artist Jeanne Boylan so she could talk to the eyewitness. Klaas gave Boylan, who had helped in his own daughter's kidnapping case, an enthusiastic endorsement. So, for that matter, did the producers of *America's Most Wanted*, who had originally tried to bring Boylan in as a consultant. Ed and Lois, unaware of my earlier comments that the family did not want to work outside organized law enforcement channels, particularly when it was the media that would be bringing in the specialist, initially agreed with Klaas that bringing in Boylan sounded like a good idea, unwittingly setting the stage for later conflict with Fox.

Adding to the Saturday urgency were growing concerns about a man who lived near Ed and Lois who hadn't been seen at home or in the neighborhood since Elizabeth disappeared. This person was described by neighbors and, more significantly, by members of his family as a loner with a "questionable lifestyle." First, search dogs had taken hits (that is, smelled Elizabeth's scent) on the street near the man's residence. Then, members of the man's extended family came to the search center and said they thought he ought to be investigated. Finally, the man's lawyer, striding dangerously close to violating lawyer–client privilege, but willing to take the risk, stepped forward and, without going into the specifics of the man's background or criminal history, told us that police should question him.

It dawned on me that it was possible that the harp suspect, whose composite sketch was now public record, and the unaccounted-for neighbor, could be one and the same. If so, and if Elizabeth was hidden in his home, the question became how much danger Elizabeth might be in if police, or, worse, volunteers, stormed the house. Jeremy Utter, with the Abby and Jennifer Group, was coordinating the volunteer dog rescue groups at the search center, and was urging that the dogs go back to the man's street. The thought of the volunteer searchers acting without assistance from law enforcement was terrifying to me. I may have already jumped ahead of the police in questioning Bill Krebs, but now I wanted to do just the opposite. If Elizabeth was in that house, I did not want her to be harmed during a misguided vigilante invasion.

Convinced that the police needed to know about all this right away, I grabbed my brother-in-law Doug, and we headed for my car. "Come on," I said. "There isn't time for this information to travel through the bureaucracy. Let's go to the top at police headquarters. We'll tell the police everything we know."

It was nearly 11:00 P.M. when we got to the police station, which was nearly deserted. We contacted the night watch commander and I asked him to call Don Bell at home. At first he refused. It was late and he didn't want to bother the lead sergeant late on a Saturday night. I insisted that I had very important information. The more I thought about it, the more I believed the harp guy and the neighbor were the same person and we were about to crack the case. Finally, after enough haranguing, the night patrolman contacted Bell, handed me the phone, and I was able to tell him my theory.

When I finished talking, a clearly upset Bell said, "Tom, it wasn't him."

"What?"

"It wasn't the guy in the sketch. That guy already turned himself in. He did it within three hours of us releasing the sketch. He has an absolute alibi. He couldn't have done it."

It turned out that the beret-wearing man with the missing front tooth had seen his sketch on television and contacted police almost immediately. He told them he was the man they were looking for, and yes, he had indeed attended the harp concerts. But he insisted he had nothing to do with the kidnapping and said he was in the hospital the night of the abduction. The police checked with the hospital. His alibi was airtight.

It wasn't until after I hung up that what the sergeant said started to sink in. Now it was my turn to be upset. First, the police hadn't bothered to tell the family ahead of time that they were going public with the sketch, and then they hadn't bothered to tell us that the sketch had resulted in clearing the suspect. They had briefed the newspapers in time for them to make their late-night deadlines—the news would be the next morning's lead headlines—but they hadn't found time to tell us. As a family, we were cooperating fully, telling the police everything we knew. It was becoming clear the street didn't always run both ways.

Disappointed that another lead had disappeared, and discouraged about the behavior of the police, Doug and I drove back to the search center and broke the news to those who were still there. We told them that it wasn't the harp guy. That didn't rule out the unaccounted-for neighbor. But it was late, and that lead would have to wait until morning.

Saturday had long since turned into Sunday when Heidi and I drove home in the darkness. Not that time mattered much under the circumstances.

The later the better was how I looked at it. I wasn't sleeping anyway. When we were ready for bed, I asked Heidi to do something we had never done in our marriage: kneel down and pray. It wasn't easy for me to ask that. It had been more than twenty-five years since I thought it might be important to get down on my knees. I didn't have any answers, but I didn't want to stand in the way of any spiritual aid. We prayed to God, if indeed there was one listening, for help. The events that were happening were extraordinary; there seemed to be a higher power at work. When we got back on our feet, I looked up. I couldn't help wondering where Ira was, and what he was thinking.

The search effort suffered its one and only fatality that Saturday—Kiera, a German shepherd search dog, collapsed and died of heat exhaustion after a hard day in the mountains above Arlington Hills. Kiera was part of Intermountain K-9 Search & Rescue, a nonprofit group whose members had come to the search center when it opened on Thursday and had been pulling steady duty ever since.

For best results, the dog handlers explained to us, a search dog should get to an area before it becomes contaminated. Once additional humans are on the scene, it becomes difficult, if not impossible, for even the very best search dogs to sniff out the designated scent. Such was the case with the search for Elizabeth and her kidnapper. By the time police sealed off the trails and hills behind Ed's house on the day of the kidnapping, any number of people had already covered the ground with their footprints and their scent. In subsequent days, the best chance for the dogs was to find new, unpolluted evidence of Elizabeth's scent—in a stream, perhaps, below where she might have recently washed or walked, or on a trail where she or someone who had made contact with her had recently traveled.

It was a long shot for the dogs to come upon such a situation three days after the abduction, but no more of a long shot than human searchers finding Elizabeth and her kidnapper. There were a number of promising moments, including a brief but exciting chase Saturday afternoon. Three handlers and their dogs—Linda Sosa with a golden retriever named Maverick, Cody Richmond with a German shepherd named Leroy, and sandaFer loGan with a bloodhound named Speed and a German shepherd named Heidi—were searching in the foothills east of Ed's house in the vicinity of the Shoreline Trail when the dogs got excited.

"All four dogs started acting funny as they were going up the dirt road and along a stream," Linda remembered. "Leroy was more in the water, Speed on the other side, and Maverick on the road. All were on a dead run up the canyon."

Linda called Jeremy Utter at the search center. Jeremy instructed the handlers and their dogs to return to Shriners so they could be teamed up with police. About two hours later, six police officers, including two SWAT officers wearing black pants and gear, accompanied the handlers and dogs back to where they had been searching. "Go find Elizabeth," Linda said to Maverick, and she and the dogs resumed their earlier enthusiasm and continued to move upstream, repeatedly finding new hits.

But it was hard, tiring work, and at around 6:00 P.M. the police stopped the search. "They said, 'We've walked enough today,'" Linda remembered. "We were disappointed. We wanted to keep going. But as soon as they said no, we had to stop. That's our chain of command, our protocol. When the police tell you to stop, you stop."

At the calls of their masters, Speed, LeRoy and Maverick turned around and made their way back down the faint trail and to the cars, abandoning their progress up Red Butte Canyon, just one ridge south of Dry Creek Canyon.

8

My little sister Cynthia stood her full height of five-foot-four and, while ostensibly addressing the assembled media outside the Federal Heights wardhouse on a drizzly Sunday morning, she spoke directly to whatever decency there might be in the man who had stolen Elizabeth from her bed.

After sleeping on it—in my case, I use the term loosely—the family felt even more strongly about acting on the unexpected advice from the old gentleman the day before. It wasn't empirical evidence that Elizabeth was alive. It would not hold up in court. And it wasn't something any of us wanted to spell out for the media. In some ways it was no different than the psychic tips that had been flooding in ever since news of the kidnapping had spread. Nonetheless, on a deeper level than what could be explained by the normal senses, it meant something to us. The words Cynthia enunciated at the press conference, Brent Cook's words, rang true.

Reporters had only three questions:

"What was that all about?"

"Does this mean you think she's alive?"

"Do you think you might know who this person is?"

Without going into detail we said that, yes, we felt Elizabeth was alive and based on a number of clues we thought it possible that the person who had her—and we had no idea who it was—wanted to let her go. At least his good side did. We could only hope the kidnapper was hearing the message.

I made a brief comment at the press conference and did some one-on-one media interviews later, after which David pulled me aside. "Tom, I'm going to tell you something that is going to make you feel really good," my brother said.

"What's that?"

"I hear what you're saying, and I think you're thinking more clearly than any of us," he said. "I realize that your apparent craziness is directed. You know what you are doing." He paused. "But a lot of people aren't hearing what you're saying. They're looking at your delivery. You're jumpy and you're rambling. You can't stand still. Tom, people are starting to wonder if you're losing it."

In truth it was hard to focus on normal things, and not just because of the sleep psychosis (Saturday night had been my third straight without sleep). All of us in the family were so deeply absorbed in our one quest that we let everything else slide. None of us were looking completely sane to the outside world, especially not after our "appeal to the good" press conference.

Not long after David talked to me about my craziness, I had talked to Ed and learned, for the first time, the detail that Mary Katherine thought the kidnapper was carrying some type of knapsack or small duffel bag. All my siblings were anxious to hear this latest information, but there was no place to talk privately. Every available room in the building was being used for the search. So the five of us slipped into a small bathroom just off the main hallway, where we spent about fifteen minutes discussing this latest clue, along with all the others, as we played Hercule Poirot, totally oblivious to the outside world—until a knock came at the door. David opened it to find a woman standing there. Somewhat reluctantly she asked, "Is everything all right in there?" He opened the door wider and we saw a long line of people waiting to use the bathroom.

Sunday afternoon my sister Angela and Karen Hale, a friend of the family who had been helping with the media, pulled me aside at the search center. "Tom, we need to bring in some help to work with the media. You can't do it yourself anymore," Angela said.

Without a doubt, she was right. Everyone in the family had taken leave of their daily activities to work full-time on the search, and the continued strain was starting to take a toll. The question of who to bring in did not take long to answer. Many had volunteered for the task, including a longtime friend, Vicki Varela, who had been Governor Leavitt's trusted aide for years. I had already consulted with her, and I would continue to do so throughout the search. Mike Grass and Missy Wilson Larson were partners with Chris Thomas in a public relations firm called Intrepid. My oldest daughter, Sierra, who was just finishing her communications degree at the University of Utah, was interning for them. Along with most of their staff, the Intrepid owners had been helping us since day one, primarily by searching on the trails. Missy, daughter of former Salt Lake City mayor Ted Wilson and his wife, Kathy, had been helping with the media and anything else she could while her parents were heading up neighborhood searches. Mike Grass had been out on the trails with his dad, Ray, the outdoor editor at the *Deseret News* and a longtime close friend of mine. I knew Chris Thomas the least, but I had worked with him on a commercial photo shoot. When Intrepid's owners stepped forward and offered to take over the public relations, we quickly accepted their offer. Still, on Monday when I talked to them about their role, I was adamant about one thing: "No one handles me."

I had started out as the main family spokesperson, the media-savvy veteran news photographer, the oldest brother, the uncle in total control. When a microphone appeared, the family pushed it toward me. Now, less than a week into the case, I was becoming the crazy uncle, the person being steered away from the microphones. Fortunately, everyone in the family did their share in front of the media and their sincerity came across to the public. David, who ended up doing most of the interviews as the months wore on, had never done a media interview in his life until the day Elizabeth was taken.

My biggest problem was a lack of sleep. None of us had slept much, but there was a big difference between not much and none. As spokespersons, the others came across as articulate and believable, whereas I was starting to seem more like Herman Munster. Michael Janofsky, a *New York Times* reporter I had worked with previously, had interviewed me earlier in the week. In his article he described me as behaving like Al Pacino in the movie *Insomnia*. (In the movie, Pacino plays a cop who gets obsessed by a case and can't sleep.) Janofsky told me his editor took out the Pacino reference before the article ran in the *Times*. Perhaps it was too glib for a story about an unsolved kidnapping, but I had seen the movie and the description couldn't have been more accurate.

But my obsession had a lot of company. On Sunday, another 1,900 volunteer searchers registered at the search center despite rain and cool temperatures. It was the first rain in two weeks, and it effectively wiped out any remaining footprints from June 5. The Sunday volunteers included a group of kayakers, organized by Wasatch Touring, who swept the Jordan River. In just four days, more than seven thousand people had registered to search for Elizabeth.

And that was just the support we could see. The ElizabethSmart.com Web site, secured by John Smith and now maintained by David, was receiving more than eight million hits a day. All over the world, people were downloading posters of Elizabeth and information about the case, while the media were downloading high-resolution images to go with their stories. Cards, letters, faxes, and e-mails flooded into the search center. Strangers wrote in for no other reason than to say they cared and they were praying. "The Girls," Mindy and Christy, began printing and storing the e-mails, separating them by the thousands into large binders. One of their favorites was one that read: "I don't believe in God, but I'm praying for you." Another came from an eight-year-old boy in Ohio, who wrote that he was searching his backyard every day, looking for Elizabeth.

There were the neighborhood girls who sold lemonade and donated the money they collected to help with the search. There were the senior citizens who sat in chairs outside the wardhouse all day long, acting as security. Many people from out of state drove to Utah to help with the search effort. And there was Carl Cook, the mentally challenged young man who showed up every single day wearing the medals he'd won at the Special Olympics. Carl emptied the garbage cans and picked up litter on the grounds. At night, after the center closed, he would go out and search on his own. At about 4:00 A.M. one day Carl was walking along the I-15 freeway. A police officer pulled up as Carl was looking under a cardboard box on the side of the road.

"Son, don't you think it's a little late to be out here?" the officer asked.

"No, I'm working the case," said Carl.

"What case?"

Carl turned and showed him the "Please Find Me" Elizabeth button on his shirt. "She could be anywhere," said Carl, turning his gaze on the cop. "Why aren't you out searching instead of doing this?" Carl spent so much time working and looking that his mother finally called and asked if someone at the search center would please tell him there was a two-hour time limit on searches.

Elizabeth Smart had become everybody's daughter. Her home videos and her shy, endearing smile had entered millions of households that wanted nothing more than to turn on the evening news and hear that she was safely back home.

As the hours turned into days with still no sign of her, the rising frustration was palpable—with the public *and* the police. A high-profile case—and no one could remember a more high-profile case in Salt Lake than this—demands results. In an attempt to ease the pressure, officers in both the police and the FBI encouraged the family to scale back the media attention. As a family, of course, we were trying to keep the pressure and awareness high.

Out on the street, the police were leaning hard. They rounded up ex-cons for questioning. They sent parolees, especially anyone who had ever been charged with a sex offense, back to jail for minor violations—unless they could shed any light on the kidnapping. The police offered deals in exchange for information. The Utah crime rate for the year would drop dramatically. The word was out. Until the Elizabeth Smart case was solved, life would be as miserable as possible for the bad guys—all in an effort to squeeze out a rat.

The police were obviously willing to go to great lengths to crack the case, the public was willing to comb all of northern Utah by hand if it had to, the family was willing to beg and plead and forgo sleep—and, still, by the time the sun went down Sunday night, all anyone could do was pray.

I joined the family and community for a candlelight vigil in Liberty Park organized by Mayor Rocky Anderson. I drove to the park with Ed and Lois after their brief but emotional meeting with Jeff Runyan and his son, Justin. Jeff was the father of Rachael Runyan, the three-year-old girl who had been kidnapped and murdered twenty years earlier and for whom

Utah's Rachael Alert system was named. For years, the Runyan family had been crusading to get a system in place that would quickly alert the public and all law enforcement agencies about child abductions. The system was inaugurated at 7:21 the morning of Elizabeth's abduction, which marked a triumph in their crusade—although the delay of nearly three and a half hours between Ed's 911 call and the sounding of the Rachael Alert effectively took some of the "quick" out of the quick-response system.

The Runyans wanted to do what they could to help Ed and Lois. Justin Runyan, who had witnessed his sister's abduction years earlier, had volunteered at the search center at Shriners. The first day, memories of his sister's kidnapping were so overwhelming that he collapsed and had to go home. But he returned the following day to help.

Abductions exact a huge toll, with fallout that reaches far beyond the original horror of the kidnapping. Life will never be the same, but life does move on, and the world is full of good people to help make sure it does. That was the message Jeff Runyan delivered to Ed and Lois.

About a thousand of those good people came to Liberty Park to light candles and pray for Elizabeth. After a musical number, Mayor Anderson spoke briefly and pledged his and the city's support. Members of our family also spoke, reiterating the pleas to the kidnapper to "Do the right thing" and "Let her walk." To everyone's relief, I stayed in the background and didn't say a word. I mostly spent the time hugging people—people I knew well and people I didn't know at all.

David was the only member of the family who missed the prayer vigil. John Smith had asked him to meet with him that night to brainstorm about the case. Smith was doing everything possible to help, and we were grateful to him. He had boundless energy and suggestions, which were most often helpful. No one doubted that his heart was in the right place.

While they were working together on the Web site Sunday afternoon, David and Smith had started talking about the cut window screen. Their discussion led them to visit a nearby Home Depot so they could examine a variety of window units in an effort to determine how the screen at Ed's house might have been accessed and cut. Later, they went to Ed's house to look for more clues. Then Smith invited David to an all-night session with

Smith's friends. Smith wanted David to promise that he would come to the meeting with an open mind and be willing to think outside the box. He also got David to agree that no matter what the group's conclusions, he would be willing to take them, as a member of the family, to the police. "Anything to find Elizabeth," Dave replied.

Before he left the search center, David told Sergeant David Craycroft, who was stationed at the center, about his discussions and investigations with Smith that day and about the meeting he'd been invited to that night. Craycroft asked David how much he trusted Smith. David said he trusted him implicitly; he'd been working on the search harder than anyone he knew and had been an acquaintance of his for years. But just to be on the safe side, they agreed that Craycroft would call David on his cell phone at midnight to make sure everything was all right.

Smith had told David to park his car on a street several blocks from Shriners, where Smith would pick him up and take him to their meeting. "It was a little too cloak and daggerish for me," David remembered, "Like something out of a spy novel." But he went to the rendezvous just the same.

As David stood waiting, a black Cadillac slowly passed him, after which Smith pulled up in his car and motioned for David to climb in. As he drove away, Smith informed David that he'd rented a room at a nearby motel for the night so they could meet in private. He said two trusted friends would be joining them—Doc, the psychologist I'd met, and Dave, a programmer who had been helping Smith with the Web site. David asked Smith why he'd had his friend drive by in the Cadillac to check him out. Smith was stunned to hear David had picked up on that. He gave a simple answer that the friend had been helping stake out the house of a suspicious neighbor and was on the way back to resume. Smith mentioned that Doc and Dave would add a lot to their discussion. He dropped David off at the motel room, and said he would return soon with Doc and Dave. He suggested that in the meanwhile, David ought to try to get some rest.

David lay down on the bed, but he began to freak. "My mind was running a hundred miles an hour about everything that was going on," he remembered. "I suddenly thought to myself, 'What if this whole thing is a setup; what if there's a body or a person hidden in the room and they've gone to call the police and act as if I had Elizabeth in this room?' I thought I better get up and check the room so I wouldn't go nuts thinking about it. I checked the shower, the closets, under the bed. I said out loud, 'Get a grip, you're not being set up.' Then the door opened and John, Dave, and Doc came in. They sat down and we started to talk."

Smith put two large pieces of poster paper on the wall to write notes and draw diagrams, and the discussion began. At midnight, right on cue, David's cell phone rang. It was Sergeant Craycroft. "Everything is fine," said David.

A long talk ensued about the cut screen. The four men discussed how it would have been necessary to cut at least part of the screen from the inside because the screen was on the kitchen side of the window and the window, which cranked open to the outside, got in the way when cutting across the bottom from outside the house. They then talked about the security system in the house and how most of the doors had an alarm that would beep when opened, but the kitchen door did not have one. They theorized that the kidnapper apparently had inside knowledge about that. It seemed too coincidental to explain it as just dumb luck.

Smith then shifted the discussion to people and motives. He said it was important to leave no one out, including Elizabeth's parents and her uncles and aunts. They asked David about Ed's financial situation and also about mine. David told them he didn't know many details but he knew both Ed and I were currently involved in deals that weren't going as well as we would like. It was at this point that Smith openly wondered how I was able to come up with great sums of money to help the search when I was apparently so far in debt. David asked him what he meant by that and Smith brought up a discussion he'd had with me on Saturday. He had commented that there was a growing need for a larger capacity server for the Elizabeth Smart Web site, which would mean we might need more money. I had answered, "What do you want? I'll get you whatever you need. If it's $30,000, $40,000, whatever it is, I'll get it."

Without my knowing it, Smith had taped my comment. Although I had only meant that I was committed to find whatever money we needed to keep the search alive, Smith had for some reason thought I was trying to bribe him. Just before dawn, Smith, Dave, and Doc told David that they had concluded the kidnapping was an inside job, that the window screen had been cut to make it appear that someone had entered from the outside, and that Ed and I were the two primary suspects, because we needed money to pay bills. Their hypothesis was aided, apparently, by information Doc had received that the police also suspected the kidnapping was an inside job. Smith, Dave, and Doc added that they thought Ed's body language during television interviews was suspicious, indicating he might be hiding something. They further theorized there might be a third person involved, partnering with Ed and me, who was probably guarding Elizabeth.

David didn't know what to say. They were accusing his brothers. If money was the motive, he said, then he ought to be a suspect, too. He tried to move the discussion to other possibilities. What about all the handymen Ed had hired to work on the house? But all Smith, Doc, and Dave wanted to know now was whether David was going to keep his word and take their conclusion to the police.

"When I said I would like to meet again and discuss the situation further, they acted like I had insulted them to even bring it up," David remembered. "That was it. The meeting was over."

From the motel, David went straight to the search center and talked to Sergeant Craycroft, who had returned for the morning shift. At David's urging, Craycroft scheduled a meeting for later that morning with Don Bell. Not long after that, David's cell phone rang. It was Smith, saying they needed to talk. They agreed to meet for breakfast, but then Smith called back a few minutes later and said he didn't feel comfortable meeting at a restaurant. "John sounded very offish so I asked him what was going on," said David, "but he didn't want to elaborate and said he needed to go."

Alarmed, David drove to Smith's house and found a police squad car parked in front. When he knocked on the door, a uniformed officer answered and said Smith didn't want to talk to David. Now completely confused, David drove the few minutes back to the search center to again talk to the detectives there. As they were talking, David got another phone call from Smith. "He was hysterical, sobbing to the point I couldn't make out exactly what he was saying, other than 'What have I done?'" said David. "I looked at the detectives and asked one of them to go with me to John's house. Upon arriving at John's we found him sitting in his front room repeating over and over, 'All I've tried to do is help find Elizabeth.' It was apparent that he was in a total meltdown and the only thing that might help him was sleep. Smith calmed down enough to say that he had not had any sleep since the day Elizabeth went missing. I learned that he was so scared that his life was at risk that when he hung up the phone, canceling our breakfast meeting, he called 911, for himself! That was why the police were at his house. The detectives asked Smith if it would be all right to perform a quick search of the house. Smith gave his approval. They found no sign of Elizabeth or anything else that looked suspicious."

After the police sorted it all out—and it took a while—David was taken to police headquarters, where the FBI and SLCPD interrogated him. He told the police everything, including, as he had promised, Smith, Doc, and Dave's absurd theory about Ed and me concocting the kidnapping scheme for financial reasons. After the interrogation, David, completely spent and exhausted, commented to an FBI agent who was ushering him out of the room that he would do anything he could to help find Elizabeth. The agent patted him on the back and said, "You can help by getting some sleep."

It was the last any of us would see of John Smith in the investigation. Despite his big heart and good intentions, his fervor to crack the case and his inability to get a proper amount of rest had flipped him right over the edge. The Elizabeth Smart kidnapping was quickly claiming its share of victims. As Jeff Runyan had said to my brother not many hours earlier, child abductions exact an awful toll.

9

On Sunday, June 9, 2002, four days after the kidnapping, at about the same time Salt Lake City was convening its candlelight vigil for Elizabeth Smart in Liberty Park, the high council of the Butler West Stake of the Church of Jesus Christ of Latter-day Saints met in a quiet room at a large wardhouse in the southeast foothills of the Salt Lake Valley to determine whether Brian David Mitchell and his wife, Wanda Eileen Barzee Mitchell, should be allowed to retain their membership in the Church. It had come to the attention of LDS leaders that Brother and Sister Mitchell were engaging in actions not in harmony with Church doctrine. The matter needed to be discussed.

A Church court, officially called a disciplinary council, was convened, with Gregory A. Schwitzer, president of the LDS Salt Lake Butler West Stake, presiding. As is customary in proceedings of this nature, there were no spectators for the hearing; only the twelve members of the high council were invited, along with President Schwitzer and his two counselors in the stake presidency—and in this case there were no defendants present.

It isn't preferred LDS procedure to hold a disciplinary council without the accused present. But it happens, and more often than one might think. For a number of reasons, people at odds with the Church sometimes choose not to plead their case in front of the high council. Maybe they think their fate is already decided, or they might be embarrassed. Perhaps they simply do not care what the Church does. Whatever the reason, the hearing takes place with or without defendants. But it is important that the members in question are made aware of the date of the proceedings and invited to attend.

Informing Brother and Sister Mitchell of the court had proved difficult. The Mitchells had no known address and were believed to be homeless. They no longer lived with Brian's aging mother, Irene, a member of the Butler Eighteenth Ward. For the last few years, Brian and Wanda had come and gone from Irene's house. They stayed with her for varying lengths of time. However, a month earlier, after a domestic dispute, they had been ushered off Irene's property by county sheriffs and ordered not to return. Still, because it was their most permanent address, the Church kept the Mitchells' records in Irene's home ward. For the past several years, the Mitchells had become completely inactive. They never went to church. That in itself isn't grounds for excommunication—if it were, at least a third of the membership of the LDS Church would be gone—and neither was standing on the streets of Salt Lake City dressed in robes and calling people to repentance while begging for money, a regular habit of Brian's.

What did qualify as grounds for excommunication was actively preaching doctrine contrary to the accepted canons of the Church. The LDS faith is based on revelation from God to, and direction from, living prophets, and has been ever since fourteen-year-old Joseph Smith, Jr., went into a grove of trees to pray in upstate New York in 1820, and came out with the news that he had seen and talked to God and his son Jesus Christ. To LDS Church faithful, every successor to Smith, down to and including current LDS Church president Gordon B. Hinckley, is considered a prophet, seer, and revelator of God. Through these prophets, and no one else, God directs his church. This principle of revelation is how faithful members believe the Book of Mormon came forward, as well as the other scriptures; it is how temples came to be built and how the unique LDS doctrine of salvation for the dead was instituted; it is the basis for assigning more than sixty thousand full-time missionaries to their posts throughout the world. Revelation from God to the leader of the LDS Church is the very foundation of Mormonism. And it is not to be trifled with by its members.

But Brian and Wanda Mitchell had trifled with it. Brian had recently made public a manuscript that purported to be a collection of revelations he had personally received from God over the course of the past eight and a half years. Not personal revelations he might apply to his own life, but revelations he said all mankind, and in particular members of the LDS Church, must hear. He called his manuscript *The Book of Immanuel David Isaiah*—that was the new name he said God had chosen for him—and in it he revealed how he had been directed by God to do a number of things to restore righteousness and order. Included was a command to establish "The Seven Diamonds Plus One Study and Fellowship Society" for the express purpose of studying several secular books of philosophy and theology, including the *LDS Hymnbook*; Betty J. Eadie's bestselling book about her near-death experience, *Embraced by the Light*; *The Golden Seven Plus One*, by C. Samuel West; *The Literary Message of Isaiah*, by Avraham Gileadi; and *The Final Quest*, by Rick Joyner. According to Mitchell, God wanted these books added to the LDS Church's recognized books of scripture, the Bible, Book of Mormon, Doctrine and Covenants, and Pearl of Great Price.

Although this content was disturbing, it would perhaps have been borderline tolerable to the Church. But where the twenty-seven-page *Book of Immanuel David Isaiah*—the original of which had been handwritten by Wanda Mitchell in artistic calligraphy—crossed the line was in its denunciation of LDS president Gordon B. Hinckley's leadership. Near the beginning of the manuscript, after establishing that the world was in serious peril under Satan's reign, came these words: "For this cause I have raised up my servant Immanuel David Isaiah, ever my righteous right hand, to be a light and a covenant to my people—to all those who will repent and come unto me, for in my servant, Immanuel is the fullness of my gospel, which I, the Lord brought forth out of obscurity and out of darkness through my servant Joseph Smith, Jr." Then, a few paragraphs later: "One who is mighty and strong I have ordained in the stead of him who was ordained of God. For he, who was ordained of God and is sustained by the people, has acted deceitfully and is lifted up in the pride of his heart, and he has rejected the fullness of my gospel, even the new and everlasting covenant, and he seeks the praise of the world and exalts himself, and he leads the children of the promise with a flaxen cord down to their destruction."

It didn't take the greatest of scholars to get past the run-on sentences and misplaced commas to realize Immanuel David Isaiah was trying to take over for Gordon B. Hinckley.

Mitchell finished and dated his work on April 6, 2002, after which he and Wanda began distributing photocopies of the text to members of their families and other close associates. The reception was less than warm. Typical was the scene that took place at the home of Wanda's mother, Dora Corbett, on April 9. As members of Wanda's family gathered there following funeral services held earlier that day for Wanda's stepfather, Glenn Corbett, who had died at the age of ninety-two, Brian rang the doorbell. Brian's brother-in-law, Dick Camp, answered the door.

"This is for thee," said Brian, thrusting forward a copy of the manuscript.

Camp, an ex-Marine, looked at the title and the first few lines, then said, "Who is this Immanuel David Isaiah?"

"He stands before you," said Brian, dressed in his robes.

"No shit," said Dick. "Why don't you come on in and we'll talk about it?"

But Brian was already backing away. "I must flee," he said, and ran off the porch.

Where, why, and how it had all unraveled for Brian and Wanda Mitchell was a source of much family discussion, consternation, and, ultimately, bewilderment. The first eight years of their marriage had been, if not entirely normal, at least outwardly sane. When they married in November 1985, Wanda had six children and an ex-husband, and Brian had four children and two ex-wives. That was a lot of baggage for the tiny Salt Lake City apartment that Wanda had rented while finalizing her divorce, and that Brian moved into once they were married. Brian, who was thirty-one when they married, and Wanda, who was thirty-nine, gradually began to distance themselves from their children, their families, and nearly everything to do with their former lives. But the church they both belonged to was an exception. As they drifted away from everything else, they drew closer to their religion.

From 1985 through early 1993, Brian and Wanda were extremely active Mormons, even by demanding LDS standards. Living in a succession of wards within the boundaries of the Salt Lake Park Stake, one of the city's—and the LDS Church's—oldest stakes (collections of wards), they accepted all church callings that came their way. As a priesthood holder, Brian rose rapidly through the lay leadership ranks. He was a counselor in the stake mission presidency, then a member of the stake high council, and finally a counselor in the bishopric of the Salt Lake First Ward—the same ward President Hinckley attended as a young boy. Wherever they went, Wanda was ward organist. In 1991, Brian also accepted a call to serve as an ordinance worker in the Salt Lake Temple, the most sacred sanctuary of Mormondom. Wanda joined her husband working at the temple in 1993.

Brian Mitchell held a steady job as a die cutter at the O. C. Tanner Jewelry and Recognition Company factory in South Salt Lake. At work, Mitchell's strict LDS persona stood out even among coworkers who were regular churchgoers themselves. His intolerance for worldly things was well known, if not particularly well received, at the plant. Annoyed by the pop music piped in on the building's speaker system, Mitchell would sit at his desk and sing LDS hymns to drown out the lyrics. He brought a miniature hymnbook to work and made a plastic hymnbook holder that he mounted in his work carrel. Off-color jokes, stories, and cursing made him sing louder. Coworkers who keyed into Mitchell's prudishness made it a point to tell crude stories within earshot of his workstation, hoping to get a rise out of him.

Mitchell had few friends at O. C. Tanner, but he did manage to find a kindred spirit in Doug Larsen, a fellow die cutter and ultra-conservative Mormon who would talk philosophy and religion with him for hours. The two spent so much time sharing their thoughts that it wasn't uncommon for the foreman to remind them, "More work, less talk."

They read the same books and then discussed them. Included was *Called to Serve*, the autobiography of Bo Gritz (both men would vote for the anti-tax crusader and Libertarian Party candidate in the 1992 U.S. presidential election), and, with the exception of *The Final Quest*, all of the books that Mitchell would designate as scripture in *The Book of Immanuel David Isaiah*.

Mitchell and Larsen engaged in long discussions about the undisciplined nature of the world and a general lackadaisical attitude they saw in most practicing Mormons. Even their humor was serious. As they went about their die-cutting duties, shaping molds for trinkets and pendants, they would joke that they were "making idols for Babylon," and when they would occasionally break from their disciplined regimen of consuming only healthy foods and dive into a box of Oreos, they would laugh that they were eating "poison wafers."

But if all appeared rigid and solid on the surface, the foundation was buckling. Mitchell's impatience with the world, a place where he never seemed to fit, led him further and further from the religious mainstream. Sometime in the late 1980s or early 1990s, he began delving into the philosophies of rigid, conservative Mormon groups that focus on the U.S. Constitution. These so-called fringe or patriot Mormons place an emphasis on individual freedoms, gun rights, tax inequities, personal discipline, and the need to get back to the basics. A common theme of the patriots is the belief that the warnings of Ezra Taft Benson—the thirteenth president of the LDS Church, who served from 1985 until his death in 1994—went largely ignored by the membership. Another common theme is pondering the meaning of Section Eighty-five in the Church's book of modern revelation, the *Doctrine and Covenants*. Verse seven of that section refers to "One mighty and strong who will come to set in order the house of God." Mainstream Mormon belief is that the "One mighty and strong" refers to the living prophet presiding over the church, or perhaps the Savior upon his Second Coming. But among the splinter groups outside the Church, there is a belief that the "One mighty and strong," also known as the Davidic Servant, refers to a person outside the Church oligarchy who will be called prior to the Second Coming to rescue the Church before its leaders blithely steer it right through the gates of hell.

In addition to attending his regular ward meetings on Sunday, Mitchell attended study group discussions and lectures sponsored by the ultra-conservative groups at various locations around the Salt Lake Valley. These discussions flourished in the early 1990s. Guest speakers such as *Embraced by the Light* author Betty J. Eadie and prolific LDS authors Duane Crowther and Cleon Skousen attracted crowds in the hundreds.

Brian Mitchell's departure from conventional Mormonism accelerated when he made the acquaintance of one C. Samuel West, a radical LDS thinker who moved from Arizona to Orem, Utah, in the 1970s to preach and teach a brand of quasi-religious healing he called lymphology. In 1981, West published his book, *The Golden Seven Plus One*, which proclaimed lymphology as the secret to life. In his book and lectures, West contends that the oxygen in cells, when fired by cellular pumps kept dry by lymphatic vessels, generates electrical power that is the key to perfect health and the end of all disease. His findings are based on a combination of science—West studied chemistry and naturopathy in college—and his own self-proclaimed divine revelation. West claims that he wrote all 319 pages of *The Golden Seven Plus One* during a continuous fifteen-day stretch with a man named Billy Gonzales, who acted as his scribe. West says not a word was changed after the first draft. "That book was produced not by my power," he declares. West promises that his lymphatic formula for disease-free living—breathe deep, eat right, and avoid anger—will "save the righteous" and produce a healthy earth for the Savior's Second Coming. In addition, it will render such things as prescription drugs and conventional medical practices obsolete. As a result, he believes that the American Medical Association and large pharmaceutical companies want to run him out of business. In ads he placed in *The Spotlight*, a magazine of the ultra-right published in Washington, D.C., he once labeled the AMA and drug companies as mass murderers.

In constant danger of being shut down, fined, or both, by government medical regulators, West confines his practice to his home about thirty-five miles south of Salt Lake City, offering his book, pamphlets, videotapes, and cassettes through toll-free lines and pages on the Internet. His clientele tends to be those looking for alternative approaches to healing after conventional medicine either failed them outright or limited their options. In the early 1990s, this clientele included Glenn Corbett, Wanda's stepfather, who investigated West's unorthodox claims of healing after being diagnosed with cancer. While lymphology did not cure Corbett, it did provide West with an introduction to Corbett's son-in-law, Brian Mitchell.

West's impact on Mitchell was immediate. He left his job at O. C. Tanner soon after meeting the lymphologist, and he and Wanda went to work for West, peddling his books, seminars, and videotapes. West's endorsement of natural healing methods resonated with Brian, whose father, Shirl, raised his family to stay away from conventional medicine and the physicians who practice it. The Mitchell children were taught to cure themselves with nutrition, body cleanses, and other holistic remedies, a notion that Brian carried into adulthood. Wanda, on the other hand, was raised to depend on conventional medicine; she used doctors to battle her illnesses, which tended to be mentally and emotionally based. For Brian, the idea of treating Wanda's mood swings with diet and deep breathing was particularly attractive. Lymphology offered a much cheaper alternative to prescription drugs.

In 1993, West took Mitchell into his Orem home and they worked together in West's office, answering toll-free calls side by side. Mitchell, West said, "really had the gift." West soon declared his protégé a certified lymphologist, fully authorized to heal lymphatically and to recruit others to do the same—if they would first make a $500 donation for a set of C. Samuel West's instructional tapes and videos.

Enmeshed in their new careers as health missionaries, the Mitchells moved out of their apartment in Salt Lake City, stopped buying Wanda's prescription drugs, sold most of their belongings, including Wanda's beloved piano (which she sold back to her mother), purchased a fifth-wheel trailer (with financing help from Shirl Mitchell), and left behind their old life as practicing Latter-day Saints in the Salt Lake Park Stake.

They spent the spring and summer of 1994 camped at a trailer park below the dam at Jordanelle Reservoir near Heber City, a farming town forty miles east of Salt Lake City. They lived next door to Wanda's sister, Evelyn, and her husband, Dick Camp. About the time of LDS president Ezra Taft Benson's death at the end of May 1994, the Mitchells made one memorable appearance as speakers in a sacrament meeting at the Heber Second Ward, where they scolded those in the congregation for not living up to their covenants. After that they stopped going to orthodox LDS services entirely. Brian grew out his hair and beard. His priesthood blessings to Wanda, his use of lymphology (he massaged the family dog's lymph nodes to help it heal after it was hit by a car), and his railing against income tax and tithing (paying 10 percent of one's income to the church) all became constant.

After Ezra Taft Benson's death, Evelyn and Dick Camp watched as Mitchell's behavior grew increasingly bizarre. He and Wanda had come to Heber "on the edge" but by June, they had fallen over the side. "Earlier in the spring, he would sometimes go off for an afternoon of fishing with me," remembered Dick. "He was still Brian. But by the summer he just wasn't normal anymore."

One day as fall neared, the Mitchells simply hitched their trailer to an old truck they'd acquired, and drove off. Dick and Evelyn followed them the short distance to Heber City, where they bought them lunch at a café in farewell. "I cried for a week after that," remembered Evelyn. "I'd lost my sister."

After leaving the trailer park, the Mitchells spun further into their antisocial, ultra-zealous orbit. They moved first to a rural part of Idaho, near Grangeville, where they lived in an area populated by far-right constitutionalists. But Mitchell's incessant preaching soon wore thin even with people who liked to hear extreme preaching. On the run from their neighbors, the IRS, and welfare services for failure to pay child support, the Mitchells abandoned their debts, and their dog, and left Idaho to wander up and down the eastern part of the country, from New York to Florida. Wanda's occasional postcards and letters to her mother were the only clue to their whereabouts.

When they returned to Utah about two years later, their behavior was no longer just odd; it was bizarre. They had taken to wearing robes, and Wanda carried baskets with baby dolls she talked to as if they were real. The Mitchells also called themselves by new names. At first, Brian wanted to be called Shirlson, a literal reference to his father (who wasn't talking to Brian because, among other things, Brian had defaulted on the trailer loan and left Shirl holding the note). Then he wanted to be known as David, which he pronounced "Dawveed." If anyone who knew him tried to call him Brian, he would not answer. Later, as *The Book of Immanuel David Isaiah* would record, Brian David Mitchell became Immanuel David Isaiah and Wanda became Hephzibah Eladah Isaiah.

By this point, they no longer had their trailer. They lived wherever they could—sometimes with family (most often with Irene Mitchell), sometimes in Sam West's basement in Orem, sometimes in homeless shelters, and sometimes in a teepee camp they set up in the mountains above the University of Utah, although no one in the family knew exactly where it was because Brian kept the location secret. He even built a miniature wooden house. It was eight feet tall, sat on regular-size car wheels, and could be pulled by hand. He called it a hand house and, sometimes, the Ark of the Covenant. But the hand house was heavy to pull. It stayed parked in Irene Mitchell's driveway much of the time.

Dressed in his robes and biblical-style cap, Mitchell began begging on the streets of Salt Lake City. He became a regular fixture in the downtown area. He just held out his hand and stood mute. He explained to family members that it was now his life's calling to give others the opportunity to provide service. That's why he begged. Wanda, however, did not beg—she tended to her dolls and sometimes spent long hours in the Salt Lake City Library writing down her husband's revelations in calligraphy.

As the years passed, Mitchell claimed a number of revelations, which, according to him, "commenced in the year before the death of Ezra Taft Benson [who died on May 30, 1994] and continued after his death." The thread woven throughout the laborious, self-serving writings in *The Book of Immanuel David Isaiah* was that Mitchell was greatly favored of the Lord, who had seen his faithfulness, forgiven him his sins, and handpicked him to clean things up after the people refused to listen to Benson. "Yea, they did outwardly feign support and pretended to uphold my prophet Ezra but inwardly they accused him of treachery because he testified against their weakness," Mitchell wrote. "And lo, they are the treacherous ones...therefore, I took my prophet Ezra unto myself...and I gave the keys of priesthood power and authority that Ezra held into thy hands, Oh Immanuel!... Even as I chose Abram and named him Abraham, and even as I chose Jacob and named him Israel, even so I have chosen thee, David, my son; and I name thee Immanuel David Isaiah, for thou wast foreordained to be a light upon a hill, an ensign to the nations."

It is toward the end of *The Book of Immanuel David Isaiah* that Mitchell, again presuming to speak for the Lord, reveals to his wife, Hephzibah, that she, too, was foreordained to greatness, "to be the Mother of Zion, and the New Jerusalem, and of the Kingdom of God in this the dispensation of the fullness of times." Among other delusions of grandeur, Mitchell's book promises his wife that "thine own mother shall weep upon thy neck and plead for forgiveness" and that she "dost delight in being meek and submissive and obedient and humble and of broken heart and contrite spirit, even as a little child. . . . Therefore, Hephzibah Eladah Isaiah, thou art called and chosen to be a helpmeet unto my servant Immanuel David Isaiah, and to be his wise counselor and best friend, and to be submissive and obedient unto thy husband in all righteousness, and be a comfort and a strength and a companion to thy husband in every time of trial and affliction until the end."

Then comes the part about the sister wives.

"Wherefore, Hephzibah," wrote Mitchell, "my most cherished angel, thou wilt take into thy heart and home seven sisters, and thou wilt recognize them through the spirit as thy dearest and choicest friends from all eternity, and they shall bring thee great joy. . . . And thou shalt take into thy heart and home seven times seven sisters, to love and care for; forty-nine precious jewels in thy crown, and thou art the jubilee of them all, first and last, for thou art a Queen, Oh Hephzibah!"

With this writing, Mitchell opened the door to one of Mormondom's oldest and most controversial tenets, that of plural wives. For nearly a half-century in the early days of the LDS Church, a small percentage of the membership (including both sides of Brian's heritage, the Mitchell line on his father's side and the Bates line on his mother's side) practiced polygamy until it was outlawed by a cease-and-desist manifesto issued by LDS Church president Wilford Woodruff in 1890. After a fourteen-year transition period resulting in a second manifesto, any LDS members who insisted on continuing what became known as "The Principle" were excommunicated. Over the years, many of these disaffected Mormons formed into splinter groups, known generally as fundamentalists, and down through the decades any number of men professing to be prophets emerged to lead these fundamentalist sects and defy not only the church that had spurned them but also the laws of the state of Utah and the United States of America, which prohibit plural marriage.

Brian David Mitchell was the latest in a fairly lengthy line to declare himself a fundamentalist prophet.

The Mitchells made their first serious attempt at polygamy in late 2000 after visiting a shoe store in the Fashion Place Mall in suburban Salt Lake to look at sandals. The young woman who waited on them, twenty-year-old Julie Adkison, displayed an interest in their unusual dress, and expressed a curiosity about their religious beliefs. Adkison had recently broken off from a sizeable fundamentalist group based in Utah, the Kingston Clan, and was considering baptism into the LDS Church. Naturally inquisitive about religion because of her background and the life change she was considering, she asked the robed couple what church they belonged to.

"He said they weren't with any organized religion but they believed in Christ," said Adkison. "I told him that I was a Kingston. He looked at me real weird and I asked him if he knew what they are. He said he did. After that he said that he didn't just believe in Christ but that he was Christ. I figured he meant in the sense that he followed Christ's teachings but the more he spoke the more I realized he actually believed that he spoke for Christ."

Adkison didn't see the robed man again until a few months later, after she had been transferred to work at a branch of the same shoe store at the Crossroads Mall in downtown Salt Lake City, a frequent begging location for Mitchell. By now, Julie had been baptized into the LDS Church and was also engaged to be married. She said hi to Mitchell one day as she passed him on the sidewalk and they casually talked some more about religion. Adkison, a polite young woman by nature, thought no more of it until a few days later, when both Brian and Wanda Mitchell showed up in the shoe store and asked if they could make an appointment to talk to her. It was important that she hear what they had to say, they insisted. Not wanting to offend them, Julie scheduled a time to talk to them later in the month. They agreed to have their meeting in a public park near Temple Square.

"On the day we agreed on, they came to the store dressed in their robes and told me it would only be a few hours," Julie remembered. "I had my assistant cover for me, and he said he'd call the cops if I didn't come back soon. They walked me out and we went to the park. They sat me in the middle of them, both talking to me. After a while he started saying how he felt like it was time for them to start living polygamy and that I was the one who made them realize it; that they hadn't felt they were ready until now. I thought like uh-oh, where's this leading? He looked at my engagement ring and said, 'That's a pretty ring.' I said, 'Thanks.' He said, 'I'll bet that's worth a lot of money.' I said, 'I guess.' Then he said to sell it and go into the mountains and live with his wife and him. He told me that Hephzibah [Wanda] said that he needed to ask me. She was obviously 100 percent for this, too. I just kinda laughed at him. I was shocked. He told me not to answer, but to think about it."

A few weeks later, on March 1, 2001, Brian and Wanda appeared in the shoe store and handed Julie a letter. "I want you to read this and God will testify the truth to you," Mitchell told her. Then he turned and walked away.

The four-page handwritten letter began in Mitchell's voice. "God sent us to you Julie," it began. "Hundreds of special women have honored us in a similar manner as yourself, but you are the only woman that God sent us to testify of those things sacred and holy which you received." About halfway through the letter, the voice changed to that of God. "Can you deny my spirit, that it is I that speaks to you thru my chosen servant Immanuel?" The letter admonished Julie to "Seek ye to be one with Immanuel and with Hephzibah that ye also may be one with me."

"I didn't scorn them, not to their face," said Julie, who married her fiancé that May. She didn't respond to the letter, and she never saw Mitchell or Wanda again. "But we laughed about that letter for a couple of months," she said.

Thwarted in their straightforward appeal to Julie Adkison, and perhaps to others, the Mitchells shifted their strategy at finding Wanda's sister wives. If they couldn't get them to come willingly, then it would have to be by force. The potential sister wives would have to be young enough not to be set in their ways.

In the summer of 2001, not long after Julie Adkison's rejection, the Mitchells were staying in Sam West's home in Orem.

"We were watching the news when a story came on about a little girl who had been taken from her parents," remembered Sam West's son Karl, who had recently moved back in with his parents after going through a painful divorce that involved temporarily losing custody of his young son. "I said something to the effect that anybody who takes a child from her parents deserved to go to hell. Mitchell disagreed, and started talking about it in terms of 'What if she wanted to go and she leaves on her own behalf and she is much older?' What would I say to that? I said, 'I guess only God could judge that.'"

Karl remembered that Wanda tried to shut Brian up when he started to talk about taking the hypothetical girl. "It was clear they knew they were going to do something," said Karl. "He even said he had a special name for the girl he was going to take. He said he was going to call her Augustine."

As they made the progression from zealots to fanatics, the Mitchells systematically alienated all those they had close contact with, including family members. They lost patience for anyone else's point of view; they had no capacity for compromise. Quick to take offense, ready to sever relationships at the slightest hint of disagreement, they left behind them a string of estrangements. They indignantly stormed out of the home of Brian's brother Tim in Logan, Utah, late one night after Tim told them he thought lymphology was nothing more than glorified massage and they were being deceived by a false spirit. They left Wanda's mother's house in West Valley City, Utah, in a huff one afternoon because Dora Corbett would not allow them to use her home for group preaching. They even had a falling out with Sam West when West would not acknowledge Mitchell's prophetic claims or condone his outright apostasy from the orthodox LDS Church.

Their final and most violent break came on April 18, 2002, at Irene Mitchell's house. For the better part of five years, her home had served as a refuge for Brian and Wanda. It was where they returned when they were tired of wandering and sleeping on the ground. Although they were often gone for long periods of time—in the winter, especially, when they would go to warmer, unspecified climates in the south—eventually they would reappear on Irene's doorstep.

Retired from teaching school and long since divorced from Shirl, Irene was used to living alone and would from time to time suggest that perhaps her son and daughter-in-law shouldn't wear out their welcome by staying—and preaching—too long. But Irene was not a confrontational person, and her suggestions were always gentle and subtle. She wrote her most straight-forward requests in letters, which Brian and Wanda never opened.

But when Brian's sister Laurie was diagnosed with cancer in late 2000, things changed. Irene spent most of her time helping Laurie and her hus-band with their six children in Washington, Utah, a suburb of St. George three hundred miles south of Salt Lake City. That left Brian and Wanda in charge of Irene's house for what turned out to be the better part of a year and a half. The situation worked out well enough; Irene had someone in the house, so it wasn't abandoned, and Brian and Wanda had free rent.

Still, tensions mounted. Brian and Wanda didn't do much to take care of the place—a problem compounded by the fact neither of them had a job. When Laurie died in February 2002 at the age of forty-three, Brian and Wanda did not attend the funeral. Brian's only real involvement with his younger sister's illness had been to try to heal her through lymphology. When his technique was rebuffed, he took offense and added yet another family estrangement.

Irene moved back to her Salt Lake home for good around the time when Brian unveiled *The Book of Immanuel David Isaiah*. The lack of positive response to their writings only furthered Brian and Wanda's conviction that it was them against the world. Everywhere they distributed the man-uscript they were met with either scorn or indifference. Sam West, whose book Brian declares Holy Scripture, burned the four copies given to him and his family and chastised Brian for his apostasy. Shirl Mitchell, with his own thousand-page manuscript collecting dust, complimented his son's writing skills, but it was a backhanded compliment; he labeled the book's content Mormon plagiarizing.

Wanda's family laughed after Brian dropped off copies of his book at Dora Corbett's house on the day of Glenn Corbett's funeral. Earlier that afternoon, Brian and Wanda had arrived late for the funeral, attracting attention because of their strange dress. Before the services ended, they got up and left. Wanda's children, who hadn't seen their mother in years, went running after her. Her youngest daughter, LouRee, whose two children had never seen their grandmother, called out, "Mother," in an attempt to get Wanda to stop. Brian turned and coldly said, "That's not her name." "I'm not talking to you, I'm talking to my mother," said LouRee, at which point both Brian and Wanda yelled out, "Repent! Repent!" as they ran off.

As for Irene Mitchell, when the onetime high school English teacher received her personal copy of her son's book she didn't ridicule the writing, but she didn't praise the religion in it either. She just put the twenty-seven-page manuscript on the shelf as her houseguests continued to preach to her.

Over the years, Brian and Wanda had often verbally abused Irene with their aggressive preaching. On the morning of April 18, the abuse turned physical. When Irene told them she had to go out and did not have time to listen to them, Brian and Wanda became incensed. Brian took hold of one of his mother's arms, and Wanda took hold of the other. As they held Irene's arms they preached in her face. When Irene resisted and screamed for help, they pulled harder. The louder she shouted, "Let me go! Let me go!" the harder they pulled. Finally, the seventy-six-year-old woman screamed, "Help! Someone call the police!" and Brian and Wanda released her. Irene ran out the door to a neighbor's house and called her youngest daughter, Lisa, who didn't hesitate in urging her mother to call the police.

Two Salt Lake County deputies responded to the call. After discussing the domestic disturbance with Irene on the front porch, the deputies entered the house and ordered Brian and Wanda to pack up their things and leave. The deputies recommended to an obviously distraught and frightened Irene that it would be a good idea to take out a protective order. They gave her a pamphlet with instructions on how to obtain one. By now Lisa had arrived to drive her mother to the county courthouse in Salt Lake City to file for the order, which allowed Brian and Wanda time to vacate the premises. It was nearly 4:00 P.M. when the paperwork was completed. On the drive back to Irene's house—an older home in an established residential neighborhood twenty minutes from the city center—Lisa and Irene picked up Lisa's husband, Tom Holbrook, who worked at LDS Church headquarters in downtown Salt Lake City and was just getting off work.

When they got back to Irene's, Brian and Wanda were still there. Hearing them in the basement as she entered the house, Irene retreated to the neighbor's with Tom and Lisa to call the sheriff again. Another pair of deputies responded and personally escorted Brian and Wanda out of the residence and off the premises. They were dressed in purple robes and when they crossed the lawn and saw Irene, Lisa, and Tom, both Brian and Wanda began yelling at the top of their lungs, "Repent sinners! God will get you and your families for what you have done! You will be destroyed, your family will be destroyed, your home will be destroyed!" The deputies twice had to order them to be quiet before Brian and Wanda finally turned and walked away, each carrying a small rucksack.

Inside the house, Irene, Lisa, and Tom discovered a mess. "Brian and Wanda had taken their possessions and basically destroyed them," remembered Tom. "The garbage can was full of broken dishes, bent knives and forks, smashed pots and pans. All of Wanda's sheet music was cut up and lying on the floor. They'd sliced their shoes with razor blades and soaked their clothes in water and cut them up and left them in a pile in the garage. They'd taken all their flour and sugar and salt from their food storage and dumped it in a big pile in the backyard. Everything they owned was destroyed. They busted all of the china Wanda had been collecting and they had taken some of her collectible porcelain dolls and broken the faces and torn the dolls up. There was obviously some real anger and rage going on. But they didn't destroy anything of Grandma's, just their things. They were leaving all their worldly possessions behind."

After straightening up a bit, Tom and Lisa left with Irene for their home in nearby South Jordan, where Irene had decided to spend the night. As they turned north on 1300 East, then west on 6400 South, they looked down the block and saw Brian and Wanda boarding a bus that was headed in the direction of downtown Salt Lake City. It was the last they would see of them. Two weeks later, on May 2, Brian and Wanda were supposed to appear, along with Irene, for a hearing on the protective order at the Third Judicial District Court of Salt Lake County. When only Irene appeared, the judge ordered an extension of the protective order, keeping it in full effect until notice could be officially served on Brian and Wanda.

Tom Holbrook urged Irene to take her copy of Brian's book to her bishop, which she did. The bishop in turn gave it to Gregory Schwitzer, the stake president. Meanwhile, Tom took his copy to his office at LDS Church headquarters, where he delivered it to the committee on apostate activity. The LDS authorities determined that the content of *The Book of Immanuel David Isaiah* was inflammatory, and the author of the book should be disciplined. They recommended that President Schwitzer inform Brian and Wanda of the need for a disciplinary council as quickly as possible.

President Schwitzer scheduled the hearing for the evening of Sunday, June 9, 2002, more than a month away, but the Mitchells were nowhere to be found. They seemed to have disappeared from the downtown streets and malls where Brian regularly begged for money. Tom Holbrook was given a copy of the LDS court notice and asked to keep a lookout for Brian when he went to work downtown. Tom also asked coworkers at LDS headquarters to keep an eye out for his brother-in-law. No one needed a description. Everyone knew the Jesus Man.

At the end of May, less than a week before Elizabeth Smart went missing and just as President Schwitzer was beginning to think they might have to postpone the disciplinary council, he came across Mitchell by accident. Schwitzer had visited a favorite shop on Main Street. As he exited the store, a newly purchased tie in his hand, he looked across the street and saw Mitchell in his muslin robes and cap sitting on the pavement.

Schwitzer crossed the street and kneeled down by the begging man. "Hello, Brian," he said. He received only silence in return. The stake president continued to talk pleasantries. He got no response. Finally he reached in his pocket and produced the notice of the disciplinary council. He explained what it was and handed it to Brian. When Brian wouldn't take the paper, Schwitzer dropped it beside him and informed him he hoped he and Wanda would come to the stake center to be heard on June 9. At that point, Brian became enraged and screamed at Schwitzer to repent. Then he stood up and walked off, leaving the notice lying on the sidewalk.

All this history was presented to the Salt Lake Butler West Stake High Council on the evening of Sunday, June 9, before a vote was taken regarding excommunication. In addition to a copy of Mitchell's book, letters from Dora Corbett and Irene Mitchell were entered into evidence. Each detailed the heartbreaking slide into fanaticism and apostasy of their offspring. "They think we are all Babylon because we have homes and cars and so many worldly possessions [but] I can't believe my daughter puts up with her way of life," wrote Dora Corbett. "I wonder sometimes if Brian has her hypnotized. She thinks he's a wonderful man. She told me that anyone could be a prophet. I'm sure Brian thinks he is. Wanda used to have such a beautiful smile and one could feel her spirit. She sure doesn't look like that anymore. I feel so bad that they are like they are. How must Heavenly Father feel? I just pray for them."

After kneeling in prayer, the brethren of the high council voted unanimously to take away the LDS membership of Brian David Mitchell and Wanda Barzee Mitchell.

And no one had a clue where they were.

10

Monday morning brought a return to the network morning-show routine. We used to start the day watching the news; now we *were* the news. The Elizabeth Smart kidnapping had become a national story and a national concern, and inside the family we wanted to do whatever we could to keep it that way. No interview was too small, no hour too early or too late, and no media request unreasonable. Every microphone, camera, and reporter's notebook was a way to keep the search alive.

That meant intense scrutiny from the media, and not just on the case, but on every member of the family.

After our round of talk shows Monday morning, Heidi and I and our three daughters, Sierra, Nicole, and Amanda, drove toward town to get something to eat. It was a little after 5:30 A.M. when we pulled into the empty parking lot of a breakfast place. The restaurant didn't open until 6:00.

Emotionally spent after the television interviews, we decided to wait in the car. We discussed how in one way it was easy talking about Elizabeth, knowing the potential for reaching vast audiences; but it was also a wrenching experience, a constant reminder that she was really gone.

After a few minutes I opened the car door and stepped out. "I can't wait till they open," I muttered. "I've got to go."

As I moved toward the relative privacy of a dumpster in the corner of the parking lot, my three daughters shouted in unison, "Dad, don't!"

I turned around to see them staring at me in disbelief. Didn't I realize that whatever I did—whatever any of us did—had a strong chance of winding up on the evening news? I walked back to the car, deciding that I could wait after all.

We ordered huge quantities of food for breakfast, reasoning that we needed to keep our strength up. Then we barely touched a thing. We just talked and choked back tears, the same thing we'd been doing for nearly a week. After pretending to eat for a while, Heidi got up to pay at the register and came back crying. "They won't take my money. They won't let us pay." The restaurant staff knew who we were. Good luck and God bless, they told us. On our way out we walked past fliers with Elizabeth's photo that someone had taped to the restaurant's front windows.

We returned to the search center, which had moved overnight from Shriners Hospital to the Federal Heights LDS wardhouse across the street. For four full days, Thursday through Sunday, Shriners had donated its grounds, parking lots, meeting rooms, and even some of its staff to the search effort. Nearly ten thousand volunteers had used the hospital as a search head-quarters. But if the search was going to be longer term—and much as any-one hated to admit it, the absence of any significant leads or so much as the hint of a ransom demand indicated that it might be—the hospital needed to get back to normal operations.

Zeke had met with local LDS leaders Sunday and they offered the use of the Federal Heights facility to the family "for as long as you need it." A large room at the west end of the building, the place where the stake high council meets, was given to us as a headquarters. It was our war room. For the Smart family, the building had a feeling of sanctuary. We had all grown up going to church here. When my parents first built their home on Chandler Drive in the late 1960s, the entire residential area—from the block U on the mountain to the University of Utah campus below—encompassed one LDS ward, or congregation, the Federal Heights Ward. When the Arlington Hills development came about, LDS created the Arlington Hills Ward. That's the ward my parents and Ed's family attended, but both the Federal Heights and Arlington Hills wards used the same building, and the entire area felt like home.

During our first family meeting Monday morning in our new search headquarters, I stepped out of the room to call Jeanne Boylan, the sketch artist Marc Klaas had been lobbying the family to retain. She tried to explain to me exactly what she did and I replied that I had been assured that the best people in the country were already working on ascertaining how much Mary Katherine, the only eyewitness, had seen of the kidnapper and whether it was enough for a sketch. I had serious doubts that Mary Katherine had seen enough for a good sketch, and we didn't want that information to be made public. Boylan was trying to be as helpful as possible, but when she said that "Fox would fly me in," I ended the conversation. It didn't feel right to override law enforcement, especially by using someone who was coming in as part of the media. My instincts told me not to bring in Jeanne Boylan. I encouraged Ed to avoid her as well.

After I hung up, I went to the downtown police station with several relatives of the suspicious Arlington Hills resident about whom Doug and I had talked to the police on Saturday night. The man still hadn't returned and his home had not been searched. The purpose of our visit was to again try to impress on the police the urgency of this lead. On paper, it added up that this could be the answer. I told homicide detective Mark Scharman, "I think I know who did it." It was my third such proclamation in five days.

While I was at the station, the police, who wanted fingerprints and blood samples from all family members, asked if I would stay long enough for them to print me and draw some blood. I was quickly fingerprinted, but after waiting forty-five minutes for someone to take my blood sample, I told them I would not wait all day on a bureaucracy when Elizabeth was still missing. Then I left.

Making decisions based on pure instinct was standard procedure during the first frantic week of searching. Even though the search effort had become sophisticated in its organization, the decision about where to search next was most often based on nothing more than a gut feeling. Despite leads coming in at the rate of more than one per minute, none were substantive enough to point out where Elizabeth might have gone. Once the vicinity around Kristianna Circle had been searched, it was anybody's guess where to look next.

On Monday, we expanded the search to the desert southwest of the Great Salt Lake in a desolate area known as Skull Valley. At our morning press conference we asked for anyone with an ATV to meet at a freeway exit near the abandoned town of Delle, Utah, about fifty miles from Salt Lake City. As soon as we made the appeal, dozens of all-terrain vehicles converged on Delle, with the media right behind.

We sent Scott Thornton and Mike Freed to Delle in a pickup truck to coordinate the search. "When I got to Delle it was like a Harley convention of ATVs," remembered Freed, who was still recovering from the disappointment that he hadn't cracked the case with the harp suspect. "The (local) police were acting kind of concerned, so I was trying to get everyone on their way, and that's when I looked up and saw about twenty-five microphones in my face and a couple of news helicopters overhead. 'Can we talk to you?' they asked. 'Not right now,' I said. 'We've got to get these people out of here.' So they asked if they could put a microphone on me while I worked and I said OK."

After most of the ATVs were on their way, Freed stopped to give the media some direct quotes. "This is something we're not going to allow to happen," Freed said as the cameras rolled. "The people of Utah will not put up with this. The Olympics were just here and everyone lined up to help and now they're lining up again just like the Olympics. We're going to find her. My friend Tom Smart told me she's alive and we're going to find her and that's good enough for me."

Tall, lean, and athletic-looking, Freed is photogenic; the image of a determined man with a set jaw standing next to a pickup truck framed by the wild Utah desert was something no decent video editor could pass up. All across America, Freed was on that night's newscasts, and for months to come his "we're going to find her" clip could be seen on cable news shows and *America's Most Wanted*.

But if Tom Smart's word was good enough for a trusted friend, I was about to find out that law enforcement felt very differently.

Throughout Monday, the question that began surfacing in every media interview was about lie detector tests. Had the family been polygraphed? Had I personally been polygraphed? I was first asked that question at the search center by Darin Mackoff, the Fox News producer. Mackoff said he had a source saying that Ed had taken a polygraph, but that the test had not been administered by the SLCPD. I said I was certain the family had not brought in a polygrapher—as Congressman Gary Condit had reportedly done in the well-publicized case involving the disappearance of his legislative intern, Chandra Levy. But, I hastened to add, as a family we would all welcome the opportunity to take lie detector tests administered by law enforcement. Shortly after that, the polygraph question came up again during an interview I did with Sean Hannity on his national radio show. No, I had not been polygraphed, I told him, and, to my knowledge, neither had anyone else in the family.

A little later that afternoon, just before I was about to do an interview with local radio station KSL, Ed called my cell phone. "Tom," he said, "I had a polygraph. They did it yesterday. It was four hours of hell." Just after he told me that, the call-waiting signal beeped on my phone. It was KSL, who wanted to follow up on the polygraph questions I had already discussed on the Hannity show.

I answered, again, that I had not personally been asked to take a polygraph, but added the detail that Ed—who had not had time during our short conversation to inform me that law enforcement wanted the news to remain confidential—had gone through one Sunday afternoon and had described it to me as four hours of hell.

Not long after making that public declaration, I found myself at FBI headquarters in downtown Salt Lake City sitting across from the FBI's top polygrapher, with wires attached to my chest and hands. Before starting the first lie detector test of my life, the polygrapher leaned toward me and said, "By the way, your brother Ed's polygraph lasted two hours and forty-five minutes, and he passed fine."

The long arm of the law had reached out fast. After my KSL interview, Heidi had driven my sister Cynthia and me back to the police station so Cynthia could talk to a detective and I could give my blood sample. The next thing I knew, I was all wired up.

I was in no shape for a polygraph test, or much of anything else. It had been five and a half days since I'd had any sleep. Cynthia pleaded with the officers to first let me get some rest. No attorney worth his bar membership would have let me submit to a polygraph in my weakened state, that's for sure. But when they asked me to be polygraphed, I just said, "Let's get this over with." I had no idea of the pain I was in for. Later, I would learn that it is against international rules of war, according to standards adopted by the Geneva Convention, for interrogators to interview prisoners of war after seventy-two hours of no sleep. Not only is interrogation of the seriously sleep-deprived deemed cruel and inhumane, but it is also unreliable, as people in this weakened state are likely to say anything the interrogators want them to say.

As unprepared as I was for the interrogation, law enforcement was even less prepared. No one had taken the elementary step of asking my wife, Heidi, if I was with her the night of the kidnapping. I probably had a better alibi than most of the investigators. The same was true of my brothers Chris and David, who would be polygraphed during the next two days. But as we would also discover later, the intent of a polygraph test is not to determine whether a person is telling the truth, but to provide a chance for law enforcement to dissect that person when he or she is vulnerable. The idea is to pick up on some hidden evidence.

I was escorted across the street to the FBI offices, where I was instructed to go to the restroom. "And before you use the bathroom, wash your hands in warm water," the officer said. "Even if you don't have to go, that will make you go."

I was handed a consent form, which, although I was too whacked out to read properly, I signed anyway. I was told that anything I said during the polygraph would remain strictly confidential.

When I was about seven years old, I learned how to clean a fish. You stick a knife in the lower part of the fish and cut up the belly to the gills, grab inside the fish, and rip its guts out. Then you take your thumb and scrape the very core of the vein on the fish's backbone until there is nothing left but meat and bones. That's similar to the process I went through during my polygraph. It is a fillet of your soul. Anywhere the polygrapher wanted to take me, I was willing to go—anything to help find Elizabeth—and if that meant crawling into the darkest part of my psyche, I stepped into the void willingly.

It started out with a simple question, "Do you lie to your wife?"

"No," I answered. Then I added, "I lie for sport and I lie for love but I don't lie for real." I was trying to be honest. To explain further, I told the polygrapher that I had once told Heidi very honestly that her new haircut made her look like a Mormon Relief Society president—not a compliment—and that I think I've liked every haircut she's had since. And when I gamble, I continued, my wife and I have an agreement that I have to give her half my winnings and match my losses. Strangely enough, I've been breaking even for years—but she can read me like a book. Those are lies, but they're not real lies. I'm an honest person. I tried to explain it all to the polygrapher but things quickly became complicated.

"Do you lie to your wife?" was one of the easiest questions. What was hard was when they asked if I'd ever hurt anyone. Ask yourself that question. Have you ever hurt anyone? Yes or no?

They don't shock you with questions. They go over everything they're going to ask you beforehand so you know exactly what's coming. There are no surprises. They get everything down to a yes or no answer while they have these probes wrapped around your chest and fingers.

A lot of the questions are completely innocent. "Were you born on your birthday?" "Do you reside on Moose Hollow Drive?" "Is today Monday?" Questions they know will have a positive response. The point is to get a physiological reaction to the questions to determine if you're telling the truth. And even if you pass the test, that's no guarantee you told the truth. Polygraphs aren't admissible in court because there are too many ways to fool the test and too many instances where a polygraph casts suspicion on completely truthful answers. When you're sleep-deprived or traumatized there's about a 45 percent chance the test will be inconclusive.

After about four hours of intense probing, the polygrapher—who sat behind me while he asked the questions—came around and looked at me and said, "Well, we're done, but we have a problem. You're inconclusive."

I said, "There's nothing else I can do. I've been honest with you. I've told you everything I could as honestly as I could. The ball's in your court."

He replied, "No, the ball's in your court."

I guess he wanted me to go on talking and try to pass the test, but at that point I really had nothing left. Again, I said, "No, there's nothing else I can do," and I stared him in the eye. I know eye contact is important in interviews, so I just looked at him for what I was sure was more than an hour (I later heard it was over two hours). Neither of us said anything. I had tears streaming down my face, and if I remember correctly the polygrapher had tears in his eyes. About halfway through this stare-down I heard a voice outside the door in the outer FBI offices. "We found her," I heard someone say excitedly. I didn't react. I just kept looking at this man I did not know.

Finally he broke the silence and said, "Well, it's getting late and we need to move on." Then he asked me what I had been thinking about during all that time we had been looking at each other.

I said, "Didn't you hear them outside the door say they found her?" He said he hadn't. Then he stood up and walked over and opened the door to an empty office. "There's no one out there," he said. I was simply hearing voices at that point.

After that, he gave me a yellow legal pad and said they needed a time line. He wanted me to list where I'd been and what I'd been doing from eight o'clock the morning before Elizabeth was abducted. I must have looked at that blank legal pad for twenty minutes. Finally I started piecing together what I had done and where I had gone. I wrote that I had been shooting a baseball game for the newspaper that Tuesday night, which in fact was not correct. I had shot the baseball game Monday night and a basketball game Tuesday. The next thing I remembered was Ed calling me early the next morning. I put "3:30" with a big question mark next to it because I didn't know exactly what time it he had called; I just knew it was dark. I wrote that I had then driven to Ed's house but hadn't gone in at first because the police tape was there, which wasn't true either. I was just too sleep deprived to remember anything very accurately. I wasn't overly concerned because I had nothing to hide and everything I said could be checked. My photo assignments at the newspaper could be confirmed easily, the exact time of the phone call could be established through phone records, and my wife had been with me when we woke up and drove to Ed's house.

When I stopped writing I thought we were finally finished, but then the polygrapher hooked up the wires again and asked me some of the same questions he'd asked before. "Do you know who took Elizabeth?" "Did you take Elizabeth?" "Is today Tuesday?" By this point I don't know if they were trying to break me or what. Inevitably, the interview takes you where your deepest fears or thoughts are hidden. Anyone who goes into a situation like I did, without an attorney, is helping to bring about his own emotional suicide. But the last thing I was thinking about was myself.

Ironically enough, the polygrapher doesn't always tell the truth himself. For example, he might ask, "Why do you think so-and-so thinks you did it?" even though so-and-so never made such an accusation. The polygrapher tries to blow your mind, although my mind was pretty well blown before I even got there.

The polygrapher did not tell me my final result. The very last thing he told me was that I should not talk about my polygraph.

I didn't see anyone on the FBI floor when I left the building. Ed's description of "four hours of hell" was amazingly accurate, although my hell had been nearly double that. I reached for my cell phone and called Heidi.

Heidi hadn't known I was still at the station, and for hours she had been calling my cell phone, which I had shut off. At about 11:30 P.M., after the search center shut down, she had gone to the police station, where they told her they hadn't seen me. Finally she drove to Ed and Lois's house. There she was directed to an FBI agent who told her where I'd been all night.

It was after midnight when the headlights of Heidi's car shined on me, carrying my cell phone, walking aimlessly along the street away from the FBI building. I'm sure my wife of twenty-three years had never seen me as beaten down as when I dropped into the passenger seat beside her and we started the long drive back up Parleys Canyon to home.

We had put everything else aside for six days. Finding Elizabeth had become our only focus. And now that mania to find her seemed to be backfiring. The police had turned on us, and the media was starting to turn. It can be a crazy world sometimes. It was about to get crazier.

11

It was noon on Tuesday, June 11. Day seven. I was in the basement of my parents' house, where I had just completed a questionnaire for the FBI. Everyone in the family had been given an identical sheet of printed questions that morning. The questions got right to the point. "Did you kill Elizabeth?" "Who do you think could have taken her?" "If you had taken her, what would you have done?"

After I filled out the questionnaire I was interviewed by two FBI agents, Juan Becerra and the unfortunately named Ken Crook. There were no wires or probes this time, and no stare-downs. The agents were very professional in their questioning.

Agent Crook was a no-nonsense type I took to immediately. "Look, Tom," he said, "when a girl is taken, usually they grab her, they duct tape her mouth, and it's over." He asked me why I thought the kidnapper told Elizabeth to bring her shoes. The only reason I could think of was that he was taking her someplace where she'd have to walk. I added that I thought the shoes represented the most practical reason to think she might still be alive. Crook was curious why I thought the kidnapper was able to select an exit door that was one of the few not equipped with an alarm. "Dumb luck" was the best I could come up with.

As with the polygrapher the night before, I know I didn't wow the agents with my sharp intellect. Once again I hadn't slept at all the previous night. By the time Heidi and I got home from my polygraph it was already after 1:00 A.M. We had to leave in a little more than two hours for the early news shows. I had tried to get some sleep, but soon gave up and crawled into the hot tub.

We were at the Sabalas' home in time for the live feed for *Good Morning America*, when Charlie Gibson interviewed our daughters. The girls were, in my biased view, nothing short of fabulous. Due to concerns about copycats and the possibility that a serial kidnapper might be targeting the family, none of Elizabeth's cousins had appeared in front of the media until now. But it made sense to appeal to the kidnapper with a more youthful approach, and since they were the oldest cousins, Sierra, Nicole, and Amanda were the obvious choices. They are bright, personable girls and they made excellent television guests. Sierra echoed the now-familiar family appeal to the kidnapper's good side, and asked him to let Elizabeth go. I remember sitting there with Heidi, watching our daughters talk about the love they share for their cousin. I can't imagine any father being more proud.

Media interest in the story was still huge, but the absence of hard news meant plenty of airtime to fill, a fact that increased the demand for interviews with family members. Early Tuesday, Fox producer Darin Mackoff approached Mike Grass to set up an interview for that day's edition of *The O'Reilly Factor*. The show's host, Bill O'Reilly, specifically wanted an interview with me. But by this time, the family had established what was euphemistically called the four-hour rule but could have been more accurately called the keep-Tom-away-from-all-live-microphones rule. The edict was that no family member could talk to the media without having had at least four hours of sleep the night before. As I hadn't had four hours of sleep for nearly a week, the family told Bill O'Reilly I was not available.

Mackoff said O'Reilly was insistent: Tom or nobody. "Then nobody," the family responded. As much as everyone wanted to accommodate the media, there was also a point where there was a potential to do more damage than good. Why risk attracting negative attention by pushing sleep-deprived family members, who were emotionally traumatized as it was, in front of the public?

So the crazy uncle was banned from O'Reilly—and everything else—that afternoon. No sooner had the FBI agents left my parents' house than Heidi appeared with a glass of water and a pill. "Why don't you take this Ambien," she said, "and get some sleep?"

With my wife holding my hand, I took the sleeping pill, sure it wouldn't work, and then…blackness. After one hundred and fifty-two hours—just sixteen hours short of a full week—after running around Salt Lake like a cross between Sherlock Holmes and the zombies in *Night of the Living Dead*, after telling the police no fewer than four times, "I know who did it," after dozens of print and broadcast interviews, after a seven-hour polygraph, I finally went to sleep.

As their ultimatum had failed to produce results, *The O'Reilly Factor* producers asked who in the Smart family might take my place. When Sierra and Amanda—fresh from their *Good Morning America* success and a number of equally impressive media appearances that morning—were suggested, the O'Reilly people said fine; if they couldn't have Tom, they'd take Tom's daughters. They arranged for the girls to be interviewed mid-afternoon on the lawn outside the search center. Sierra and Amanda would be miked and wired; Bill O'Reilly would ask them questions from his New York studio. Heidi and Mike Grass escorted Sierra (age twenty-one) and Amanda (age seventeen) to the interview tent.

It had been a hellish week for all of Elizabeth's cousins. Most of them had slept every night since the kidnapping either in their parents' room or with their doors and windows double-locked. This wasn't just any girl who had disappeared, this was someone they knew intimately—and someone who looked like them. In fact, on a trip with Elizabeth's brothers and sisters to the pet store over the weekend to buy supplies for two new dogs Ed and Lois had bought after the abduction, three-year-old William had looked up at Sierra and asked, "Are you Elizabeth?"

All three of my girls were working as hard as they could. Amanda, who was in her last week of high school in Park City, was hurrying to the search center from school one afternoon when a motorcycle cop pulled her over for speeding. Her car had Elizabeth posters on every window and a baby blue ribbon on the antenna, and Amanda was wearing a "Pray for Me" Elizabeth button. When the officer came to the window, Amanda said that she was Elizabeth Smart's cousin and that she was hurrying to the search center. The officer asked her for her license, looked at it briefly, handed it back with the words, "I am so sorry; I hope you find her," and then let her go.

Without bothering to tell the family, Mike Grass, the girls, or anybody, Bill O'Reilly had Marc Klaas join him for the interview. The two men opened the segment by discussing "the questionable tactics" of Tom Smart.

In hindsight, we should have seen it coming. Not only is *The O'Reilly Factor* known for its in-your-face confrontational style, with a heavy spin factor, but also we had already had our share of borderline adversarial moments with the Fox network. First there had been the problem in setting up the interview with Marc Klaas and Ed and Lois. Then there had been Klaas's suggestion that the family bring in forensic sketch artist Jeanne Boylan, followed by Boylan's own overture. Finally there was Darin Mackoff's question to me the day before about the family taking polygraphs. By now it was clear that Klaas was a paid correspondent and that his primary goal was to get the story, not to help the family.

Bill O'Reilly, in New York, and Marc Klaas, in San Francisco, clearly wanted to challenge me directly as to why I had declined Klaas's initial suggestion that the family bring in Jeanne Boylan and why I was being, in their view, an impediment to the investigation. I could not defend my position on not bringing in a sketch artist without compromising the investigation by saying that Mary Katherine had not seen well enough to produce a good sketch. We didn't want the kidnapper to know how much, or how little, she had seen.

The fact that I was sleeping and my daughters had taken my place did not deter them. After opening the show with "Hi, I'm Bill O'Reilly, thanks for watching us tonight," O'Reilly launched right in. "Now for the top story tonight. Salt Lake City police are heavily hinting that the person who kidnapped fourteen-year-old Elizabeth Smart was known to her. Joining us now from Salt Lake are Elizabeth's two cousins, Amanda and Sierra Smart, and from San Francisco, Marc Klaas, who launched the Klaas Kids Foundation after the kidnapping and murder of his twelve-year-old daughter, Polly. Mr. Klaas, first up, how do you see this case? Are there problems here?"

"Well, there've been many problems from the inception," Klaas answered, "least of which is the fact that they seem to have absolutely nothing to go on. And the one piece of solid evidence that might exist, which is burned inside the mind of the little nine-year-old sister, had not really been followed up on until today, I guess, when they finally reinterviewed the young lady, or the young girl, and they've gotten some new information, which apparently is leading them directly toward one of perhaps several individuals that are on the radar screen."

Klaas went on to inform O'Reilly of his opinion that Mary Katherine's mind could best be probed by Jeanne Boylan, but her services had not been solicited and were not being used.

"I understand that the uncle, Tom Smart, Amanda and Sierra's father, is against that," O'Reilly said to Klaas.

"Apparently so," replied Klaas.

"And the uncle has been against some other things as well, correct?" asked O'Reilly.

"Well, it's been difficult," said Klaas. "Tom has been a challenging individual, yes, sir."

"And do you know why?"

"No, sir."

O'Reilly then turned to Sierra and Amanda, who, with growing incredulity, had been listening to the exchange between O'Reilly and Klaas via their headphones.

"Now, Amanda and Sierra, you just heard Mr. Klaas, who's an expert on this, say that your father has kind of been not really on the same page as Mr. Klaas, at least. Do you have any reaction to that? Amanda?"

Although the question was directed to Amanda, her older sister, Sierra, answered first, "On the same page?" she said, followed quickly by an echo from Amanda, "On the same page?"

From O'Reilly, "Yes, I mean, well..."

Before he could finish, Sierra interjected, "What do you mean by that?"

"What I mean is that Mr. Klaas says he's trying to set up an artist coming up there, trying to do a rendition with the little girl. But your father doesn't want that to happen."

Sierra and Amanda knew nothing of Jeanne Boylan or of any previous exchanges between Marc Klaas and myself. They had no idea Klaas would be joining O'Reilly on the program. "We thought it would be just us and O'Reilly," Sierra remembered. "We could hear the show in our ears and all of a sudden we heard him talking to Marc Klaas. We didn't know who Marc Klaas was; we didn't know his story or anything about him. Amanda and I were getting really nervous because they're saying Tom is interfering with the investigation. We really started freaking out because we were miked and couldn't say anything. We had been told it would be a straight interview. Then, he asked that first question and it was such a strange question that we both started talking. We were shocked. You almost forgot you were on national television because it was so weird to be there and to be asked such questions. Then we were fighting for our dignity."

The girls did their best to defend the family and me, but it was O'Reilly's show and he did not retreat, leaving Elizabeth's cousins with this closing line: "Look, I'm not pushing you ladies, and I know you're here because you want everybody in Utah and across the country to keep an eye out for your cousin, and we want Elizabeth to come home. But it is a little strange that in a close family like the Smarts, that you wouldn't discuss this case with your dad in very specific terms."

O'Reilly then went back to Klaas, dismissing Sierra and Amanda before they had a chance to respond.

"I thought about just entering in," Sierra remembered. "It just really ticked us off that after searching twenty hours a day anyone would think that we'd all get together at home and have a long talk about what everyone was doing. You don't talk about it because you don't have time. That's just common sense, the kind of common sense O'Reilly doesn't seem to use on his show."

Heidi was the first to notice something was wrong. Sierra moves her foot and taps it when she is agitated, and from that and other negative body language she could tell her daughters were in trouble. "They're badgering the girls," she said to Mike Grass, who was on his cell phone. Mike turned to look, but there wasn't anything he could do.

At the end of the interview, the girls tore off their headsets, threw them to the ground, and burst into tears. That sent Heidi into tears, too, as she turned to Mackoff and said, "That's it! My kids are done! There will be no more media!" The women turned and stormed off toward the family room in the wardhouse, leaving Mike Grass to chew out the Fox crew.

No one objected to the media asking tough questions, but they should have directed those questions to people who could answer them. Beyond that, there was a serious ethical question about Klaas, a paid media consultant with his own agenda, not disclosing his relationship with the Fox network either to the family or the public.

As I slept through the afternoon, and as O'Reilly and Klaas were ganging up on the girls, the Salt Lake City police were looking in another direction altogether. At Tuesday's press conference, Chief Rick Dinse looked straight into the television cameras and declared, "It's possible we have already talked to, or will soon talk to, the suspect responsible for this crime. We believe we have an understanding of this suspect.... we think it is someone who had access to that area, who would have access to that residence."

After delivering what qualified as easily the most hard-hitting, substantive statement made by police in the nearly week-old case, the police chief added ominously, "My caution to this suspect is, we are going to get you. And if he's got Elizabeth, he'd better release her now."

The press conference came just in time for the *Deseret News* to splash Dinse's warning across the top of the front page of its Tuesday evening edition: "We are going to get you." The breaking news led every local evening newscast and was aired prominently around the country. Whoever it was Dinse was referring to—and no specific names were mentioned—he had been warned.

12

The sleep I got at my parent's house Tuesday afternoon didn't hurt, but it didn't seem to help much either. If anything, I felt worse when Heidi woke me up, about four hours after I took the Ambien, and Tuesday night in my bedroom was another sleepless affair. My body cried out for more sleep but my mind still wasn't willing and so the tug-of-war between physiology and psychology resumed. By Wednesday morning, we learned that the police had been able to follow up on the neighborhood and funeral leads; in each instance, the individuals under suspicion had airtight alibis. As for Chief Dinse's announcement that the police had already talked to the kidnapper and were coming to get him, there was no denying that it was good to hear a little Dirty Harry in the chief's voice, but no one in the family knew what that was about. And if Dinse meant Bret Michael Edmunds, there was more than a little doubt in our minds that he was the kidnapper.

Edmunds, according to the police, was the owner of the car the Winder Dairy milkman, Charlie Miller, had spotted in Arlington Hills the morning before Elizabeth was taken. From the partial license plate Miller gave them, the police had been able to identify Edmunds as the car's owner, although his whereabouts were still unknown.

At the family press conference on Monday, someone from the media had thrust a photo of Edmunds in front of me and asked if I recognized him. I studied the face and couldn't place it and couldn't put a name to it, which is what I told the reporters. But in the back of my mind I had the nagging thought I had seen that face somewhere before. Only later would I realize it was at the Sunday night prayer vigil in Liberty Park.

During the vigil, the police had spotted Edmunds, but they had made no attempt to apprehend him until after he left the large crowd. When officers tried to stop him in his car, however, Edmunds eluded them.

Bret Michael Edmunds was from Sanpete County in central Utah. He was twenty-six years old, and, according to the police, he had a serious drug habit. He had a rap sheet, mostly small-time stuff to feed the drug habit. He was wanted for aggravated assault for allegedly trying to run over a police officer. His car, a dark green Saturn, had been spotted in the circle by the block U above Ed's house more than once, and by more people than just the milkman. Edmunds parked there sometimes and stayed the night.

The main problem with Edmunds as a suspect was his size. At six-foot-four and at least 250 pounds, he did not come close to matching Mary Katherine's description of a kidnapper the same height as her brother Charles. It was possible that Edmunds might have seen something if he was in Arlington Hills in the early morning hours of June 5, and it wasn't beyond credibility to think that he might be an accomplice to the crime, although given his unsophisticated criminal history, that seemed unlikely. As far as the family was concerned, there was no compelling reason to believe he was the man who had abducted Elizabeth. The police also seemed to be of that opinion; they insisted that Edmunds was not a suspect, he was only wanted for questioning. (After the FBI mistakenly named Richard Jewell a suspect in the 1992 Atlanta Olympic bombing case, U.S. law enforcement became more cautious about calling anyone a suspect until sufficient evidence had been accumulated to support the charge. Generally a "person of interest" or a "potential suspect" is the language used until law enforcement has enough evidence to file charges.)

But the longer Edmunds remained missing, the more the media, with no other leads to chase, fixed on the elusive loner. When police reported sighting a green Saturn in the southeast corner of the Salt Lake Valley Wednesday morning, the news spread quickly. Television programs were interrupted with the breaking story, and reporters and camera crews rushed to the scene.

Most of the family was at the search center at the time. By its sheer intensity, the news was disturbing, and that intensity increased when we realized the Edmunds sighting was in the Suncrest area, not far from my brother David's house. All the kids at the nearby elementary school, including Dave and Julie's kindergartener, Konnor, and fourth-grader, Cessilee, were locked inside as police, helicopters, and dogs converged on the scene. Chris Thomas, our media adviser, came through the search center and recommended that all family members stay clear of the media until the neighborhood lockdown was over.

Heidi and I got in the car and drove the short distance to the Mill Creek Coffee House in Sugarhouse, where Sierra worked as a barista. She was at the counter when we came in. It was the first time I had seen her since the O'Reilly interview the day before. She burst into tears when she saw us and asked a coworker to cover for her so we could go upstairs and talk. After the O'Reilly interview, she told us she had been interrogated by FBI agents, who told her that they knew she had tried to commit suicide and had been sexually abused in the past—two completely false statements (lying is commonly used as an interrogation technique). Sierra had been through one of the worst days of her life. She expressed the same kind of outrage I was feeling about the FBI tactics. But her biggest outrage was over Bill O'Reilly. After I had a chance to explain the background between Marc Klaas and myself, she pulled a letter out of her purse and put it on the table.

Sierra was in her final semester of classes at the University of Utah, about to get her degree in communications with an emphasis in public relations. One of her classes, appropriately enough, was a media law class that included a section on ethics in journalism. Before studying communications in college, she had grown up watching me work as a journalist. She understood the media, what it did, how it functioned; she knew the difference between good journalism and bad journalism.

"I wrote this letter last night when I got back to my apartment," she said. "I walked right past my roommates and went straight to my room and wrote it in like two seconds flat. It wasn't a planned, calculated letter all thought out ahead of time. It was total stream of consciousness. I wrote exactly how I felt. I didn't change one word," she said, pushing the letter toward Heidi and me.

Dear Bill O'Reilly:

Never have I encountered such a self-centered, heartless human being. I gave you the benefit of the doubt for one reason only—and that was to help get our message out to bring Elizabeth home to her family.

You deceitfully arranged for my sister and me to appear on your show—but for the most evil reason—I never even knew was possible.

You had the chance to help us out—a family trying to locate our kidnapped Elizabeth. Instead, you mendaciously tried to create a "sensational" story out of information made up and meticulously arranged to presume my father was trying to hinder the investigation. And worse, you tried to put his daughters up against him. Did you not think we are dealing with enough? Has your show lowered to the point you have to pay people to create a story?

Honestly, I never thought I'd encounter someone as despicable as you, and I'm sorry your life has such a shallow meaning.

All we want is Elizabeth back, and we're all working 24/7 to find her. My dad, specifically, is doing everything in the world EXCEPT lowering himself to you and your PAID SOURCE.

The only regret I have is wasting my time with you.

My twenty-one-year-old daughter had succinctly summed up the episode. I was so proud of her I wanted to frame the letter, and I told her so. It was perfect.

"But do you think I should send it?" she asked.

Writing it was one thing, but sending it was another. From the start, our one rule was that nothing should take the focus off Elizabeth. A fight with *The O'Reilly Factor*, the top-rated cable talk show in America, could do that. And Bill O'Reilly was clearly the sort who would welcome a fight. We decided now wasn't the time. "But there will come a time to publish it," I said to Sierra. "Before this is over, the story of ethics in journalism in the search for Elizabeth will be huge."

I had no illusions, however, that not fighting back would be the end of it. I was afraid the accusations made on Tuesday night's *The O'Reilly Factor* would turn into a major ethics-in-media issue, putting the focus on me and taking it off Elizabeth. I was becoming way too visible in the investigation—

way more visible than Edmunds, who managed to baffle the police once again when the short-lived Suncrest manhunt produced nothing.

After I returned to the search center, Kevin Peraino, a reporter for *Newsweek* magazine, informed me that the polygraph I had taken late Monday night had been graded inconclusive—something even I didn't know for sure. Kevin was a clever reporter. While the other 150 or so journalists in town were gathering at the search center every day, waiting for quotes and updates at the daily press conferences, Kevin set up camp in the downtown police station lobby, where he developed contacts and watched who came and went. He knew I had been at the FBI office Monday night, he knew I had taken a polygraph, and he'd somehow managed to find out the results. So much for confidentiality.

Kevin Peraino was also the first—and to that point the *only*—person to ask my wife about my alibi for the night and early morning of June 4 and 5. Kevin called Heidi to verify my assertion that I had slept next to her that night. After assuring him that I had, Heidi was about to tell Kevin, off the record, that he was the first person to ask her to confirm my alibi. Neither the police nor the FBI had bothered to ask. But then Heidi thought better of it. We had come to realize that there was no such thing as off the record. Period.

Knowing that my polygraph results were now public, and suspecting that Bill O'Reilly was bound to keep up with his "Uncle Tom impedes the investigation" angle (which he and Marc Klaas would indeed continue for the rest of the week), I was more concerned than ever about my scheduled Wednesday night appearance on CNN's *Larry King Live*.

King's talk show had been following the kidnapping case from the beginning, to the point that the crew and even King himself had developed personal relationships with our family. King came off as a fair, impartial interviewer. I very much wanted to talk to him on national television. I felt it would be a good opportunity to clear the air about the ethics-in-journalism questions that seemed to be brewing. Due to my four hours of sleep the previous afternoon, I passed the family test for going on the air.

The show was scheduled for 7:00 P.M. in a studio on the south side of the Salt Lake Valley. I went to my sister Angela's house for some quiet time during the afternoon, but I had a hard time sitting still. Observing my agitation, my family wasn't sure I should do the show. They wanted me to get some rest instead. But I wanted to clear the air and keep the focus on Elizabeth. In my mind, going on *Larry King Live* was vital.

As I waited for the interview, the crazy sequence of events of the past week kept rolling around in my brain: Brent Cook's letter telling us to look for the good in the kidnapper, the thousands of searchers who had been scouring the valley, the warning from Chief Dinse to the abductor that "We are coming to get you," and the hunt for Edmunds who was wanted only for questioning. In all these developments I felt there was a common thread, a connection that would solve the case. I just didn't know what it was.

Because the hot news of the day was the hunt for Edmunds, the *Larry King Live* producers had also lined up an interview with Charlie Miller, the milkman who identified Edmunds's vehicle.

I only learned of the addition of the milkman when I arrived with Heidi for the taping. I also learned that Larry King had the night off and Nancy Grace, a regular on *Court TV*, would be taking his place. She would be conducting the interview from Atlanta.

Just a few minutes before airtime, Charlie Miller walked in. A man of about forty with deep smile lines around his eyes, he came across as gregarious and cheerful, the sort of guy who was willing to extend his bedtime (his workday began at midnight) so he could come on the show.

Charlie was interviewed first, and as he talked to Nancy Grace an idea began to form in my insomnia-fogged brain. In answer to a question about whether he knew the Smart children, Charlie said that he sometimes gave dairy drinks to the kids in Arlington Hills on school mornings while they waited at the bus stop. I remembered something Lois had said to me earlier in the week: "I don't know who could have taken her. She's always with me except when she goes to the bus stop and back." My mind began to race from one clue to another. This was clearly a nice man, a friendly, helpful guy. He knew the Smart children, he was familiar with their neighborhood, and he gave the kids drinks at their bus stop, long after his milk route, I reasoned, should have been finished.

I thought I just might be sitting next to the kidnapper. If that were true, I had to appeal to Charlie Miller to let Elizabeth go. Suddenly, my interview on national television with Nancy Grace was secondary. I had to speak to Charlie through my interview with Nancy. Even if there was only a tiny chance I was right, I felt it was worth it.

What follows is the transcript of the June 11 taping of *Larry King Live*.

Nancy Grace: Thanks for being with us tonight. I'm Nancy Grace from *Court TV*, sitting in for Larry King. Fourteen-year-old Elizabeth Smart, taken from her bedroom at gunpoint in the middle of the night one week, seven days ago. The only witness, her terrified nine-year-old little sister. And now, police are looking for this man, Bret Michael Edmunds, twenty-six years old. They say he's a transient, and he's got a rap sheet. Edmunds was seen in Elizabeth's neighborhood a day or so before the kidnapping. Police are not calling him a suspect. But they think Edmunds may know something about the case, and they want him. Tonight, from Salt Lake, the man who actually spotted Edmunds in this upscale neighborhood where Elizabeth lives with her family. Joining us, the milkman, Charlie Miller. Hi, Charlie.

Charlie Miller: Hi.

Grace: Charlie, a question. Everybody wants to know: what exactly did you see?

Miller: I saw a gentleman when I was dropping off a delivery. I delivered to a person a few houses down from the Smarts' home. I came up the street rather slow. As I was jumping into my truck after the delivery, he went by real slow, [I was] trying to make an acknowledgment to kind of identify with him or wave to him, like I do with most of the people in the neighborhood, and there wasn't any kind of acknowledgment. So, I continued with my route. And when I did, he happened to follow me further up the road.

Grace: That's suspicious.

Miller: Yes. Well . . .

Grace: What time of the morning was it, Charlie?

Miller: It was actually about 6:15 A.M. to 7:00 A.M. in the morning. So, when he came by the second time, I basically thought that he was going to come and steal my milk. So, I took down some information.

(Laughter)

Grace: Charlie, that's unusual. You see a car and something instinctively says this guy might steal from my truck. What led you to think that?

Miller: Well, we have cases of where that's happened.

Grace: Yes.

Miller: You know, it's just—things that you are aware of as a milkman, and you try to protect what you deliver.

Grace: You're driving along. The guy starts following you. Then what happened?

Miller: He followed me on these two blocks. Then I didn't see him anymore, and I didn't think much more of it. That following Thursday, after Elizabeth was kidnapped, I read in the paper, and her—the way her sister had described this gentleman, it was the—kind of fit the same description that I saw.

Grace: Let me ask you a question. We are showing a photo right now of the guy police are looking for. Is this the guy you saw?

Miller: You know, I can't specifically say for sure. I got more of a profile when he was coming past me. His head was down. But the clothing and the stature that she had described fit what I saw.

Grace: And what about the car, Charlie?

Miller: The car was a dark, older model car. You know, I described to the authorities that it was like a Nissan or a Honda, and I put down a license plate number. I had remembered it because it was a memorization kind of thing. I had written it down on my little box that I have in my truck that I do my deliveries with.

Grace: Charlie, you're in the neighborhood practically every day.

Miller: Yes, ma'am. Well, actually two times a week. Tuesday—Mondays and Thursdays.

Grace: I've heard that you thought this was kind of odd behavior. Something was suspicious. What raised the hair on the back of your neck? What was odd?

Miller: Well, I identify with a lot of people in the neighborhood, you know. I'm very sociable with a lot of people, and I give people different drinks and stuff, and know people that are walking or jogging or people that are going to work, and it's association with that. And this is somebody that just didn't fit for the neighborhood for that time of the day and also just wasn't the right criteria to me.

Grace: How long have you been there, Charlie? How long have you been in that neighborhood?

Miller: I've actually been there two years now.

Grace: For two years, two times a week, you've never seen this car, and he starts following the milk car. OK, that is a tiny bit unusual. Now, what led you—what connected two plus two and made you call authorities?

Miller: Well, it was the article that I read. And plus what the little sister had described. And it was like the baseball cap that she described as white, and the different type of clothing that he was wearing, and what kind of—how high he was in what she described.

Grace: Did he have on a baseball cap when you saw him in the car?

Miller: Yes, ma'am.

Grace: White?

Miller: Yes, ma'am.

Grace: And you know, it's more than coincidence. A lot of people think that this was just before the abduction. That's pretty damning in some people's eyes. Let me ask you this: you stated that you've been in that neighborhood for two years. Did you know the little girl? Did you ever deliver to them?

Miller: You know, the kids actually go up to meet at a bus stop for the bus, and when I come back around my route, I usually stop and give the kids drinks before they get on their bus. I just give them—because we have little drinkers that we have. And I feel I have, you know, to come to think of it, you know, that's the reason it touched me so much, is it's like a person I was connected to in a small way, but, you know, the kids that stop at the bus and then all of a sudden to have this happen, it's really...

Grace: You know what? Everybody that has seen that video of this little girl, it reminds them of their little sister, their little niece, somebody, their daughter. And here you have probably given her a drink, the little free drinks you hand out at the bus stop. How do you feel now in retrospect? Now that there's an all-points bulletin for this—at least a witness—based on your tip?

Miller: I'm hopeful. I'm very hopeful.

Grace: Me, too. Me, too. Charlie Miller, everyone, is with us tonight. He is the local milkman that has provided a tip in this case, the one tip out of six thousand police are honing in on tonight. Charlie, thank you. Quick break, everyone. When we come back, joining us live will be the brother of the mother [sic].

(Commercial break)

(Begin video clip)

Ed Smart: We know that we are so close, so close. And we know that because we feel it in our hearts. And we know and we plea and ask that this person please release Elizabeth. Please let her go. We've been pray-ing along with the whole nation and so many people that your heart will be softened and that you'll be able to see and do the right thing.

(End video clip)

Grace: You are taking a look at the father of the little girl kidnapped one week ago. That was Ed Smart. With us, now, his brother, Thomas Smart. Hi, Tom. Thanks for being with us.

Smart: Glad to be here.

Grace: Tom, I understand that Ed, your brother, has actually been put in the hospital at one point for exhaustion. What happened?

Smart: Well, before this incident happened on Monday, Lois's father had their [sic] funeral, and Edward's been working really hard. And pretty much, they were spent before this ever happened. And they just, of course, were so traumatized by—I mean, they just literally collapsed from exhaustion. It's pretty simple.

Grace: Tom, it's so hard for so many people to even get their mind around—you wake up in the morning and you go to wake up your daughter. She's gone. How are they holding up as of tonight?

Smart: As of tonight, I talked to my brother this morning. And he was very calm and seemed to have a certain peace. You know, we all kind of feel that. And I don't understand why. They're doing OK.

Grace: Are they really? I mean, calm, peaceful. Their daughter's gone. I'm about to jump out of my skin.

Smart: Yes, it's completely incongruous that that's the case. And I think that you know, this is—somehow we have a lot of hope still. And we've learned a lot from this. And I don't know what tomorrow brings. So, when I say this in the past tense, it's because for five days I felt very strongly that there's a happy ending and that this—I mean, I think that this—I think that we're praying for a miracle. And we are asking for a miracle. And we believe that there is a miracle there. We're just...

Grace: You know what, Tom? You're not the only one. You're not the only one praying for a miracle tonight.

Smart: I hate to say...

Grace: Go ahead.

Smart: I think that the world's praying for a miracle. I think it's important—it seems so hard to say that in the middle of the worst things—the worst nightmare—you can say that there's a peace that we kind of feel that people are people and we're learning so much from this experience. And I know that the whole nation—I feel like the whole world is praying that this person...

Grace: That she comes home.

Smart: That she comes home. That's all—that's what it's about. And there are a lot of other beautiful things they're about. But the only real important thing that we want to focus on is bring Elizabeth home. She's an angel. You know she's an angel. We all know she's an angel. And we want her to come home. The rest of that is—and we believe that's going to happen.

Grace: Let me ask you this, Tom.

Smart: OK.

Grace: A lot of focus has been placed on your brother, Edward Smart. We all know he's taken a polygraph. What was his response to that?

Smart: He said it was four hours of hell. And he's willing to go do a polygraph. He didn't know that—he didn't volunteer that. But somehow a polygraph—something got out and I said, "Ed, what about a polygraph?"

And he just went, yes, I've been through four hours of hell—and whatever. The entire family is willing to take polygraphs. We'll do whatever you want. I don't know who has and who hasn't. But the family's—the family will do anything. Just . . .

Grace: I'm trying to imagine my own dad strapped to a polygraph for four hours trying to answer questions, the whole time, wondering where the heck his daughter is, you know, taken in the middle of the night. Did he pass the polygraph?

Smart: Yes, I was told that he passed the polygraph. When you do a polygraph, and I know because I've done one just recently—I should never say that . . .

Grace: Hey, hey, hold on. Why did you have to take a polygraph?

Smart: Everybody is suspect on this. So, it's the police's job to question everybody in this situation.

Grace: Well, Tom, that is not unusual. Police start with the family and the friends and they go outward from there because statistically, very often when a child is abducted, it is someone the child is related to or knows. It is not unusual at all that you or Ed have been asked to do a polygraph. So I was very happy to hear that Ed had taken the polygraph. Let me ask about the mother, Lois. How is she tonight?

Smart: I haven't talked to her in person. I've only talked to my brother. And I talked to him about eleven-something today. And the peace that Edward has, I'm sure Lois is OK. We're just—we're praying for a miracle. And we all believe for some reason. I don't know the answer . . .

Grace: What do you think about the focus right now on Edmunds? Do you think there's a chance he may have met Elizabeth somehow? May have talked to her? I mean how the heck would a transient know how to go into a million-dollar home, three thousand square feet, go exactly to the bedroom, and find the girl, snatch her? Nobody hear a thing. Is there any way he could have had a conversation with her?

Smart: I don't know. I mean, I don't know—I don't know who this guy is.

Grace: Have they seen him? Did Ed or Lois think they had seen this guy?

Smart: Nothing that they've said to me. But I think—we're happy that Charlie's come forward with this—Charlie, right?

Unidentified male: Yes.

Smart: Yeah. With this information because we think he's the key—he may be the key to it. We don't know but we trust whatever the police say at this point and we want to do whatever we can.

Grace: Well, Tom, I would have to agree with you. If police are searching the area with helicopters looking for this guy, that leads me to think that he's got some very important information that they want. Tom Smart, message to the kidnapper tonight, what do you have to say?

Smart: I believe that this person is not a bad person at all. And our family has felt strongly for a while. And there's been a comfort here for a while. This is just somebody who actually likes Elizabeth. We don't know—we have issues. We've been ripped apart by our polygraph. I don't know who has done what with my brothers. We all have issues. Anybody's taken—we've been ripped apart to the core. And we understand that everybody has issues. And we pray hard that whoever this is will know that the family is full of compassion towards everybody because this is a wonderful story, in a lot of ways. Because it's about, foremost, a beautiful, little angelic girl. But it's also about—everybody has issues no matter what. It crosses the boundaries on everything. It's an amazing story.

Grace: Tom, thousands and thousands of people are joining you tonight in your wishes and your prayers. And I want to thank you for being with us.

Smart: Thanks so much.

Grace: Bye, Tom.

When the taping was over and we took off our headphones and microphones, Charlie stuck out his hand to shake mine. I hugged him instead, and whispered in his ear, "Do the right thing." He didn't respond to that, just gave me a kind of quizzical look, and then I let him—my latest suspect—walk out the door.

Heidi wept the entire way home. The only words she managed were, "You've screwed the family, Tom." She'd given a lot of thought to those words; they truly summed up her feelings. On national television I had betrayed the FBI's confidence by announcing my polygraph, and I had cast doubt on the sanity of the entire Smart family by babbling incoherently.

"But Heidi," I said, "I think it was the milkman."

The drive home and Heidi's displeasure did nothing to settle my mania that the milkman was a likely suspect and needed to be talked to, preferably right now. "I've got to talk to him. I've got to convince him to let her go," I said to Heidi. In my psychotic state it didn't make any sense to wait. We needed to find out where Charlie Miller lived and sort everything out now, just as John Smith and I had done with the gardener. When we arrived home I looked on my desk for the phone numbers of Pat Reavy and Derek Jensen, the reporters working the story for the *Deseret News*. I hoped they would have a phone number or an address for Charlie Miller. Heidi kept trying to talk sense to me. If there was anything to my suspicions, they could be followed up the next day. There was no need to go charging back down the canyon to Salt Lake in the middle of the night, particularly not in my state of mind. She called Doug Goldsmith, a therapist who had already been helping counsel some of the family. From her descriptions to him, Goldsmith diagnosed my problem as sleep psychosis. The only cure, he said, was sleep.

But I would not lie down. Heidi then called my father to see if he could reason with me. "Dad," I said after Heidi handed me the phone, "even if you thought there was only a 10 or 20 percent chance the milkman did it, wouldn't you go down and talk to him tonight?" I made the same argument to my sister Angela, the person Heidi called next. Both my father and my sister agreed with Heidi—that everything could wait until morning. I barely listened to them. I don't know how close I was to a complete psychotic break, but I know now that I was closer than I had been at any time in my life.

I finally promised Heidi I would not call Reavy or Jensen or the milkman that night, and I would not drive back to Salt Lake. I also promised I would try to get some sleep and went upstairs to our bedroom. About that time, Amanda and Nicole, who were both living at home at the time, came in the door. It was a little after midnight. Heidi was talking to them, giving them the blow-by-blow of the night's events, when she glanced over at the telephone in the kitchen and saw the light on indicating the phone in the master bedroom was in use.

She picked up the receiver. "Tom!" she shouted, "who are you talking to?"

She slammed down the phone before I could answer and ran up the stairs. "I can't believe you did that," she said as she came in the bedroom. "You promised you wouldn't."

"But I didn't call the reporters or the milkman," I told her. "I only called a psychiatrist."

Curled up on the bed in a fetal position, feeling more helpless than I had ever been in my life, I had reached for the phone and dialed the number of John Smith's friend Doc. I hadn't talked to Doc since we'd had lunch on the second day, but I'd kept his phone number. He'd said to call any time, for any reason. So I called. I got his answering machine. I left a one-word message. Just before Heidi picked up the phone I had whispered into Doc's recorder: "Help."

13

Heidi hadn't had much more sleep than I had. We'd both been hunting for Elizabeth nonstop for eight days. Yet, through it all she managed to keep a grip on reality and remain a master at recognizing the right thing to do. The right thing to do by the time Thursday morning rolled around was to leave me home.

I didn't want to stay home. All night I'd thought about what I was going to do when the sun came up. I got just enough sleep, maybe an hour, to help me realize that if the milkman had done it, or anyone else who was so publicly visible, the police should be the ones looking at the evidence and determining what to do after that.

A much more immediate concern had surfaced in that morning's *Salt Lake Tribune*. Under the headline "Police Eye Relatives in Probe," the newspaper's lead front-page article cited sources in "four law enforcement agencies" saying that evidence suggested the window screen at Ed's house had been cut from the inside and that the crime may have been an inside job.

Written by reporters Kevin Cantera and Michael Vigh, the article hit us hard:

> Evidence from within Elizabeth Smart's Salt Lake City home has led investigators to theorize the girl may have been abducted by a member of her extended family who staged it to look like the work of an outsider, the *Salt Lake Tribune* has learned.
>
> Since the fourteen-year-old girl's apparent kidnapping, police have scoured the family's Arlington Hills home for physical evidence. Eliza-

beth's nine-year-old sister reported a man with a gun had taken the older girl from the bedroom they shared.

Detectives have been unable to explain how the abductor—seen only by the younger girl—could have entered the house through the small window that appeared to be the entry point, according to sources in four law enforcement agencies. The window isn't in the girls' bedroom, but police have refused to specify where it is located.

Investigators have surmised that someone who was already inside the home may have tried to make the window look as though a break-in occurred there. But the screen appears to have been cut from the inside....

The article did not specifically name anyone in the family, nor did it identify by name any of the law enforcement sources. But it was clear that sources inside law enforcement were fueling the speculation that Elizabeth's extended family may have taken part in the abduction. The article went on to cite a twelve-year-old FBI study that said family members were implicated in 49 percent of kidnappings.

For the family, the nightmare had just turned even darker. It was one thing to take polygraphs and establish alibis to make sure everyone in the family was cleared so the investigation could move forward. Those things meant police were doing their job. It was quite another thing to be linked by law enforcement and the media to so-called physical evidence that suggested a family-orchestrated inside job.

In the absence of any other breaking news about the case, the *Tribune* story got plenty of attention. On NBC's *Today Show*, host Matt Lauer talked with reporter David Bloom in Salt Lake City. "Good morning, Matt," said Bloom. "NBC News has learned that while investigators still believe Elizabeth Smart could have been abducted by a stranger, there is troubling evidence suggesting the crime scene could have been staged; that there may have been no forced entry, and that someone closer to the family could be involved."

Not everyone bought the theory. SLCPD spokesman Dwayne Baird told the *Deseret News* that the *Tribune* story "had no validity" and restated that the police hadn't ruled out anybody as a suspect. Baird also said that the four sources mentioned in the *Tribune* story were not working closely with the investigation. "Whoever made reference to four law enforcement sources was not referring to the inner circle of investigators," Baird said. The *Deseret News* story also reported that one of the *Tribune* reporters had told MSNBC that their story was speculative.

Still, the idea that the family might be involved was out there, and beyond the trauma of being obliquely accused of such a thing, the potential for fading public support was enormous.

The *Tribune*, interestingly enough, had picked up on the same theme John Smith had presented to David in the motel room four days earlier. But whereas Smith's was a private theory that stayed private, the *Tribune* story was very public and was supposedly based on law enforcement sources who had examined the screen and window at the crime scene. To make things worse, since the law enforcement sources were not named, we could not challenge them directly.

And they were wrong. The physical evidence at the crime scene did not suggest an inside job. It didn't take a degree in criminology to see that to gain entry into the kitchen from outside the home the screen had to be cut from the inside, at least partially, because the screen was on the inside of the window frame and the window was on the outside. The problem for anyone trying to cut across the bottom of the screen while standing outside the house was that the window blocked the way. The best way to cut across the bottom of the screen while standing outside—indeed the *only* way—was to reach inside. But just because the screen was cut from the inside didn't mean the person doing the cutting had been inside the house.

As for the narrow window opening, it was true that at first glance the ten-inch opening did not appear to be wide enough for a human body to fit through. But in fact there was plenty of room. On Friday, two days after the abduction, my brother Chris had found that out for himself.

Chris and Ed were standing in the kitchen when Chris said, "Ed, my curiosity is killing me. I want to see if I can fit through that window."

"Ed said OK," remembered Chris. "So I went to the west window in the kitchen. It's identical to the one on the east, where the screen was cut, but I didn't want my prints anywhere near that one. I cranked open the window, hopped up on the counter and, boy, I went right through. I'm not a small guy and I was able to fit, no problem. I had to turn my body sideways but not my head."

We later found out that a law enforcement officer had tested the width of the window aperture on the day of the abduction. Like Chris, he had also used the west window. So from the start the police, despite what the *Salt Lake Tribune*'s unnamed sources were suggesting, should have been aware that the opening was wide enough for a man to crawl through.

For the family, Chris's word was all the proof we needed. He had the biggest head in the family by far. As Chris put it himself, "If my melon was able to fit through, I was thinking, that's not a problem at all."

The problem was that we weren't at liberty to discuss openly what we knew about the window opening, just as we couldn't talk about how the screen was cut or about the chair propped up outside the kitchen window or about the unidentified prints. Just as I couldn't tell Marc Klaas and Bill O'Reilly that Mary Katherine hadn't seen enough to bring any sketch artist into the investigation, none of us could tell the *Salt Lake Tribune* any details from the crime scene that might compromise the investigation.

The one thing we could continue to show publicly as a family was solidarity and strength—which was what our Thursday morning family press conference definitely called for. In light of the article in the *Tribune*, I thought it enormously important that I be there with the rest of the family. Heidi, on the other hand, thought it enormously important that I *not* be there.

My wife was determined to keep me out of public view until I got some sleep and sanity, in that order. She didn't want me talking with anyone. Unbeknownst to me, she had gone through the house after my call to Doc the night before and disconnected and hid every phone. Our house has an internal intercom system, with every room wired in via telephone, meaning a phone in all rooms but the bathrooms. That's twelve phones. Heidi pulled the plug on them all. Then she found my cell phone and hid it. I was under house arrest.

Early Thursday morning, Angela called to see how I'd fared through the night and she and Heidi started talking about who they could get to stay with me while Heidi went to Salt Lake City and represented us at the press conference. They discussed several possibilities for who might make the best "Tom handler."

"The best person I can think of is Dave Johnson," said Heidi. "Because of what he's been through, he'd understand." (As a former leader of Salt Lake City's bid to win the 2002 Winter Olympics, Dave Johnson had gone through his own media nightmare, becoming the target of innuendo and accusations because of gifts given by Salt Lake bidders to members of the International Olympic Committee. He was later acquitted of any wrongdoing.)

Angela called Dave, who was on his way to work. He did a U-turn and drove to my house.

We drove to Charleston and I showed Dave my horse property development. We had lunch and discussed the strange twists and turns of life, and Dave kept me sane. At one point, I did steal his telephone, but only to call Heidi and let her know we were OK: We were driving around Soldier Hollow, when I said, "Look, there's a moose over there!" Dave looked and said, "Where?" and I reached over and grabbed his phone and called my wife. I hadn't completely lost my sense of humor.

In Salt Lake City, Heidi had sought out Cynthia, my doctor sister, to see if there might be something I could take to get some sleep. It was either that or commit me. After consulting a psychiatrist, Cynthia sent Heidi home with two prescriptions—one she said was "strong," and the other "really strong."

When Heidi got home that night and after Dave left, she gave me a choice. "Do you want the strong or the really strong?" she asked.

"The really strong," I answered.

She handed me the bottle containing what she said Cynthia told her were the really strong sleeping pills and I took two of them.

The rest of that evening was relaxing, just waiting for the moment when I would drop into a deep sleep. I more or less floated around the house, eating, relaxing on the deck, talking to some neighbors who came by—everything but falling asleep. At 10:00 P.M. I put on a pair of shorts for bed and turned on the news. During the newscast, I watched as Ruth Todd, nighttime anchor on the local ABC affiliate and a longtime friend of min. interviewed Kevin Cantera and Michael Vigh of the *Salt Lake Tribune* about a big follow-up story the two had written that would be in the *Tribune* the next morning. The reporters said they had additional information from their police sources that further pointed to the possibility of family involvement in the kidnapping. The family member they were describing sounded a lot like me.

I remember lying in bed in a somewhat existential trance, thinking how uncomfortable it must be for Ruth Todd to talk about a story indirectly fingering me as a kidnapping suspect. Vigh said to the television audience, "We knew full well what the reaction would be to this story...but it's our job to report what we know, and we know that there's a police theory being bandied about that perhaps it's a family member.... I mean, that's our job." Vigh ended the interview by saying, "I guess all I can say about tomorrow is make sure you buy the paper...it's very provocative."

I mused about how important it was for journalists to be careful about reporting what was being "bandied about," particularly when it wasn't being bandied about on the record. Unnamed sources aren't necessarily always taboo, but they should be used with great care. The general rule is that they should only be used when it is for the public good and when the information will do minimal harm.

I also mused, quite serenely, thanks to my medicated state, about the fix Cantera and his partner Vigh were getting themselves into. They were coming after me and I knew something they didn't—I was innocent.

"Pity the fools," I said out loud to the empty room. I shut off the television and stared at the ceiling. Later I feigned sleep as Heidi slipped into bed. I wanted to make sure I qualified under the four-hour-sleep rule for the next day's events even if I had to cheat a little.

The truth was that I still could not fall asleep. It wouldn't be until the next morning that I would examine the prescriptions Heidi got from Cynthia. The prescription that was "strong" was Ambien, the same sleep aid I'd taken in the past. The "really strong" pills were Zyprexa. I read the label: "May repeat up to one or two tablets twice daily."

How can these be sleeping pills if you're supposed to take them during ..e day?" I called out to Heidi. It turned out they weren't sleeping pills at all. They were anti-anxiety medication. Zyprexa doesn't put you to sleep; it just makes you feel like nothing really matters.

During my day of house arrest and mellowing out, the rest of the family had been busy. Late Wednesday night, my brothers and sisters had met at Angela and Zeke's house after Kevin Cantera and Michael Vigh's first appearance on KTVX, where the following morning's *Tribune* article was hyped. Chris, David, and Cynthia's husband, Doug, were there, along with Angela, Zeke, and Chris Thomas, who took charge of the meeting. They discussed ways to combat the growing public relations storm caused by the *Salt Lake Tribune*'s article. The fact that the press didn't know the facts didn't seem to matter. My alibi, for example, could easily be verified by talking to my wife. But beside the *Newsweek* reporter, no member of the media or law enforcement had done that. The so-called suspicion about my alibi was based on nothing but unsupported conjecture. But when sharks smell blood, they often work themselves into a frenzy, to the point where they simply attack, often missing their mark and injuring whatever is in the way. The media can act in a similar manner when an unnamed source gives false or incomplete information, especially in a high-profile case with few answers.

"The press thing was scaring us. We knew it was a double-edged sword and things could turn," remembered Angela. "We were all so disheartened that a local paper was taking a *National Enquirer* approach to the story, that they'd put such a spin on something this tragic. We were just so pure in what our goal was, and we were already so torn apart—and now this."

The group drafted a family statement, signed by the Smart and Francom families, expressing "disappointment" in the *Tribune* reporting, labeling it "highly speculative.... It implies that it is unusual to investigate the family in this type of case. Investigating the family is common procedure. We continue to fully cooperate in every aspect of the investigation and urge the public and media to avoid distraction from what is most important."

They made copies of the statement very early Thursday morning and

Chris Thomas and Mike Grass delivered them to the various news outlets at the search center, including the network morning shows. It was a small counterstrike to the *Salt Lake Tribune*'s 130,000-plus statewide circulation. It was after 3:00 A.M. when the job was finished. No one was getting any sleep.

14

Friday morning's *Tribune* hit the doorsteps of Salt Lake City—and the Elizabeth Smart investigation—like a wet rag.

Sister Didn't See the Face of Abductor
Police ruling out nobody, including family members
By Kevin Cantera and Michael Vigh

The only known witness to the abduction of Elizabeth Smart—her nine-year-old sister—did not see the face of the man who took her because the bedroom the girls shared was in darkness, the *Salt Lake Tribune* has learned.

Among other avenues of investigation, police are looking at whether an extended family member may have participated in the kidnapping of the fourteen-year-old girl.

Law enforcement sources say the young sister's inability to see the man's face means investigators cannot rule out the possibility the crime was committed by someone she knew.

On Thursday, police continued to say they had not ruled out any suspects, including members of Elizabeth's family. The girl's June 5 disappearance sparked a large-scale search and has made headlines around the globe.

David Smart, Elizabeth's uncle, told reporters Thursday the family understood that its members were a necessary focus of the probe and they were willing to sit for lie-detector tests. "If they did not investigate us, they would be negligent," he said.

The *Tribune* has confirmed an NBC report Thursday that the responses given by one member of Elizabeth's family during a polygraph test raised investigators' suspicions about his alibi…investigators have surmised that someone who was already inside the home may have tried to make the window look as though a break-in occurred there. But the screen appears to have been cut from the inside.

The reference to the suspicious alibi was from the time line I filled out for the FBI. Details of my polygraph were obviously making the rounds. But while I knew that the *Tribune* report alluded to my confusion over where I was and what I did the night before and the morning of the kidnapping, I also knew that no one from the newspaper had bothered to check my alibi. Just as law enforcement had failed to check with my wife concerning my whereabouts the night of the kidnapping, or with the newspaper to verify my assignments, no *Tribune* reporters had made contact with me.

As Heidi and I prepared to leave for Salt Lake City—my house arrest over, at least for a day—I wasn't particularly concerned about my personal welfare, despite the attacks on my credibility. I knew I had not kidnapped my niece. I knew that no matter how suspicious I might appear to the *Salt Lake Tribune*, Marc Klaas, Bill O'Reilly, and probably Nancy Grace after my bizarre performance with her on *Larry King Live*, if it ever came to any kind of serious investigation, I would be cleared in no time.

What did concern me was how the negative press was affecting the search. Since Tuesday, the day *The O'Reilly Factor* began its attacks, the numbers of volunteers at the search center had been dropping dramatically—400 on Wednesday, 300 on Thursday, and less than 250 on Friday morning. The decline wasn't all attributable to negative public relations. Some attrition was bound to occur over time. But hints that the family had been in on the kidnapping certainly did not help.

It was a shame to see public perception hurt a search that had been such an unqualified triumph of human spirit, determination, and stamina. By Friday 8,115 registered volunteer searchers had participated in 877 recorded group searches. Thirty-three fixed-wing aircraft and seven helicopters had flown more than 300 missions. Searchers used trained search dogs, more than 150 all-terrain vehicles, and more than 100 horses. Another 135 amateur radio operators also helped. Businesses from all over the valley contributed food, equipment, vehicles, and workers. All told, police detectives had received 3,324 leads, and the ElizabethSmart.com Web site had recorded 56,000,000 hits.

Families, church groups, and service clubs came. For days on end, various members of the Wasatch Front Chapter of Bikers Against Child Abuse (BACA) rode the Wasatch. Larry and Charlene Holmstrom, the neighborhood volunteers who directed many of the search assignments, sent the bikers to some of the more difficult locations.

"We went to some places that were a little rough at like three or four in the morning," remembered Paul "Bomber" Dubois, BACA's leader. "A couple of times the windows were open and nobody was there. We weren't supposed to, but we'd go in anyway. We hit some cabins in the canyons that way."

One night, acting on a tip, the BACA riders went to a warehouse on the west side of town, where they heard noises inside. "It was about four in the morning and those warehouses should have been empty," said Bomber. "We had everybody leave but Larry and me. We stayed behind and kept quiet and waited. Next thing we know the police are showing up. It turned out some old night watchman had holed up in the warehouse to drink and he heard us outside so he called the cops. 'It's OK, we're on a search,' Larry said to the police."

Larry and Charlene Holmstrom were part of a group of about thirty loyal neighborhood volunteers who were at the heart of the search—friends and neighbors of Ed and Lois's who responded early the first morning and never stopped. The sleep deprivation among this group during the first eight or nine days was just unbelievable. They were walking zombies.

Every day someone new would take a turn as the search center cheerleader, urging the others to keep going. "Today's day seven!" they would say. "Good things happen on day sevens! We're going to find her!" We were simply trying to keep each other's hopes up, and that was a full-time job. I remember confiding in Ted Wilson at the search center one day that I really felt a sense of purpose and faith about what was happening. He said,

"I don't know Tom, I've been pretty pissed off at God lately, I just don't understand it." Maybe Ted was right, but I couldn't afford to go there. The love and support from the community was a testament to faith in humanity, and all of us felt a sense of purpose. While some had a faith-promoting experience, others had their faith tested.

The family meetings were a model of efficiency, thanks to Phil and Suann Adams. My father had suggested we ask Ed and Lois's friends to be the leaders of our group. When I asked why, he said, "Because Phil Adams is the smartest guy I know." In daily and sometimes twice-daily meetings that involved the Smart and Francom families, Ted and Kathy Wilson, Chris Thomas, and others, Phil and Suann ran through the agenda as if they were running a Fortune 500 company.

One item of business that almost routinely came up was whether we should hire a private investigator or an attorney. At least one person close to the investigation, off the record, encouraged us to do so. But most warned us that if we did hire our own investigator he or she would not be given complete access to information the police had gathered on the case. Most of law enforcement seemed threatened by the suggestion. Phil Adams did a considerable amount of research and compiled a list of some of the top private investigating agencies in the country, but in the end, we decided to continue to support law enforcement and do our own amateur investigating.

Another important item was money. We had originally asked that all donations to help with the search be made to either Shriners Hospital or the Laura Recovery Center. We believed the search effort wasn't going to last more than a week and we wanted to help compensate both entities not only for their expenses, but also for their immeasurable kindness. Plus, we had initially been told that we could use the LRC as a pass-through for funding, but soon found out that was only true while the foundation had staff working the search, which was only the first few days. With the help of Mayor Rocky Anderson, my sister Angela worked with Gordon Hoskins, who worked for the city, to lay the groundwork for a Child Abduction Fund that would allow people to receive tax deductions for their donations.

Everyone came together and everything clicked. Thousands of people worked at thousands of tasks that had been unfamiliar to them only a week before; they did it all with grace and efficiency. That was the miracle of the search center and the community. It just worked.

By Friday, however, with the volunteer numbers dwindling, we all recognized the need for a change in our search philosophy. After discussing the matter during the family's morning meeting, we made the decision to keep the search alive but to place the emphasis on community searches beyond Federal Heights and Arlington Hills. No longer would volunteers report to a central location. Through the Web site and with the help of packets David and others were assembling, people around the Wasatch Front, the state, and the country, could organize their own searches and coordinate them with the main search center. Two of Lois's brothers, Stan and Myron Francom, volunteered office space at their business in nearby Sugarhouse where we could move the phone banks, desks, maps, and other search items.

While these logistics were being worked out, my brother Chris pulled me aside. My normally outspoken brother was subdued and apologetic, almost to the point of tears. "Tom," he said, "during my polygraph they kept asking who would be the most likely person in the family to have an affair. I told them that I didn't think anyone in the family would, but they kept insisting I answer, so I finally told them, probably you." Chris had felt terrible about it ever since. He explained to me his reasoning that I had traveled and lived around the world covering the Olympics and consequently I'd had more potential opportunity to fall from grace. Chris had obviously beaten himself up pretty badly; we just hugged and said we loved each other. Chris finally chuckled and told me, "Don't feel too bad, I told them that because of having lived in Las Vegas with the environment there, I was probably the next most likely to have made that mistake."

On that note, I left the search center and went to the *Deseret News* building downtown. I hadn't been back to work since the ordeal began. The newspaper is my extended family; I've worked there on and off since I was a seventeen-year-old copy boy.

I walked into the building feeling like a hunted animal. However, photographers, reporters, secretaries, and editors all made it a point to come up to me and offer their support. Angie Hutchinson, a city editor I'd had newsroom battles with in the past, hugged me in tears. Linda Thomson, a reporter who had a young child, came up to me and said, "I just want you to know I'd trust you with my daughter anywhere." It was a real outpouring of love and support. You could tell that the hell we were going through as a family, after the *Tribune* started publishing its articles, was being felt by my newspaper family as well.

Reporter Derek Jensen wanted to hear my side of things, so he drove home with me and we talked. As a photographer, I was in the habit of driving and talking with the paper's reporters, often for long hours at a time as we traveled on assignments. I'd been doing it for twenty-five years. But never had the reporter started the conversation by asking, "Tell me, Tom, exactly what were you doing the evening of June fourth?"

Amanda's high school graduation was scheduled for late that afternoon in the football stadium at Park City High School. Heidi and I had become so paranoid by now that we debated whether we should even go to the graduation, out of fear that the media might show up and make a scene. After everything that had happened over the past few days, it certainly wasn't out of the question. We ended up going to the stadium very early so we could slip in without causing a commotion. We saw no sign of the press. As it turned out, some members of the media did show up, but by the time they arrived, we were safely inside the stadium and they were turned away at the front gate.

The graduation went off fine, with syrupy speeches and rosy forecasts. It was a clear June evening in the mountains, the kind that make Park City summers famous, and the focus was all on Amanda and the rest of the graduates—just as it should have been. I started crying during the national anthem and was a complete basket case through the whole thing as we watched our youngest daughter graduate from high school. I realized how important it was for us to be there. It was vital that we not lose sight of the children who *weren't* missing. As a family we needed to keep it together and not let life stop. Amanda had a party at our house afterward. About fifty people came. We ate hot dogs, hamburgers, and potato chips, and toasted the family's newest graduate.

15

After about a week, the searchers stopped combing the mountains and the helicopters and small airplanes could no longer be heard overhead in Dry Creek Canyon.

It hadn't always been like this. Mitchell had made stabs at normalcy. The first attempt at settling down and having his own traditional family life came shortly after he turned nineteen, when he discovered his sixteen-year-old girlfriend, Karen, was pregnant.

Mitchell and Karen got married. He went back to school and obtained his high school equivalency degree and even attended some classes at the University of Utah. Karen gave birth to a baby boy in 1972. They named the child Travis.

But between drugs, drinking, and charges of infidelity, playing house was problematic. After a second child, a daughter named Angela, came along, the young couple split up. Brian was only twenty-two when he was awarded temporary custody of Travis and Angela. With them, he moved back home to live in his mother's house and, occasionally, his father's as well.

The temporary custody did not last. Karen wanted the children, and in a later court hearing to determine permanent custody and visitation privileges, Brian failed to show up. In his absence, the judge awarded custody of Travis and Angela to Karen, who had by then remarried.

But Brian, who still had the children, had no intention of turning them over to their mother. He ignored the court order, took the kids, and fled the state. He didn't stop until he got to New York, where he found a new girlfriend, an African American woman named Alyson. He took her and the children to Portsmouth, New Hampshire, where they moved into an apartment. Mitchell got a job in the service department of an automobile dealership and started to pay a few bills. He kept his whereabouts hidden from the authorities, but not from his family. His mother visited him in New Hampshire, as did his father, who was following Irene because she had separated from him yet again. It was a dance that had gone on for years. Shirl Mitchell didn't want to be with Irene until Irene didn't want to be with him.

In New Hampshire, Mitchell found spirituality of sorts—during an LSD trip. As he would later relate to family and friends, he was standing in front of a mirror, stoned out of his mind, when he saw a reflection of what and who he was supposed to be—and it wasn't a pot-smoking, LSD-tripping, long-haired, drugged-out fugitive from Utah social services. The hallucinogenic epiphany turned him around. He loaded the kids, but not the girlfriend, into his car and headed back to Salt Lake City.

In Utah he found even more religion—the same one he'd started out with in the first place. The conversion came not long after he, Travis, and Angela moved back in with Irene. Brian struck up a relationship with his younger brother, Tim, who was still living at home. There were eight years between them; many of Tim's early memories involved watching his older brother trying to outrun his father's anger and beatings. But now, Tim was eighteen and Brian twenty-six. They could relate.

As a teenager Tim Mitchell had gone astray from the LDS Church standards he'd been taught in his youth. But after graduating from high school and a short stint in the army, Tim had experienced his own spiritual awakening, repented his wild ways, and returned to full activity in the LDS Church. He encouraged his older brother, who had openly admitted that he was searching for spiritual stability after his unsettling drug trip, to do likewise. But Brian wasn't as interested in rejoining the old fold as he was in getting out of town before his ex-wife discovered he'd returned to Utah and came to take away the children.

He heard about a man who was starting up some sort of religious commune near the town of Escalante in southern Utah. Escalante was remote enough that his ex-wife might not find him there. "Maybe I'll go to Escalante and check it out," Brian told his brother. Tim said he'd like to ride along.

"Mom let him borrow the car and we took some camping gear and left," remembered Tim Mitchell. "On the way down we had these long, drawn-out discussions about the gospel, belief in God, and faith in general. I was still trying to talk him into coming back to the Church. We spent one night at an uncle's cabin on the way and the next morning we went up to this place Brian had heard about. We walked around and looked at the buildings, but no one was around. It got dark and we built a campfire and kept talking. I said, 'Look up at those stars, can't you see that there's something eternal about us, that we're children of God?' and all of a sudden Brian just started crying and he said, 'You're right, it's true.' He had a pack of Marlboro cigarettes in his pocket and he threw them into the fire. He said, 'This guy down here isn't a true prophet, he's a false prophet; what are we doing here?' So we got in the car and drove back to Salt Lake that same night. We got back home around two in the morning."

A new, orthodox Brian Mitchell emerged. He cut his hair and beard, swore off cigarettes, stopped drinking, and headed straight to the bishop's office in the wardhouse to confess his sins. He started attending LDS Church meetings. For the first time in a decade, he began reading his scriptures. He didn't take the sacrament for several Sundays until he'd fully repented, and he got sick for a couple of weeks as his body weaned itself of its craving for nicotine.

A few weeks later, Mitchell's ex-wife finally showed up, Tim recalled, and asked to see Travis and Angela. Mitchell was still afraid she would take them away, but he had decided he wasn't going to run anymore. He was going to do the right thing. Karen came to see Travis and Angela, but she left them to stay with their father. Righteous living, it seemed, was already paying dividends.

That winter, Tim left on a two-year LDS mission to California. Almost twenty-seven, Brian was well past his missionary days, so he set his sights on meeting and settling down with an active LDS woman. He found her while attending an Old Testament lecture given by noted Mormon scholar and onetime Salt Lake City police chief W. Cleon Skousen. The woman's name was Debbie Woodridge. She was three years older than Mitchell and had three young daughters from a previous marriage. She owned a small house in Sugarhouse and had a steady job with the government. She was estranged from her family in Colorado because they disapproved of the LDS Church. When Debbie met Mitchell, he was working at a Montessori children's daycare center. A working mother, Debbie could not believe her good fortune. She had managed to find a single man who went to church and worked in child care. He was the answer to her prayers.

After about a dozen dates—most of them at Debbie's house with her three girls because neither Debbie nor Brian had any money—they were engaged. Not long after that, in a low-key, low-cost wedding, Debbie's bishop performed their February 1981 marriage at her LDS ward. Debbie's estranged family didn't attend the wedding and reception that followed because they didn't approve of her religion; and while most of the Mitchell family did attend, they did not approve of Debbie. The Mitchells did not hide their feelings that they thought Brian—once divorced himself, and a reformed drug abuser—could have done better. To their minds, he'd married beneath him. During Brian and Debbie's marriage, Irene Mitchell never once visited in her daughter-in-law's house.

Beyond the mother-in-law issue, the marriage had numerous other problems. To begin with, there were too many children. Mitchell's two plus Debbie's three made five, and they were all under the age of eight. It was the Brady Bunch without the comfortable house. The bungalow Debbie owned had just one bedroom, one bathroom, a kitchen, and a living room on the main floor, with two more small rooms in the basement, both unfinished and one with a dirt floor. Soon, all the rooms were filled, and that was before the two children Mitchell and Debbie had together arrived—Joey in 1982 and Sarah in 1983.

From the start, the relationship between Mitchell's oldest two children and their new stepmother was problematic. In the first days of their unfamiliar new life, Travis and Angie just stared at the floor. Debbie responded to their lethargy by having them pick up lint from the carpet. An unworkable situation only got worse: depressed kids, disapproving in-laws, money problems (Mitchell quit his job to be home with the children while Debbie continued to work at her job outside the home), and no room to breathe. No one was happy.

In an attempt to save the marriage, Mitchell and Debbie put Travis and Angela, then ten and eight, into foster care. Because he was upset at his mother, Mitchell would not let Irene have his children, and his ex-wife was not in a position to take Travis and Angela back. The only option left to him was the state. The Utah Department of Social Services placed Travis and Angela Mitchell with a family that subsequently adopted them and changed their last name. Just like that, Mitchell lost the son and daughter he had once traveled all the way to New Hampshire to hang onto. In his brother Tim's opinion, giving up Travis and Angie in an attempt to fix his second marriage produced a long-term heartache from which Brian never recovered. "My theory is that he had deep-seated guilt feelings about his failure with Travis and Angie," said Tim Mitchell. "He loved Travis and Angie so much. He'd sacrificed his life for them. And then he let them go. He did not know how to deal with that torment. I think it had a lot to do with what happened later."

But getting rid of the two oldest children didn't improve conditions on the home front. Things just got worse. It was about the time that the older children left the home in Sugarhouse that the allegations of sexual, physical, and emotional abuse began—first from Debbie and later from the children.

Outside the walls of the tiny house, at church services on Sunday and in interactions with the neighbors, Mitchell was soft-spoken, easygoing Brian. But inside, according to his wife, he was mean and aggressive. Debbie said there were times when Mitchell struck her with his fist, but it was the psychological terror that was the worst. Mitchell, she said, would put his face inches from hers while she was sleeping and then, when she opened her eyes, he would let out a scream. He knew she was terrified of mice, so one day she opened the oven to find he had filled it with dead mice.

When Joey had just turned one and she was two months pregnant with Sarah, Debbie gave Brian an ultimatum: "Leave until you can be nice." He stayed away until after Sarah was born and then moved back in for seven more months, until Debbie threw him out again—this time for good. It was all over except the custody battles.

While they were fighting for the kids, Debbie became concerned about what she considered abnormal sexual behavior by the younger children. Fearing that Mitchell had abused them, she filed sexual abuse charges against her soon-to-be ex-husband in June 1985. A caseworker from the state Division of Child and Family Services came to Debbie's home and interviewed Joey, who was three, in an attempt to determine the truth. While there was no direct evidence of sexual abuse, the state worker recommended that any further visitation between the father and Joey and Sarah be supervised.

After Mitchell was gone the last time, Debbie's daughters from her first marriage also complained to their mother that he had touched and engaged them in sexually inappropriate ways. They said the abuse started even before Mitchell and Debbie were married, and continued after that. Debbie got the three older girls into counseling and made it her personal crusade to make sure Mitchell would have no further contact with them, and that he would lose all custody of Joey and Sarah.

Mitchell denied to authorities that he'd abused any of his children, in any manner, and attempted to maintain a relationship with Joey and Sarah. But troubles persisted, and not just with Debbie, but with Joey and Sarah, who would scream at the door and beg their mother not to make them go with Mitchell when he came to collect them for his supervised visits. Debbie tape-recorded the tantrums and played them for the state social workers assigned to her case. As a result, she got permission from Family Services not to send Joey and Sarah against their will. They didn't have to go with their father if they didn't want to.

Rejected by Debbie and his children, Mitchell eventually faded out of sight. He saw Joey and Sarah sporadically for a few months, then not at all. Instead, he moved on and began a new life. He met Wanda Barzee, who was also going through a separation and divorce. He began seeing her regularly. By November 1985, only hours after his divorce with Debbie was finalized and less than six months since he'd been charged with sexual abuse of his children, he and Wanda were married. Mitchell moved into Wanda's tiny apartment, two miles north but a galaxy away from the little home in Sugarhouse. He would not see Joey, Sarah, or Debbie's three girls again.

16

Eternity is a difficult concept to define, but ten days with no trace of Elizabeth seemed to sum it up. It was as if time had stopped and shot forward both at once. The minutes went too slow and the hours too fast.

We held our family press conference Saturday morning, June 15, but there wasn't much new to report. The whereabouts of Bret Michael Edmunds remained the media's top focus. The twenty-six-year-old drifter had somehow managed to stay one step ahead of law enforcement. The police had found his license plates abandoned in a field near Centerville, Utah. Then they'd gotten a tip about him—he'd ordered takeout food at a Chinese restaurant. In each instance, they arrived too late. They thought they had him cornered in Texas, but after a daylong manhunt that included Salt Lake City police officers who flew to the scene, it turned out the man they were chasing wasn't Edmunds after all.

The attention on Edmunds had helped take some of the heat off me. So had Derek Jensen's article in Saturday morning's *Deseret News*. Under the headline "Elizabeth's uncle finds speculation ludicrous," Derek's story printed my defenses: that I had nothing to do with the kidnapping; that even if my memory had been faulty due to trauma and sleep deprivation, my alibi was rock solid; and that I had not interfered with the police investigation in any manner. Derek's story quoted the police regarding my status in the investigation. "Tom Smart is no more a suspect than you or I," stated department spokesman Dwayne Baird, adding that any reports implicating me as a suspect were "sensationalized speculation." In sharp contrast to the *Salt Lake Tribune*, the *Deseret News* police source was on the record and clearly identified.

With the weekend looming, after the morning press conference, Heidi and I decided it would be a good time to load up the horses and take them to the pasture by the family cabin on the Weber River, where they always spent the summer grazing. We could get away to gain perspective and recharge.

We drove to Charleston to collect the horses: Diva, Moscow, Sky, and Ranger, the little colt. A trip to the Weber cabin meant high grass and a lot of attention for the horses—although with Elizabeth gone, riding time during the summer of 2002 would probably be minimal.

While I was loading the horses, my cell phone rang. When I answered, the woman on the other end said she was with the *Washington Post* and wondered if she could have a couple of minutes of my time. I wasn't supposed to be talking to the press until I got some sleep, but this was the *Washington Post*, one of America's major newspapers and, more than that, part of a nationwide syndicate that distributes stories to publications around the country. I decided to go ahead and talk.

I'd done some work for the *Washington Post* over the years. I knew a photo editor there, Linda Seeger Salazar. So I asked the caller if she knew her. When the name didn't produce any response, I should have been suspicious, but in my sleep stupor I went blithely on, rambling as much as talking. I sensed I was being pretty incoherent and told the reporter that I hadn't had much sleep and it would probably be better if we talked later.

After about twenty minutes of me begging to get off the line, the reporter finally thanked me for my time and hung up. I hoped I'd done some good in making a contact with the *Washington Post*.

It turned out I had managed to do just the opposite. I would later discover that the woman wasn't with the *Washington Post* but the *National Enquirer*, the notorious supermarket tabloid. Her name was Courtney Callahan, and not only had she lied about her name and the publication she worked for, but she'd also apparently taped our conversation and shared my ramblings with the police in an effort to convince them that I should be considered a viable suspect.

Although the Weber cabin is only seventy miles east of Salt Lake, it might as well be in the Klondike. The last six miles are a dirt road on the other side of a locked gate. A handful of cabins, including ours, are surrounded by thousands of acres of pristine forests, lakes, streams, and mountains.

I heard Heidi breathe a sigh of relief after we crossed the bridge and locked the gate behind us. The cell phone said "No Service." Sierra, Nicole, and Amanda were with us, along with Sierra's boyfriend, Chase Campbell. And we had the four horses. My family knew where to reach us, but we left the rest of the world behind.

At the cabin I got my first full night's sleep in ten days. I'd like to attribute it to the clean mountain air and the soothing quiet, with no telephone or television. But I had also brought along a prescription of Tomazipan, a sleeping pill stronger than Ambien. I took one pill and was out before my head hit the pillow. I did not move until morning. I woke up with a sleeping pill headache and a body wanting more sleep. But it still qualified as the most welcome night's sleep of my life.

Sunday morning, I found Diva in the pasture and saddled her up. There isn't much about horses I don't love. They're challenging but rewarding. If you treat them right and try to understand them, they'll respond accordingly. The key is never to let the horse forget who's in charge. As I mounted Diva I thought about the need for a similar attitude in the search for Elizabeth. Even though the kidnapping, with all its unknowns and mystery, might seem bigger and stronger than all of us, we had to stay in charge.

I rode Diva for hours. We spooked some deer and other wildlife but saw no other horses or humans. I let the sturdy mare, nicknamed the "hell bitch" after the high-spirited and not always cooperative horse in Larry McMurtry's *Lonesome Dove*, run through some long meadows, working off her winter fat, as I reined her toward the top of Moffit Peak. Riding the horse was good therapy, but several times I found myself breaking into tears without warning. I thought about my grandfather Ira, and Avon, my grandmother. Other than my parents and Ira, Avon had been the strongest influence in my life. She was a favorite with all of the great-grandchildren, including Elizabeth. There's something about being alone in nature where you can just think without straining and try to sort things out. At the summit of Moffit Peak is a special spot our family calls the "Hot Rocks." It is where a pile of rocks surround the elevation marker and where my mom and dad first kissed and where they got engaged. A calm feeling came over me as I rested there. But then, as I gazed out at the peaks around me, with the expansive, lush forests below them in all directions, I got a sobering glimpse of just how large the world is—and how many places there are to hide.

"Elizabeth!" I yelled, sitting on that peak atop my horse. "Elizabeth!" The only answer was the whistling wind and the creaking of the leather saddle.

It was Father's Day on Sunday, and more than on any other Father's Day in memory, I appreciated having all my children with me. Sierra brought a VCR and a video, which we turned on in the afternoon. It was a film called *Monster's Ball*. It wasn't exactly your family come-together type of film, more theater of the absurd, a hard, edgy movie with strange plot developments and bizarre turns. But at least when it ended you could say that it was only a movie.

In the Salt Lake Valley, the investigation and media frenzy went on without us. An unexpected development occurred Saturday when the police hastily convened a press conference at the unlikely hour of 8:00 P.M. Detective Dwayne Baird stood in front of the media holding a tan English-style golf hat, the kind with the flap that folds over in front. Baird said that Elizabeth's abductor had worn a hat of this style and this color.

"It's a golf-type cap, tan in color. This information was developed by our detectives," said Baird. "It's based on their further investigation in this case. They didn't give me any details as to how they came to the conclusion."

Baird cautioned that the golf hat had nothing to do with the continued search for Bret Michael Edmunds. "We haven't connected this cap or this style of cap to Mr. Edmunds," he said.

A reporter asked about the curious timing of the press conference— long past the regularly scheduled times. "Have you, because of the amount of the press attention on this, felt pressure to—I don't want to sound ungrateful, because we've got to get any information obviously that you develop—but to call a press conference on Saturday night at 8:00, you know,

I'm just curious if you're eager to give, to produce us with the latest on the search," the reporter asked.

"I was told to provide any information whenever I got it, and I want to do that as part of your benefit," said Baird. "If someone knows someone who would have been up in this area dressed like this with that kind of a cap, it would be beneficial for us to know who they are and what business they had up here."

The police didn't have a suspect, but they knew what style of hat the suspect was wearing. What exactly were they saying? And what weren't they saying? In a case full of strange developments, this was yet another bizarre turn.

17

The longer the kidnapping went unsolved, the more apparent it became that law enforcement's failure to react quickly and appropriately the morning of the abduction had resulted in myriad problems. As a family, we were aware of some of what law enforcement had and had not done in those first few critical hours. The two biggest problems were their failure to identify the crime as a kidnapping right away and their failure to secure the crime scene. Other details about what had and had not happened didn't come to our attention until later. But later we were able to piece together a fairly precise picture of how the investigation had fallen into the hole police had been trying to dig out of ever since.

The police's slow response may have been due, at least in part, to the rarity of the crime. Despite the headlines they generate, this type of kidnapping is not common. There are only about one hundred cases of children forcibly abducted from their houses by strangers in the United States each year. By comparison, twice as many people are struck (and killed) by lightning each year. To the one hundred children and their families, that is no consolation, but because of the relatively small number of home abductions, few of the law enforcement officers who responded to Ed's 911 call on the morning of June 5 had any experience with such a crime. The goal among law enforcement was to hunt for Elizabeth, not preserve clues and evidence that might identify who took her.

It didn't help that the police also fumbled when it came to determining exactly who would take charge of the investigation. When the SLCPD watch commander first received the call from Ed's house at 4:01 A.M., he did not follow protocol and contact the lieutenant in charge, Cory Lyman, apparently because Lyman was on light duty at the time, recovering from recent knee surgery. Instead, the watch commander called the acting captain, who called Don Bell, head of the department's sex crimes unit, to oversee the investigation with detectives from a different unit, homicide. The early watch commander never went to Ed's home, and by the time Bell arrived on the scene, two crucial hours had already passed.

Even slower to get involved was the Federal Bureau of Investigation. The SLCPD didn't call the FBI. Jake Garn called them sometime before 5:00 A.M. Garn, a former U.S. senator and former Salt Lake City mayor, as well as a longtime neighbor and friend of Ed and Lois, got involved after receiving an early distress call from Ed. "The police are here but the FBI is not," Ed told Jake. "Can you help?" Jake called the FBI, but the message apparently got lost. The FBI didn't make any assignments until the Assistant Special Agent in Charge (ASAC), Dan Roberts, turned on his television about 7:00 A.M. and learned about the kidnapping on the news.

Despite a police presence at Ed's house from 4:13 A.M. on, it wasn't until Sergeant Bell arrived around 6:00 that anyone began to take control, and there was no attempt to secure the crime scene until homicide detective Mark Scharman arrived a little after 6:30. Alarmed at the number of friends, family, and neighbors milling about the house, Scharman started a log of people who had been in and out of the house that morning. By 6:54—nearly three hours after Ed's 911 call—Scharman managed to clear everyone but official personnel from the premises. One of the officers inside the house tried to contact Cory Lyman, who was in physical therapy rehabilitating his knee. Not until mid-morning did Lyman check his messages and hear: "The crime scene is shot to shit. Get up here as soon as you can."

The early chaos may have contributed to errors in the official police report, which stated: "The parents contacted several neighbors and then contacted the police." This erroneous statement led to the false assumption that neighbors and family contaminated the crime scene before police arrived. The truth was that the police were the first to arrive and could have sealed the house right then, at 4:13 A.M., and not let another person enter. When that did not happen, and when, as a result, evidence was compromised or destroyed, the crime scene opened itself more to speculation than to scientific analysis.

SLCPD investigators were the first to begin processing the crime scene, but they soon called in the state crime lab, which had more resources. The work the state did would tell more about what went on during the chaotic hours immediately following the reporting of the kidnapping than about what happened during the break-in and abduction. Photographs taken mid-morning by a state crime lab photographer of the cut screen and the kitchen window showed a much different scene than photographs taken by an SLCPD officer who had arrived earlier. The crime lab photos clearly showed a number of items on the dark marble kitchen counter below the open window, including a knife, an open bag of flour, and bits of scattered flour—none of which was there when the SLCPD photographs were taken. Later speculation as to how the intruder could have managed to avoid the flour and not leave obvious footprints may have contributed to the suspicion that the window screen had been cut as a ploy to disguise an inside job. No one ever determined how the flour and the knife got on the counter, although it had to have happened fairly soon after police and neighbors began arriving, as I remember seeing the flour on the counter when I got to Ed's house around 5:00 A.M.

Also muddying the scene was a crime lab photo of the kitchen counter area that made it appear that a decorative vase holder on the counter was centered in front of the window—another apparent deterrent to anyone entering the house through the cut screen. But the photograph was taken from about a forty-five degree angle and created an optical illusion that the vase holder was blocking the window opening. A photograph taken from the outside during that same early-morning sequence showed the vase holder's location—well to the side—more accurately.

Any possible footprints had been destroyed by the many people who had walked through the kitchen before Scharman closed it off, but the crime lab did manage to preserve a palm print from the window frame. Technicians also found a partial fingerprint on the bedpost in the girls' bedroom that matched a fingerprint on the backdoor handle. Because of these prints, hundreds of neighbors, family members, construction workers, and others had to be printed in the months to come. While the media would report that law enforcement was fingerprinting anyone who had been in the house, as well as most males in the neighborhood, the police were careful never to make public the reason for taking the prints. Throughout the investigation, law enforcement kept the existence of the prints they found that first morning a closely guarded secret. They represented, as one officer speculated, "the key to the case."

Within the first few hours, dozens of officers and several K-9 units started following three scent trails—one that ended above the house at Tomahawk Circle, a second that went to the bottom of the driveway and ended in the gully on the west side of the property, and a third up a nearby canyon. While the dogs followed the scent in the canyon, a helicopter got a visual of two joggers farther up the trail. After an officer on the ground ran ahead and confirmed that neither of the joggers was Elizabeth, nor had they seen her, handlers called the dogs back.

The first federal officer called to the crime scene was FBI agent Augustus "Mick" Fennerty IV. His boss, Dan Roberts, reached him at his home in West Jordan on the west side of the Salt Lake Valley a little after 7:00 A.M. and told him to get to the Smart home on the double. Fennerty was the coordinator of Crimes Against Children for the FBI in Utah and as such would become the case agent on the kidnapping. Fennerty had been up late the night before, reuniting a family with its missing child at the airport.

While rushing to the Smart home, Special Agent Fennerty made two calls. The first was to Ken Hansen, a retired SLCPD officer who was serving as director of the Internet Crimes Against Children task force. Hansen could bring a vast amount of expertise to the case; unfortunately, he was at the airport on his way out of town for several days. Fennerty next tried to call SLCPD's Heather Stringfellow. In 1999 she became the only SLCPD detective to complete the weeklong course on child abuse and exploitation at FBI headquarters at Quantico, Virginia. That training was primarily so she could be the liaison with the FBI, and understand the resources available to local law enforcement in the event of a child abduction in Salt Lake City. He couldn't reach Stringfellow, who was out of the country until the following Tuesday. When she returned she informed Fennerty that the previous year she had disagreed with the way the Sex Crimes Unit department was being run and had asked to be transferred out.

When Fennerty arrived at Kristianna Circle, more than three hours after Ed's 911 call, the home was sealed. The FBI Agent asked Sergeant Bell how the neighborhood canvas was going. Bell told him it was already complete. The comment alarmed Fennerty because he reasoned it simply was not possible to canvas the entire neighborhood so quickly, especially when many of the neighbors were out searching. Fennerty didn't know if Bell was being careless or if that was just his way of telling the FBI that the situation was under control.

But the FBI was not staying out, and while it would defer, as protocol required, to the local police and not take over the case, the federal agency would nonetheless pursue the investigation. Barred from entering the house while the state crime lab did its work, Fennerty spent the day at the base of the driveway making phone calls. He set up an Elizabeth Smart Hotline 800 number, started checking on family financial records and credit card transactions, and helped assign FBI agents to work with the SLCPD. He also called FBI headquarters in Washington, D.C., to request a team of specialists.

Fennerty also stayed in contact with authorities in Idaho Falls, Idaho, where another kidnapping, eerily similar, had occurred the same morning. At 5:30 A.M. a family discovered their fourteen-year-old daughter was missing. The girl, who was also the oldest daughter of a large LDS family, had been taken while sleeping with her little sister on the backyard trampoline. After a terrifying ordeal, the girl managed to escape from her abductor's home and call her mother around 3:00 P.M. She led police back to the home of a forty-two-year-old traveling tool salesman named Keith Hescock, where they waited for him to return. When he arrived, he led officers on a high-speed chase, which resulted in a shootout. Hescock shot an officer in the leg, killed a police dog, and then shot and killed himself. After searching his home, investigators found physical evidence related to two girls who had disappeared in the previous three years. They also found Hescock had been arrested with a friend in 1997 for illegally killing six elk and a deer. His friend was from Salt Lake City. Officers were later dispatched to drive to Idaho Falls—about three hours by freeway from Salt Lake City—to see if Hescock, who fit the description of Elizabeth's abductor, would have had sufficient time to make the round-trip drive to kidnap Elizabeth as well as the other girl.

Another disturbing piece of potential evidence was a faint trail of dried blood investigators found in the driveway of Ed's house. Within days, however, lab analysis determined that the blood was not Elizabeth's. It belonged to Bill Krebs, the gardener John Smith and I had questioned the second day. Krebs had cut himself while working at Ed's home the day before the kidnapping.

By Thursday, the four FBI specialists Fennerty had requested arrived in Salt Lake City, among them one of the top profilers in the country (the agent was part of the team that worked the Unabomber case), and Kim Poyer, who teaches the course on child forensic interviews at Quantico. On Friday, Fennerty took them through and around Ed's home to study the crime scene and what little evidence remained. On Saturday, the FBI specialists reviewed the videotape of the initial interview of Mary Katherine. They agreed it was a solid interview, but they thought that as long as they had one of the FBI's best interviewers in town, it would be prudent to do another. They believed that a woman interviewer might make Mary Katherine more comfortable. They requested the follow-up interview, but Sergeant Bell denied the request adamantly enough that Poyer left town the next day. A day later, Bell had another detective from his unit interview Mary Katherine. He did so again a few days after that.

Sunday night the FBI specialists again studied the crime scene. When it was dark, they noted that, from the outside, the home was like a fishbowl with no curtains on the windows and plenty of places for a stalker to hide in the cover of the scrub oak. Before the agents left, they came up with a profile of the person who kidnapped Elizabeth and left that profile with the task force. Their assessment was that this was a sex offense, that the crime was premeditated, and that the abductor would have taken Elizabeth to a predetermined place. They believed he would be keeping track of the case through the media, he probably had previous sexual issues, and he may have been arrested for sexual offenses such as voyeurism.

The FBI's opinion was find that man, find Elizabeth.

But whoever took Elizabeth was keeping a very low profile. In the absence of any contact between the kidnapper and the family, law enforcement officials thought no tip too wild to consider. On Tuesday, June 11, six days after the abduction, a schoolmate of Elizabeth's told investigators that Elizabeth had been talking to someone on the Internet at school, supposedly a boy. The schoolmate said she didn't know who the boy was, but that he was a student at the school. Investigators responded by confiscating the hard drives of nine computers at Bryant Middle School. They never found anything to substantiate the girl's claim.

Also on Tuesday, June 11, beginning at 10:00 P.M. and continuing until 10:00 A.M. the next day, SLCPD set up a roadblock near Ed's house. The purpose was to stop all vehicles traveling through the neighborhood exactly one week after the kidnapping in the hope of learning something from the traffic patterns. Several people, upon seeing the roadblock, turned their vehicles around and bolted. Police gave chase and later made dozens of arrests for varying offenses. But as with the school computers, nothing they found pointed to any involvement with the kidnapping.

As the case moved forward and the various law enforcement agencies closed their ranks, it became clear to the family that it was going to be up to us, not the authorities, to determine the role we would play in trying to find Elizabeth. At first, it was natural to see a police officer, or an FBI agent, and assume we were all working toward the same goal. But we came to realize that, as members of Elizabeth's family, we were in many ways outsiders in the investigation. The alliance between law enforcement and family, if it could be called that, was one-sided. This was the police's investigation. They were in charge. They would do it their way.

There was no formula telling us what we should or shouldn't do, or, for that matter, what we could or couldn't do, on our own. We could have chosen to leave the case to the police, assist them when asked, and otherwise returned to our normal routines. This hands-off approach was one that many of our friends, coworkers, and sometimes even strangers recommended to us. But deep down, we all knew nothing would be routine in any of our lives until Elizabeth was found.

With the decentralizing of the search center and the distancing of the police, we had to figure out what to do next. It was my dad who led the way. He turned to the pile of paperwork—the result of nearly a thousand official searches, several of which he had taken part in. After each search, the designated team captain had written down where the team had gone and anything noteworthy that they had seen or found. It was amazing how many homeless shacks, articles of clothing, recent campfires, kitchen appliances, wrecked bikes, and other items searchers had discovered in the forests and open spaces in and around Salt Lake City. One search group found a perfectly good car sitting in a river. All of it had been documented on search center debriefing forms, or, barring that, on napkins, menus, and other scraps of paper.

Few were better suited to the task of organizing the mess than Charles Smart, a pioneer in the field of computerized medical data.

Both my parents had developed a particularly close bond with Elizabeth and her older brother, Charles. Shortly after Dad moved to Maryland to work for the Cancer Institute, Ed and Lois followed with their family—at the time they had just the two children—so Ed could finish his college degree, and go on to get his graduate degree, at George Washington University in nearby Washington, D.C. Ed, Lois, Elizabeth, and Charles moved into the basement of the house Dad and Mom had bought in Rockville, Maryland. Elizabeth was two at the time and Charles was four. During the day, while Dad and Ed were at work and school, Mom, Lois, and the kids toured the East Coast to see the sights. They would take day trips to the Amish country in Pennsylvania one week, Mount Vernon the next, and Gettysburg the next. Dad bought a twenty-six-foot boat to explore the Chesapeake Bay. The two families spent a lot of time together during Elizabeth's early years. Later, they spent more time together when Ed's family moved into the basement of the Chandler Drive home while Ed started the house at Kristianna Circle. Even when the families separated, they lived less than a mile apart. My parents developed close relationships with all their grandchildren, but none closer than with Elizabeth.

Dad recruited half a dozen neighborhood volunteers and four laptop computers to help him with his data-programming project, and went to work.

Elizabeth Smart, 13, stays dry under a tarp during a family trip in the summer of 2001.
Family photo

Elizabeth in December 2000. George Frey

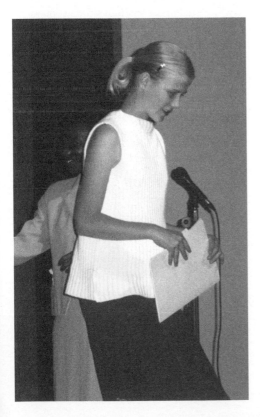

Elizabeth at the Bryant Junior High awards ceremony hours before she was kidnapped.
Connie Smith

Exterior shot of the kitchen window and chair against the wall in this photograph taken by the Salt Lake City police within the first hour of their arrival.

Exterior shot of the kitchen window, photographed by the State Crime Lab later in the day of the kidnapping. A flour sack is shown in the background that wasn't in the earlier photos.

The partial palm print on the window, shown in this photograph taken by the State Crime Lab later in the day of the kidnapping.

Interior shot of the kitchen window area taken within the first hour by the Salt Lake City police.

More than 1,800 volunteers registered at Shriners Hospital to help in the search for Elizabeth Smart on June 6, 2002, the day after she was kidnapped. Laura Seitz, *Deseret Morning News*

Elizabeth's grandfather Charles Smart takes a moment of quiet reflection while riding Moscow along one of the Green River Lakes in August 2002. Tom Smart

Volunteers search the brush in the foothills above Salt Lake City on Friday morning, June 7, 2002. Laura Seitz, *Deseret Morning News*

Lois and Ed Smart, Elizabeth's parents, attend the candlelight vigil for their daughter at Liberty Park on Sunday night, June 9, 2002. Michael Brandy, *Deseret Morning News*

Larry Holstrom speaks to media and volunteers before a search outside the Federal Heights Ward. Johanna Kirk, *Deseret Morning News*

Ed speaks. He is backed by his five siblings (from left, David Smart, Tom Smart, Cynthia Owens, Angela Dumke, and Chris Smart), and, in the back row, you can also see Elizabeth's brother Charles, grandfather Charles, and Zeke Dumke III. Johanna Kirk, *Deseret Morning News*

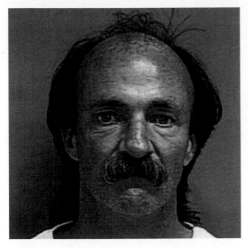

Richard Ricci's booking mug shot. Salt Lake City Police Department

Richard Ricci enters the Utah Third District courtroom in Salt Lake City on July 31, 2002, to go before Judge Randall N. Skanchy for his initial appearance on charges of theft. Jason Olson, *Deseret Morning News*

Richard Ricci leaves the court just hours before he suffered a ruptured aneurysm in his prison cell on August 27, 2002. Jeremy Harmon, *Deseret Morning News*

Angela Ricci, Richard Ricci's wife, on the day Elizabeth returned home. Scott G. Winterton, *Deseret Morning News*

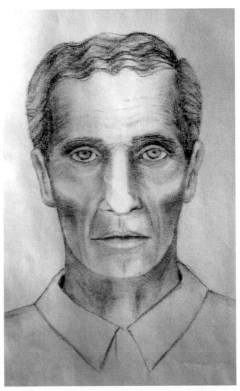

Sketch of "Emmanuel" by Dalene Nielsen based on Ed's year-old memory of the time he spent working with him at the Smart home.

Brian David Mitchell and Wanda Barzee Mitchell walk down the Salt Lake Temple stairs after being married in the Mormon temple in 1987, two years after their civil marriage. Dora Corbett

Brian David Mitchell and Wanda Barzee Mitchell in their handmade clothing. Dora Corbett

Shirl Mitchell, Brian David Mitchell's father. Tom Smart

Photo of Brian David Mitchell from September 27, 2002, taken after stealing items from an Albertson's Food Store. This is the photo Mick Fennerty sent to *America's Most Wanted*.

The lean-to and the tree where Elizabeth was chained with a cable much of the time.
Tom Smart

A tent was pitched in the flat area of the foreground; the lean-to is in the background.
Tom Smart

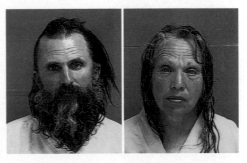

The tree where Elizabeth was chained with a cable much of the time. Tom Smart

Mug shots of Brian David Mitchell and Wanda Barzee Mitchell from March 12, 2003.
Salt Lake County Sheriff

Ed, ecstatic, greets the media saying, "It's real! It's real!" during a press conference at the Federal Heights Ward of the Church of Jesus Christ of Latter-day Saints on March 13, 2003, the day after Elizabeth was found alive in Sandy, Utah. Keith Johnson, *Deseret Morning News*

Grandfather Charles Smart is reunited with Elizabeth. Tom Smart, *Deseret Morning News*, Getty Images

Elizabeth holds her youngest brother, William, as she sits with her sister Mary Katherine the morning after her return. Tom Smart, *Deseret Morning News*, Getty Images

Lois, Elizabeth, and Special Agent Mick Fennerty are all smiles at a celebration to thank the volunteers in April 2004, one year after Elizabeth's return. *Tom Smart*

The rest of us envied his transition. We all wanted—we all *needed*—something new to keep us busy in the search for Elizabeth. We differed on how to keep looking. Chris and David felt we should keep physically searching, while others felt the physical searches should be discontinued except in cases where there was a compelling reason. So much publicity had been given the kidnapping that thousands of hikers, bikers, and hunters would provide more watchful eyes than the organized searches. If someone really wanted to hide a body, it was doubtful the searchers would find it anyway. For example, a decomposed body of a man in a sleeping bag was accidentally found by hikers in Big Cottonwood Canyon after two search parties had already canvassed the area. Angela and I felt strongly that the searches were losing credibility and at our family meeting on Monday morning, June 17, we passed a resolution that all future searches involving family members had to be based on solid leads. We would make public the need for a heightened awareness rather than continued random searching.

David and Chris weren't there for our vote. They came in late for the meeting because they had spent all day Sunday searching around Bear Lake in northern Utah, 150 miles from home, based on a psychic-type lead.

"You did what?!" demanded Chris when he learned we had passed a motion to limit future searches. A debate followed. Voices were raised. Chris ended the debate by asking Ed if he wanted us to stop searching, to which he of course replied what any parent would: no.

After everyone had a chance to express exactly how he or she felt, we stopped shouting long enough to realize that *everyone* was right. There was only one wrong way, and that was to do nothing. What mattered was that we continued our efforts, whatever form they took. It was fine if we each had our own idea about how to go about finding Elizabeth. None of us had backgrounds in law enforcement. We didn't have degrees in forensic science. We hadn't been trained at Quantico. We had no idea how a kidnapper thinks, or where best to look for one. All we had was our determination to not let up—whether that meant turning over every rock, programming computers, working the media, praying, or something else, we needed to follow our hearts and do it.

From the outside, I'm sure there was a perception that the Smarts had total unity and solidarity in our overall goal, and that was absolutely true. But behind the scenes we didn't always agree. We were often quite frantic about what to do next, and we clashed frequently.

We each had our own challenges, our private down times and tests of faith. I remember that Cynthia became very discouraged after her earnest appeal to the kidnapper's good side, following the advice in Brent Cook's letter, failed to produce the hoped-for results. Cynthia had felt so strongly that was the answer. When day after day passed without progress, she really struggled. She didn't pull out of her despair until one day she opened her scriptures and read the forty-ninth chapter of Isaiah. One verse hit her especially hard:

> But thus saith the Lord, Even the captives of the mighty shall be taken away, and the prey of the terrible shall be delivered: for I will contend with him that contendeth with thee, and I will save thy children.

"That passage just seemed so incredibly applicable that I typed it on my computer and printed a copy that I posted above my sink to give me hope," Cynthia remembered. She also sent a copy to Ed and Lois.

Each of us was being constantly reminded that in addition to searching for Elizabeth, we had to seek inspiration wherever we could find it so we would stay positive and productive. A day rarely went by without the family expressing our love for one another.

On Tuesday, June 18, SLCPD Captain Scott Atkinson told the media that, contrary to initial reports, police now believed that Mary Katherine had not been threatened directly by the kidnapper, and, furthermore, that the kidnapper probably did not even know she'd seen him.

An outcry went up from the press corps. NBC correspondent Shellee Smith asked Atkinson how the police could have let the media misreport this basic information for nearly two weeks. Others fired similar questions at him. Atkinson explained that the false information about Mary Katherine being threatened was what Ed reported the first day. He did not mention that Ed's confusion had been quickly cleared up, nor did he explain why the police had not corrected it publicly until now. (After learning of the correct facts from the family, *America's Most Wanted* had reported in its broadcast on Saturday, June 8, that Mary Katherine had not been threatened. But except for television critic Scott Pierce of the *Deseret News*, no other media had followed up on that report; the public perception two weeks after the kidnapping was still that the kidnapper had threatened Elizabeth's sister.)

Atkinson also announced a new estimated height of the suspect from five-foot-eight to a range of five-foot-eight to five-foot-ten. (Mary Katherine never gave a height in feet and inches, she only said the kidnapper was the same height as her brother Charles.) No one in the media asked about the reason for the height adjustment. Atkinson told reporters that Mary Katherine had seen the kidnapper in two different parts of the house, that Mary Katherine had said the suspect had what she described as dark hair on the back of his hands, and that Mary Katherine had heard him threaten Elizabeth. This, too, riled the press corps. Why hadn't this information been released earlier? What kind of game were the police playing? Why had they waited so long to put this on the record? The questions became accusatory and heated. Hearing reports that the press conference was getting out of hand, Chief Dinse called Detective Fred Louis on his cell phone and told him to get Atkinson to stop the conference. But Atkinson could not see Louis giving him the kill sign by slashing his hand across his throat and raising his cell phone in the air; Louis was hidden behind the wall of press.

The following day, in an attempt at damage control, Chief Dinse addressed the press personally. He took general questions about the investigation. Frustrated reporters again wanted to know why the police had waited two weeks to reveal that Mary Katherine had not been threatened. And why hadn't the other details from the first morning been disclosed? The chief didn't offer any more answers than Atkinson had the day before. He finally said, "There is no conspiracy here. We are not telling you everything.... If you haven't figured that out by now, that's the truth."

The police weren't about to tip their hand to the media, or the family, about a potential suspect they had quietly taken into custody—a person

Mary Katherine would have recognized if she had been directly threatened by him, and who was much taller than her brother Charles. What the police *were* willing to disclose were details that would help strengthen their case later on.

One reporter who seemed particularly agitated by Chief Dinse's comments—or noncomments—was Kevin Cantera of the *Salt Lake Tribune*, who grilled Dinse so relentlessly that the chief finally asked Cantera to quit interrupting. After two weeks of provocative reports in the *Tribune*, Cantera and his reporting partner, Michael Vigh, had become mini-celebrities as in-the-know journalists when it came to the Elizabeth Smart story. It was heady territory for the two relatively young and inexperienced reporters, who had been openly bragging at a Utah chapter of the Society of Professional Journalists banquet about which famous news anchor or commentator they would make time for.

Thirty-three-year-old Vigh had come to the *Tribune* five years earlier from a small semi-weekly newspaper in the nearby city of Tooele. The only stop for thirty-four-year-old Cantera between journalism school at the University of Utah and the *Tribune* was a stint at a weekly Salt Lake City tabloid. Some veteran journalists at the *Tribune* questioned putting two relatively green reporters on a story as major as the Smart kidnapping, but the newspaper's editor, Jay Shelledy, favored the two brash and eager reporters. In fact, he took to calling them "Vigtera," combining their names as legendary *Washington Post* editor Ben Bradlee had when he called Watergate investigative reporters Bob Woodward and Carl Bernstein "Woodstein." Other editors at the *Tribune* watched as Shelledy pushed Cantera and Vigh, as well as others assigned periodically to assist in covering the kidnapping, to come up with scoops, encouraging them to, as one *Tribune* editor put it, "not report on the case as much as solve it."

Shelledy may have pushed so hard because he thought the *Tribune* was at a disadvantage due to my affiliation with the rival *Deseret News*. This, of course, was not true. The last thing the Smart family was going to do was play favorites with any media. But there was no question that the *Tribune* was pushing to take the lead in investigative reporting. When Cantera and Vigh responded as Shelledy ordered, with their highly speculative stories pointing at the family, Shelledy prodded them on. Some editors at the *Tribune* had serious concerns about Cantera's and Vigh's use of unnamed sources, but Shelledy backed his reporters and told editors to quit pressing them for their sources. The reporting hit its nadir on Sunday, June 16, when the *Tribune* ran a front-page article with a headline that read "D-News Puts Girl's Uncle in Spotlight," along with the subhead: "Tom Smart, called focus of probe by paper, proclaims his innocence." The story, written by Cantera and Vigh, exposed me by name as a potential suspect by citing the *Deseret News* article of the day before in which I explained my alibi and expressed my innocence. Charging that the rival newspaper—the newspaper I worked for—put me in the spotlight after merely responding to the *Tribune*'s own reporting required a deft bit of newspaper gamesmanship Jay Shelledy was obviously not above. At least one editor called it the "dirtiest piece of journalism" that staffer had ever witnessed.

For the *Tribune* not to acknowledge that its own reporting had prompted me to defend myself was an insult to readers' intelligence, as well as a serious lapse of ethical responsibility. Not everyone at the *Tribune* agreed with Shelledy, who reportedly reviewed the June 16 story while on vacation in Idaho and forbade anyone to change the first few paragraphs. *Tribune* deputy editor Vern Anderson called the story "a goddamned piece of shit" and as the *Tribune* went to press Saturday night, he walked out of the paper's offices physically ill.

There was little if any fallout for crusading journalists Cantera and Vigh, whose stock and stature continued to rise. Only hours before Chief Dinse met the press for his damage-control session Wednesday morning, Cantera and Vigh had been on ABC's *Good Morning America*, appearing live from Salt Lake City with host Charlie Gibson. Gibson had led his report about the kidnapping with the "interesting new development" that Mary Katherine had not been threatened. He then directed a comment to Cantera. "Kevin," he asked, "bottom line, though, it makes the Salt Lake City Police Department..., it doesn't make them look very good."

"No, it certainly doesn't," said Cantera. "I'll tell you one thing, though. I have covered Salt Lake City police for going on three years now. I know that they've got their way of doing things. They may look a tad incompetent right now, but that may be the image they're trying to portray. For all we know, they may want some suspects out there to think they're incompetent and they're dropping the ball so that that person lets down their guard."

"Yesterday," continued Gibson, "the police spokesman said they believe that this kidnapper was someone trusted in the community. On what do they base that?"

"I believe they've based that on the fact that whoever pulled this abduction had some pretty good access inside the house and likely began the action from inside the house," said Cantera. "We have a screen that was actually cut from the inside of the house, as we reported last week, leading them to believe it's an inside job of some kind. When they say a trusted person in the neighborhood, I think they're trying to say this is somebody who has a position of respect in the family, who would have had some kind of access to the family. Whether that's an extended family member, a trusted neighbor, it's hard to say right now."

Cantera's comments on national television, as in his newspaper reports with Michael Vigh, suggested a close connection between the *Tribune* reporters and what was going on inside the police investigation. When Chief Dinse spoke about "not telling you everything," it suggested otherwise. Anyone watching Kevin Cantera's leg shake nervously up and down as he grilled Dinse for details, could see either a journalist scrambling to stay in the know or one who was nervous about whether what he'd reported was as inside the investigation as he'd hoped.

By Thursday, June 20, the police had finally found one person they were looking for, although it would be more accurate to say Bret Michael Edmunds found them. Despite a nationwide manhunt, Edmunds wasn't caught until he got sick. Early Tuesday, he checked himself into a hospital in Martinsburg, West Virginia, complaining of symptoms that appeared to be related to drugs. He gave the hospital a fictitious name, Todd Richards, but hospital workers discovered his true identity when they called Edmunds's mother, whose name the fugitive had listed as his emergency contact. The mother lived in Sterling, Utah, a small town in Sanpete County. She contacted law enforcement authorities in Salt Lake City, advising them of her son's whereabouts.

The police announced Edmunds's arrest on Friday, June 21. By that time, an SLCPD detective and an FBI agent were already on the way to West Virginia to question the fugitive—who was in bad shape and remained hospitalized. They searched Edmunds's car, which Martinsburg police had found in the hospital parking lot, bearing Washington plates. Investigators once again cautioned that Edmunds was not a suspect; they only wanted to question him.

Talking to the media, the police mentioned an article they said was about to appear in the *National Enquirer* that focused on allegations of family involvement in the kidnapping. Captain Scott Atkinson and Detective Dwayne Baird both referred to the tabloid article in interviews with the Associated Press and the *Salt Lake Tribune*. How the police knew about the as-yet-uncirculated article and why a comment lending credibility to a *National Enquirer* news story made its way into police interviews at all was puzzling. But we were soon to discover that this was no false tip. On Friday, copies of the July 2 issue of the *National Enquirer* hit newsstands nationwide. On the cover was the headline "Utah Cops: Secret Diary Exposes Family Sex Ring." Inside, the article ran the width of two tabloid pages. The following was the lead paragraph:

> Police probing the mysterious abduction of fourteen-year-old Elizabeth Smart have made a discovery that's rocked them to the core—a shocking gay sex scandal involving her father Edward and two uncles, the ENQUIRER has learned exclusively.

The article cited "police sources" that claimed Ed, David, and I were part of a gay sex ring, that our wives knew of our deviant behavior, and that during a search of an unspecified family member's home, police had found "a horrifying journal" that detailed the brothers' "mind-boggling activities." The tabloid's sources, all unnamed, said that police had searched my home and confiscated my computer, discovering hundreds of "homosexual pornographic pictures."

Suddenly, the accusations from the *Tribune*, Bill O'Reilly, and Marc Klaas looked like kid stuff. The article quoted more unnamed sources that alleged Elizabeth was "troubled."

The police had never even been to my home, or David's, let alone searched them or confiscated any of our computers. Earlier, Ed had turned over his computers voluntarily, and Chief Dinse was quoted by Ashley Broughton in the *Salt Lake Tribune* on June 21 as saying, "we have found nothing on the computers that creates a nexus to this crime."

The *Enquirer*'s police sources were quoted as saying my polygraph was "inconclusive" and my alibi for the night before the crime was "not solid"— the same information that had been reported earlier in the *Salt Lake Tribune*, and could have been easily explained with a modicum of checking. To jump to the conclusion that I was somehow involved with my niece's kidnapping was a classic case of using a smidgen of truth to perpetrate a mountain of lies. The *Enquirer* even managed to get a photograph wrong. A photo identified as David Smart was in fact David Francom, Lois's brother. Of course all of it was in keeping with the sensationalistic journalism that has always been the *Enquirer*'s trademark.

The only good thing about the article was that it was so ludicrous it destroyed its own credibility. None of the legitimate media organizations in Utah, print or broadcast, publicized or followed up on the *Enquirer* article to any significant extent, and the same was true for the mainstream national news organizations. What's more, many Utah stores that regularly stocked the *National Enquirer* pulled copies of the "World Exclusive" on the Elizabeth Smart kidnapping off the shelf. At some stores, the July 2 issue was stashed behind the counter, available only by request. Other stores returned their copies, refusing to sell them at all. That didn't stop the spread of the story at supermarket checkout stands around the country, but at least it helped contain some of the pain closer to home.

To discuss how to combat the *Enquirer*'s lies, and any resultant fallout, Chris Thomas organized an emergency meeting with members of the family at Angela's house. We had recently hired Chris as our full-time public relations advisor, after his partners at the Intrepid Group agreed we could use his professional services for as long as we needed him.

Chris instructed us to respond publicly that the article did not warrant discussion. To get into a public debate with the tabloid would only blow the story up further, and, worse than that, it would steal focus from the search for Elizabeth.

I agreed with Chris that a fight with the *Enquirer* was not in our best interests at the moment. But I filed the date in the back of my mind, knowing we had a year to bring a lawsuit for libel. (Beyond all the untruths, the article was filled with bigotry and hatred, not to mention a bit of irony when it came to the gay issue. It seemed to me that a gay man would be less likely to be involved in the kidnapping of a young girl, not more. The whole episode was a particular insult to the many gay friends who had been helping with the search.)

As untruthful as the *Enquirer* story was, it was propped up by one disturbing truth: the tabloid's gossipy "police sources," whoever they were, represented at least two people in law enforcement, and maybe more, who were willing to point fingers at the Smart family.

With the *Enquirer*'s story the latest buzz in the Elizabeth Smart kidnapping, and with Edmunds awaiting extradition to Utah from his hospital bed in West Virginia, a lone report that aired Sunday night, June 23, on KSTU, the local Fox News affiliate, was nearly lost in the commotion.

Scott McKane, KSTU's lead reporter on the kidnapping, announced that police had a new person of interest they were looking at—and it was not Elizabeth Smart's father, her uncles, or any other relatives. It was a handyman named Richard Ricci, a man Ed Smart had once hired on the recommendation of another contractor. Ricci, McKane reported, lived with his wife, Angela, in a trailer park in Kearns, on the west side of the Salt Lake Valley. But he wasn't living there now. He was locked up in the Salt Lake County Adult Detention Center—and he had some explaining to do.

18

By Monday, June 24, Scott McKane's Fox exclusive had ballooned into front-page news. The Smart kidnapping, nearly three weeks old, finally had a new face to look at. The police made it clear that Richard Ricci was not officially a suspect. His arrest was for an unrelated parole violation—while he was in custody they wanted to question him about the kidnapping because of his association with Elizabeth's father.

Ricci made an intriguing prospect. He was an ex-con with a long record, and he had worked for the Smarts. To add to the intrigue, by early Monday afternoon a West Valley City auto mechanic had come forward to tell reporters that Ricci had brought his Jeep in for repairs in late May. But someone had taken the Jeep from his shop for ten days, including the day of the kidnapping. Ricci was the one who brought it back. When he dropped off the car, he removed a few items, including a machete-style knife and a posthole digger.

And there was one more interesting detail: the Jeep had once belonged to Ed Smart.

Richard Albert Ricci had been out of prison just six months when he first met Ed Smart in early 2001. A contractor friend of Ed's recommended Ricci for basic carpentry work and other relatively unskilled construction labor Ed needed done on his house. Ed didn't know that Ricci had been behind bars and was currently out on parole, and Ricci never volunteered the information. In time, two of Ricci's buddies from prison, Rex Young and John Remington, would join Ricci working on other homes in Arlington

Hills—jobs secured at least in part because of Ricci's working relationship with Ed. Young and Remington kept their prison records quiet too.

It wasn't that their presence in the neighborhood was unusual. Workmen in the Federal Heights/Arlington Hills area are as ubiquitous as BMWs and new Chevrolet Suburbans in the driveways. Established homes in the exclusive residential area are constantly being remodeled, while new ones, like Ed Smart's, are being finished. There is always plenty of work. Many a handyman's kid goes through college on the jobs from Federal Heights and Arlington Hills.

Some workers keep to themselves, do their jobs, and move on. Others get to know the people and families they work for. Ricci was part of the latter group. He took an interest in Ed and Lois and their children as he worked on a semi-regular basis on the Smart house for about three months. He got to know the family and called everyone by their first name. He was outgoing, friendly, charismatic, and easy to like. When it became obvious that he didn't have a car, Ed offered him one of his—a white 1990 Jeep Cherokee he'd been thinking of selling—as payment for his work. If Ricci was willing to work it off, he could take possession of the vehicle immediately.

Ricci made a big mistake with Ed when he stopped showing up for work after getting the Jeep. After a couple of missed shifts, Ed went straight to Ricci's apartment. Because the ignition was broken and didn't require a key, he knew he could repossess the Jeep easily. But when he got to the apartment, he found the Jeep sitting in the driveway with the engine running. Ed jumped in and started to drive away.

Ricci appeared and said, "What are you doing?"

Ed replied, "What do you think I'm doing? I'm taking back my Jeep." And he drove off. Within a couple of days, Ricci was back at Ed's, apologizing for what he called a misunderstanding, and asking if he could get back to work and take back the Jeep, no hard feelings.

Ed accepted Ricci's apology, and the work proceeded. But a couple of months later Ed fired Ricci and two other workers when one of Lois's favorite bracelets turned up missing from the jewelry box in her bedroom. The workers were the likeliest suspects, and Lois had a feeling that Ricci was the culprit. Ed confronted all three workers, and when each denied taking the bracelet, Ed told them he couldn't chance having a thief in the house and dismissed them all. He filed a report with the Salt Lake City police, who also questioned the workers without success. The police failed to inform Ed that one of the people he had employed was a lifelong criminal currently on parole.

It was the last time Ed saw Ricci until he came to the house in the early fall of 2001 to pick up the Jeep registration, which had been mailed to Ed's address. Ricci drove to Kristianna Circle in the Jeep and chatted with Ed on the front steps. He thanked him for the help getting a car and made a point of again stressing that he had not taken Lois's bracelet. He told Ed he had even taken a polygraph at the police station to prove his innocence. "I would never steal from you, man," he said, raising his right arm as if testifying in court. "It's important to me that you know that."

On the morning Elizabeth disappeared, Ed compiled for detectives a list of workers who had helped him on the construction of his house and were familiar with the floor plan and the family. It was the likeliest place to start, and it was not a short list. Ed came up with the names of dozens of workers with no more than a look at his checkbook. Ricci's name was among them, and while Ed, lacking knowledge of Ricci's criminal past, gave him no special notice, the name jumped to the top of the list when *police* noted his record. Since the age of nineteen, when he was first tried as an adult and given a one- to twenty-year sentence for second-degree felony burglary, Ricci had spent three-quarters of his life behind bars. The convictions were for fraud, burglary, shooting at a police officer, and parole violation. At least those were the legal reasons. Underlying them was the root cause: a long-time addiction to heroin.

To the police, this was a con's con and a drug addict. Even before they knew about Ed firing him, they knew they would need to question Ricci.

The police first interviewed Ricci on the afternoon of June 5, less than twelve hours after Elizabeth was reported missing. A group of six parole workers and police officers drove to Ricci's house in Kearns to pick him up for the questioning. He was not surprised to see them. That morning, as news of the kidnapping spread, he had told one of his neighbors that he knew the police, given his past and his working relationship with the Smarts, would want to question him. He told the officers who conducted the interview he was sorry for what had happened, he felt terrible for the Smarts, and he hoped they'd quickly find whoever did it. But he did not know who could have done such a thing, and it certainly was not him. He loved the Smart children and would never hurt them. He said he'd been in bed with his wife throughout the night of the abduction.

Angela Ricci verified her husband's alibi, adding in her police interview the details of how distraught he had been when he'd seen the news of the kidnapping on television early Wednesday morning. She explained that they were sitting on the couch, drinking their morning coffee, when the breaking news came on TV. "He put his head in his hands and said, 'I hope that's not Ed's daughter,'" Angela Ricci said. "When they said that it was Ed's daughter, he said, 'I feel so sorry for that little girl; she's such a pretty girl.'"

After talking at length at the police station, the officers closed their notebooks and thanked Ricci for his time and cooperation and let him go back home. He wouldn't hear from the authorities again until nine days later, when, on Friday, June 14, he got a call from his parole officer. The police wanted to talk to him again. The parole officer said he had no idea why, but Ricci needed to get to the downtown station right away.

After verifying Ricci's alibi with his wife, the police had not thought much more about him until they talked further with Ed. Ed gave police details about Ricci that Ricci hadn't provided, including the repossession of the Jeep and the circumstances surrounding the missing bracelet. When Ed told them about Ricci's theatrics on the doorstep the day he came to get the Jeep title, raising his arm to proclaim his innocence and volunteering the information that he had taken a police polygraph, investigators got very interested. The police didn't know if Ricci had taken Lois Smart's bracelet, but they did know he'd never taken a polygraph to prove he hadn't.

There was more. Ricci had also worked for Ed at a Federal Heights home where Ed was supervising a remodeling project. The home belonged to Phil and Suann Adams, the couple now heading our family search organization. In the early morning hours of April 4, 2001, someone had broken into the Adams residence by jimmying a sliding glass door and had then stolen three hundred dollars in cash and several items of jewelry. The burglar took the cash and jewelry from a bedroom where a houseguest was sleeping. The guest, a woman from Vietnam, awoke to a rustling noise and, thinking it was a family member, mumbled that it was OK to turn on the light. All she got in response was a cough. The next morning, Phil, Suann, and their guest discovered the jimmied sliding glass door and the missing items. The first person they suspected was Ed's handyman, Richard Ricci, who had been doing electrical work in the bedroom the day before.

Phil and Suann filed a report with the Salt Lake City police and put Ricci down as a suspect. Just as he would when questioned about the loss of Lois Smart's bracelet two months later, Ricci, when confronted, denied any involvement in the burglary. Phil and Suann remained unconvinced. In an incident prior to the April 4 burglary, they had also lost a laptop and other computer equipment from another room in the house—and Ricci had been hanging a door in that room the day those items went missing.

June 14 was the day police discovered the Adams burglary report—and the name of Richard Ricci as a suspect—after compiling every criminal complaint from the Federal Heights area over the past five years.

For the police, it was all too coincidental. Three burglaries, all of them occurring when a man who had served more than his share of jail time was on the premises. More unsettling was the fact that one of the burglaries included entering a dark bedroom while someone was sleeping there. The police call that a thrill burglary.

Finally, as the police more closely examined Ricci's alibi for the night of the kidnapping—that he'd been home in bed alongside his wife—they found out Angela Ricci had a history of using a prescription drug called Soma, which produces deep sleep. If Angela was in a Soma-induced slumber, her husband could have left her side without her knowledge, gone to the Smarts' house, returned later, and acted the next morning as if nothing happened. Richard Ricci was a notorious liar.

The police needed to get him where they could squeeze him. When Ricci reported to the downtown station early on the afternoon of Friday, June 14, he was asked several questions while a medical technician drew a blood sample. After Ricci's repeated denials of guilt, the police again released him and allowed him to drive back home to Kearns. But a couple of hours later two law enforcement officers were back at the trailer. "I wonder what they want now," Ricci said to Angela, seconds before one of the officers slapped cuffs on his wrists. Police told him that they'd found alcohol in his blood sample, which constituted a violation of his parole. He was to stay away from all addictive substances; those were the rules. The technicality was enough for them to haul him off to jail. Ricci was arrested for drinking a beer.

As police read Ricci his rights in the driveway, one of the officers approached Angela and said, "You better tell your husband that he better start talking before somebody starts talking about him."

Angela had no idea what he meant. "Well, can I give him a hug?" she asked.

"No," the officer told her. "Once he's in handcuffs you can't touch him."

Then the officers put Ricci in the backseat and drove him to the Salt Lake County jail.

It turned out the police were right. Ricci had burgled the Adams house twice, and the Smart house once. He confessed first to stealing money at the Adams house after the police informed him they had his fingerprints from the scene. What they didn't tell him was that the prints were only partials, unidentifiable and incapable of convicting him. But Ricci took the bait and admitted to breaking into the sleeping woman's room, although he said he only got one hundred dollars in cash, not three hundred. Four days later, after two searches of the Kearns trailer (with Ricci's consent) produced items from both the Smart and Adams heists (including the earlier burglary of the Adams's laptop), Ricci also admitted stealing Lois's bracelet, along with several other items the Smarts never reported missing, including a perfume bottle, a wine goblet, and a skateboard.

But though he was willing to admit to being an unreformed thief, he wasn't willing to admit to any connection whatever to the real, if unofficial, reason the police had hauled him in. He was no kidnapper, he told them time and time again, and he was willing to take a polygraph to prove it.

The police finally let him take the polygraph. He passed. Not satisfied, they polygraphed him again. This time the result was inconclusive. He voluntarily submitted to a third polygraph, but that time he failed it. Ricci's wife, Angela, also took at least one polygraph and passed.

With Ricci behind bars, the police went to work trying to find evidence to connect him to the kidnapping. After running forensics on the two vehicles the police found parked at Ricci's trailer—a Ford Taurus and an Oldsmobile Cutlass—and coming up with nothing, the police and FBI hunted down the couple's third car, the 1990 Jeep Cherokee that had once belonged to Ed Smart. They found it at Neth Moul's Auto Repair in West Valley City, about three miles from the Ricci's trailer.

Shop owner Neth Moul, a refugee from Cambodia and now a naturalized U.S. citizen, got the officers' attention when he told them that on May 30, a woman had called inquiring about keys to the Jeep. Moul said the vehicle had been taken from the parking lot at his repair shop later that night. He said he had no idea who took it. He said the Jeep wasn't returned until June 8, when Ricci brought it back. The normally gregarious Ricci barely spoke to him that day, the mechanic told investigators; he seemed agitated and appeared to be in a hurry. According to Moul, Ricci was covered with dirt. A machete knife in a camouflaged sheath hung from his belt. Moul also told police that Ricci had said something about being in Spanish Fork Canyon. After Ricci parked the car, the mechanic said he watched him fill two black plastic garbage bags with the seat covers from the front seats, and also carry a posthole digger from the Jeep. He carried the bags and the posthole digger across the street to a gas station, where another man met him. Moul said he assumed the two men drove off together.

At first police said there was between 500 and 1,000 extra miles on the Jeep. The mechanic later produced a work order with what he said was the odometer mileage on the Jeep when Ricci first brought it in to repair a fuel pump. The mileage recorded on the shop order was 134,341. Now, investigators noted that the Jeep's odometer showed 135,373 miles—a 1,032-mile difference. Wherever the Jeep had picked up the extra miles, must've been muddy, Moul said, because the Jeep came back with mud caked all over it—mud that the auto mechanic said he had personally hosed off. Besides the fuel pump, the Jeep had been brought in for a safety inspection, due in May so the registration could be renewed—meaning that while the Jeep was allegedly off the premises, its plates had expired.

Neth Moul claimed to know nothing of Ricci's possible involvement in the Elizabeth Smart kidnapping. He told police he'd heard about the kidnapping on the news, but only in passing.

When confronted with Neth Moul's story, Ricci told the police he had no idea what the mechanic was talking about. He hadn't gone to the garage, period. He and Angela didn't have the money to pay for the repairs so they'd just left the Jeep in the shop. He said he'd been driving the Taurus for the past few weeks. As to his whereabouts from May 30 through June 5, he said he'd been working his day job at Mitchell's Nursery and spending time at home with Angela and her eleven-year-old son. The son was preparing for baptism in the LDS Church; after working the day shift on Tuesday, June 4, at Mitchell's Nursery, Ricci said he sat in on a lesson at the trailer that evening with two full-time LDS missionaries and his stepson. He'd even cooked dinner for the missionaries before the lesson. After they left, the boy went to bed and Ricci and Angela stayed up watching television for a while before they turned in. It was the next morning that they heard the news about the Elizabeth Smart kidnapping.

Ricci said he had the day off from Mitchell's that day. When Angela went to work around 8:30 A.M., he puttered around the yard, weeding and patching a hole in the side of a neighbor's trailer that adjoined the Riccis' property. A little later, he said, he and another neighbor drove to a pawnshop so the neighbor could hock his guitar to get money for his son, who wanted to go to the movies with Ricci's stepson. The men came back with the cash and then drove the boys to the theater and returned to pick them up when the movie was over.

After his interview that afternoon with the police, Ricci said, he went back to the trailer. The LDS missionaries returned to teach his stepson another lesson. The next day, Thursday, June 6, Ricci said, he went back to Mitchell's and worked from 10:30 A.M. to 7:00 P.M.

The story checked out. Police talked to Ricci's coworkers and supervisors at the nursery, to his neighbors, and to the missionaries. All agreed he was where he said he was when he said he was. But there were still gaps of time unaccounted for, not to mention the alleged mystery miles on the Jeep, the posthole digger, the machete knife, and the missing seat covers.

Police and FBI decided to try to break Ricci with solitary confinement intermixed with intense interrogation. FBI profilers flew back to town to help prepare a verbal game plan for the interrogations. For hours on end, Ricci was pressured to come clean with information about returning the Jeep and where he had been; after all, why would the mechanic lie? "We know you did it," investigators told Ricci.

Through tears, Ricci held firm—he never had the Jeep and had nothing to do with Elizabeth's kidnapping. Finally a frustrated Don Bell lost patience and went after Ricci himself. The veteran cop told Ricci that he knew he was involved with the kidnapping, he wasn't 100 percent sure *how* he was involved, but he knew he was. Ricci answered that he wouldn't be there on his own accord, without an attorney, giving up information on crimes that he had done if he was the kidnapper. Bell told Ricci that police were going to charge him, that they had fibers from Elizabeth's clothing in the car, and that he was going to face a white, middle-aged, female, Mormon jury. Bell outlined his theory that Ricci would kidnap Elizabeth, if she had awakened during a burglary, to avoid going back to prison for life. A clearly broken Ricci could only reiterate that he had nothing to do with the kidnapping, he didn't take the Jeep, and he had no idea who would want to set him up. He said he wanted an apology from Bell once they found the kidnapper. The interview session ended soon after that when Ricci finally demanded a lawyer and stopped talking entirely.

Exasperated by Ricci's continued insistence that he never took the Jeep, police finally offered him immunity from any criminal activity short of kidnapping and homicide. If he was doing something illegal with the Jeep during the ten days from May 30 to June 8, Ricci could tell them and they'd check it out. If it had no connection to the Elizabeth Smart investigation, he would not be charged. Ricci held firm.

▪   ▪   ▪

This drama unfolded completely out of the public awareness; and, for that matter, out of the family's awareness as well. Ed was aware that Ricci had confessed to the home burglaries and that the police were leaning on him hard about the kidnapping, but he didn't know how hard. Fox's McKane was the only person in the media who knew what was going on, and he'd agreed to keep quiet. McKane had received a tip about Ricci the day he was arrested, June 14, and was at Ricci's trailer with a camera crew the next day when police and the FBI came to conduct their search. Not wanting to risk jeopardizing their case by going public just yet, law enforcement asked McKane to hold the story. They promised that if he agreed they would grant him an exclusive when it was time to go public, and they would throw in a one-on-one interview with Chief Dinse.

When McKane finally got the OK from police to go with the story on Sunday night, June 23, nine days had passed since Ricci's arrest and five days had passed since Scott Atkinson had first told the media the details that the kidnapper hadn't threatened Mary Katherine, and the height range of the suspect was raised—two pieces of information that strengthened the case against the six-foot handyman.

Even as McKane's Sunday night report aired, police had already finalized plans to move Ricci to the Utah State Prison the next morning. They no longer needed the beer-drinking charge to keep him behind bars. He was now up on three more counts of theft—more than enough to send him back to prison.

Through his lawyer, David K. Smith, Ricci delivered a public statement proclaiming his innocence in the kidnapping of Elizabeth Smart:

> First, I would like to say I have no knowledge of Elizabeth Smart's abduction, disappearance, or whereabouts. I want to say to the Smart family from my family, Angela, my stepson, and myself, that we pray for her safe return. I have cooperated fully with FBI and police and APP (Adult Probation and Parole). I have taken polygraph tests, been through twenty-two hours of questioning, given blood, DNA, and surrendered my vehicle. The police and FBI have searched my home and shed and have even dug up my garden—and they have found nothing. I think the reason I'm involved is because of my past.

Ricci's statement was printed in all the local papers and broadcast on every TV newscast.

For their part, law enforcement supplied the media with details of Ricci's extensive record: the twenty-three years and six months he'd spent behind bars since 1972; the five paroles, all of them broken; and the incorrigible pattern of criminal behavior. His most serious crime was in 1983 when he shot back at a police officer during a foiled pharmacy heist; the most unflattering blemish on his record was a 1996 conviction for helping steal thousands of dollars' worth of food from a welfare food bank in central Utah.

Finally, the police released information to the public that a search of Ricci's father-in-law's trailer and an adjoining shed had produced two suspicious items—a long, machete-style knife and a tan Scottish-style golf cap. Dave Morse, Sr., Ricci's father-in-law, told reporters that to his knowledge Ricci had never used or been in possession of either item. But the police confiscated the knife, which bore a resemblance to the machete Neth Moul had described (although there was no camouflaged sheath), and the cap, which looked like the one Detective Baird had showed the media earlier. Police said forensic technicians would examine both items.

As Richard Ricci was settling back into prison life at the state facility at the south end of the Salt Lake Valley, a grand jury was scheduled to determine if there were sufficient grounds to charge him with the kidnapping of Elizabeth Smart. Angela Ricci was among those asked to testify, as was auto mechanic Neth Moul.

Sergeant Don Bell and Detective Mark Scharman of the SLCPD made it a point to come to our family meeting at the search center on Tuesday, June 25, eleven days after Ricci's arrest, to tell us personally of the grand jury scheduled for the next day. They arrived wearing coats and ties; they looked like two attorneys about to close a case. They sat at one end of the high council table, and Ed and Lois sat at the other end. It was the first big meeting involving both extended family and the police since the investigation began twenty days earlier. Bell started it off by reciting his credentials, which included working on virtually every major crime in the Salt Lake Valley over the past twenty years, including the Unabomber case (the elusive mail-bomber had struck in Utah in 1981 and 1987). Bell explained to us that the grand jury was a tool that wasn't often used in Utah, but that it was an extremely effective way to get people to come forward quickly. The grand jury was top secret, he emphasized, and we were advised not to tell anyone about it. Bell talked about the evidence stacking up against Ricci. He said he felt strongly that Ricci was the kidnapper. Scharman didn't say much; occasionally he nodded as Bell talked. He also agreed with Bell that someone in the family was interfering with the investigation and it was causing a lot of harm. Everybody in the room knew the detectives were talking about me.

We had many questions. Most of them had to do with the auto mechanic and Ed's old Jeep. According to what we'd read, the mechanic said Ricci met another man when he left the repair shop. Did the detectives know who the second person was? And what did they know about Neth Moul? Was he credible? Bell said he wasn't sure that there even was a second person, and he saw no reason not to believe Neth Moul. Bell talked extensively about Ricci's criminal habits, how he broke into people's houses at night—houses of two families in this very room, he pointed out, looking at Ed and Lois and Phil and Suann—and how he was a habitual criminal and lifelong con man. It was almost as if we were a jury he needed to convince (and a skeptical one at that; while Bell was talking, my sister Angela whispered to me, "It wasn't Richard Ricci").

Still, a somber mood inevitably enveloped the room as Bell continued to paint a noose around Ricci's neck with his words. He praised Ed and Lois for being two of the best people he had ever associated with under such difficult circumstances. But he added that they would probably hate him by the time this was over. We got the feeling that the case was moving into the past tense, that Bell was trying to tell us that the authorities might never prove who did it, and that they may never find the body. But they knew who the kidnapper was—and he was safely behind bars—so we could at least put our minds to rest about that.

In his summary of the investigation, Bell told us that every male inside the crime scene that first morning and in the days leading up to the kidnapping, with the possible exception of one construction worker, had been fingerprinted. Although no one contradicted him at the time, the remark alarmed many throughout the room. Most of the people sitting there had been in the home, and a majority had not yet been fingerprinted. Either the police were lousy record keepers or they were simply ready to button up the case. With Elizabeth still nowhere to be found, neither prospect was at all encouraging.

19

The phone call came Sunday afternoon, the last day of June. Heidi and I were at my parents' house, talking about the case. The Ricci grand jury, the one Don Bell told us was strictly confidential, had been playing out in the courthouse during the week and was all over the news.

The Richard Ricci angle brought a new and different focus to the case. The handyman seemed the likeliest of suspects. He knew the family, he knew the neighborhood, he knew the house, and he easily could have acquired a key to Ed's back door when he worked for him. He was a known burglar who didn't steal just for money, but for the thrills, as evidenced by his bold nighttime burglary at the Adams's house, and by the odd collection of things he stole; the wine goblet police found while searching Ricci's trailer, for instance, came from a set of twelve belonging to Ed and Lois. It was filled with sand and a seashell Ed and Lois had once brought home from a family trip. Richard had left the other eleven goblets and stolen just the one, and then filled it with Smart family memorabilia. The police referred to that as trophy stealing. It wasn't about possessing something for its material value; it was a manifestation of power. Then, too, Ricci was knowledgeable about things like security alarms—he had gone into the Adams's house when he knew the alarm wasn't on. This was something that Elizabeth's abductor seemed to know about as well; he had exited out one of the few doors in the Smart home that was not hooked up to the alarm system.

Beyond the mountain of circumstantial evidence, there was no arguing that Ricci fit the profile police had been publicly nurturing. A review of statements made during three weeks of law enforcement press conferences seemed almost enough to convict Ricci without further deliberation. At various times, police had said, "We may have already talked to this suspect," "We're looking for someone who knew the house and neighborhood," "It's possible that Mary Katherine may have known the abductor because she didn't see his face," and "The kidnapper did not threaten Mary Katherine." Each of those statements fit the case against Ricci.

Then there was the golf cap. The cap police confiscated from Ricci's father-in-law not only looked nearly identical to the cap Dwayne Baird had displayed at the late-night press conference on June 15 (the day after Ricci was arrested), but, of greater significance, it matched the kind of cap Mary Katherine claimed the kidnapper had worn. In an attempt to help Mary Katherine identify the "strange cap" she had seen on the kidnapper's head, one of the investigators had collected about a half-dozen different styles of caps and hats and placed them in a row. Then he had Mary Katherine look at the hat lineup. The golf cap, she told them, was the closest to what she thought the kidnapper had worn.

It wasn't much of a stretch to imagine that Ricci, wearing his father-in-law's cap, could have slipped out of his trailer in Kearns the night of June 4 while his wife was under the influence of prescription medication, traveled across the valley to the Smarts' for a nighttime thrill burglary, and inadvertently awakened Elizabeth in the process. Perhaps he panicked and abducted her because she could identify him, which under the three-strikes law would have sent the perennial con to prison for the rest of his life.

But problems persisted in fitting Ricci to the crime. Ironically, the assistant district attorney, Kent Morgan, and Chief Dinse made statements to the media that compromised the case against Ricci. Morgan told the *Salt Lake Tribune* that there was no physical evidence connecting Ricci to the crime scene, and Dinse told the same publication that Mary Katherine hadn't seen enough to warrant a sketch.

Morgan's and Dinse's comments begged answers. If it was a burglary gone bad, where was the physical evidence linking Ricci to the crime scene? Was he such an accomplished thief that he could enter and leave without a trace? And wouldn't Mary Katherine, who was quite familiar with the friendly handyman, have recognized him, even in the dark and even if he hadn't directly threatened her? And finally, how could police account for the fact that Ricci was more than six feet tall? If Ricci was Elizabeth's abductor, the smoking gun was yet to be found.

I told Heidi that I would like to talk to someone in the FBI about the case, particularly after Don Bell's visit to our family meeting. The SLCPD sergeant hadn't left much room for the possibility that the abductor was anyone other than Ricci. But what if the police were wrong? Shouldn't there be a B scenario out there? Shouldn't all leads be exhausted?

That's when the phone rang. FBI agent Mick Fennerty was on the line. He wondered if Heidi and I could pay him a visit at his office downtown.

Although the case was nearly four weeks old and Agent Fennerty had been working it since the first day, we had not met before. Special Agent Ken Crook had been my main FBI contact, but he was being taken off the case. Crook had always been helpful and forthright. He didn't brush me aside when I asked him a question. In my view, he was a standup guy. I hated to see him go.

Mick Fennerty was Utah's lead Crimes Against Children agent. That was about all we knew about him prior to our meeting. It was my first visit to the FBI office since my seven-hour polygraph. I hoped this visit would be more pleasant, and much shorter.

Fennerty met us at the door and got us through security. Tall and lean, he had a runner's build. There was no tough-guy look to him, and although he was in his mid-thirties he could pass for much younger—and he sometimes did, he told us, when he went on Internet porn stings dressed as a thirteen-year-old boy or girl.

There was almost no one there that Sunday. Heidi and I pulled up some chairs around Fennerty's cubicle and got acquainted.

"You might see some bad things here," Mick said. He told us about the serious effort that the FBI was making to bust cybercrimes. His department had won the FBI Directors Award in 2002 and there had been widespread coverage of a couple of its big stings that resulted in the arrests of a nationwide web of pedophiles. Within five minutes of meeting him, one thing was clear about Mick Fennerty. He hated people who hurt kids.

We started to talk about the case and, to our surprise, he talked as much as we did, maybe more. The usual routine with law enforcement was we'd ask questions and they'd answer them in short, cryptic sentences, giving away no more than they had to. When we were out of questions, the conversation was over. But our conversation with Fennerty was a two-way street. When he couldn't answer a question, he wrote it down, so he could answer it later. Heidi and I found ourselves relaxing. We felt we could talk freely.

We brought up Richard Ricci. "Interesting possibilities there," said Fennerty, but he did not believe Ricci was the kidnapper. In fact, Ricci wasn't even among his top ten suspects, but somewhere farther down the list— maybe closer to my name, he joked. Fennerty had been through a couple of heated discussions about Ricci with others on the task force. He was decidedly in the minority in his belief that Ricci wasn't the abductor. Some of his colleagues had even wanted to indict Ricci. Fennerty had challenged one of them to write up an indictment; he knew there was no physical evidence. The prints from the crime scene were not Ricci's, and after hundreds of male neighbors, construction workers, family members, and friends of Ed and Lois had been printed, they still had not been identified. More significantly, the only eyewitness, who knew Ricci well, said it wasn't him. Mick had suggested that the investigators play a recording of Ricci's voice to Mary Katherine since she said the voice of the kidnapper was familiar, and Ricci had a very distinct voice. "Play a recording of his voice for her and if she says it is not him, then let's end the investigation into him and move on." he said.

Many of Fennerty's fellow investigators laughed at the idea of taking Ricci off the suspect list, but they did take his suggestion of playing a voice tape for Mary Katherine. Don Bell took recorded excerpts from Ricci's police interviews and played them for Mary Katherine. She told him that the voice on the tape was not the kidnapper's. Rather than removing Ricci from the suspect list, however, the agents rationalized that a hushed voice during the kidnapping wasn't comparable to the voice from the interview. For Fennerty, the voice experiment was enough to put Ricci way down the suspect list.

Fennerty explained that there should be trust between law enforcement, the family, and to some extent the public and the media. He said that

even though law enforcement had to look at the family because of the likelihood a family member might be involved, the family also may have the
clues necessary to solve the case. He also told us that it isn't necessary to
find a body to solve a case. As much as he wanted Elizabeth returned, he
said his main focus was finding the perpetrator before he did it again. He
shared with us a personal experience his own family had gone through with
a kidnapping. I got the impression he was being as open with us as he could
because he wanted us to work together and be allies. The longer we spoke,
the clearer it became that this guy was obsessed with solving this crime. He
looked tired and drawn, and, working Sunday, he clearly wasn't worried
about working overtime; all that seemed to matter to him was the investigation.

After talking for more than two hours, he said, "Now for the reason I
called you down here." He looked directly at me. "Do you know Herb
Pavey?"

I said, "Yeah, he's my neighbor."

"How well do you know him?"

"Pretty well. We had dinner with Herb and his wife, Patti, just last
night."

Fennerty rustled through the papers on his desk and came up with a
photocopy of a cancelled check I'd made out to Herb Pavey. In the "For" line
I had written, "Sexual favors."

"What's the check for?" Mick asked.

Heidi and I both burst out laughing. I told Fennerty that a few months
earlier I had bought some horse panels from Herb. The "sexual favors" line
was a joke, I explained—an old, well-worn (Heidi would say worn-out) joke—
and maybe not particularly funny given that the edition of the *Enquirer*
about the Smart family sex ring was still on America's newsstands.

"Is there anyone else you've written checks like this to?" Mick asked.

I named off four or five of my best friends. I said, "If I'm actually going
out for sex I don't think I'm going to be putting that in the memo, Mick."

"Yeah, I know," he said. "I just had to ask."

■   ■   ■

Receiving a positive reception at the FBI was encouraging, and Heidi and I left Fennerty's office with new hope about working with law enforcement.

At a meeting prior to our next family press conference, we told the rest of the family about Mick Fennerty. They all had a good laugh about my being questioned by the FBI for the "sexual favors" notation on my check. All except Dad, that is, and he didn't find it amusing at all.

"Dad, you can cut my right arm off," I replied, "but please, don't take away my sense of humor."

My siblings wanted to meet Agent Fennerty and have a chance to express their concerns to him. I called Fennerty and told him I was coming down. When he opened the security door he was clearly taken aback when he saw that I had brought along Heidi, Chris, and David. "Wow, almost the whole crew," he said.

We sat down in a back cubicle. One by one, and sometimes at the same time, we fired away at Fennerty, telling him our frustrations and our fear that some people in the Salt Lake City Police Department were trying to close the case. As we talked, he quietly jotted down notes on a pad. After more than an hour there was a collective sigh of relief. This guy was being straight with us and treating us like members of his team. We got the clear feeling that we could ask him anything. After spending time with Fennerty, our question about whether to hire a private investigator ended—we couldn't hope for a better liaison.

The latest lead that had come to our attention involved a person who lived near Ed who was being questioned about several catalogs police had found in his possession, including some that featured bondage pornography. As had happened several times before, we learned about the lead in a roundabout way. A mutual friend had called Zeke, my sister Angela's husband, to ask if we knew about the pornography and its possible connection to the kidnapping. Zeke called Ed, who called the SLCPD and received a confirmation that the police knew all about the lead and had been working on it for more than a week. Because it sounded as if it might be a substantial development, we asked Fennerty what he knew about it.

"What are you talking about?" he asked. He'd heard nothing about it.

Publicly, the FBI and SLCPD did whatever they could to promote the image that they were working well together. In some instances it was true; they often teamed up for interviews, and most of the management of both departments bought into the Ricci theory. But there were still leads and evidence that were not being shared, the pornography lead (which soon dead-ended) being the latest example. It alarmed us, we told Fennerty, that the FBI and the SLCPD seemed unaware of each other's activities. We told him about the family meeting with Don Bell and Mark Scharman when we had been assured that all members of the family who had been in Ed's home had been fingerprinted, even though we knew that wasn't the case. Fennerty told us the FBI was getting that same incorrect information from the SLCPD.

In addition to our concerns about the fingerprints and the lack of cooperation, there was also the persistent nagging concern about the unnamed law enforcement sources the media used to cast suspicion on the family.

While it was true that the *Enquirer* story had never made its way into respected media reports, locally or nationally, the collateral damage was nonetheless considerable. An undercurrent suggested the Smarts were not what they appeared to be. Not long after the article appeared, Heidi and Nicole were at an auto repair shop near our home picking up one of our cars. When they told the counter man their last name to get the car, a discussion began about the kidnapping, which was not unusual. But this time an older man in the reception area overheard the conversation and piped in. "I know who did it," he said. "It's that weird uncle. The gay one. She's probably not alive at all." Heidi and Nicole left the repair shop in tears.

Just after the *Enquirer* article was published, Tom Smart got a knock on his door. Not the Tom that surprises me in the mirror every day, but Thomas Toland Smart, a former classmate of mine at East High School. His father, William B. Smart, is a distant cousin to my father and was also the bishop in the Federal Heights Ward to whom I had to confess after "borrowing" my scoutmaster's car when I was fourteen. Our lives were further entwined when I started working at the *Deseret News*, where Bill was the executive editor. Over the years we have remained good friends and shared many adventures.

When the knock came on Tom's door, it wasn't the first time he had been mistaken for me. His visitors introduced themselves as reporters for the *National Enquirer*. One had an English accent and said he wanted to talk about the kidnapping. They showed him their press credentials and, in comradely tones, said something about journalists needing to stick together. Tom told them they were obviously mistaking him for Elizabeth's uncle. He explained our relationship and told them he didn't know anything about the kidnapping other than what he read in the papers. The reporters didn't believe him. They got pretty pushy until, finally, after Tom almost started shouting at them, they accepted his word. They asked if he knew where they could find me, but Tom said he didn't think I would want to talk to the *National Enquirer*, and they left. Tom told me that after they took their leave he kicked himself when he realized he'd missed an opportunity to take part in the *Enquirer*'s world of checkbook journalism. He later joked, "What I wish I'd said was, 'Yes, I am Tom Smart, give me a thousand dollars and I'll tell you everything I know.'"

In an effort to stop the false information and law-enforcement rumors and leaks that were the source of so many problems, Ed and I made an appointment to meet with the mayor of Salt Lake City, Rocky Anderson. We also wanted to speak about our concerns that the SLCPD was not sharing some very significant information with the FBI, and that the police seemed to be trying a little too hard to close the case with Ricci.

To our relief, the mayor, a talented politician and formerly a tough civil trial attorney, not only agreed to see us, but could not have been more sympathetic. A decade earlier, Anderson had represented, pro bono, families and friends of three girls—Lisa Strong, Tiffany Hambleton, and Christine Gallegos—who were murdered, along with a fourth victim named Carla Maxwell, between 1985 and 1986 in the Salt Lake City area. Two SLCPD investigators, Don Bell and Jim Bell (no relation), handled the case and for years no one was convicted. The cops seemed certain the murderer was a convict named Paul Ezra Rhodes who was already serving time in Idaho. Anderson and his clients didn't believe the evidence pointed to Rhodes. They thought the police had conducted a sloppy investigation and were covering their mistakes and ignoring clues that might bring the killer, or killers, to justice. Anderson filed a memorandum with the court that included blunt accusations that "evidence reflects that Sergeant Don Bell had lied to his superiors in the SLCPD about investigative efforts and the information provided to the Homicide Task Force." Largely because of the persevering families and friends, the help of senior SLCPD personnel, and Anderson's efforts, Forrest Whittle was ultimately convicted of Lisa Strong's murder. The murders of Tiffany Hambleton, Christine Gallegos, and Carla Maxwell remain unsolved.

The similarities between the investigation of the murder cases and Elizabeth's kidnapping alarmed the mayor. In both instances, it seemed that Don Bell and other investigators were so rigidly committed to one theory that it prevented them from aggressively pursuing other avenues. Mayor Anderson said he would not tolerate any kind of railroaded conviction of Ricci or anyone else, nor would he put up with departmental leaks to the media.

Within a day of our meeting, the mayor sent a memo to Police Chief Dinse outlining "significant concerns about the numerous apparent leaks of information...during the course of the investigation in the Elizabeth Smart case. Those with information have been provided it because of their position of public trust. Any unauthorized disclosure of information constitutes a flagrant breach of that trust." The mayor's memorandum referenced the earlier murder cases and stressed his concern that a repeat of past mistakes should not be permitted. The meeting with the mayor took place just before the Fourth of July, and we felt encouraged. Anderson's support made a huge difference.

We found it was much better to celebrate our small triumph than to dwell on thoughts of the previous Fourth of July, when the entire family had spent the holiday together, with Elizabeth right in the middle of the action. My parents had paid everyone's way to Boston and then we'd rented a tour bus to visit LDS Church sites across the eastern part of the United States. Back then, at age thirteen, Elizabeth was in the middle of the cousins' pack—a quiet, unassuming member of the crowd, popular but unobtrusive. As usual, she shied away from any unnecessary attention. It was difficult to single out Elizabeth at any particular event, other than the time her swimsuit turned from red to pink because of the chlorine in a pool.

One month after the kidnapping, a day after the Fourth of July, Larry King flew to Salt Lake City to tape a special *Larry King Live* broadcast on the status of the case. He arranged to interview family members at Angela's home. Ed, Lois, and my parents, along with all of Ed's siblings and two of Lois's brothers, Stan and Dave, were there. Eleven is a large group to set up and it's difficult to mike everyone properly. I'm sure I didn't merit a mike because of the four-hours-of-sleep rule. I think my family was also trying to spare me a repeat of my embarrassing interview on *Larry King Live* three weeks earlier.

My brother Chris and I were the only ones not miked for this taping. All the family members were articulate whenever King called on them. The show centered mostly on Ed and Lois and my parents, with occasional comments from all who were wired. During the program King talked about the faith of the family and asked if everyone would be in church worshipping on Sunday.

I couldn't help myself, "All but one," I answered.

"Well, you don't have a mike on, so you don't count," joked King. As he left the house after the interview, he whispered to me, "That's all right, I won't be in church either."

The following Sunday, Angela had the entire Smart clan over for dinner in her backyard. It was great watching the cousins enjoying each other's company, playing soccer and basketball, swinging from the trees—just as they had before the kidnapping.

To be together and escape the craziness for a few hours was comforting, but it was hard not to discuss the case. After a while I walked into a corner of the yard with Ed and started talking about the latest news. One by one, each of our siblings noticed our conversation and wandered over and joined the group, until all six of us were standing together in a tight circle sharing information. After a while, we heard Lois shout from across the yard. We looked over to find all of our spouses gathered in a similar circular formation performing an impromptu parody of us, including hand signals to accentuate our intensity. "Hey, how's it going?" they shouted. "We have the 'out-laws' over here and the 'in-laws' over there. The 'non-bloods' here and the 'bloods' over there." We all burst out laughing as our spouses, who had endured the Smart mania for more than a month, sent us the not-so-subtle message, "Can't you just let it go for a few minutes and enjoy the day?"

Don Bell came to meet again with the family on Monday, July 8. Kathy Wilson had asked for the sergeant's assistance in coordinating regional searches. She hoped to get police input on new places to look. Based on Bell's attitude about Ricci the last time he met with us, I chose to stay away from the meeting. It turned out to be a wise move for my blood pressure.

From the reports I got after the meeting, the discussion had soon moved from where to look for Elizabeth to where to look for a body. "I asked him to give us a number," remembered Kathy. "I asked him to tell us what were the percentages that it was Richard Ricci. He said there was less than one-half of 1 percent chance that it wasn't. When Bell left, everyone was just devastated."

But while most of law enforcement, the auto mechanic, the media, and public opinion continued to focus on Ricci as the kidnapper, he did have one significant person on his side.

While Ed and Lois did their best to keep news about the investigation from their children, it wasn't always possible. One afternoon, that first week of July, the television was on during the day when a teaser for that night's newscast came on. Mary Katherine was sitting near the television and saw a familiar face flash on the screen. It was the man who used to work on their house. Mary Katherine looked up with a quizzical expression. "They don't think it's Richard, do they?" she said.

A day or two after that, Mary Katherine was playing in the yard with a cousin when the two girls started talking about the kidnapping. In a conversation the other little girl's father later relayed to Ed, who in turn notified the police, Mary Katherine confided to her cousin, "They think it's Richard. But it isn't."

20

In the third week of July, about a month after the family's meeting with Bell, we were on a search of the desert about a hundred miles west of Salt Lake City. We were working out of makeshift headquarters at a place called Simpson Springs, one of the original Pony Express stops. From 1860 until the invention of the telegraph in 1861, Pony Express riders from Missouri to Sacramento stopped every twelve to twenty-five miles for a fresh mount and a plate of beans. The trail out of Salt Lake City steered due west to the sagebrush, on the way to Reno, the Sierra Nevada, and the California coast. It was as crowded as the western Utah desert ever got.

About a month before our search, a trucker had called in a tip to police about a light-colored Jeep he'd spotted heading out of the desert. After subsequent reports about Ricci and his white Jeep, police considered the information worth checking out. Cory Lyman, who had taken over as task force commander of the Elizabeth Smart investigation, and Don Bell alerted the family about the trucker's tip and said they felt it was a place we might want to organize a volunteer search. They handed out maps of the area between Delta and Rush Valley, roughly a hundred square miles of sagebrush and little-traveled back roads.

It was the first time I'd met Lieutenant Lyman. He was a towering presence, about six-foot-five and solid. I sat down after the meeting to talk to him. If Ricci was the kidnapper, I told him, I thought it would be important to locate the posthole digger Neth Moul said Ricci had lifted out of his Jeep on June 8. I asked Lyman a number of questions. Had the police searched for the posthole digger along the route from the mechanic's shop to Ricci's home, about fifteen blocks away? Had they checked with Mitchell's Nursery, Ricci's employer, to find out if the company was missing one? If Ricci owned a posthole digger, where was it now? Had it been checked for DNA evidence?

After I asked my questions, Lyman leaned forward and informed me that the posthole digger wasn't important. "Almost everyone has one of those, including me," he said.

I was surprised. Whenever I worked on a fence, I was always looking for some rancher or farmer to borrow a posthole digger from. I did not own one. Neither, based on my experience in trying to borrow one, did almost anyone I knew. What was clear to me was that Cory Lyman didn't need or want any input from me. That was the last time I tried to have any serious discussion with the police. The rest of the family watched my interaction with Lyman and had the same impression; he was trying to put me, an outsider, in my place. It became something of a joke; the family had a standing offer that anyone who would go to Lyman's house and find out if he actually owned a posthole digger would get fifty dollars.

We organized a volunteer search around Simpson Springs for the next day, a Saturday. I knew that this search was based on a substantial lead. Was this where Ricci had put the thousand miles on his Jeep? Was this where he had used the elusive posthole digger?

The land around Simpson Springs certainly qualified as a place you might discard something you never wanted to see again. Except for the commemorative Pony Express markers, the road that passes Simpson Springs is nothing but dust all the way to Nevada and beyond—a lure for dirt-bikers, ATVers, government chemical testing, and the occasional horse club reenacting the old days. It's not the kind of place anyone stays for long.

About thirty volunteers showed up riding ATVs, dirt bikes, and SUVs. Rob Birkinshaw, a dedicated volunteer and sympathetic father of nine who had lost two of his daughters to an incurable disease, had put out a call on www.utahatvtrails.com; overnight he had recruited most of the motorized searchers. He had done the same with the first big ATV search at Delle and many others over the past month.

The night before, Mike Freed, my father, and I met with a geographic expert, sectioned maps into grids, and made copies for the volunteers. It looked a lot easier on paper than it was in reality. The desert is vast, and when you're looking for something specific, it's even more so. But we spread out from Simpson Springs, and a little after noon the small group searching with my dad found something worth investigating—an indentation in the ground, not far from a burned-out campfire. The slightly sunken area was roughly six feet long and had some Visqueen plastic sheeting sticking out of one end. It looked like it might have been dug within the past few months. It also looked like it might be a shallow grave. Larry Holmstrom—or Agent Holmstrom, as we affectionately called him—wanted to dig immediately. But cautious minds prevailed and we called the FBI and police.

During the ensuing three-hour wait, my dad's cardiac arrhythmia started acting up. The strain was getting to him. For more than a month he'd scoured the streets of Salt Lake, the banks of the canyon streams entering the Salt Lake Valley, the forests in the foothills, and many other areas around the state. This was his third trip to the western desert. But waiting for the police outside Simpson Springs finally broke him. He was still physically capable of more searches, but emotionally he was finished. He watched as hawks circled in the desert sky high above him, and then he stared down at the mysterious hole at his feet. He realized that if there was a body down there, he didn't want to be around to see it. He wasn't sure his heart could take it.

Finally several law enforcement officers and a cadaver-sniffing dog arrived from Tooele, the nearest city. After the dog poked around the dirt and raised no alarms, we dug up the long, narrow hole. All there was inside was garbage—leftovers from campers who had packed it in but hadn't wanted to pack it out.

Relieved but exhausted, we got into the trucks and headed back to our cars at Simpson Springs, which is when I happened to find out that there was a special name for what law enforcement was doing to Ricci.

For the past month, they had held Ricci in the state prison, where they denied him visitors, phone calls, shaves, haircuts, hot water, hot meals, and yard time. He was confined to a hot cell in the maximum-security unit. There he spent twenty-three hours a day. His only contact with the outside world was his lawyer, and when they met at the prison, the guards shackled and cuffed Ricci and put a hood over his head to deliver him to the sessions.

Ricci had spent three-quarters of his adult life at the state prison, but it had never been like this. Although his cell was not far from the mainstream prison population, where he had many friends and associates and knew most of the guards by name, he might as well have been on the moon. Not even his mother could visit him.

Into this isolated state of confinement, interrogators tried a variety of tricks to convince their captive that he had no choice but to confess. They pressured him to get the inevitable over with. Only then would he regain a few prison privileges or the option of serving time in a less unforgiving institution.

"Know what we call that?" said one of the law enforcement officers as we drove together across the dusty desert. "Excuse the language, but we call that the Jedi mind fuck."

Being an inmate was the one thing Ricci had managed to do with sustained success in his otherwise troubled, addicted life. His weakness was drugs; his strength, his personality. If people didn't like what he did, they tended to like him personally (as Ed and Lois could attest). He was a lovable bad guy.

Richard Albert Ricci was born in December 1953 to Richard and Katherine Ricci. He grew up a middle child with a sister four years older and a brother ten years younger. His father had two sons from a previous marriage, Ricci's half-brothers, whom he didn't see much. The Riccis lived in the Millcreek area of the Salt Lake Valley, a place of developing middle-class neighborhoods in the 1950s. Ricci's dad was a truck driver who spent a lot of time on the road away from home. As compensation, his stay-at-home mom doted on her son.

Wiry and always on the move—what his mother called, in the vernacular of her day, her "active" child—Ricci played baseball, skied, and joined the

Boy Scouts. When he was eight he was baptized into the LDS faith, the church to which his mother also belonged.

It wasn't exactly a formula for juvenile delinquency, and the two other Ricci children gave their parents no more than the normal challenges, but over the years Richard graduated from being an active child to a problem child. "Every family has one to some extent, I guess," remembered Katherine Ricci. "He just started hanging out with the wrong crowd. And then, what really did it was the drugs. Oh, how I hate those drugs."

As a teenager, Ricci developed closer relationships with the local cops than with his teachers. He dropped out of school before completing his first term at Olympus High School, a fifteen-year-old on the streets. His youth saved him from serious trouble for a few years and then, after he turned eighteen, he joined the U.S. Navy and successfully completed basic training. But what might have developed into a prolonged period of structure and discipline turned into a discharge. Ricci contracted hepatitis and the Navy had no choice but to send him back to his home and his habits. Less than a year later, he went to prison for the first time on a second-degree burglary conviction. He did two years and two months of hard time before winning the first of his five paroles.

After his initial twenty-six month stay at the Utah State Prison, he walked back into freedom and stayed out long enough to marry and father a son, Richard. They called him Little Ricky.

In February 1977, Ricci returned to prison for attempted burglary and parole violation. He was paroled two years later but was back behind bars six months after that for another parole violation. Eleven months later he was out again.

His criminal offenses to that point had been relatively minor, but Ricci hit the big time in 1983 when he was convicted of a first-degree felony for shooting at a police officer while trying to escape after a botched pharmacy burglary. In that case, SLCPD officer Michael Hill fired at Ricci and Ricci fired back with a sawed-off shotgun. The blast grazed Hill's head, leaving five pellets in his hand and one in his scalp. Ricci was convicted of attempted criminal homicide and aggravated robbery, both first-degree felonies for which he was sentenced to serve consecutive five-to-life sentences.

Two years into his sentence for shooting the police officer, Little Ricky, at the age of eight, was hit and killed by a drunk driver. According to those close to him, Ricci took the death very hard despite, or perhaps because of, not having spent much time with his son. He was not released from prison to attend the funeral.

He remained in prison ten more years, until the summer of 1995, when he presented himself, at the age of forty-one, to the parole board as clean, sober, and reformed. His prison record seemed to back him up. He had become something of a star inmate. He was part of the prison firefighter's group, an elite team, by prison standards, of fit men sent to fight forest fires and work on conservation projects outside the prison walls. He practiced his guitar; wrote songs; played football, basketball, and baseball; was a work-out room regular; and even got serious about school, completing a degree in botany. Prison also got him off booze and heroin. He won his fourth parole.

This one lasted seven months, until he was convicted of a third-degree felony for stealing hundreds of cases of food from the Central Utah Food Sharing facility. Ricci argued that he didn't actually steal the food, he just stored it, but he went back to prison nonetheless for another three years. At the age of forty-six, he won parole for the fifth time. When he stepped out of the prison on September 12, 2000, he promised he would never return, and the parole board promised that if he ever did, he would be locked up for good.

The conditions of his parole stipulated that he abstain from all drugs and alcohol, that he avoid association with anyone he'd known in jail—essentially all his friends of the past quarter-century—and that he find a legal way to support himself. It wouldn't be easy.

As a law-abiding citizen, he failed miserably—and that's counting only the Smart and Adams burglaries. He also slid back into heroin use in December 2001. Probation reports show that he was nearly sent back to prison, but went instead for rehab at Valley Mental Health.

By 2002 it was looking as if Ricci just might outrun his past and make it on the outside. He was regularly attending a twelve-step program in an attempt to overcome his addictions; he secured steady employment; and, most significantly, he found his soulmate.

He and Angela were married on Valentine's Day at a casino reception hall in Mesquite, Nevada, just across the Utah border, where Ricci's sister, brother, mother, and father were all living. Angela and her eleven-year-old son had a trailer in Kearns, next door to Angela's parents, which is where the new family of three set up residence. Ricci romanced his new wife and spoiled his stepson. He spent a good deal of time gardening, cultivating his yard using botany skills he'd learned in prison. He even made an occasional appearance at the local LDS congregation, the Kearns Tenth Ward, where he developed a friendly relationship with the bishop, David Morrow. Angela's son began the missionary discussions to prepare for baptism. The Riccis, trying to make ends meet but not quite getting there, accepted welfare assistance from Bishop Morrow. In return, Ricci did janitorial work at the wardhouse and worked at the LDS food bank in nearby Magna. It was a big turnaround for an ex-con who six years earlier had done time for stealing from just such a place.

Finally, on May 17, 2002, Ricci landed a steady job when his botany teacher in prison, Lee Mitchell of Mitchell's Nursery, hired him to wait on customers and work with the plants at his business on the east side of the valley, not far from where Ricci was raised.

People who associated with Ricci at the twelve-step meetings, at the Kearns Tenth Ward, at Mitchell's Nursery, and at the trailer park in Kearns didn't see a drug-abuser and a thief; they saw a devoted husband, father, citizen, wage-earner, and taxpayer.

When law enforcement came by Mitchell's Nursery, not only was Ricci's alibi confirmed—yes, he worked all the shifts he claimed he worked—but also his good character. His coworkers gave him glowing reviews. "A pleasure to work with," "Real good with the customers," and "No problem at all" were some of the comments. It was the same at the Kearns Tenth Ward. Bishop Morrow told investigators Ricci was a likeable man who was willing to do whatever was asked of him.

"I really think he was trying to turn his life around," said the bishop. "We got acquainted from various discussions in my office. He talked a lot about the son he lost. He was very interested in his stepson's missionary lessons. He wanted him to be involved in Boy Scouts."

After he was sent back to prison, Ricci sent Bishop Morrow a letter, which the bishop shared with authorities.

"Bishop," he wrote, "I testify I have nothing to do with kidnapping any of our Father-in-Heaven's children. I love children. I would never do anything like that."

By far his biggest advocate was Angela, his bride of four months who vigorously defended her husband and herself. She never wavered in her testimony that she and Ricci were side-by-side in bed the entire night of June 4 and the early morning of June 5, and that neither of them had touched the white Jeep since dropping it off for fuel pump work at Neth Moul's shop in mid-May. As for Moul's statement that seat covers had been taken from the vehicle, Angela insisted there were no seat covers in that Jeep, the mechanic's story couldn't be correct. On television, in the newspapers, anywhere she could spread the word, Angela Ricci stood by her man.

When Angela learned she was not permitted to visit her husband, she wrote the prison, begging officials to reconsider. Ricci was yet to be arraigned on any of the new burglary charges and hadn't yet been convicted of anything. The letter came back from the prison stamped, "Request Denied! Try Back in 2005!"

No phone calls were allowed. Ricci could only write and receive letters. In his letters, Ricci described in detail what the authorities were doing to him. He told Angela of the denial of normal privileges such as hot showers and shaves, of his separation from the rest of the prison population, of the loneliness of his cell, the oppressive heat, and the constant interrogations and accusations.

On the outside, too, the momentum in the case against Ricci was building. Added to the Smart and Adams burglary charges came a federal bank-robbery charge for an armed holdup of the Far West Bank in Sandy, Utah, in November 2001. John Remington told authorities he had robbed the bank with Ricci and Rex Young. Remington said that Ricci was the lead person in the bank robbery, that Ricci entered the bank wearing a ski mask and a light-colored jump suit, that he demanded money by waving a nine-millimeter handgun, that he pushed a pregnant woman onto the floor, and that when he collected $1,713 in cash he fled out of the bank and into a stolen white Honda Accord. Remington was the getaway driver. Young was in another vehicle and his role, according to Remington, was to disrupt anyone who might try to follow the getaway car.

Remington also provided the authorities with another intriguing piece of information regarding Ricci. He said Ricci had once mentioned that if he ever again encountered an eyewitness during a burglary, he would kill the witness rather than risk being identified. This information from one of Ricci's longtime criminal companions not only corroborated the law enforcement view that Ricci was a man capable of kidnapping and murder, but it was also distinguished by an unusually high degree of credibility. Remington had nothing to gain from divulging the information. At the time of Remington's meeting with police he was not charged with the Far West robbery. Remarkably, his own remarks actually caused him to be charged with that crime, to which he later pled guilty and received a prison sentence of forty-six months from U.S. District Court judge Dee Benson. According to the assistant U.S. state's attorney who prosecuted the case, and Remington's own lawyer, Remington's revelation of what he knew about Ricci came solely from his genuine concern for the welfare of Elizabeth Smart.

Despite the mounting circumstantial evidence against him and his less-than-desirable living conditions, Ricci refused to admit to knowing anything about the kidnapping. But law enforcement was not out of tricks.

The plan was to make sure Ricci became aware, through the prison grapevine and the media through his attorney, that famed forensic sketch artist Jeanne Boylan had come to Salt Lake City to interview Mary Katherine and, as an outcome of that interview, had produced a likeness of Elizabeth's abductor.

Only part of that story was true. Jeanne Boylan had, at the SLCPD's request, flown to Salt Lake City during the first part of July. She had interviewed Mary Katherine. However, after the interview, which took place at Ed's house, Boylan told the FBI and police that in her opinion there wasn't enough information for an effective sketch. If a sketch were done, in fact, she said it could have a counterproductive effect by distorting Mary

Katherine's sharp but fragile memory. Boylan said that although it was very dark, Mary Katherine had a brief frontal glimpse of the man. She also described a hat consistent with the golf cap, but that the brim was pulled down unusually low on the forehead. Mary Katherine didn't mention facial hair and said that the abductor's hair was short. She thought she could see the back of his hairline. Boylan concluded that it was better to leave Mary Katherine's mind alone and not risk confusing any images locked inside.

Ricci wasn't told any of this. He was told just the opposite: that after talking to Mary Katherine, Jeanne Boylan had produced a sketch law enforcement was going to use to catch the kidnapper. After letting him stew on that news for a few days alone in his cell, FBI and police investigators showed him a bogus sketch—one that looked very much like Ricci.

Because they were convinced Ricci was the kidnapper, the police considered their subterfuge fair play. The fact that Mary Katherine, who continued to insist that Ricci was not the kidnapper, hadn't seen enough of the kidnapper to produce a reliable sketch helped bolster the police's theory that even someone the little girl knew fairly well could have been the perpetrator.

Investigators reasoned that it wouldn't have been out of character for a con man like Ricci to know of the need to disguise his voice, and even to hunch down so he looked shorter. That would explain why Mary Katherine failed to identify a recording of Ricci's voice as that of the kidnapper, and why she thought he was shorter than he really was.

But the fake sketch did not work. When Ricci looked at the drawing of himself he scoffed at it. He refused to take the bait. He reacted by reiterating he had not kidnapped Elizabeth Smart, or anyone else, and he did not know who did. He sent word back to his wife, warning, "Don't let them trick you."

Ricci's letters were his only connection to the outside world. He wrote to members of his family and others, but especially to his wife, whom he referred to as "My best ally!"

"This is no joke," he wrote Angela, but then he made a joke of his own. "I was thinking here's something for a tee shirt: 'Ricci Didn't Do It.' And then on the back side 'Where Were You On June 4th?'"

He never wavered in maintaining his innocence of the crime. As he wrote in a letter Angela made available to the media:

I guess the only thing I would like the public to know would be I really don't know anybody who would kidnapp [sic] a child.... They need to focus their suspicions on real leeds [sic]. I had nothing to do with abductions. What is their problem? The FBI and police have Ed believing I had something to do with this. I think it lies in the neighborhood somewhere, or club, or even church!

21

In the state of Utah, July 24 is known as Pioneer Day. Businesses close and work shuts down, as Utahans commemorate the 1847 arrival of 148 Mormon pioneers in the Salt Lake Valley. They were the Great Basin's first permanent settlers and the lead wave of thousands of members of the Church of Jesus Christ of Latter-day Saints who would travel twelve hundred miles from Illinois, many on foot, to flee religious persecution. The Mormons chose the place by the large salty lake because they believed God wanted them to—and because no one else wanted it. Even the local Indian tribes, the Shoshone and the Ute, avoided permanently settling in the barren valley, which was known for its harsh, cold winters and hot, dry summers.

The Mormons dammed the mountain streams to water their crops, built cabins with thick mud between the logs to keep out the winter winds, and stayed. One hundred and fifty-five years later, more than a million people, two-thirds of them with Mormon roots, lived along the ninety miles of the Wasatch Front. As usual, many would watch the annual Days of '47 Parade in downtown Salt Lake City and stay close to home to celebrate the holiday. But we knew many others would take off for the mountains or the deserts or the National Parks, increasing the chances of someone seeing something that might lead to locating Elizabeth.

Heidi and I left for the Weber River cabin on Tuesday night, July 23. There we joined Mom, Dad, David, Julie, and their children. Ed, Lois, and their children stayed in Salt Lake City Tuesday night, with plans to join us the next morning. But it wasn't until late afternoon that we heard their car pull up outside the cabin.

"You're not going to believe what happened," were the first words out of Ed's mouth. "There was an attempted break-in at Steve and Jenny's house."

Jenny is Lois's sister and Steve Wright is Jenny's husband. At 3:00 A.M., a picture frame fell off the cedar dresser underneath a window in nineteen-year-old Jessica Wright's bedroom. When Jessica awoke, she saw what looked like a thin object retreating back through the window. Jessica's scream brought her dad running. They collided at the entrance to her bedroom. Together they went over to the window, where they saw that the screen had been cut. The window had been open about six inches at the bottom, stopped by a set screw for security purposes, and there were blinds on the inside. Whoever cut the screen wouldn't have been able to see the set screw, or the picture frame that gave away the intrusion.

Jenny Wright immediately called 911. She was patched into dispatch at 3:10 A.M. "Someone just tried to break in," she blurted out. "They just cut the screen in my daughter's room, and there is a chair at the window. We let the dog out, but we don't see anyone."

"All right, we will get someone there as soon as possible," she was told.

After fifteen minutes and still no response, Steve called 911 again. "It hits home because our niece is the Elizabeth Smart kidnapping," he said in a frenzy, jumbling his words. "My wife is crying…it's the same scenario as what happened to her. Our screen is slit."

The Wrights' house is in the southeast part of the Salt Lake Valley, which places it in the jurisdiction of the Salt Lake County Sheriff's Department, not the Salt Lake City Police Department. When sheriff's deputies arrived at 3:40 A.M., they dusted for prints around the windowsill and on a chair that had been dragged across the lawn and propped up against the wall directly underneath the window. It was a scene eerily similar to the night of Elizabeth's abduction, replicated in almost every detail. The first deputies who investigated the scene were of the opinion that it was someone's sick idea of a prank. But the existence of the chair at the Smart crime scene had never been made public. Only the police and a few people inside the family knew about it. Another thing that wasn't widely known was the relationship between the Smarts and the Wrights.

That information narrowed the prank theory to family insiders and a few close friends, which, if true, made it an even sicker joke. The sheriff's office called SLCPD, but the information was either ignored or lost, as Cory Lyman knew nothing about it until Ed called him nearly four hours after the attempted break-in, around 6:30 in the morning.

The Wrights were frantic at the thought of what could have happened. They remembered back to the evening before and realized there had been signs of an intruder that they had ignored. When Steve and Jenny had returned to their home after an evening out, a ladder was outside the garage. Jenny asked Steve why he had the ladder out. Steve said he hadn't put it there and put it back in the garage. Then, after they turned in for the night, their dog, which was outside, wouldn't stop barking. Steve brought the dog inside to keep the neighbors from complaining. Jessica, who had switched bedrooms with her fourteen-year-old sister, Olivia, just a few months before, said that all night she'd had the feeling she was being watched.

The deputies questioned Jessica, her boyfriend, members of the Wright family, neighborhood friends, residents up and down the street, and anyone else they thought might know something. In the meantime, Steve and Jenny called Ed and Lois, and the two couples talked at length, commiserating with each other while trying to determine if the attempted break-in, with all its similarities, was related to Elizabeth's abduction.

By about 9:00 A.M., Ed started to worry, based on previous experience, that no one had called the FBI. Ed's premonition proved correct. He called Mick Fennerty, who had run the annual *Deseret News* 10K race that morning. Ed's call was the first Fennerty, or anyone in the FBI, had heard about the break-in.

After rushing to the Wrights' house, Fennerty made a quick study of the crime scene. "There are two scenarios here and only two," he said. "It's either a really sick prank and a really ballsy one—or it's the guy." It was the propped-up chair that most intrigued the FBI agent. Fennerty was aware that few knew about the chair at the Smarts' house, and Jessica's bedroom window was not high enough off the ground to need anything to stand on to be reached. "It was like someone was purposely rubbing it in our faces," Fennerty said.

■　　■　　■

As Ed and Lois told us the story, we were each asking ourselves the same questions. Did this mean that whoever took Elizabeth was after her cousins, too? Did it mean she was still alive? Or was it one more sad coincidence?

One thing we knew for certain: Ricci didn't do it. He was in maximum security at the state prison—the ultimate alibi. There was a Ricci wrinkle to the story, however. Steve Wright had an adopted brother who had spent some time with Ricci—at the state prison. As far out as it seemed, the police suggested that Ricci might have orchestrated the whole thing from behind bars. Steve's brother would have to be checked out.

Ed told us that the police preferred to keep the news of the break-in quiet. They wanted to conduct their investigation outside of the media. Since there wasn't an obvious relationship between the Wrights and the Smarts, they were confident it could stay that way, as long as no one in the family said anything.

For a family that had gotten way too used to publicity—and damaging leaks—it wasn't a problem keeping it quiet. But inside the cabin, it was all anyone could talk about. The break-ins were too similar for comfort. If it was just a coincidence, it was a most unsettling one, one that succeeded in terrifying Elizabeth's cousins all over again. You could see it in their eyes as they stayed close to the cabin and talked about it among themselves. Most of them had just started sleeping in their own beds again, six weeks after the kidnapping. For Elizabeth's five brothers and sister especially, the very real fear of being taken rushed back to the surface.

Not all of Elizabeth's siblings were at the cabin. Sixteen-year-old Charles had gone with Angela and Zeke and their family to their cabin near Yellowstone for the holiday. That afternoon, Ed called Angela and asked to talk to Charles so he could tell him what had happened at his cousin's house. Charles's reaction was interesting. He said news of the break-in gave him hope he hadn't felt in weeks. "That gives me hope that she's alive," Charles said to his Aunt Angela after the phone call. "Olivia is Elizabeth's best friend in the family. If she were alive and chose anyone to be with her, Olivia is who it would be." He thought there was a strong possibility that it was Olivia, and not Jessica, who was the target.

The FBI worked the case hard. At Fennerty's direction, dozens of agents canvassed the Wrights' neighborhood, interviewing hundreds of people while scouring the streets for physical clues. They went over the crime scene exhaustively. Amazingly, the sheriff's deputies had told the Wrights that it would be OK to hose down the chair. It was washed clean before the FBI could examine it.

The cut screen intrigued Fennerty, who believed that not many burglars cut screens anymore. Don Bell and Cory Lyman of SLCPD disagreed, insisting that screens were cut all the time in burglaries. (Later, David called several experienced law enforcement personnel who had worked hundreds of breaking-and-entering cases. "Screens are usually popped out. If you are dealing with an old house, with the old-time screen, they may be cut, but if you have an aluminum frame screen, they usually pop them out," one e-mailed back.) Fennerty thought the chances of two screens being randomly cut with a knife at the houses of girls who were cousins were extremely slim at best.

But in the end, no substantive clues were found. No one in the area remembered seeing anything suspicious that night, and in the absence of any real damage, loss, or injury, the sheriff's department passed the incident off as a prank. The case was quietly set aside as inactive and unsolved.

The reality, of course, was that someone had cut the screen and propped up the chair—indisputable facts that left family members more spooked than ever. Both the Smart and Francom families began to take even more aggressive security measures. David and Julie installed a new security system in their home and bought a dog. Others did likewise. At our house, Nicole chose to sleep upstairs for several nights instead of in her downstairs bedroom. When she did return to her room, she took our golden retriever, Mozart, with her. Lack of clues notwithstanding, no one in the family was quick to dismiss the July 24 break-in as a neighborhood holiday prank; after that night, no one related to Elizabeth Smart went to bed without double checking that all the windows were locked.

It wouldn't be until two weeks later that the public would learn about the attempted break-in. On the night of August 7, Scott McKane broke the story on Fox KSTU, scoring an exclusive as he had a month and a half earlier with the Richard Ricci story. Whether it was because they were tired of being scooped by McKane, or jealous, or simply content to believe law enforcement's conclusion that it was a harmless prank, the rest of the local media barely reacted to the news. The early morning incident at Elizabeth Smart's cousin's house was duly reported by the newspapers and television and radio stations, but without any real enthusiasm. Two days after the story broke it was gone.

For the media, as for the police, Ricci remained the likeliest of suspects. At task force headquarters, police made a list of the reasons for and against Ricci being the kidnapper. It was a lopsided list.

PRO	CON
• Neighbors said he could have done it	• Home in bed with wife
• Worked in house, familiar with it	• No record of sexual assault
• Thrill burglar	• No physical evidence linking him to scene
• Friends say they thought he did it	• Mary Katherine didn't recognize him
• Willingness to kill	
• Known to wear type of hat	
• Had the Jeep	
• Stole from Ed's house	
• Stole from the Adams's house	
• Lied to Ed	

At a meeting in mid-August, the task force took an impromptu vote to see how many in law enforcement thought Ricci was the kidnapper. Cory Lyman asked the group of about twenty detectives, police officers, and FBI agents—all of whom knew the case well—to raise their hands if they thought Ricci had something to do with Elizabeth's kidnapping. With the exception of a few who apparently preferred to abstain, every person in the room raised his or her hand. This was followed by another vote: who thought Ricci had nothing to do with the kidnapping? Only one hand was raised—it belonged to Mick Fennerty.

For the family, it was a different story. There were those among us who had never believed that Ricci had anything to do with the kidnapping. The rest of us vacillated between thinking he was not involved at all to thinking he could have been part of a bigger conspiracy. By far the prevailing feeling in the extended family was that Ricci was innocent of the crime.

Ed and Lois tended to think Ricci was involved. Both were influenced by their association with members of the SLCPD, who seemed almost certain it was Ricci. Beyond that, Ed and Lois had personal reasons. As a mother, Lois desperately wanted closure, and Ricci's guilt would at least give her that. As for Ed, his background with Ricci was extensive. He'd employed him, worked alongside him, and sold him a car. He'd trusted him. When Phil Adams lost his computer and said it was Ricci who stole it, Ed accepted Ricci's word that he didn't do it. When the Adams's guest room was broken into and cash was stolen, Ed again believed Ricci when he said he wasn't involved. And when Ricci swore to Ed's face that he hadn't stolen Lois's bracelet, even though Lois felt it was Ricci, Ed accepted him at his word.

Ricci had lied to Ed the entire time they'd known each other; why wouldn't he be lying now? Ed wasn't about to be fooled again. "I don't need any more lies. I need to know the truth," Ed told the newspapers. When Ricci was arraigned in late July on burglary and theft charges, Ed went to the courthouse in downtown Salt Lake City on his own, unannounced, looking for the truth.

The marshals brought Ricci into the courtroom shackled at his wrists and ankles, and wearing an orange prison jumpsuit. His cheeks were sunken, his stringy hair fell nearly to his shoulders, and his beard was starting to fill out. He was pale and had lost quite a bit of weight. He looked like a refugee, not an inmate. When his wife, Angela, sitting in the public gallery, first saw him she gasped audibly. It had been six weeks since he had been taken to prison. She turned away and began to cry.

Ricci was in and out of the courtroom in seconds, saying nothing except for a mouthed "I love you" to his wife on his way out. Denied a chance to talk to Ricci, Ed sought out Angela, who agreed to talk to him. Courthouse administrators found them a quiet room where they could talk privately.

Ed asked Angela to please tell him why Ricci wouldn't explain the extra miles on the Jeep and where it was when he took it out of the repair shop.

"Richard never touched that Jeep," Angela answered, holding Ed's hand. "He can't say what happened to it because he does not know. He's told the police that but they don't believe him." Unnerved by what she had just seen in the courtroom, Ricci's wife pleaded with Ed as much as he pleaded with her. "He didn't do it, he couldn't have done it," she said. "He lost a son once, he wouldn't put a hole like that in anyone else's heart."

To Ed, Ricci was an accomplished con man, he could fool anyone. And it didn't help that Angela had been his wife for less than six months; she didn't know about the break-ins and the bank robbery. What else didn't she know? To Angela, Ricci was the best thing that had ever happened to her and her son. They were both right. The skateboard Angela Ricci's son was riding was the skateboard Ed had bought for his son.

If the police were right and Ricci was the kidnapper, it seemed to me that the best place to look for a trail of evidence was at Neth Moul's auto repair shop. Don Bell had said that Ricci might not have met anyone when he returned the mud-splattered Jeep to the shop. But I went back and read news accounts that quoted the mechanic as saying Ricci did meet another person. If that were true, the person he met might have been an accomplice in the kidnapping—Neth described the mystery man's height as about five-foot-eight, which fit with Mary Katherine's description. In light of almost universal condemnation of Richard Ricci, and with Ricci no longer talking, it seemed of paramount importance to find that person if we wanted to solve the case.

Waiting on the police to solve the mystery became increasingly frustrating. "What is the truth about Neth Moul?" Ed said impatiently one afternoon. "I'd like to go down and find out for myself." He knew the police would not be happy with him if he questioned the mechanic on his own. They wouldn't be happy with me, either, but I was already on their blacklist.

"I'll go talk to him. This is still America," I told Ed. "We aren't trying to obstruct anything; we're just trying to find the truth." David and I stayed after the family meeting and created a list of questions we wanted to ask the mechanic.

Neth Moul was busy when I walked into his shop but he was willing to talk to me when he found out who I was. He was very kind and spoke with a thick Cambodian accent. I had to concentrate to catch his exact meaning. The story he told of Ricci dropping off the car on June 8, three days after the kidnapping, was basically the same one I had heard reported in the media, with two major discrepancies. First, he said the car was covered with a light dust, not "splattered with mud as though he had been four-wheeling" (which is how he was quoted in earlier media and police reports). This was a big contradiction. We had searched throughout the state based on the initial reports and had asked police to clarify what type of mud it was to help in the effort, but we never got a straight answer.

The second difference was when Neth said Ricci not only waved to a man across the street, but that he also observed Ricci and the man walk toward a blue van in a parking lot. Moul also offered other points of clarification. He said there was a small pine bough about twelve inches long stuck in the Jeep's front grill that he removed when he washed off the dust. He showed me the receipt that indicated the extra mileage. He said he'd offered Richard a ride when he returned his Jeep, which was declined. "What's the matter?" Moul said he had asked Ricci, trying to joke with him. But he said Ricci didn't joke back as he usually did. Instead, Ricci removed the machete from the car and put it in a camouflaged sheath, then he got the seat covers and posthole digger and stuffed some of the gear in two plastic bags and waved to the unknown person across the street, who waved back. Toting his gear, Moul said Ricci walked across four lanes of traffic on 3500 South. I asked Moul if the person across the street was either Remington or Young, the two men he occasionally worked with and had allegedly robbed a bank with. Moul said he knew both Remington and Young and the person who met Ricci that day was neither of them.

After listening to the mechanic, I walked away with a new perspective. Maybe it was Ricci. Moul was definitely convincing. I typed up a report of my visit and forwarded it to both SLCPD and FBI, which made Cory Lyman furious. Several officers wanted to arrest me for obstruction of justice. Lyman told Ed that I could have hurt the case by tampering with a witness, and that my report had details that weren't in the official reports from law enforcement. My report and Ed's insistence that there was more to Moul's story led Lyman to take Detective Scharman, who Lyman considered one of his best interviewers, back out to the mechanic's garage. The information they received concurred with mine, leaving Lyman to question the quality of the first reports he'd received. I'd like to think that my background as a journalist made me more observant than law enforcement, but then again, maybe the mechanic's story had changed since he'd first talked to investigators.

With August slipping away and questions still far outnumbering answers, we became more determined than ever to solve the case with brainstorming. We scheduled a family meeting at the Federal Heights wardhouse to thrash out everything we'd learned so far. In advance, Kathy Wilson and I stayed up late several nights, reviewing hundreds of tips from the search center, the We're Neighbors lists, and various police investigations. Hidden in all the minutiae, there had to be a clue.

Someone brought a pad of yellow sticky notes to the meeting, and we began putting them on the walls, listing all known suspects, past and present, and all theories, however implausible.

Through this process, we were able to identify the two questions that bothered us most. Who did Ricci meet, if anyone, after dropping off his Jeep at the auto mechanic's shop? And who tried to break into the Wrights' house?

We decided to offer money for information. We unofficially called the program tips-for-cash. Anyone providing information about the person Ricci purportedly met outside Neth Moul's repair shop on June 8, or any information about who broke into the Wrights' house on July 24, would get three thousand dollars, each, no questions asked. Our theory was that if anyone out there knew what Ricci was up to in the Jeep, three thousand dollars should be enough enticement for that person to come forward, particularly with Ricci behind bars; and if the attempted break-in at the Wrights' house was, in fact, a prank, three thousand dollars ought to be plenty of incentive for the perpetrators (or for those who knew the perpetrators) to admit it and pocket the cash, especially now that weeks had passed. We wouldn't even have to tell the police; the source of the information would remain confidential.

We alerted the media about the tips-for-cash rewards, and sat back with our fingers crossed, heads bowed, and yellow sticky notes everywhere.

22

As soon as they walked through the door, Lindsey Dawson wondered where her robed customers had been keeping themselves. Dawson was manager at the Souper!Salad!, an all-you-can-eat buffet restaurant in the Salt Lake City suburb of Midvale, and she was used to seeing the man and woman in their flowing white robes. They had never been regular customers, but during the past few months they hadn't been in at all.

Dawson had gotten to know them by making it a point to come by their table to ask if everything was all right. She asked them if the fruit was fresh enough—that's what they mostly ate—and if there was anything else she could get for them. Lindsey's personality was nonthreatening, she didn't smirk at what they said, or gawk at what they wore, or visibly recoil at their smell. Over the months a casual sort of friendship had developed. They told her they were messengers of the Lord Jesus, preachers to the downtrodden. The man and woman usually came in during the afternoon, when there were few customers in the restaurant. Lindsey never asked, but she guessed it was to avoid the stares people who dressed like Joseph and Mary unavoidably attracted.

But on this day in early August 2002, Joseph and Mary had walked right in with the 5:00 P.M. dinner crowd. Souper!Salad! was hopping. Dawson had no idea why they had broken their routine. Nor did she have any idea who the third member of their little group was. The new addition was taller than the other woman, and, obvious from her posture and carriage, younger. Maybe she was their daughter, although it was hard to tell because in addition to the robes, the women were wearing veils that covered their faces. Only their eyes, along with a patch of forehead underneath their muslin head coverings, were visible. Dawson had not seen the veils before.

Lindsey Dawson was not alone in noting the return of the robed people to the Salt Lake Valley in early August 2002. After being absent most of the summer, it was suddenly as if the Jesus Man and the woman who walked behind him had never left. At markets, laundromats, bus stops, public parks, all-you-can-eat restaurants, convenience stores, homeless shelters, soup kitchens, and especially on downtown street corners, they were back at their usual haunts, and they had a new follower.

At the city library, a haven for the homeless, the librarians didn't flinch when they saw the Jesus Man again. For several summers now, the man and his female companion had been coming to the library, although they did not check out books and, as far as the librarians knew, they didn't possess a library card between them. They usually sat at a table in the common area on the main floor. The man normally wouldn't stay long. He left the woman for long stretches of time as he went out to the streets to beg (so the librarians learned through the grapevine). The woman would read and knit, and sometimes she wrote page after laborious page of beautiful calligraphy.

But the third woman with them was new, as were the veils that covered the women's faces. That part was unsettling to the librarians. But more than their dress, there was something about these people's body language that made it seem as if they were hiding something. Who was the new, obviously younger, woman? Why was she all covered up?

News of the Elizabeth Smart kidnapping had the people of the Salt Lake Valley on edge. More than two months had passed since the fourteen-year-old had vanished from her home in the middle of the night. The massive community searches had died down, but "Please Find Me" fliers were still ubiquitous, and billboards throughout the city continued to advertise the $250,000 reward for her return. Until she was found, no possibility was too remote, which is what prompted a discreet call from someone at the library to the Salt Lake City Police with a tip that a young woman was there who could be Elizabeth Smart.

Shortly after the call, a Salt Lake City detective arrived at the library. The detective walked directly to the robed man and women. When he asked them who they were, the man told him that they were Peter and Juliette Marshall, traveling with their daughter, Augustine, as servants of the Lord Jesus. The man did the talking, while the veiled women stood behind him and nodded their heads in agreement. Hearing nothing to suggest the Jesus Man was lying, and failing to notice the grip the older woman had on the younger woman's wrist, the detective finally turned to the younger woman and, while looking directly at her, asked, "Are you Elizabeth Smart?"

"No," Elizabeth replied, "I am Augustine Marshall."

Two months and counting since she'd been kidnapped, Elizabeth was free of the cable and shackles that had once kept her tethered to the trees in Dry Fork Canyon. She'd tried to escape from the remote camp once. It happened when she was untied briefly early in her captivity. The Mitchells got into an argument that distracted them for a moment. But an enraged Mitchell saw what was happening and chased Elizabeth down before she got far. As he forced her back to camp, he lectured her about her ingratitude. If she tried anything like that again, he said, he would kill her and then he would hunt down her family and kill them.

Over time, and after dozens more stern lectures, a much stronger restraint than the steel cable took hold of Elizabeth. This cable was attached not to her ankle but to her mind. During the long days and nights of her captivity in the mountains, while she was physically restrained, Mitchell systematically stripped away Elizabeth's identity, just as he had stripped away his own and Wanda's. He had been sent to save her from herself, he told her. He had come to rescue her from the world. She was evil. She came from an evil family. Her parents were lifted up with worldly pride and sought only the praise of man. They worshipped idols and chased worldly riches. The world had corrupted them and they had corrupted her, but he would have patience with her, and he would save her. He was her salvation, he told her.

He gave her a new life and a new name. She was no longer Elizabeth Smart. He called her Augustine, a name he said God had directed him to use. He forcefully subjugated her will to his. She would be obedient, sub-missive, and dutiful. And she would be grateful . . . or else.

Through June and July, the brainwashing continued. There was no escaping the constant verbal barrage, the language sprinkled with "thee," "thou," and "thine"; the constant references to "God's will." Elizabeth was a prisoner of war—a casualty of Mitchell's personal war against society, against family, against God, and against himself. Minute by minute, day by day, Mitchell pecked away at Elizabeth's sense of what was true and real. It was up to him whether she ate, whether she had shelter, whether she lived or died.

And how could she doubt his power? How else, he told the terrified girl, could he have walked through her home, equipped as it was with the security devices of man, and taken her away without a single sound of alarm? He boasted how he had walked through her parents' own bedroom before coming to hers on the morning he took her, and her mother and father hadn't so much as stirred. He boasted that he had kept her hidden at their camp in the mountains in spite of the whole world looking for her. On his trips into the city in the days immediately following the kidnapping, Mitchell brought back newspapers that detailed the massive search for Elizabeth Smart. Planes, bloodhounds, hundreds of police officers, and thousands of searchers had all tried to find her. But God's messenger had lifted her out of the world, and the world would never find her. As he told her all this, his cold, piercing eyes drove home the point.

He showed Elizabeth newspaper photographs of her distraught parents. He made her burn the newspaper clippings while telling her they were no longer her parents. She had a new family now that would shield her from worldliness. The newspapers reported that the Lord had even brought forth a man, a sinner, to account for her disappearance. Richard Ricci was a bless-ing from heaven, a validation that God was pleased with what Mitchell had done.

Playing his role as a prophet of God, Mitchell continued to terrorize Elizabeth, painting a picture that made black into white, and white into black. Up was down and down was up. Now she was Augustine. Elizabeth Smart was dead.

To prove it, Mitchell unhooked the cable from her ankle and they walked to town.

They took the path that led along the dry streambed to the south end of Dry Creek Canyon. At a large scrub oak tree just before the lightly used canyon trail merged with the Bonneville Shoreline Trail, they took off their hiking boots and hung them on the tree's branches. They put on sandals and walked a half-mile along the popular trail until they reached the paved road above the university. There they caught a bus near the hospital. They were less than a half-mile from Elizabeth's house. If the bus had turned right instead of left, Elizabeth could have been home in five minutes. But the bus did not turn right, and as they rode through the city streets to the heart of downtown, they passed fliers and posters with Elizabeth's face on them.

But no one recognized her behind her veil.

From the bus, they stepped into the heart of the place that was feverishly hunting for Elizabeth Smart—and still no one noticed.

And if someone should happen to notice, Mitchell told Elizabeth, he had his knife and he would use it. If he would kidnap for God, he would also kill for God. He would kill anyone who interfered with them, just as he would kill her and her family. He instructed the women to keep quiet; if anyone asked anything of them he would do all the talking. As long as they stayed veiled and silent, they would not be bothered.

The more trips they took into the city without incident, the more it appeared Mitchell was right.

By mid-August they moved to a new campsite closer to the city, only a half-mile up Dry Creek Canyon and no more than a mile and a half from Elizabeth's bedroom. It made for an easier commute to town, and the lower elevation made the nights marginally warmer for sleeping. Mitchell had spent the summer sawing logs and notching branches on his underground lean-to at the upper camp—the structure it appeared they would stay in through the winter. But just when the lean-to was nearly complete, Mitchell abruptly packed them up and moved them to the new site. The lower camp was also located on the west side of the canyon, halfway up a very steep hill and, like the previous camp, well camouflaged. The small sleeping area was set up on a relatively flat piece of ground in a stand of scrub oak. From the edge of the trees, the lights of the Salt Lake Valley were visible to the south during the evenings, while in daytime the bright red seats in the University of Utah football stadium—the site of the opening and closing ceremonies of the recent Salt Lake Winter Olympics— gleamed in the sunlight.

Throughout August 2002, the Jesus Man returned to all his old habits and hangouts. He knew how to use the city to survive. He turned the money he collected from begging into food and drink for his "family." In addition to the soup kitchens and homeless shelters in the downtown corridor, he was no stranger to the markets and convenience stores. Among his regular stops to use the restroom and purchase beverages were the four Maverik convenience stores—particularly the one at 300 South and 500 East, with its large walk-in beer cooler in the rear of the store. It wasn't unusual for Mitchell to leave with a six-pack of beer—something the clerks always found amusing: Jesus buying beer.

The more he walked the women through the streets of Salt Lake City, the bolder Mitchell became in public. He had kidnapped a teenage girl from the bosom of the mother church and, he believed, was parading God's power in front of all those who would one day bow before him. To the congregation of two that walked silently behind him, he mocked the efforts of those who searched for the girl who had once been Elizabeth Smart. In a laundromat one afternoon, he picked up a newspaper and after a few moments, leaned toward Elizabeth. "I see your Uncle David is organizing another search," he scoffed, pointing to the article.

On another day Elizabeth saw good friends of her family, Phil Adams and his son Jeremy, drive down the street, passing close enough that she could have easily waved or shouted to attract their attention. But caged in silence by Mitchell's threats, she only watched from behind her veil as they drove by.

Another time she was eating at the Chuck-A-Rama Restaurant on 400 South when Russell Banz, a youth leader in her LDS Stake, came in with his family and sat at the next table. A month before the kidnapping, Banz had been with Elizabeth on a youth outing. Through the summer, he and his family had participated in numerous searches, and every night his family prayed that Elizabeth would be found. In his day job as the Web site director for KSL-TV, Banz posted story after story about the kidnapping and worked with dozens of images of Elizabeth so others could be on the lookout for her. He had also helped set up a link to download posters from the KSL Web site. He knew Elizabeth's face well. As the young girl passed his table with the older woman, Banz could not help thinking there was something about the eyes behind the veil. It even appeared for a moment, when their eyes briefly met, that the girl might be trying to signal him or connect with him in some fashion. Banz considered for a moment going over and talking to the threesome. But the urge passed, and he didn't.

With every such encounter, the psychological leash on Elizabeth tightened, and both Mitchell and his captive became more convinced of his invincibility. Toward the end of August, Mitchell was emboldened enough to bring the three of them out of the mountains to live in the city. For five nights they stayed at a downtown apartment located only one block from the Salt Lake City police station. Twenty-four-year-old Daniel Trotta, a cashier at the Wild Oats Market, a natural food store on 400 South, had befriended the trio during their frequent visits to the store. After learning that they slept in the mountains, he told them that if they ever needed a place to stay in town, they were welcome to crash at his place. Trotta lived in a $600-a-month basement apartment at the Oxford Place Apartments, and often let people sleep on his floor or couch. He was happy to let what he viewed as fellow free spirits stay for a few days. He showed them his closet, filled with outfits from gothic to punk, and said, "I like to dress up," figuring the robed people would relate.

Trotta and Mitchell had some conversations, but the women mostly kept quiet, according to Trotta's later interviews about what went on inside his apartment while he hosted the three. The women, he said, kept their veils over their faces even while they were in his apartment. Occasionally, they sang hymns and they listened to his music—he had a shelf full of Depeche Mode records—and they all talked about music. Trotta said the younger woman talked about her school classes, but when he asked her name, Mitchell interrupted them. "Just call her 'My joy in her,'" he told Trotta. Elizabeth did not protest.

On the evening of August 24, Trotta took Mitchell and the two women to a party at a house east of downtown, about a mile from his apartment and not far from Federal Heights. The owner of the house, Vincent "Bub" Farrell, was throwing a going-away party for his daughter, Leah, who was about to leave for the fall term at New York University. Farrell hosted numerous parties at his house, which was painted blue and was once owned by Asians, accounting for its nickname, China Blue. The parties at China Blue attracted an eclectic mix of artists, musicians, actors, and assorted nonconformists. Most were friends of Bub's or Leah's, or friends of friends, but Bub Farrell didn't care who showed up, as long as they behaved themselves.

More than a hundred people were already crowded into the house on a pleasant summer evening when Trotta showed up with his robed guests. As they approached the front door, Mitchell said, "We must go in and assess the spirits." At the vestibule, Mitchell and the women had to wait for the crowd to thin to enter. The vestibule was known as the hell room and was painted in black with red flames on the walls. "We must cry repentance to these people," Mitchell said as he was made to wait in hell. The partygoers looked at him sideways, not sure if he was kidding. Hell soon gave way to the living room, painted in light blue with white fluffy clouds on the walls and ceiling—the heaven room.

Mitchell left the women by the food and made his way to the beer cooler in the back. Various people who were there remember that he started chugging down can after can of Miller Genuine Draft as he moved from room to room preaching Jesus's gospel. One of the partygoers, Pamela Een, became curious as she heard Mitchell's preaching, which she found remarkably one-sided. "He would not listen to anything anyone else said," Pamela remembered. "He was on this big rant. It was very Old Testament bent, saints and sinners, and he put himself in the position like he had this great new wisdom we hadn't heard before."

Pamela and her friend Amber Merriweather listened as Mitchell stopped and talked in hushed tones to the veiled women who had come in with him, telling them to "get what you can out of this place, food and whatever." The buffet table was loaded with vegetarian gumbo, sausage gumbo, and salads. After Mitchell was out of earshot, Pamela and Amber approached the women, who hadn't said a word. "Are you both OK?" they asked. "What's going on here? This guy seems a little strange, are you sure you want to be here?" To the tall younger woman, who they guessed to be about nineteen, they asked specifically, "Who are you, what is your name?" By way of response, both women dropped their eyes and remained silent.

A little later, there was a commotion in the back of the house, and Mitchell was right in the middle of it.

"It was about midnight and the women weren't directly with him," remembered Pamela. "He was out back and there was a big crowd gathering around him. He had been drinking and was getting louder about his religious inclinations and people didn't want to hear it anymore. He was in the middle of a bunch of guys and they were telling him to shut up and he wouldn't, and they were getting out of their seats to get physical with him. I saw this going down and I walked over and grabbed his arm and looked at him with this 'come hither' look because I knew from when I met him that that's all it would take. Because he was already sizing me up. You can tell when someone is looking at you that way. I led him to the street and the two women followed and I said, 'Look, you have to leave.' The whole way out he was like 'You're my angel, you're the one,' just going off about how great I was and how chosen. But once I got him out on the street and informed him he wasn't getting laid, his whole tune changed. He tried to call me a sinner when he had just called me an angel so he kind of stopped and stumbled over his words for a minute. Then he started to yell from the street. I yelled back, telling him he needed to go or the police were going to come."

At least one person at the party that night knew Elizabeth. Joe Lenge was a substitute teacher who had once taught Elizabeth's math class at Bryant Intermediate School the year before. Another partygoer, Tim Hollinger, left the party early that night because he had to get up early the next morning—he was going out on yet another search to try to find Elizabeth Smart.

23

The search for Elizabeth was like walking through a maze. The more people we talked to and the more places we searched, the more the maze seemed to expand.

Perhaps the most difficult part of what we called "search madness" were the psychic leads. The vast majority of these came from people who sincerely wanted to help, and who we sincerely, but skeptically, hoped *could* help. When you are desperately clinging to faith and prayer, the line between the religious and the psychic world is foggy at best. Maybe there is no line at all.

From the beginning, we were inundated with psychic leads. They started on the very first day after Elizabeth went missing. A close friend of the family called and said she knew a Native American woman who had helped locate a body in the Southwest through her spiritual powers. This woman had helped our friend through some extremely difficult times and she deeply believed in her abilities. The Native American woman, who came from a tribe noted for its spiritual beliefs, wanted to remain anonymous and wanted no payment. She relayed her impressions about a handyman, perhaps a gardener or someone with a light uniform, and a shed of some sort. We listened to what the woman said, but, given that we had no more information to go on, we could do nothing. That same day, my friend Tom Fenske called from Billings, Montana, and offered to fly his company's jet down so we could "put the best psychic we can find in the plane and cover the state in a grid until we find her." I thanked Tom for his offer, but said we were not quite ready to do that yet. At that point, Angela, Cynthia, Heidi, and Kathy Wilson took over management of the psychic leads.

There is a coven of witches about thirty-five miles south of Salt Lake City, and Cynthia received information that they might have kidnapped a blond virgin to be sacrificed on the summer solstice. This information, which was never substantiated, disturbed many in law enforcement. At one point Ed got a call that the police were going to Utah County to dig up a body where these witch leads had pointed. As it turned out, there was nothing there but a load of frustration.

Everyone in the family got a taste of the psychic world. One friend of my parents related a dream about Elizabeth being in a basement in West Valley City. My mother got so nerved up over this news that she suggested recruiting members of the LDS wards in the area to go door to door to search the basements. Once the possibility was rationally discussed, we didn't implement that plan, but such was the initial urge to believe the psychic leads. The truth is, when it's your family member who is missing, you are not apt to discount anything, at least not on the first several hundred leads.

One day, Dad and I drove through the central part of the state on Highway 6 checking out specific information from a prisoner whose mother had had a vision and described a white truck parked in a driveway on the side of a home along Highway 6. Chris and David each spent hours on searches that were based on nothing but vague psychic impressions. Chris climbed Elizabeth Mountain on a psychic tip and spent a couple of days searching with David in the areas of Bear Lake and Chalk Creek. Chris and Lois's brother-in-law, Steve Wright, also spent a day searching near Delta, Utah, based on information a water-witcher had given them. But it was all to no avail.

Because David and Julie ended up running the search center from their home, they got the brunt of the outer-orbit leads. Among the most extreme came from a group called PSI Tech that believed we could find Elizabeth through what they called technical remote viewing. They formulated a sketch of the location of her body based on their "viewings" and, in a report they forwarded to David, concluded: "Sadly, we found her dead.... Preliminary analysis concluded that her body is likely located near Big Mountain Pass along Highway 65.... She was driven up a mountain and thrown out of a vehicle at the point where the temperature drops and begins to feel cold.

Her body rolled down a ravine or side of a mountain and now lies (crunched up) near an opening that resembles a funnel or a mine entrance." David, Chris, and Angela organized several searches in the Big Mountain area, taking their lead from rock patterns that were outlined in the PSI sketch. Several times the searchers spotted areas that looked like the sketch, but, once again, they found nothing.

The PSI Tech lead took a major turn toward the bizarre when the psychics suggested that the drawing might be the entrance to a sacred Native American burial vault at the base of Emigration Canyon, across from Hogle Zoo on the east side of the Salt Lake Valley. Because there had been previous leads in the same general area, the SLCPD organized an investigation in conjunction with the state archeologist. When the investigation turned up nothing, PSI Tech started criticizing the police and questioning their motives.

The most unsuspecting victim of the psychics was my cousin Mike Sweet, a colonel in the National Guard in Carson City, Nevada. Mike organized volunteer searches in that area and at times had as many as 250 National Guardsman working during their off hours with dozens of other volunteers. Mike worked closely with Marvin Morton, the Elko County sheriff. Morton worked with local FBI agents, one of whom got a lead from an elderly mystic, a Native American woman whose psychic information had reportedly been accurate in a previous investigation. This person said the key to the mystery had something to do with sweet or sugar. When the sheriff told the FBI agent about Mike Sweet being involved with all these searches, the agent's radar went off. When Mike returned home from a short family trip, he had two messages waiting on his phone, both from the FBI. They wanted to talk. Mike had been involved with investigations when he worked at the Pentagon in Washington; he knew that anyone who got passionately involved in an investigation was likely to become a suspect. As a preemptive move, he called my dad and asked him to write a letter explaining Mike's role in the searches. The next morning, two FBI agents, thinking they had a hot target, greeted Mike. He pulled out the letter from Charles Smart and handed it to them. They read it, sighed, made a copy of the letter, and left.

The most dangerous moment we ever encountered from a lead, psychic or otherwise, came not from the lead itself, but from Ed's driving. He'd received a tip from a man who had found some red material he thought might be Elizabeth's pajamas at the base of an ancient sunstone carving in Spanish Fork Canyon. The four of us brothers left a Sunday family dinner early one evening to make the sixty-five-mile drive and meet the man before dark. It was the only time we had all gone on a physical search with Ed, and it felt good being together. But as Ed tried to pass a semi pulling a double trailer at the entrance of the canyon, he found he couldn't power past, and as he turned the corner an SUV came at us head-on. Fortunately, the other vehicle was able to drive off the road without hitting us.

"All we need is to get everyone killed in a car crash now," I thought. We all agreed it was stupid to let someone as distracted as Ed drive and decided one of us would drive on the return trip.

We met the man, who took us climbing through the canyon to a spot with huge, intricate carvings and, sure enough, we saw red fabric poking out of some mud underneath. The man had already arranged to send a piece of the material to the police evidence lab, and it would later prove to have nothing to do with Elizabeth. But the pain of uncertainty hung in the air as we stood there, trying to imagine if this was where Elizabeth had met her demise. It upset us all to the point that we completely spaced out and let Ed drive home—luckily without incident.

Besides the psychic madness, there was the craziness of the searches in our own neighborhoods. Angela and Cynthia both participated in several in their respective neighborhoods, but I think it was harder for us boys because we'd had the finger of suspicion pointed at us. Chris helped organize a search in Farmington Canyon, near his home, where searchers found a shallow, foul-smelling grave. Chris and Ingrid watched as law enforcement processed the site. They hoped that it would prove to be another animal grave, but when one of the officers jumped up from digging, ran to his vehicle, grabbed a briefcase, and returned, Chris felt physically ill. It did turn out to be a dog's grave, but his actions made Chris think otherwise. A little while later the sheriff came over and said, "I have good news and bad news. The good news is it's not Elizabeth. The bad news is it's not Elizabeth," by which he meant that there would be no closure for the family that day. Chris said that when he and Ingrid left, he was shaking all over.

David had a similar experience when his friend Todd Kim told him that dogs who had been given a piece of Elizabeth's clothing had gotten a positive hit on a mound of dirt at a new construction site near David's home in the south end of the Salt Lake Valley. Police brought in three more K-9 units and ended up at the same mound of dirt. Soon the sheriff's department arrived and everyone braced for the worst. David's angst grew when he called Ed to inform him of the developments and Ed asked, "Do you really think it could be Elizabeth?" Dave silently prayed that it was not, but he gave the only answer he could, "I don't know." By 10:00 A.M. the next day, the search was complete. Again there was nothing.

There were dozens of searches in the Park City area where I live. Through the Catholic Church, Tim Petracca organized more than twenty searches. One lead we received was about a rough-looking man in an old SUV who was wearing a white cap; someone spotted him trying to open a locked gate next to East Canyon Creek, below my house. The caller thought it might have been Richard Ricci. The lead made me smile. I knew the caller was describing my neighbor David Bernolfo, one of the wealthiest men in Utah, who owns eight thousand acres next to my property. When he isn't wearing a three-piece suit at his office at Bamberger Investments, he often comes up and works on his ranch. We had spent many hours together rounding up cows on horseback. While he was fiercely protective about keeping trespassers off his land, he opened up his ranch for the search. About a hundred volunteers combed the banks of East Canyon Creek, while my dad and I took a horse group through the various canyons. Mike Sibbett, a neighbor and the chairman of the Utah Board of Pardons, arranged to have helicopters drop searchers along the ridge lines to make their way back to the canyon bottom. (In hindsight, I wish we had done the same thing in the mountains around Ed's home.) Searchers found articles of clothing and garbage but nothing of significance. It was a terrible feeling, looking for Elizabeth's body in my own backyard.

Almost all of the searches with credible leads pertained to Ricci. Reports of a white Jeep Cherokee came from hundreds of places. The FBI spent a long day with dozens of agents in central Utah near the town of Price, tracking down acquaintances of Ricci's and looking in several places where a body might be hidden. Other leads took investigators on searches all over the state.

Near the end of July, Ed and his son Andrew participated in an air search aboard a surveillance aircraft piloted by Jamie Gutierrez, the coordinator for all air searches organized by the Elizabeth Search Center. The search focused on the Moab area in the southwest corner of the state. Jamie later recounted to me the difficulty he'd had in explaining to Elizabeth's father and brother what they were looking for. "There was a time when I was trying to point out what we were trying to spot, a mound of dirt, or suspicious area where a body might be," he said. "Then I cut myself off, realizing what I was saying." Jamie remembered that Ed sensed his uneasiness and asked him to please not worry. "I have never forgotten the kindness Ed expressed to me that day," Jamie said.

Don Bell and Cory Lyman asked us to organize a search in the area near Ricci's previous home near Monroe, Utah. Mike Freed and I made several maps and drove down with Rob Birkinshaw, who sent out a call for searchers on his utahatvtrails.com Web site. More than a hundred volunteers responded, including about two dozen trained search-and-rescue personnel. After an exhausting day, we met to sort out the various leads, one of which was a hidden campsite with items that had been stolen from town a few months before. One area had Jeep tracks that ran over small trees, which we thought could have accounted for the pine bough Neth Moul claimed he saw in the grill of Ricci's Jeep. The seasoned searchers, including Sheriff Barney, discussed the need for more information. "Look, Tom," one said, "This is a big country with lots of different types of soil. If that Jeep came back covered with mud, they should at least be able to tell you if it is light colored, sandstone, or rich brown. That would help us here. Even if it was washed, you should be able to tell from the undercarriage." I told them I couldn't agree more, but explained that the police would not share with us that kind of detailed information. I thanked them for their efforts and gave Sheriff Barney the phone numbers for Don Bell. I hoped that he would tell another law enforcement officer about the forensics on the Jeep.

24

Around the middle of August the *Deseret News* ran a story about how members of our family were trying to return to our regular jobs and put a sense of normalcy back in our lives. To some extent that was true. Chris had stayed away from his job with Duke Energy for weeks and was long overdue to return. Physicians at Cynthia's clinic had filled in with her patients, but she had to get back to her practice. Angela had helped manage the day-to-day business of running the search center with Suann Adams, but she needed to take care of her children.

David, who was self-employed, continued to run the search center from his home in Draper, but there were no longer enough tasks to warrant all of us missing work. We continued our regular family meetings and organized press conferences at least once a week, and we all tried to work out schedules so we could attend, but most of the family made an effort to return to a daily routine.

The *Deseret News* had been extremely understanding and all summer had let me have time off to work for the search. But after reading the article, my editor, John Hughes, cornered me and asked when I would be coming back. "It might be good for you," he said gently.

With some reluctance, I went back to full-time work at the paper. While it was actually good to shoot photos again, I was still totally absorbed in the investigation. David and I continued to spend anywhere from three to seven hours a day on the phone, discussing the case with each other, law enforcement, family members, and others. Heidi and I no longer had the responsibility of maintaining a daily routine for Sierra, Nicole, and Amanda, who had all moved away from home, which gave me more time to spend on the case.

Any time Mick Fennerty, Ed, or one of my brothers or sisters called with new information, I put everything else on hold. I had lost about fifteen pounds in the two and a half months since Elizabeth had disappeared, and while many friends at the paper welcomed me back, they were clearly concerned about my health and obsessive behavior. Several of them encouraged me to talk to a therapist. For the most part they were convinced that Richard Ricci had kidnapped Elizabeth and that I was simply unable to face that reality.

The hardest part about going back to work was that I was now somewhat undependable because the search for Elizabeth was my top priority. Photo editor Ravell Call and *Deseret News* management were willing to be flexible.

I love my job. Even when I go on what some might consider an uninteresting assignment, the opportunity to interact with all types of people is one of the great aspects of being a photojournalist. That said, when I got back to work, one of my first assignments was so emotionally draining that it made me question if I could go back to work after all. Early on the morning of August 19, a man named Javier Sickler grabbed the eleven-year-old daughter of his longtime friend from her Midvale home. A neighbor heard suspicious noises coming from the backyard and called the police. When officers arrived, Sickler was sexually assaulting the girl and beating her repeatedly in the face. Sickler left her unconscious and fled the scene, but an officer with a dog chased him down. The alert neighbor and quick police response undoubtedly saved the young girl's life. Ravell asked if I could cover the press conference at Primary Children's Hospital that afternoon, which I thought would not be a problem.

After nine hours of surgery, a visibly shaken doctor stood in front of the press outside the hospital and told us that the little girl was going to live but that she'd been through the worst beating he'd ever encountered, and she would probably lose her sight. The girl's father stepped out from the hospital to thank the medical staff and read a statement. Heartbroken, but grateful to still have his daughter, he thanked God for her life. Then he thanked the Smart family for helping raise the awareness about missing children; he said he was praying for Elizabeth. I hid behind my camera as the tears flowed. His grief was all too familiar; it echoed Ed and Lois's pain, and my own. I slipped back from the crowd of press and moved to the lobby of the hospital. When the injured girl's father came back into the hospital from the press conference, I told him who I was and that we were praying for his family also. We hugged for a brief moment and then he went back to his child.

Toward the end of August, Dad's heart palpitations increased and Mom's blood pressure hit dangerous levels. We were worried that the stress, grief, and anxiety over Elizabeth might kill one or both of them—especially when they each suggested privately that dying wasn't such an awful thing. They said that at least then they'd know where Elizabeth was and if she was all right.

Earlier in the year, Dad and I had planned a summer trip with the horses into the Wind River area of Wyoming. The kidnapping disrupted all our plans, but one day in late August, Dad suddenly mentioned that we really needed to get away. I agreed. I couldn't think of anything more necessary for Dad– and for me—at the moment.

On our third day in the Winds we took our trailer to a nearby parking lot and unloaded our horses while our outfitter, Todd Stevie, talked to another outfitter who had just come up from the nearby town of Cora. After a short time Todd walked up to Dad and me with his eyes bulging in shock. "Richard Ricci is brain-dead in the hospital," he said.

Clearly there was no escape from the case. It seemed the search for Elizabeth was just going to keep getting more bizarre. After attempting to absorb the news with a hard ride, Dad and I returned to camp for a solemn dinner and then went to sleep on the canvas floor of the tent we shared. At 2:00 A.M., Dad woke me from my Ambien-induced sleep as he rose from the tent floor and exclaimed, "Hurrah! Hurrah! She killed him!" Then he told me his theory that Elizabeth could have hit Ricci in the head and caused a subdural hematoma, which is similar to a bruise that causes bleeding between the brain and the skull. After two or three months the volume of liquid swells and causes so much pressure that it creates stroke-like symptoms, which can result in death. The next morning we headed home a day early. Ricci died the next night—not of a subdural hematoma but of a ruptured aneurysm.

Ricci's unexpected demise hit the investigation hard, scattering theories, dashing some expectations, and igniting others. On the downside, all hope of a full confession and explanation went with him. On the upside, we now hoped that Ricci's accomplices, if there were any, would feel more inclined to come forward, as they would be risking no repercussions from their deceased coconspirator.

Ricci had been back in court the day it happened. He appeared in the chambers of Judge Paul G. Maughan in the Third District Court in Salt Lake City on Tuesday, August 27. Ed and Lois were in the courtroom, along with Ricci's wife, Angela. Ricci came in with his attorney, shackled and cuffed as always, his hair still long and stringy, his face pale and even more sunken. The hearing had to do with the burglaries and bank robbery charges and took no more than a minute, after which Ricci left, making eye contact with Angela but avoiding looking at Ed and Lois. It was the last time any of them would see him conscious.

A few hours after arriving back at the prison, Ricci punched the intercom button in his solitary cell and told the guard he was having trouble breathing. The guards were there within two minutes and watched as Ricci collapsed onto his bunk. Paramedics administered mouth-to-mouth resuscitation and called for a medical helicopter.

After the short flight to University Hospital, Ricci underwent a four-hour surgery that relieved fluid pressure and bleeding from his brain. He remained in a coma and was put on a life-support system. A spokesman for the prison said Ricci had a history of hypertension but he had not been on medication while in custody. The spokesman added that the prisoner had seemed healthy enough. Until he pushed the intercom button, he had showed no signs of distress.

With his hospital room flanked by guards from the FBI, SLCPD, and Utah State Prison, the life-support system stayed on until Friday night, when Ricci's family decided it was time to pull the plug because there was no chance of his recovery. Twelve minutes later, at 7:28 P.M. on August 30, 2002, Ricci was dead.

Angela was in his hospital room, holding her husband's hand, when the end came. She went to close the privacy curtains around the bed, but the guards blocked her way. "Prison policy," she was told. "We can't risk an escape." Surrounded by uniformed officers wearing pistols, the new widow broke down and wept.

But not everyone was weeping. The public's lament had nothing to do with the fact that Ricci had gone to his grave. It had to do with what he took with him. SLCPD's Rick Dinse said it now might be impossible to clear Ricci in the kidnapping case. Department of Corrections spokesman Jack Ford said, "We hate to have somebody pass away when they're in our custody, and it's unfortunate because he was still being investigated by a couple of other law enforcement agencies."

In its Sunday edition two days after Ricci's death, the *Salt Lake Tribune* ran a front-page story, "Why Ricci Topped Cop List." Reporters Michael Vigh and Kevin Cantera, still using unidentified police sources for their speculative reports, outlined the case against Ricci, claiming that "among the inner circle of investigators there remains scant doubt that the career criminal, who died Friday, somehow managed to snatch the girl without a trace."

The article went on to describe a hypothetical scenario of how and why Ricci kidnapped Elizabeth. It rehashed all the circumstantial evidence of the past three months. Ricci was familiar with the home, he knew how to get in, he knew the girls had small yet valuable items on their dressers—but his plan was foiled when Elizabeth, who was a light sleeper, awoke. The reporters noted the lack of physical evidence tying Ricci to the crime scene, but they didn't let that get in the way of their insinuation that Ricci had to be the kidnapper. Ed called me the day after the article came out and asked what I thought of it. We both agreed that certain people were really stretching things to make the Ricci theory fit.

Ricci's body was cremated a week after he died, at the Peel Funeral Home in Magna on the valley's west side. At an evening memorial service, attended by about fifty people, there was not a disparaging word about the forty-eight-year-old son, brother, father, and husband. A number of Ricci's old friends from prison were there, mixed in with family, neighbors, members of the Kearns Tenth Ward, coworkers from the nursery, and media. Rick Olsen, a former guard at the state prison, spoke about Ricci's popularity with prisoners and prison staff alike. Bishop Morrow of the Tenth Ward spoke of a loving husband and father who helped clean the church and supported his stepson's recent baptism. Angela Ricci eulogized her Sagittarius soulmate, the person she was destined to go through life with, even if life only added up to six months. There was a silver lining, she said, because now big Rick was reunited with the other love of his life, his son, little Ricky.

No one mentioned the Smart kidnapping in their formal remarks but the walls of the funeral home foyer were lined with poster-sized blow-ups of e-mails that had been pouring into Angela's computer ever since her husband's death. The e-mails, which came from all parts of the country, were full of condolences, comfort, and support. One, from KK in Salt Lake City read: "Please trust in the fact that there are more people than you can imagine that believe in you and Richard." Another, from Lisa in West Valley City, read: "Angela, you seem to be a wonderful woman that truly stood by your man." And one from Barbara in Elkhart, Indiana, read: "When I first saw Rick's picture of his eyes, I thought this man did not kidnap anyone."

As mourners grieved the death of their friend, FBI agents Mick Fennerty and Juan Becerra collected license plate numbers from the vehicles in the funeral home parking lot, and took photos of those attending the service. The most interesting guest was Steve Wright's adopted brother and former Ricci prison acquaintance.

Angela gave half of Rick's ashes to his family and took the other half back to her trailer, where she put them in a vase and placed them on the coffee table beneath a picture of a muscular Rick in a tank-top playing his electric guitar. It was what he looked like, she told guests as she touched the vase, before they took him away that last time to prison. "When he left this house in June," Angela said, "there was nothing wrong with him. He was healthy as a horse."

■   ■   ■

With Ricci deceased and the tips-for-cash reward program underway, we had renewed hope that someone, somewhere, prodded either by guilt, relief, greed, or all three, would emerge with information.

We had a brief expectation that the mystery might be solved in the rugged mountains in the central part of the state, above the town of Fairview. Like so many leads, this one was as convoluted as it was bizarre. On Sunday, June 9, two Boy Scout leaders had scared off a man who had been digging a rectangular hole that measured six feet long, two feet wide, and eighteen inches deep. They reported it, but SLCPD detectives didn't drive to the scene (about a hundred miles from Salt Lake City) until nine days later. The detectives collected evidence at the campsite next to the hole, including several tissues scattered about the area that contained DNA. Subsequent DNA lab tests, however, did not match the DNA of any suspects, or potential suspects, in the Smart case, including Ricci. The detectives then faxed several mug shots, including one of Ricci, to Deputy Mark Robinson of the Sanpete County Sheriff's Department so he could show them to the Scout leaders, Dean Kleven and Keith Brotherson. When neither man identified any of the mug shots, the police ended their investigation.

That might have been the end of it if Robinson hadn't asked Kleven, a professional artist, to draw a sketch of the mystery man and, further, if that sketch hadn't made its way into the local newspaper, the *Manti Messenger-Enterprise*, a month later. Manti resident Karen Christensen saw the sketch and contacted David at the Elizabeth Smart Search Center with the information, which was the first anyone in the family had heard of the lead. For several reasons, we decided that the area around the so-called grave should be searched extensively, particularly because Kleven and Brotherson described the man they'd seen as about five-foot-eight, and said he drove a light-colored SUV.

Mick Fennerty and many others in law enforcement thought this was a viable lead and Mick asked me to do whatever I could to get the sketch into the Salt Lake City newspapers. We held a press conference and as a result most of the Salt Lake City television news stations, as well as the *Deseret News*, carried the sketch. In a subsequent development, Karen Christensen helped organize a search that brought more than fifty people, including

David and Chris, to a place called Miller's Flat in Fairview Canyon on August 31, the day after Ricci died. The searchers examined the rectangular hole, which had partially collapsed in the months since it was first discovered. They spent the day scouring the area. But in the end, they uncovered no evidence that Elizabeth, Ricci, or anyone else connected to the case had ever been there.

Instead of shaking things up, Ricci's death seemed to cast an even greater pall over the investigation. The tips-for-cash rewards went untouched. No one called in with even a wild guess or a theory, let alone any concrete information. In another effort to shake something loose, Ed decided to go public with news of the chairs propped against the walls outside the windows at both his house and the Wrights'. In an interview with Derek Jensen of the *Deseret News*, Ed provided these previously unknown details to try to generate interest in the tips-for-cash program. When you added together the cut screens, the chairs, and the early-morning break-ins, the similarity of the two crime scenes became, as Ed put it, "very unnerving."

But the new crime scene details produced no response, and the police continued to maintain that the Wright incident was simply a neighborhood prank with no further ramifications. "[Investigators] really don't believe it has anything to with Elizabeth Smart's kidnapping," responded Peggy Faulkner, spokesperson for the Salt Lake County Sheriff's Office, in answer to Ed's comments.

The summer had been long for everyone, but in mother time it had gone beyond eternity. Lois Smart had somehow survived the discovery of the cut screen and open window and the horror that her daughter had been stolen. She had managed to make it through the hot, empty days of June, July, and August, clinging to circumstantial clues and assurances from investigators that the handyman had done it. But when Labor Day came and the leads had dried up and Ricci was dead and the neighborhood kids were trotting out to the bus stop wearing their new back-to-school clothes, Elizabeth's mother bottomed out.

She put on Elizabeth's favorite red boots and quietly headed for the mountains. My father accompanied her. They saddled two horses and rode to the Hot Rocks at the top of Moffit Peak, the same spot where I had sat astride Diva nearly three months earlier and called out "Elizabeth" at the top of my lungs.

The ride to the peak was Elizabeth's favorite, so that's where Lois went. When she got to the top, she unclipped the "Pray for Me" button with Elizabeth's face on it that she had worn since her daughter had disappeared, got off her horse, and buried the button under a rock cairn. As her tears flowed, she said a prayer, meditated for a while, and then left. It wasn't a funeral service, nor was it an admission that Elizabeth was dead; it was simply a mother's acknowledgment that she loved her daughter with a fervor that was slowly paralyzing her. The more Lois dwelled on where Elizabeth might be, on who had her, on how she was being treated, the more she neglected herself, her husband, and her other children. She couldn't abandon the rest of the family, or continue to neglect them; that would be tantamount to the kidnapper taking them *all* away from her. So she came to the mountaintop, in boots a size too small that were killing her feet, and she made her peace with it. It was an uneasy peace but a peace just the same.

Not long after Lois's ride, President George W. Bush invited Ed and Lois to Washington, D.C., for the President's Conference on Child Protection. John Walsh of *America's Most Wanted* and Senator Orrin Hatch, who was working on child pornography Internet legislation, urged Elizabeth's parents to accept the president's invitation. They could use the trip to keep attention on Elizabeth's case and help raise awareness about the need for tougher child-protection laws.

Ed and Lois accepted the invitation and took Chris Thomas, Heidi, Angela, and David with them to the conference. They figured the trip might do them good. And it did. Although Ed and Lois only briefly shook President Bush's hand, after standing in a long reception line, they used the trip to expand on the personal relationship Ed had started with John Walsh earlier in the summer. It was a relationship that would prove enormously helpful in the days to come.

Another unexpected benefit of the trip was that we became aware of the wealth of resources available to parents and families of missing children at the National Center for Missing and Exploited Children (NCMEC) in Alexandria, Virginia.

The idea and push for the National Center came from John Walsh and his wife, Reve, following the tragic abduction and murder of their six-year-old son, Adam, in 1981. Adam was abducted from a Sears store while Reve was shopping. His severed head was discovered weeks later, but the rest of his body was never found. Investigators never convicted anyone of Adam's murder, although Walsh believed his son was killed by a drifter who was later convicted of multiple murders and sexual crimes and died in prison.

Walsh turned his grief into a crusade. He started foundations; organized parents; lobbied Congress; put in place the groundwork for the NCMEC; wrote a book, *Tears of Rage*, which became a national bestseller; and started a hit television show, *America's Most Wanted*, to help law enforcement catch the kind of criminals who murdered his son.

Walsh took Ed aside in Washington and talked to him as one grieving father to another. Ed needed to keep trying to solve the case, Walsh counseled, but it was also important that he move on emotionally if he didn't want his life destroyed by the kidnapping. Walsh also encouraged Ed to become involved in the child-abduction activist community—with Ed's high profile and sympathetic situation, he was in a position to do a lot of good.

At a tour of the NCMEC, Ed and Lois met the director, Ernie Allen, who gave them an encouraging statistic. Ernie said that the center's numbers showed that of the children abducted in the manner Elizabeth was taken, 40 percent were dead within the first week, but of those who made it beyond the first week, 60 percent returned home alive. If Elizabeth was still alive, the odds of her safe return were for her, not against her—a hopeful bit of news for a change.

The National Center had been working hard to find Elizabeth; from the first day of the kidnapping, the center had assigned a caseworker, Charles Pickett, to the search. The family had been unaware of Pickett, as well as the NCMEC itself, because the SLCPD had insisted that NCMEC personnel work through law enforcement channels only. Pickett explained to Ed and Lois that he had talked with Don Bell immediately following the abduction and Bell had given him contact numbers for police investigators but not for the family. Pickett said he had quickly posted the kidnapping at Utah's Clearinghouse for Missing Children and that within the first two weeks the NCMEC had processed 145 leads as a result. Elizabeth's parents also learned that Pickett and the NCMEC had been responsible for getting Elizabeth's photo on the ADVO direct-mail cards that are sent to households across the country with information about missing children.

Had the SLCPD allowed Pickett to contact the family directly, we no doubt would have found out much earlier about a handbook that helps families who are going through a kidnapping crisis. We had found the booklet, entitled *When Your Child Is Missing: A Family Survival Guide*, through Phil Adams, but not until August. Published by the U.S. Department of Justice, the book is written by the parents of five children, all victims of abduction: Shelby Cox, Morgan Nick, Jimmy Ryce, Tiffany Sessions, and Jacob Wetterling. Two were found murdered, and Tiffany, Morgan, and Jacob are still missing. The manual guides families through the unimaginable. It provides information on polygraphs, sleep deprivation, working with law enforcement, the role of the media, reward money, dealing with psychics, and a victims' bill of rights—virtually everything we had needed. At the end are quotes from the writers:

"The media are your best friends. Use them, don't let them use you."

- Claudine Ryce

"It's okay if you can't tell me everything, just don't lie to me."

—Pat Sessions.

For our family, Pat Sessions's quote, "One shot on the evening news is worth twenty thousand posters," came at a time when some of us wanted to wind down the press conferences. Since the second week of the kidnapping, investigators in the FBI and SLCPD had encouraged us to "let the media die down." Reading *When Your Child Is Missing* reinforced our determination to keep the case in the media as much as we could. The fact that The National Center had been asked not to contact us early on was clearly more about law enforcement ego than about helping with the case.

Pickett, who was familiar with other cases from Utah, told Ed and Lois he believed there could be a religious fanatical link, and when that happens it almost rewrites the book on child abductions. He told Ed and Lois that he believed firmly that "some fool" still had their baby.

"Don't be trying to bury her yet; it's not time," he said.

The visit to the NCMEC also helped Ed and Lois see that their efforts to bring awareness to a systematic alert system were already getting positive results in what the media was calling the summer of missing children.

The California Amber Alert, a version of Utah's Rachael Alert and a prototype that was being pushed for a national model, was barely a week old when, during the first week of August, Roy Dean Ratliff, a felon who was wanted on rape charges, abducted Tamara Brooks and Jacqueline Marris seventy miles north of Los Angeles. Due to the alarm sounded by the Amber Alert, a tip came from Bonnie Hernandez, an animal control officer, who spotted the car off a rural road in a remote desert region about one hundred miles from where the abduction occurred. After the driver refused to surrender he was shot to death by two sheriffs deputies while the girls hid inside the car.

The press asked members of our family if we felt bad that other cases were getting solved while ours seemed to be at a standstill. The answer was a resounding no. I doubt there was anyone, outside the family and friends of those kids, who was happier about their rescue than our family. We knew the massive amount of media attention the Elizabeth Smart case had generated was in part because the Smarts were an affluent, well-connected Caucasian family. However, kidnapping crosses all boundaries and all children deserve the same resources. It was gratifying to see other cases solved quickly because of a heightened awareness about *all* missing children.

While they were in Washington, D.C., a group of parents met at a small restaurant near the National Center. Ed, Lois, Heidi, David, and Angela joined members of other families with missing children. "The Club Nobody Wants to Belong To," they called themselves. Despite the morbid membership qualifications, the gathering let everyone know that they were not alone.

"Sitting at the table and listening to the exchange of stories was just heartbreaking, absolutely heartbreaking," remembered David. "But I think it also brought comfort to Ed and Lois just knowing there were other individuals who were going through the same type of situation."

The trip east managed to put aside briefly the ongoing question about how actively involved the Smart family should be in the investigation. It had been a month since Ricci's death. Public sentiment that it was time for us to move on was stronger than ever. Lois's family, the Francoms—and to some extent Lois herself—shared this sentiment. The Smarts, on the other hand, wanted to forge on. We agreed with Mick Fennerty's assessment that Ricci's death meant the case might finally be solved. "So many people were fixed on Ricci that they weren't looking anywhere else," Fennerty said. But now, the doors might open to new possibilities.

Chris, Angela, Cynthia, David, and I met at least weekly, and often daily, with Fennerty, who told me he thought the case would be solved by the end of October. In an attempt to avoid overloading him with calls, we had a system by which one of us, usually David or I, would call with questions, take notes, and then fill in the others.

David was going through hell because he and Julie were running the search center and Web site from their home. The psychic leads alone were enough to put them over the edge. But unless we could find a compelling reason that lent the lead credibility, we didn't share it with other family members, especially not Ed and Lois. We shared everything we thought was important, but we spared Ed and Lois most of the search insanity—the hell of missing their child was more than enough for them to deal with.

Ed and Lois worked, for the most part, with Cory Lyman—"Ed's handler," as we called him—and it was obvious that Ed felt good about their relationship and the information he got from Lyman. The Francoms got their information from Don Bell in the beginning, then later, after Bell left the active investigation, from Lyman. The rest of us got our information from Fennerty.

Sensing that our constant meetings and phone calls with Ed about the case might be causing too much strain on Lois, David decided it was important to ask Lois directly if she was OK with how hard we were pushing.

"Do you want us to stop investigating and searching?" he asked.

"Absolutely not," answered Lois. "I do not want you or anyone else to stop looking or trying. I want to bring Elizabeth home."

■ ■ ■

A few days after returning from Washington, D.C., David's phone rang. It was Fennerty. His tone was sober. He said he'd heard from a hiker who had just returned from the mountains in the northeastern part of the state and believed he had discovered Elizabeth's grave. He gave David the hiker's coordinates and told him a search party was being organized. David hung up and called me with the information.

"Phone Mick back," I responded as soon as I realized the coordinates, "and tell him to call off the search."

David and Fennerty were unaware of Lois's recent horseback ride to the Hot Rocks. What the hiker had found, as he climbed to the top of Moffit Peak, was the "Pray for Me" button Elizabeth's mother had weeks earlier buried under the pile of rocks.

25

Fifty-two dollars' worth of beer, gum, batteries, and a flashlight. That's what the man who looked like Jesus had tried to steal from Albertsons. The supermarket was only half a block up from the downtown Salt Lake City police station, next to the cash-a-check storefront that used to be a Winchell's. (The police were glad to see the Winchell's go. They could do without the doughnut jokes, just as they could do without busting the homeless on shoplifting charges that would go nowhere. A warm night in jail and three hot meals wasn't punishment for these guys; half the time "three hots and a cot" was exactly what they were after.)

SLCPD patrolmen Randy Marks and David Greer responded to the call from the store security officer who had confronted the shoplifter as he attempted to leave with the unpaid items. The store's security officer took a Polaroid of him in his robes and long beard as they waited for the officers to arrive. Marks and Greer didn't bother to take the accused down the block to the station. They just cited him and filled out a field card with the date, September 27, 2002, and the man's thumbprint.

There was some difficulty determining the man's identity. When police first asked his name, he said "Go with God." Guessing that wasn't the name he was born with, the officers persisted. The man said, "David Immanuel Isaiah," which they also guessed was not on his birth certificate. They wrote it on the Polaroid's margin anyway, with Immanuel spelled phonetically: David *Emanuel* Mitchell. Finally, the man told them the name his parents had given him—Brian David Mitchell—and, after setting the arraignment date for two weeks hence, they let him go. The security officer kept the Polaroid for the store's files.

■ ■ ■

Shoplifting was a sideline for Mitchell, something he resorted to only when panhandling and odd jobs failed him. In a place as large as Salt Lake City, more often than not, he did pretty well. Doors were always opening.

It had been the previous autumn, just before Thanksgiving, that Lois Smart had seen Mitchell begging for money downtown by the new light-rail train station on Main Street outside the ZCMI Center. The line from the University of Utah had just opened and Lois had taken her children, including Elizabeth, to try it out. In a sharp departure from his usual appearance, Mitchell had no beard and no hat. He wore no robes. It was shortly after the September 11 attacks and, besides the fact that he was often hassled and called Osama bin Laden, a drastic drop in donations had forced him to change his image temporarily.

Lois responded positively to Mitchell's clean-cut appearance and quiet, courteous manner. He seemed too clean to be homeless, she would later tell her husband. After a brief discussion, the central theme of which was the Lord Jesus, Lois Smart handed Mitchell five dollars and a scrap of paper with her husband's phone number. She told him he could call if he was willing to work for additional money.

Within days, Mitchell was at the Smarts' house on Kristianna Circle, introducing himself as Immanuel. He raked leaves, did some other yard work, and helped Ed repair a skylight. Although he knew the area well—the house was near the trail he and Wanda used when they lived in their teepee in Dry Creek Canyon—Mitchell kept that information as secret as his identity. He worked for about five hours. Ed had forty dollars in cash on hand, enough to pay Mitchell for four hours work, and offered to pay him the rest the next day because Mitchell said he wanted to return. But he did not come back the following day or the day after that. Ed figured he'd never see the man again.

Mitchell had had Elizabeth now for four months. Soon it would be Thanksgiving again, a year since their first encounter.

To Mitchell it was all God's will—the lying, the begging, the shoplifting, and the kidnapping. He functioned because of one all-encompassing holy diplomatic immunity that was his personal fantasy. Members of his own family who loved him, worried about him, sheltered him, humored him, indulged him, and even agreed to call him "Dahveed" and "Immanuel" when he insisted, would not join his church or bow to his greatness. Even his father—a man who had once thought he heard a voice tell him he was Jesus—did not support his son as Immanuel.

But there was one person who did, and she walked behind him. Wanda was his convert, his congregation of one, his devout follower who subjugated her will to his. Wanda, the one Mitchell called Hephzibah ("My delight is in her"), namesake of the mother of King Manasseh.

They hadn't married until she was thirty-nine and he was thirty-two. They met in 1985 at a therapy session on divorce fallout. Neither of their divorces was final at the time they met. Both were involved in a bitter fight for custody, material belongings, and, if they got lucky, maybe a shred of dignity when it was all over. He was looking for something to cling to. So was she.

Wanda was living in a cramped apartment a mile east of downtown Salt Lake City across the street from Trolley Square, a former trolley barn that had been renovated into an upscale mall. She had traded in her large home on the west side of the valley, filled with six kids and a husband, for this. She moved in with just a few pieces of furniture and a baby grand piano, her greatest love.

Wanda's first husband was Talmage Andrew Thompson, an aspiring educator who met her when she was a high school senior and married her just months after she graduated from Salt Lake City's South High School in 1964. She was eighteen, and he was twenty-seven.

Wanda was the second of three daughters born to Dora and Marvin Barzee. Janice was two years older; Evelyn was two years younger. Wanda was a good student and showed flashes of brilliance at sewing, art, cake decorating, and especially music, flashes that were put on hold when she began having children soon after she married Tal Thompson. They had three children in their first three years of marriage, then three more children over the next seven years. Wanda had three daughters and three sons before she turned thirty.

Tal alternated between going to school and teaching it. He taught physical education and driver's education at a variety of high schools throughout Utah. In twenty years of marriage, the Thompsons moved thirty-three times.

Tal and Wanda were both raised in the LDS Church. During their marriage they were a going-to-church-on-Sunday kind of family; their public image was that of a typical devout family. But at home the marriage was loud, tumultuous, and violent. "A roller-coaster with huge emotional binges," remembered Vicki Cottrell, a close family friend, describing the atmosphere inside the Thompson home. "Wanda and Tal had these huge fights. The kids didn't know how to respond appropriately, even in public or with friendships, because their lives at home were such a wild ride."

Cottrell and other outsiders noted that both husband and wife were prone to gigantic mood swings, a key sign of mental or emotional disorder. Another sign of chemical imbalance was Wanda's capacity to go without sleep for two or three days at a time. She would sit at the keyboard of her organ or piano and play for hours on end.

Music was her obsession and her escape. As a child, she had just one year of formal training in piano, but as an adult, she took lesson after lesson. Eventually she studied with Dr. Paul Pollei, a professor of piano at Brigham Young University. Her organ teacher, Clay Christiansen, one of the official Salt Lake Tabernacle organists, allowed her to play the organ in the Tabernacle. She gave public recitals on both piano and the organ, which became her favorite instrument. "Johann Sebastian Bach was such a love of hers," remembered Vicki.

But there was little balance. When Wanda went on her frequent music binges, she ignored everything else—kids, friends, husband, church, and housework. This led to conflict with Tal. "There was just so much violence," said Vicki.

In 1983 Wanda suffered what was then commonly referred to as a nervous breakdown. She had to be hospitalized. She stayed for more than a week; doctors finally released her after treating her with an antidepressant medication.

"I remember she came to my house after she got out of the hospital, and she talked for three hours straight," said Vicki, who later became the director of the Utah chapter of the National Association for the Mentally Ill. "I thought it was so strange how she talked so incessantly. Now I would say it was paranoia. She was suspicious of everybody—doctors, family, everyone— and she'd say, 'I'm not taking that medicine they gave me.'"

The mental collapse ushered in the final breakdown of the Thompson marriage. Wanda moved to the apartment across from Trolley Square, and Tal Thompson filed for divorce. This led to a brutal fight over custody of the children and division of the couple's joint property.

It was then that Wanda met Brian Mitchell, a man emerging from his own sad story. The short, bespectacled, matronly woman and the slender, boyish-looking man needed each other. In November 1985 they got married—on the same day Brian's divorce became final. They were married by Wanda's LDS bishop in a civil ceremony. Less than two years later they went to the Salt Lake Temple, where they were sealed, as is the LDS way, for time and all eternity.

They moved into Wanda's tiny apartment, quickly crowding it with their pasts. Between them they had ten children ranging in age from two to twenty. Periodically, one or more of the offspring would come to live with them. Wanda's youngest son, Mark, and daughter, LouRee, and Mitchell's son, Travis, all lived with them for brief periods in a succession of apartments and houses in Salt Lake. These parent-child reunions rarely lasted long, chiefly because the old volatility was still there. Mitchell and Wanda argued loudly and constantly. Wanda's children, who had seen Mitchell as a quiet, easygoing sort when he was dating their mother, were greeted now by a louder, more aggressive man who had strongly held opinions on just about everything, especially religion, a man who would padlock the television set to prevent the ways of the world from penetrating his home. Mitchell's older kids saw a demure Wanda turn into a raging harpy, a woman who would often flee to the wardhouse to play the organ for hours.

But if chaos was the order of things at home, the world beyond caught only rare glimpses of it. To those on the outside, Brian and Wanda Mitchell were responsible newlyweds, fearlessly striking out yet again to patch up their lives. Mitchell had his die-cutting job at O. C. Tanner, where he collected twice-monthly paychecks, with child support dutifully taken out by the state and sent to his ex-wife. Wanda worked too, although sporadically, to help make ends meet. And on Sunday, they always went to church.

Church work was their constant. The more the kids came and went, the more they argued, the more they slid into debt and emotional disarray, the more the Mitchells clung to the LDS Church. They lived in three different wards in the Salt Lake Park Stake—the Tenth Ward, the First Ward, and the Princeton Ward—and were very active in each one. Wanda was the ward organist, while Brian willingly accepted every calling offered. Wearing the uniform of the obediently converted—white shirt, conservative tie, dark suit—he answered yes to all the worthiness questions in his temple interviews with the bishop and stake president and went through the temple for the first time in 1988. No one knew of his past as he made his way through the ranks: stake mission president, member of the high council, ordinance worker at the Salt Lake Temple, and, finally, member of the ward bishopric.

"He was kind of a quiet guy, very respectful, always on time, always did what you asked him to do," is how Dru White, president of the Salt Lake Park Stake mission in the late 1980s, remembered Mitchell. "I knew they had a little friction in their marriage but it didn't show with Brian. Wanda was very quiet. He was very diligent."

The tighter he held to the church orthodoxy, the more Mitchell retreated from his former life, which included his own family. It was while he was a temple worker—participating in ceremonies that stressed the importance of eternal family relationships—that he severed almost all ties with his parents and siblings. He was upset by his mother's allegations that his oldest children, Travis and Angela, had been turned against the LDS faith by the family that adopted them.

"My mom said to Brian, 'How could you have let these kids be adopted and then let that happen?'" remembered Tim Mitchell. "Brian became very, very upset and it was after that confrontation with my mom that he wrote a letter to everybody in the family. In it he said something to the effect that 'I have been in the stake high council and I have done this and that in the church and I will be in charge of my children.' It was a lot of self-righteous condemnation. It was like something had snapped in him. Some emotional trauma had happened."

That trauma might have had to do with the fact that Brian was not called as the new bishop of the First Ward. Bishop Don Lane and his two counselors—Brian Mitchell and Dean Oliver—were released from their positions on Father's Day, 1991, when a new First Ward bishopric was put in place, with Rudi Mueller as bishop and Mack Roundy and Patrick Orr as his counselors.

In the LDS religion, where there is no paid professional ministry, the bishop holds authority over each individual ward. Only bishops hear confessions, allocate welfare, conduct disciplinary hearings, and direct the ward affairs. It is no small calling. A typical LDS bishop spends between twenty and thirty hours a week doing church work. But there is power and prestige associated with the position—a fact that often attracts the more zealous members of a ward—which rotates roughly every five years. A bishop's counselors, his right-hand men, generally are considered candidates to replace an outgoing bishop, and it is not uncommon for a counselor to be called to replace the bishop he has served with. The ultimate decision, however, according to Mormon dictates, is in the hands of the Lord, who inspires the stake president, or overseer of a group of wards, as to who should become the next bishop.

Mitchell reacted bitterly to being passed over as bishop of the First Ward. The rejection threw him into a deep funk, a fact Wanda shared with close friends and her sister Evelyn. "Wanda said she had never seen Brian so angry or unhappy," remembered one ward member. "He was really upset about not being named bishop."

Mitchell continued to work in the temple until early 1993; near the end, Wanda joined him, acting as an organist for the temple workers in addition to officiating alongside her husband in ordinance work. But during the same period, their attendance at conservative "Mormon patriot" study groups increased. The more Brian studied, the more he became convinced that the LDS Church, the one that failed to call him as bishop, was drifting from its true and eternal principles, and someone needed to set things straight.

Making the acquaintance of naturopath C. Samuel West further fanned the fires of unorthodoxy, prompting the Mitchells to flee their old ways and become health missionaries for the self-proclaimed doctor of lymphology. They peddled West's tapes and books to friends and acquaintances. Doug Larsen, Brian's friend from O. C. Tanner, remembered when the Mitchells made an appointment to talk to him at his home in West Jordan in early 1993.

"They'd been on some kind of fast and he told me how happy they were to be healthy," said Larsen. "They both dressed like they were going to church, looked like a million bucks. They gave their pitch. They wanted a three-hundred-dollar donation for Sam West's book and some other literature. I thought three hundred was a bit steep. I told them I'd have to think about it."

Larsen was concerned for his friend. He had changed in the months since they'd worked together at O. C. Tanner. He was "a little smiley," remembered Larsen, "like he'd found an answer no one else understood." During their many conversations over the years at work, Larsen had heard Mitchell complain from time to time about the cost of Wanda's medication for her mental illness. Larsen worried that they might have dropped her medication in favor of West's lymphatic healing.

From all indications, it appeared that Larsen's suspicions were accurate. By 1994, the Mitchells had dumped most of their possessions and moved into their fifth-wheel trailer outside Heber, where, according to Wanda's sister Evelyn Camp, who lived next door with her husband, Dick, Wanda's mood swings escalated to levels reminiscent of the darkest days of her marriage to Tal.

"Brian and Wanda would have these huge fights," remembered Evelyn. "Wanda would be yelling and screaming, they'd really be going at it. It was one thing or another. Brian kept trying to grow a beard and different things and Wanda would throw a fit."

But if Wanda was unmedicated, she now had a different kind of controlling drug in her life—her born-again husband, who increasingly resorted to using the power of his priesthood to keep her in line.

"Brian would give her a blessing and the next thing you knew, she was OK with what he wanted to do," said Evelyn.

"He could get her to do anything he wanted by laying his hands on her head and guiding her in any direction he wanted her to go," said Dick Camp. "Brian knew Wanda, being a good and faithful servant, would obey the spirit, so he gave it to her."

After they left the Heber area in the fall of 1994, followed by a brief stay in Idaho, they traveled the country, subsisting for long stretches of time on only fruit. Wanda wrote her mother postcards bragging that she'd performed organ recitals at several churches in New York City, Boston, and Philadelphia. She confided, though, that no one actually attended the recitals—at least no living people. But when she looked out at the seats she said she saw her father, grandfather, and other family spirits from the other side, listening intently and adoringly. As she wrote to her mother on November 27, 1995, two days prior to the tenth anniversary of her marriage to Mitchell:

> We are on our way to Florida to continue the work in the service of our God. Thru [sic] many trials and great opposition in a wicked world we have grown tremendously in our faith and are continually sustained and protected thru [sic] our obedience to every word that proceedeth forth from the mouth of God in living the laws of the gospel: Sacrifice, consecration, and obedience. Witnessing the great wisdom and power of God & his promises are true and sure. Eating only fruit for 5 months, enjoyed a Thanksgiving meal of a wonderful variety of ALL FRUIT. May God be with you, Love, Brian and Wanda.

Nobody remembered seeing the Mitchells in Utah again until 1997. It wasn't long after they returned that they took their new names and put on their robes, which Wanda designed and sewed at her mother's house.

The first time Doug Larsen saw Brian dressed like Jesus was during the summer of 1998. For months, Larsen had been hearing that his old friend from O. C. Tanner was dressing in robes and begging on street corners. He wondered if it was just mean-spirited gossip at work until one day he rounded a corner in downtown Salt Lake City, across from the Salt Lake Temple, and there was Brian with his hand out.

"Can you help me with my needs?" Mitchell asked.

"Hey, Brian, how you doing?" said Larsen, who had his young son with him.

Mitchell moved away from them. He gave no indication that he and Larsen had ever known each other, let alone that they had worked side by side and joked about making idols for Babylon.

"I knew instantly it was him and the rumors were true," said Larsen. "I tried to get him to talk to me and he never gave a hint he knew who I was. I followed him all the way around the block. I physically grabbed him twice. He would stop and hit up other people for money and then move on. Finally I stuffed a five-dollar bill in his hand and left."

Less than a week later, Larsen and his wife were driving along State Street by the Hansen Planetarium in downtown Salt Lake City when Larsen looked up and saw Mitchell again. This time Wanda was with him. Larsen pointed them out to his wife, but, stung by the recent snub, he did not stop. From then on, Larsen periodically saw Mitchell around town; he called these episodes "Brian sightings."

Larsen had another Brian sighting on September 27, 2002, when he spotted Mitchell, alone, in the food court of the Crossroads Mall. By now he was used to seeing him on the downtown streets; the friend who ignored him had become a genuine Salt Lake City oddity. "He was leaning against a pillar, not doing anything," remembered Larsen. "I didn't even bother going up to him. I just kept on walking."

A week later, Mitchell's sister Lisa was in the same mall, standing with a nephew in a line at the food court, when she saw her brother leaning next to a post several feet away. "Look, there's Dahveed," said the nephew. Lisa had not had any contact with Mitchell since the problems the past April that resulted in her mother getting a protective order against him. All summer, she had worried about her older brother. She hoped he and Wanda were all right. Relieved to see him, she called out, "Hi, Brian."

Brian turned and their eyes met briefly, but instead of returning his sister's greeting, Mitchell said nothing, turned around, and walked away.

The Brian sightings in and around Temple Square the first part of October coincided with the LDS Church's semiannual general conference. This practice dates back to the 1840s, when the Mormon pioneers first came to Salt Lake City. Every six months, on the first Sunday in April and October, the LDS Church's general authorities assemble to speak on gospel topics. Their talks are televised worldwide, and thousands of Mormons come to Salt Lake City to hear them live. The conference typically attracts detractors of the LDS faith as well, people who stand on public property outside Temple Square and the adjoining 21,000-seat Conference Center and yell warnings to the thousands flocking inside. No one remembered seeing Mitchell or his alter ego, Immanuel David Isaiah, preaching openly during conference weekend, 2002, but several people remembered him being in the vicinity.

In the conference's aftermath, with winter on its way and a shoplifting warrant hanging over his head, Mitchell collected the woman he called Hephzibah and the girl they called Augustine, and directed them to the bus station a block west of Temple Square. There the three of them boarded a bus headed south.

No one bothered them as they boarded, just as no one had bothered them throughout the summer and early fall. For more than four months, Mitchell had hung onto Elizabeth in the shadow of her home, her family, her friends, and her community. No one had lifted her veil.

As the bus pulled away from the curb, Elizabeth looked behind her out the window, bidding a silent goodbye to the city that had always been her home. She had no idea whether she would ever see it again.

26

"Tom, you're not going to believe this!"

Ed was on the line. He had started a lot of conversations that way during the past four months. It was what he said before talking about the break-in at the Wrights', about Richard Ricci's death, and about the article in the *National Enquirer*. I braced myself for what was coming, instinctively preparing myself for more bad news. It was almost the middle of October, Ricci had been dead for a month and a half, and nearly $300,000 in reward money remained untouched. The case was more stagnant than ever.

"What won't I believe?"

"Mary Katherine said she knows who it was."

Like most moments of clarity, the epiphany came unannounced. Mary Katherine Smart, now ten years old, had been alone in her bedroom. It was Saturday night, October 12, 2002, her parents were out for the evening, and she had gone to her room alone to read. She ignored her schoolbooks, picked up a copy of the *Guinness Book of World Records*, and started thumbing through the pages, randomly scanning the stories and the pictures. She turned a page and a muscular-looking woman stared out at her. In that moment a flash of memory hit her.

Mary Katherine waited until her parents came home and were getting ready for bed. By that time, she had collected her thoughts to make sure of what she was about to tell them. She went to their bedroom and said, "Dad, I know who took Elizabeth."

"Who?" her dad asked.

"It was Emmanuel."

And again Ed asked, "Who?"

It took a moment for what Mary Katherine was telling her parents to register. It was late, and they were all tired. What, again, had she been reading? Did she know what she was saying? But as they continued to talk, Ed and Lois felt a vague memory begin to surface—the memory of a man who had once briefly entered their lives, a man who called himself Emmanuel.

He was the one Lois and the kids had met downtown by the mall, where he asked for a handout, and Lois had given him five dollars and invited him to come to the house to work. But that was a long time ago. And he only came one day for just a few hours. Was that who Mary Katherine meant? Was that the man who took Elizabeth? Was that Emmanuel? Was she sure?

She nodded her head yes, explaining that she remembered his name and the day he came to the house and the backpack he was carrying. She also remembered his voice. It was the same voice she'd heard that awful night in the bedroom.

Ed and Lois walked with Mary Katherine to her room so she could show them the picture that had jarred her memory. She didn't know why, but it had. She had been looking at it and suddenly she just knew.

The police had said this might happen. In June, Don Bell had specifically cautioned Ed, Lois, and the extended family to be careful not to fill Mary Katherine's head with theories and suggestions about who or what she saw. Because sometimes, a moment of truth could arrive months down the road, and when it did, it was usually unbidden. In a July 19 press conference, Chief Dinse had said, "We've had four formal interviews with her [Mary Katherine], and we are confident we have a good piece of information. We may learn more from her as time goes on because of the ability to remember and recall a traumatic situation, particularly with a child of her age."

Ed and Lois continued their questioning. This Emmanuel—that's the only name he'd given them—was such a fleeting part of their lives and it had been almost a year ago. His stay was so short and of such little consequence that Ed had not included him on the list of workers he'd given to the police. It was not a conscious omission. Ed had simply kept no memory of the man.

Despite the clarity of Mary Katherine's recall, on paper it didn't add up. It seemed unlikely that a person who came and went from their lives that quickly, and that long ago, would be Elizabeth's kidnapper. Ed and Lois could not recall ever seeing the man again or hearing another thing about him. Neither could Mary Katherine—until the night Elizabeth disappeared.

On Sunday morning, October 13, Ed and Lois called Cory Lyman. Then Ed called me and asked if I would please keep the new development quiet until the police had a chance to size it up.

The police scheduled an interview with Mary Katherine, her fifth official interview, not counting the times when she was shown the lineup of hats or the tape of Ricci's voice. Her last major interviews had been in early July with Jeanne Boylan and again shortly thereafter when an attempt to hypnotize her failed. All who had interviewed her had been impressed with Mary Katherine's consistency and forthrightness. In a television interview, Jeanne Boylan stated, "I'm delighted to report that she's a very strong child. She's very committed to assisting in this search for Elizabeth. She's very alert, very astute, extremely articulate, and was quite good to work with in terms of my particular job... she's been extremely consistent."

Mary Katherine had never tried to embellish her answers to please the grownups questioning her. It was just as my father always said: "Mary Katherine doesn't talk much, but when she does, you should listen."

Still, the more adults who questioned her new information about Emmanuel—and the more rational thought was applied to a seemingly irrational theory—the more concerned she became that she might be fingering the wrong person.

"Dad," she said before her police interview, "what if it's not him?"

"If it's not, we'll find out and move on," Ed assured her. After that, to protect his daughter, Ed softened Mary Katherine's quote to, "I *think* I know who it was."

Her interview took place on Tuesday, October 15, at the Children's Justice Center, with the same detective who had conducted the previous two official police interviews. By coincidence, the interview took place the same day noted forensic scientist Dr. Henry Lee arrived in town. The police had arranged for Dr. Lee, who became famous for his role in the O. J. Simpson murder trial (one of more than six thousand cases he'd worked), to come in as a consultant on the investigation. Through an intermediary—the Fox network's Carole McKinney in Denver—Henry Lee had offered to examine the crime scene and provide advice on the case. The SLCPD accepted the offer, although some in the department, including Chief Dinse, were nervous about Lee's visit. Dinse had been working for the Los Angeles Police Department when Lee exposed many of the LAPD's mistakes during the O. J. Simpson trial. The FBI was also nervous about an independent contractor coming into the investigation. But Ed wanted Dr. Lee's input and he pushed hard for it, as did Cory Lyman. The compromise they reached was that the criminologist would fly to Salt Lake City and review the investigation only after signing a confidentiality agreement that barred him from talking about his findings to anyone other than law enforcement involved with the case.

With Cory Lyman and Don Bell, Dr. Lee watched Mary Katherine's interview from another room. Although Bell was no longer assigned to the case, Lyman still used him as a consultant. Bell disapproved of Lee, an outsider, being allowed to watch the interview, but Lyman insisted.

Mary Katherine gave the interviewer as many details about Emmanuel as she could. She recalled that he raked leaves with her brother, that he was soft-spoken, and that he carried a backpack. She recounted looking at the *Guinness Book of World Records* and how that brought the man into her mind. But while she continued to contend he was the man who took Elizabeth, she was not as forceful in her comments as she had been the first night when she told her dad. The torrent of questions from interviewers clearly unsettled her a bit.

Like Ed and Lois, the police had a hard time making it fit. If Emmanuel was homeless then he probably wouldn't have transportation. If he took Elizabeth, how did he escape? And what was his motive for taking Elizabeth? Why would he wait seven months to take her? Why had no one seen him again in the vicinity? Why hadn't he demanded any ransom?

As with the attempted break-in at Steve and Jenny Wright's house in July, the police wanted to keep this development quiet. If Emmanuel was the one, they wanted to look for him without spooking him. If it turned out that he wasn't the kidnapper, they wouldn't run the risk of looking foolish, as they had with Bret Edmunds.

Beyond the name of Emmanuel, which was almost certainly an alias, they had little to go on. Ed and Lois couldn't come up with many details from the two brief contacts the street preacher had with the family. Lois seemed to recall the man saying he was from Pennsylvania or somewhere back east, which wasn't much to go on. He had been very soft-spoken, Ed remembered, and did not volunteer much information about himself. They sat within a few feet of each other while they worked on the roof, and they talked, but their conversation was mostly about the Bible. The man did tell Ed that he was staying with his sister somewhere in the valley, and that they both traveled and preached to the homeless. Ed couldn't even remember if Emmanuel had seen all his children, although from the skylight they did have a view of the living room where Elizabeth played her harp. She may have been practicing that day. He couldn't remember. He could remember paying the man forty dollars even though he owed him fifty. Whoever he was, Ed owed him ten bucks.

No one was sure how to spell *Emmanuel*. The dictionary said the name, meaning "God with Us," could be spelled with an *E* or an *I*. Either way was correct. We decided to spell Emmanuel with an *E*.

For the police, the more pressing issue at the moment was getting their money's worth out of the famous Dr. Lee, who would only be in town for two days. After Mary Katherine's interview, the criminologist was delivered directly to Ed and Lois's house, where the crime scene was re-created for him. The patio chair was propped back up against the outer wall as it had been the morning of the kidnapping. Lee checked out the location of the screen and the way it was cut, the way the window cranked open to the outside, and other details throughout the kitchen, the girls' bedroom, and the rest of the house.

In accordance with the confidentiality agreement he'd signed, Dr. Lee did not discuss his work or findings with the media or the family, although that did not stop *Salt Lake Tribune* reporters Cantera and Vigh from reporting that Dr. Lee, in support of the pet theory they had been pushing since

June, concluded the window screen had been cut from the inside. They wrote: "Lee's examination of a kitchen window screen led him to back an early police theory that the screen was cut from inside the home, possibly as a diversionary tactic by the abductor, multiple law enforcement sources tell the *Tribune*." The sources, as usual, were not named.

The *Tribune* report flew in the face of what Cory Lyman told Ed—that Lee believed the kidnapper cut the screen while standing on the chair outside the house. Lyman said Dr. Lee believed the intruder was a man closer to six feet tall than five-foot-eight, based on the height of the incision along the right side of the screen. The upper edge of the cut was one inch short of seven feet above the chair, theoretically requiring the reach of a taller man (unless he had a longer knife). Lyman also told Ed that Lee felt the evidence suggested that the kidnapper was someone who was familiar with the interior of the house. Both conclusions had the effect of supporting the case against the late Richard Ricci, no matter how he entered the home, which led Lyman to remark that he was more convinced than ever that Ricci committed the crime.

It wasn't Dr. Lee's job to point to any suspects or potential suspects. He was a scientist, not a detective, an examiner of evidence, not theories. At dinner with Ed and Lois the night before he left, the sixty-four-year-old crime-scene veteran told them that criminal investigations rarely yield absolutes, and crime scenes are typically full of gray areas, not black-and-white evidence. The "aha" moments that solve mysteries quickly are mostly on television. In real life, criminal investigations involve a lot of work, concentration, and luck. He told Elizabeth's parents about one investigation he'd worked on that wasn't solved for thirty years.

"You have to be patient," Dr. Lee said. "You never know when that lucky break will happen."

27

Despite any doubts they harbored about a young girl's sudden recall four months after the kidnapping, the Emmanuel lead gave the police a chance to do basic investigative work, and they got busy. Because of the suspect's apparent religious identity, one of the first jurisdictions the SLCPD contacted was the security department of the LDS Church.

Almost instantly, investigators had a promising lead. LDS security produced identification information, photographs, and videotape of an anti-Mormon preacher who they said called himself Emmanuel and was often seen around Temple Square, especially at conference time. They showed Ed a photograph of the man. Ed didn't think it looked much like the clean-cut Emmanuel who had worked on his roof, but he didn't rule out the possibility. When police went to the man's house to question him, they were told he was on a long-haul trucking job. While they waited for him to return, detectives brought Elizabeth's brother Andrew, who had been in the backyard when Emmanuel raked leaves and had gotten a good look at him, to the station to work on a sketch with the department artist. (In an effort to protect her memory, Mary Katherine was not consulted for a sketch). Before starting, they showed Andrew a photo of the truck-driving Emmanuel. Not surprisingly, the drawing that was produced resembled the truck driver, who returned later in the week and was cleared with an airtight alibi.

No one in Ed's family, including Andrew, thought the police's sketch looked much like the man they remembered. Charles, Andrew's older brother, went to the station in an effort to produce a better likeness, but after a number of attempts, he got frustrated and left. The inability to produce an acceptable sketch underscored the fleeting relationship Ed and Lois's family had with the man they knew only as Emmanuel.

The task of finding Emmanuel fell to SLCPD detective Cordon Parks, who, along with Detective Bill Silver, was now doing most of the active investigative work on Elizabeth's case. Silver had the task of organizing and filing all information, including paperwork generated by more than twenty thousand leads from throughout the United States. Parks was the man on the street, the lead investigator when it came to interviews, fingerprints, and new leads. After the trucker lead didn't pan out, Parks took Andrew's sketch out on the streets. He began with the numerous homeless shelters throughout the city. One of the detective's first discoveries was that Emmanuel isn't an uncommon name. In no time, he had more than thirty leads to follow.

But while Parks was on the street chasing down his leads, he was doing it without help. The rank-and-file officers in the department, the patrolmen who worked the streets daily, were not told about the search for Emmanuel. Patrolmen Randy Marks and David Greer, to name two, never heard of a hunt for a homeless man named Emmanuel. If they had known about the search, they could have told Parks about the man they had charged with shoplifting at Albertsons three weeks earlier, on September 27. From there they easily could have produced the field card they had filled out with the man's thumbprint and his real name, Brian David Mitchell. They also could have referred the investigators to the security department at Albertsons, where a Polaroid photograph of the man was filed.

Also out of the loop was Pamela Atkinson and her homeless advocacy group. Atkinson, affectionately dubbed Saint Pamela by the city's homeless, knew the goings and comings—and the names—of Salt Lake City's homeless population better than anyone. But the police did not contact her or anyone in her organization. Neither were any out-of-state law enforcement agencies contacted. The search for Emmanuel stayed in-house, known to only a handful in law enforcement. The operation was the polar opposite of an all-points bulletin.

■ ■ ■

While the SLCPD undertook its tepid investigation of Emmanuel, the belief that Richard Ricci was the real culprit remained as strong as ever within the law enforcement community. Conventional wisdom was that the best hope for closure in the aftermath of Ricci's death was finding where he disposed of Elizabeth's body. The police were much more eager to get out the word to deer hunters to keep an eye out for a dead body than they were to look for the handyman identified by the sole eyewitness to the kidnapping. In advance of the annual late-October hunt, which attracts as many as a quarter of a million people to the hills throughout Utah, the family prepared a new flier soliciting help from anyone headed into the forests and mountains. The police were very cooperative in helping the family promote the fliers with the media. We listed the various rewards and included a photograph of the Polo athletic shoes Elizabeth was wearing when she was kidnapped. At the bottom was the toll-free number in case anyone found anything suspicious: 1-866-FIND-LIZ.

But the ten-day hunt came and went without any new leads. There were a few hours of anxiety when some hunters found a pile of bones outside Wallsburg, a small town close to the Heber Valley, especially when initial reports indicated they were human bones. But closer inspection determined the bones belonged to a dead bear. There were also anxious moments when a girl's burned body was found in a car near the Great Salt Lake and also when a young blond girl was found murdered in Brigham City and initial reports suggested it could be Elizabeth. Further investigation showed there was no connection, however.

Like the Utah weather, the trail was growing colder as Elizabeth's fifteenth birthday (November 3) approached. In honor of the day, Ed and Lois took their family to Disneyland, one of Elizabeth's favorite places. They tried their best to enjoy their time at "The happiest place on Earth." But joy was still hard to come by; thoughts drifted so easily and naturally to memories of the missing child. They remembered Elizabeth's fourteenth birthday party the year before, when she had invited twenty-three of her friends to her house. They had the party in the rec room and Elizabeth started a food fight.

At least the Disneyland trip spared Ed from having to deal with a cruel counterfeiter trying to capitalize on his family's misfortune. While Ed was with his family in California, David received an e-mail on the search center Web site from kidnapper802002@yahoo.com. A person who called himself "elizabethsmartkidnapper" wrote that he had Elizabeth and would release her for a ransom of three million dollars:

> i have Elizabeth she is not hurt yet i want to talk to ed smart when i talk to ed i'll let elizabeth go.

David forwarded the e-mail to Mick Fennerty at the FBI and Bill Silver at SLCPD. Law enforcement computer experts were able to trace its origin to a computer located in Charleston, South Carolina. The address rang a bell with David, who remembered a ransom note that had arrived at the search center's post office box in September with a Charleston, South Carolina, postmark. The content of that ransom note was disturbing but amateurish:

> To Ed Smart and family,
> We got your daughter. If you ever want to see her pretty face again you'll give us what we want. We want one million dollars or she will die. Do not send any police or we will hurt Elizabeth and we will come back for her little sister. If we don't get the money and a clean getaway like we want, our friends and us will kill Elizabeth. I will contact you later with more info. Don't try and find out who this is cause it won't do you any good.

Because the ransom note was written on the back of a search center flier that hadn't been designed until late summer—which meant that it had to have been written months after the kidnapping occurred—and because there had been no follow-up on the ransom demand, the note had been filed away and forgotten. But with the e-mail, and the increased demand for three million dollars, it appeared the person in Charleston had not gone away. Adding to the concern was that in late August, *America's Most Wanted* received a tip from a viewer who claimed he saw a distraught blond girl who looked like Elizabeth leaning against a green Volvo in the company of two boys in Charleston.

Under the direction of the FBI and SLCPD, David posed as Ed and began an e-mail correspondence with elizabethsmartkidnapper. David asked basic questions about Elizabeth's health and well-being and then queried, "If you truly have my daughter, please ask her to tell you what she tells me before she goes to bed at night." He received this reply:

> i want 3 million dollars elizabeth says she misses you and she loves u so you want me to ask her what she says to you before she goes to bed she says to say your prayers and she didn't say but i think she most likely ask you to say your prayers with her. So ed hows that, i asked her and that's what she said so now get the money ready and also tell mary kathleen [sic] her sister is fine. Ed i want this over just as much as you do now you wanted me to contact you, so here i am. You and me both know things wont never be the same but if you do what i say they will be better than they are now.

At this juncture, David called Ed and let him in on what was going on. Ed said he always told all the kids, "Say your prayers" and "I love you" before they went to bed.

While e-mails flew back and forth through cyberspace between David and the Charleston address, the FBI zeroed in on the exact location of the computer that was sending the e-mails, a residence in suburban Charleston. The FBI secured a search warrant, and when FBI agents and Charleston County Sheriff's deputies showed up at the residence on Tuesday, November 5, eighteen-year-old Walter Kenneth Holloway was at the computer in his room answering one of David's e-mails. Holloway surrendered without a fight.

The FBI found copies of Holloway's various ransom demands plus other incriminating evidence in his room, along with four rifles, but, as they expected, no trace of Elizabeth. The teenager's parents, who were home at the time of the raid, insisted they had no idea that their son was engaged in criminal activity. His mother said he spent a lot of time in his room on the computer but she thought it was just innocent Internet chat room stuff. In the garage, the Holloway family car matched the description of the green

Volvo that had been called into *America's Most Wanted*. Apparently, Holloway had called in the tip himself as part of the hoax. After Holloway was arrested, police and FBI discovered that earlier in the summer Holloway had signed up to be a team search leader on the Elizabethsmart.com Web site.

The craziness continued, but none of it led anywhere. In mid-November, out of frustration at the lack of progress, Cory Lyman did a series of one-on-one interviews with Salt Lake City's major newspapers and television stations. The task force commander talked of his desire to be more open in the investigation. "We want to make our own luck," he said as he offered to make public more information about the case. He revealed new details about the souvenir items Ricci had stolen from the Smarts' house and the information that some house keys might still be unaccounted for—another indirect indictment of Ricci, who, as a workman, would conceivably have had access to Ed's keys. Lyman said the late handyman remained at the top of the list of possible suspects. Other than obliquely reporting that investigators were still trying to track down a few men who had worked on the Smart house, Lyman did not talk about the Emmanuel lead, despite his announced intention to be more open.

As he had said on a number of occasions, Lyman told reporters that he believed the abductor's point of entry into the house was not through the kitchen window and the cut screen "The crime lab gave us a pretty strong indication that there wasn't anyone that went through that window," Lyman told Derek Jensen in the *Deseret News*. Again, the inference was it had been a perfect crime for an opportunist like Ricci who could have had other ways to enter and exit the house—but who likely used the cut screen as a ruse. Kevin Cantera's report in the *Salt Lake Tribune* seized on Lyman's remarks about the screen to validate what Cantera and his partner Michael Vigh had long contended. "[Lyman] said investigators are convinced that a window screen in the Smarts' kitchen had been cut from inside the home, as the *Tribune* first reported a week after the June 5 kidnapping," wrote Cantera. "And he provided insight as to why police scrutinized Elizabeth's family members in the days immediately after her abduction. 'We played the odds,' he said. 'We obviously put a lot of focus on family members because we very much believe [the perpetrator] was somebody familiar with the family and the home. Lyman said police have eliminated a number of potential suspects, including members of the girl's family. 'It's a big extended family and we can't completely rule some people out,' he said."

The quotes attributed to Lyman in Cantera's story bothered Ed, who for five months had been in almost daily contact with Lyman and was surprised that the task force commander would continue to speculate that the screen was cut from the inside. He also wanted to know where Lyman's comment in the *Tribune* about missing keys had come from. When Ed confronted Lyman about these points, however, Lyman denied that he had said that the screen had been cut from the inside. He also claimed that his reference about the keys was only a general suspicion that the kidnapper might have had access to keys, not that there were, specifically, keys missing. He said he had been misquoted and that he would call the *Tribune* and ask for a correction.

Ed continued to complain about the police sketch of Emmanuel. He repeatedly told Lyman that even he didn't recognize it as the man he had worked with on his roof. He wanted to work with an artist and try to do a better likeness. His nagging finally paid off when Lyman called Ed on November 15 and told him an artist had arrived at the station who might be able to help.

The artist's name was Dalene Nielson. She lived in Moab, Utah, in the southeastern part of the state, and had come to Salt Lake City to check on possible work opportunities. She stopped by the Salt Lake City Police Department and asked what it would take to become a composite sketch artist. The officer at the desk summoned Lyman. Dalene told Lyman she had never done a police sketch, but she was willing to learn. Lyman told her he had a case that could use a fresh artist right away. Cory approached one of the officers working the case and asked for his opinion about the freelance artist helping out. The officer commented, "It's as if it were meant to be."

Ed immediately drove to the station and went to a room with Dalene and they got to work. Ed thought that he himself might be the best person to work with a sketch artist, as he had spent the most time with Emmanuel. It was still a long shot—a year-old memory. They didn't have time to finish the first day but Ed was pleased with their progress and asked if they could continue the next day. Lyman agreed and Dalene, who had planned to leave town that night, rearranged her schedule to finish the sketch, which she completed at Ed's home the following day. Ed still wasn't entirely satisfied with the final product, but he thought Dalene had drawn a much better likeness than the sketch the police had been using. He thanked Dalene for her time and patience; before she left to take the original to the station, he made a copy of her sketch.

As a family, most of us wanted to see the police immediately go public with the new sketch. After a month of no results, it seemed to be the best approach. But Lyman insisted that the search remain private. Tip off this man that he was being looked for, he said, and he was liable to go so far underground that we would never find him. Among law enforcement officers, only Mick Fennerty thought they should make the sketch public, and one vote wasn't nearly enough to make it happen. As Thanksgiving approached, Detective Parks went back out on the streets with the new sketch, an assignment that didn't particularly thrill him. Others in the department weren't thrilled when word got around that Lyman had let an unproven artist work with Ed, particularly when they already had a very good artist on staff. One officer shook his head and jokingly confided to another close to the investigation, "We'd like to help, but we're too fucked up."

On the weekend before Thanksgiving, harp students who had practiced and played with Elizabeth gathered in the rotunda of the State Capitol for a performance in her honor. Throughout the fall, Elizabeth's harp teacher, ShruDeLi Ownbey, had been preparing for the concert. If Elizabeth returned by the scheduled date, the concert would be a celebration. If she was not back, it would serve as a musical tribute that she was missed and not forgotten.

Mary Katherine was one of the performers. In a salute to her sister, she played Elizabeth's harp and wore Elizabeth's black ballet shoes. She was one of dozens of harpists who performed that night, along with the bell choir from Riverton High School, a string quartet, and several flutists and clarinet players. A picture of Elizabeth playing her harp and the words "Dedicated to Elizabeth Smart" was on the front and back covers of each printed program, while Elizabeth's images were projected onto a large video screen behind the performers. A large crowd filled the chairs on the capitol's main floor while a number of visitors in the building stopped and watched from the rotunda's balcony. Many family members scanned the crowd, looking for anyone or anything suspicious.

In a final poignant tribute to Elizabeth, the harpists, dressed in black dresses with white collars and cuffs and each adorned with a baby blue ribbon, played a specially arranged spiritual medley titled "Motherless Child and Wayfaring Stranger."

28

No one around Lindo Lake Park could pinpoint the exact day the three white-robed people showed up in Lakeside. Lindo Lake Park isn't the kind of place people keep records regarding arrivals and departures.

The park and its small lake sit at the edge of town in Lakeside, California, an unincorporated community twenty-five miles northeast of downtown San Diego. Lakeside serves as a kind of buffer between metropolitan San Diego, the country's seventh most populated area, and the sparsely inhabited mountains and deserts beyond. Ten miles to the west lie malls, giant stadiums, the sprawling campus of San Diego State University, and street after street of the residential neighborhoods of El Cajon, La Mesa, Mission Valley, and Claremont Mesa. Five miles to the east is the Barona Casino on reservation land belonging to the Barona group of the Mission Indians.

It was to Lakeside that Brian David Mitchell brought Wanda and Elizabeth for the winter. The area has a diverse population of 54,000 that includes cowboys (the Lakeside Rodeo held in late April is one of California's biggest), Native Americans, motorcycle riders, a smattering of white supremacists, and assorted other individualists, including a large homeless contingent. With mild winters and multiple places to camp along the banks and underpasses of the San Diego River as it meanders on the northeast side of town on its way to the Pacific Ocean, Lakeside has gained a reputation as a friendly place for the homeless.

The unofficial center of homeless Lakeside is Lindo Lake Park, a pleasant green place close to the river bottoms and handy to the town's markets, liquor stores, and plentiful soup kitchens. When it was first developed late in the nineteenth century, the park was the center of the Lakeside Resort, a favorite escape of San Diegans, featuring a boathouse and adjoining race-track. In the twenty-first century, the lake and the boathouse remain, but the racetrack and vacation resort are long gone, replaced by a museum, a library, and tennis courts.

Clay Ruis, a Lindo Lake regular, was sitting on the grass near the tennis courts one evening in late October or early November 2002, when he looked across the park and saw the man in the white robes making his way toward him. Clay's brother Roger, their friend Ray Adame, and several oth-ers in their loose-knit group had earlier in the week noticed the strangely dressed man and the two women with him. Clay and his cronies debated as to who and what these strangers were. Muslims was the most popular guess, as the women were veiled and the man looked a lot like Osama bin Laden. No one approached the three to ask their business. They didn't appear to be outgoing and social, and if anything is respected among people without homes or much of anything else, it is privacy.

But now the robed fellow appeared friendly as he made straight for Clay, who remembered, "It was dark and his robe was flowing like something out of a Cecil B. DeMille spectacular. He asked me where a guy could get some beer around here, so I said I'd show him where the 7-Eleven was."

As they walked along Vine Street the few blocks to the twenty-four-hour convenience store, Clay asked Mitchell who he was. "He called him-self Immanuel," Clay remembered of that conversation. "At first he suggested he was Jesus Christ himself. He said, 'I am that person.' I said, 'Wait a minute, you're who?' Then he backed off and said his name was Immanuel and he was the Lord's messenger."

Clay told Mitchell that people guessed he was Muslim, not Christian, because the women with him wore veils. "He said the veils were to cover them from the sins of the world," said Clay. "He bought a six-pack at the 7-Eleven. I asked him, 'What is this, communion?' He didn't answer but after about three beers he tried to convert me. I quickly remembered a dental appointment and skedaddled."

As they had on the streets of Salt Lake City, Mitchell, Wanda, and Elizabeth quickly became familiar oddities in Lakeside because of their unusual dress and habits. But they walked the streets of the much smaller town more freely than they had in Salt Lake City. There were no posters with Elizabeth's face on them here and no billboards offering a reward for her return. Sometimes, the women would even lower their veils, and Clay Ruis remembered once seeing the three of them get off a bus dressed in regular clothes. That's when he noticed that the shorter woman looked old, weary, and very wrinkled, and that the taller woman wasn't a woman at all, but just a girl. She seemed weary too; he remembered that she did not talk and did not smile.

After leaving Utah by bus, Mitchell, Wanda, and Elizabeth traveled through Las Vegas, and then, according to a number of reported sightings, stayed for a few days in the high desert country in and around Victorville, California. Eventually, they made their way to San Diego and finally east to Lakeside, a mere three-dollar trolley fare from the bus depot in downtown San Diego.

Mitchell set up two camps in Lakeside. One was in the river bottoms, the neighborhood of choice for the homeless because water is easier to find, campsites are flat, trees and shade abound, and there are plenty of bridges to take shelter under when it rains. The other was half a mile up a steep hillside above the river. The hillside camp was wedged on uneven ground amid a stand of isolated oak trees a few hundred yards above a miniature airport for model airplanes. The upper camp was similar to the first place where Mitchell kept Elizabeth in Dry Creek Canyon; it was long on security and short on comfort. From the high ground, they could see anything approaching without being seen themselves. Because law enforcement regularly patrols the river bottoms, sometimes on horseback, and hands out hundred-dollar illegal-occupancy citations to anyone caught with messy, junk-filled campsites, Mitchell spent more time at the hillside camp, but he stored more gear and provisions at the lower camp, where he burrowed into the hard dirt to create storage compartments that were invisible to the casual observer.

The camps sat on opposite sides and were about equidistant from Cactus County Park, a rural San Diego County facility on the outskirts of Lakeside that houses a motocross track and baseball and softball fields.

Roy Miranda and Judy Gaspers were the on-site caretakers of Cactus County Park. They lived in a beat-up trailer at the park's edge, by the two-lane state highway and the dirt trail leading to the edge of town and Lindo Lake Park. Miranda and Gaspers couldn't help but notice as the robed newcomers went to and from town past the park. Miranda and Gaspers were just one step away from being homeless themselves. Their arrangement with the county allowed them to keep their trailer at the edge of the park in exchange for locking the gates at sundown and generally keeping an eye on things. There was no other pay involved, although Miranda did get to carry a gun (a .22) and wear a sheriff's shirt the county provided. It was his job to report any suspicious activity. The grounds of El Capitan High School border one side of the park, and the river bottoms border the other side. It's an attractive place for those who might want to carry out mischief or criminal acts.

The park caretakers made friends with their new neighbors. Far from reporting the squatters to the authorities, they gave them unrestricted access to their hose for water (courtesy of the County of San Diego Department of Parks and Recreation), full use of the park's bathroom facilities located next to their trailer (two decrepit toilets, one men's and one women's, in a shabby cement building), and sometimes, when Gaspers felt like cooking, dinner. Their one condition, and Miranda insisted on this, was that there be no conversation about religion or politics. "Start preaching," he told Mitchell, "and you're out of here."

A bond developed between them. When Miranda and Gaspers asked where they were from, Mitchell responded guardedly, "Up north." The park caretakers could see that these people were running from something, but, then, in the river bottoms, lots of people were doing that. They didn't know if they were running from the law or family or debts or simply from themselves, but whatever it was, they could relate. Miranda and Gaspers had their own string of failed marriages and problems with society that kept them fleeing their pasts, and, like so many homeless people, they had their fair share of addictions that kept them from moving forward. Both had turned fifty-two in 2002, putting them in the same general age bracket as Mitchell, forty-nine, and Wanda, fifty-seven, although they had no idea those were their names. Miranda called Mitchell "Chief" and Wanda "Mom." As for the young girl with them, both Miranda and Gaspers mostly called her "girl." They were quick to note that Mitchell didn't like it when the girl was asked her name, or, for that matter, any personal questions. Once, when Mitchell wasn't around, Gaspers asked the girl her name and she answered Liz. "I asked her if that was short for Elizabeth," Gaspers remembered, "and she changed the subject."

Mitchell's daily routine for the three was simple: they would walk to town past Gaspers and Miranda's trailer in the morning, spend the day preaching and begging, and then walk back to their camp before sundown. As he had in Salt Lake City, Mitchell learned the best spots to beg, and he quickly located the shelters that handed out free food and clothing.

They became a local fixture, as they paraded in their robes through Lindo Lake Park and up and down Woodside Avenue, Lakeside's main business street. They were regulars at Wrigley's, a grocery store across from Lindo Lake Park, and almost every day the clerks at the KK Market next door to Wrigley's would see them come in first thing in the morning. KK sells lotto tickets, phone cards, snacks, and alcohol. Mitchell usually walked to the cooler at the far end of the store and selected a twenty-four-ounce can of Steel Reserve, a malt liquor with 8.1 percent alcohol—nearly twice the content of regular beer. A can of Steel Reserve cost ninety-nine cents at KK. Mitchell bought soda pop for the women.

It bothered the regular clerk, Shirley Tajedini, and the store's owner, Rafe Potres, the way the man made the women stand behind him; he never let them speak as he waited to pay for the drinks.

"He weirded me out," remembered Tajedini. "He used to ask the women, 'Do you want a drink?' They'd nod. They never talked. I figured he converted them. I didn't like to wait on him. When it was his turn, I'd turn [to Potres] and say, 'You take him.' It was so weird, a man who looked like Jesus, buying beer. He bought one almost every day. That Steel Reserve that he bought, it's a really strong beer. Only heavy drinkers buy that."

Occasionally, law enforcement officials would stop the three and talk to them. Gus Kurupas and Jim Seal were county sheriff's deputies who worked out of the Lakeside station not far from Lindo Lake Park, and were assigned to keep an eye on the homeless. They periodically received calls about the people who looked like Muslims.

"There is a small Muslim community near Wrigley's Market and I remember someone called right after they got here about some suspected American Taliban type of person," said Kurupas. "But we talked to them and they seemed harmless. They were odd, but that's not illegal. The Alpine sheriff said he talked to them, so did some of the other town cops, and the high school police at El Capitan High School."

Tacit approval by the police made the arrangement even more secure, and Mitchell and the women settled into their winter home. Mitchell's only means of support appeared to be panhandling. He no longer sought out work as a handyman. Terri Sparks, the woman who ran the recycling trailer in the parking lot outside Wrigley's and the KK Market, got a lot of business from the homeless and the down-and-out who picked up cans and scrap around town, but the Muslim-looking people never brought her anything. "Almost every day I'd see them walk by," remembered Sparks. "They just looked like a regular weird-looking family. You don't ask anything 'cause someone's down on their luck. You just don't. But they never recycled."

The winter nights could get very cold, with temperatures sometimes dipping into the thirties. Occasionally, to combat the cold, Mitchell would take Wanda and Elizabeth to spend the night in an abandoned trailer on the other side of the model airplane field. "That trailer was used mostly by people stripping down motorcycles they stole," said Miranda. "They stayed there sometimes. I'd have been afraid to stay there myself." But mostly they would return from town after dark—which in the winter was any time after five—and cut through Cactus Park and either hike back up the hill to their camp or head for the river bottoms.

"I showed them how I fake-locked the [park] gate," said Miranda. "The padlock looked locked but it wasn't. It was a shortcut for them. When we heard the chain on the gate rattle, we knew it was them. They'd go to their camp and sing hymns. The sound really carries from up on that hill. When they stopped singing, we knew it was time for bed. It was kind of our routine."

■　■　■

Homeless-friendly Lakeside increased the hopelessness of Elizabeth's situation. Mitchell's threats to kill her if she spoke up remained a constant, as did his incessant preaching, berating, and insistence that she maintain a daily journal. This practice had begun the day he took her from her home in Salt Lake City, although Wanda wrote the first entries. In glowing language, Wanda wrote how wonderful and benevolent Immanuel was. Elizabeth's entries, overseen and censored by Mitchell, were complimentary, but terse. She sometimes added her true feelings of despair and her disdain for her captors in the rudimentary French that she had learned at Bryant Intermediate School.

Trapped far from home, Elizabeth could only watch as she passed the students of El Capitan High School each day on the walk to town. There on the other side of the chain-link fence were girls her age. They were laughing; going to class; running; talking; complaining about homework; and discussing boys, clothes, makeup, shopping, and weekend plans, while Elizabeth remained at the mercy of a man who had cut short her childhood.

For the most part they lived on the streets of Lakeside looking for food and money. Occasionally, Mitchell would ask Miranda if he knew of any work. "I told him I'd hire him on when I could," said Miranda, a magnanimous if hollow offer from a man not being paid himself.

A lot of the money Mitchell got from his begging went to buy booze. He was a regular customer—not just at KK and the 7-Eleven, but at various other stores in town that sold alcohol. "He drank like a fish," remembered Clay Ruis. "He could put down his cheap wine with the best of them."

Any hint of a human crowd drove the women out of the park and back up the hill. The outside world was a threat, but Lakeside was very conducive to the life Mitchell wanted for his flock of two. In Miranda and Gaspers's isolated existence looking after things at Cactus County Park, they had never heard a word about the Elizabeth Smart kidnapping.

It was in December that Mitchell showed up for services at the Santee Third Ward of the Church of Jesus Christ of Latter-day Saints. He arrived at the wardhouse on Lake Jennings Park Road in Lakeside, about a mile from the river bottoms, at 9 A.M., just as the three-hour block of meetings began with sacrament meeting. A few heads turned in the congregation as he took a seat about three-quarters of the way back in the middle section of the chapel, but they turned right back again. It wasn't uncommon, given the area's homeless population, to see a person come to Sunday services dressed in boots, jeans, and a flannel shirt, which is what Mitchell was wearing. His long hair and beard were both bunched up and each was held in place by a rubber band. He was just another man from the river bottoms looking for salvation.

To those who inquired, Mitchell said his name was Peter. He said he was not LDS and knew nothing about the religion; he just came to the church because he wanted to worship the Lord. But as Virl Kemp watched the stranger during the morning's services, first at sacrament meeting, then at Sunday school, and finally during priesthood meeting, he began to wonder. Most visitors didn't stay for all three meetings. Virl, a lifelong Mormon, long-time member of the Santee Third Ward, and group leader of the High Priest quorum, couldn't help but notice that when they sang the hymns the man in the flannel shirt joined right in as if he'd known the words all his life. "Boy, he was into the songs," remembered Virl.

At the end of the church services, Virl's wife, Peggy, suggested they invite the stranger home for Sunday dinner. She'd already invited the two full-time missionaries who were assigned to Lakeside. There was plenty of food for one more. Virl tried to find the visitor in the building but missed him. As the Kemps got in their car and turned out of the parking lot, however, they saw him walking along the street in front of the church. They pulled over and lowered the passenger-side window. "Do you have any place to go for lunch?" asked Peggy. Mitchell soon climbed in and sat in the back next to the missionaries.

The Kemps lived in Santee, about three miles west of Lakeside, in a frame house that backed onto the grounds of a junior high school. Virl and Peggy had recently married and blended their families. Virl had five children from his previous marriage (his wife had died) and the last of the five, a seventeen-year-old son, was still living at home. Peggy had a twelve-year-old daughter who also lived at home. Over dinner, the Kemps told their guests about themselves and their children. Peggy's daughter was spending the weekend at the home of her father, Peggy's ex-husband, in another town. But they did show their guests a picture of the cute blond-haired, blue-eyed girl who was about to turn thirteen. They weren't sure their indigent guest even noticed, he was so busy with lunch. "He was eating like he hadn't eaten in a while," remembered Virl. "He out-ate the Elders."

As devout LDS are inclined to do, after dinner Virl, Peggy, and the two missionaries attempted to engage their nonmember friend in a discussion about the restored gospel. "We sat in the living room and talked about the prophet Joseph Smith, the Book of Mormon, and the need for a prophet," said Virl. "He said he didn't know anything about it. But there was something about him that made me uneasy. He just didn't seem sincere."

After visiting for about an hour, the missionaries, who lived nearby, left to walk to their apartment and Virl drove Mitchell back to Lakeside, where Mitchell asked to be dropped off at Lindo Lake Park. Before he left the house in Santee, Mitchell took Peggy's hand and kissed it, thanking her for dinner. "He was very gracious," said Virl, "not outspoken or anything. The Elders gave him a Book of Mormon and I gave him a Bible when I dropped him off and wrote my name, address, and phone number on a piece of paper that I handed to him. But I didn't think we'd ever see him again. Within a couple of days I never thought about him again."

Mitchell, a.k.a. Peter, on the other hand, gave a lot of thought to Virl and Peggy Kemp—or, more specifically, to their twelve-year-old daughter. As he once had with the daughter of Ed and Lois Smart—another couple who showed him kindness—he fixated on the young girl. Back at camp that night, he told Wanda that the Lord had showed him the reason they had been delivered to Lakeside. She should prepare for another sister wife. Over the course of the next two months Mitchell would make repeated attempts to kidnap the girl. But just as he had been foiled in his kidnapping attempt at the home of Elizabeth's cousins in Salt Lake, he would be thwarted in Santee—this time by an incessantly barking Australian shepherd named Bobo, and by the unyielding spring-clipped windows Virl Kemp had installed throughout the house.

One night Bobo barked so constantly that Virl finally brought the dog into the patio area so the neighbors wouldn't be annoyed—just as Steve Wright had done in Salt Lake City the summer before. The dog's barking coincided with his stepdaughter having a nightmare so horrifying that she woke up in the middle of the night and ran down the hall and into her mother's arms, crying uncontrollably.

"She said she'd just seen the devil," remembered Virl. "It really shook her up. We thought it was just a bad dream. But after that night, she slept with the lights on."

29

By late November, Detective Parks had been looking for Emmanuel for a month and a half, but he'd turned up nothing. The new sketch hadn't seemed to help, but Cory Lyman assured Ed and Lois that the police were doing everything possible to find Emmanuel.

There was always a debate whether we as a family should try to track down the Emmanuel lead ourselves. We understood the importance of not interfering with what the police were doing. But there were times when I couldn't resist. On one occasion, Kathy Wilson and I cruised the streets on the west side of Salt Lake City looking for a couple of homeless people she had befriended, hoping that they might know who Emmanuel was. Among Salt Lake City's sizeable homeless population is a loose network of people who keep track of one another, especially around the soup kitchens and shelters. The network runs better in the warm weather, however, and as the weather was now pretty cold, we never were able to locate Wilson's friends, let alone any information about Emmanuel.

On another occasion, I was driving home from work with Heidi and, on an impulse, pulled over at the Salt Lake City Rescue Mission and approached a man who was sweeping the sidewalk. I showed him a copy of Dalene Nielson's drawing.

The man made no sign of recognition as he studied the sketch, but when I added that the person we were looking for was a street preacher who went by the name of Emmanuel, he jerked his head toward the second level.

"Yeah, he's here," he said.

"You mean here, now?"

"Yeah, he's upstairs on his bunk. He's here all the time. Do you want me to get him?"

Caught off guard, I debated what to do next. I finally said, "No, don't bother him," and went back to the car and called Mick Fennerty, who took down the information and said he'd pass it on to Parks.

The next day, Fennerty called me back. "Parks went down and talked to him," he said, "but it wasn't our guy."

Parks remained the only police officer assigned to search for Emmanuel. As the Christmas season approached, police strategy was to lay low and "wait for the holidays." Police and FBI did not send the sketch, the name Emmanuel, or a physical description to alert law enforcement agencies outside Salt Lake City. It seemed that the police, despite their insistence that they wanted to find Emmanuel as much as we did, were barely going through the motions.

Police continued to reject our entreaties to them to go public with the sketch and the search for Emmanuel. Their official position, as always, was that they did not want to spook the homeless Emmanuel. But underlying law enforcement's indifference was their conviction that Richard Ricci did it. While it's true there were investigators on the ground level who didn't buy into the Ricci theory, almost everyone in FBI and SLCPD management did.

The Ricci investigation continued, and in some ways became more intense, after his death, even though investigators found nothing substantial that might point to his guilt. Despite all the attention on the machete knife and golf-type hat police had taken from the home of Ricci's father-in-law, forensics found no DNA evidence to suggest Ricci ever wore the hat, or that the knife had ever come in contact with Elizabeth. The police's search for the camouflage knife sheath, garbage bags, seat covers, and posthole digger Neth Moul had described was unsuccessful. As for the Jeep that Moul said Ricci took from his shop, police had found Ricci's blood on the outside of the driver's door, casting doubt on whether Moul had washed the Jeep on its return, as he had maintained. Photos of the Jeep taken the year before revealed no seat covers. Angela Ricci never wavered in maintaining that not only had she slept next to her husband the entire night of the kidnapping, but that he did not have the Jeep at all after May 30, and it never had seat covers. It also turned out that there had been two other white Jeep Cherokees at the mechanic's shop at the same time Ricci's was there.

Despite all the public appeals and rewards, not a single person had come forward with any concrete information about the mystery woman Moul said called about picking up the car on May 30, or the mystery man Moul said Ricci met after dropping the car off on June 8. Police had interrogated and administered polygraphs to over a dozen people but had turned up no useful information.

The FBI polygrapher, Jeff Blevins, asked Fennerty if he could bring in Neth Moul for a polygraph. Moul refused to submit to one. (He later denied being asked to take one, but the task force discussed his unwillingness at length.) The bulk of the case against Ricci boiled down to Moul's testimony against him, but if Moul wasn't telling the truth, no one could figure out why. The lack of movement in the Ricci investigation stayed mostly in-house, however, leaving the public perception that Ricci was the likely kidnapper—a constant annoyance to everyone in the family who understood the full story.

One day David heard Bob Lonsberry, a local talk-radio host, complain about how sick and tired he was of hearing the Smarts continually talking about the kidnapping and how he wished they would just accept the fact Ricci had done it and get on with their lives. David reached for his cell phone to dial the radio station and set Lonsberry straight until his wife intervened. "You are in no state of mind to make that call," Julie told him. "You will do more damage than good." She was right, of course. What could David possibly say? In the absence of a better explanation, Ricci qualified as closure to the Smart case—and as a family we could not come forward with the case's newest lead—the elusive Emmanuel—because the police wanted it kept quiet. All we could do, if we intended to work within the system and not alienate the police, was try to create movement from the inside. We strongly supported a FBI plan to make another attempt to hypnotize Mary Katherine in an effort to unearth more details about what she saw. But the bureaucracy of law enforcement kept delaying the interview.

In the meantime, with the SLCPD's blessing, Ed gave the CBS news program *48 Hours* permission to come to Salt Lake City and film a show with the family. CBS reporter and former *Early Show* co-anchor Jane Clayson had worked previously at Salt Lake City's KSL-TV, and she used her local contacts to arrange for a personal meeting with Lois. The women bonded, and Lois agreed to let Jane interview Elizabeth's brothers and sisters on the air for the first time, on the condition that their faces not be shown and that they receive no direct questions about the kidnapping. While Ed and Lois were motivated to do the show to keep the case in the public consciousness, the police's motivation was a bit different—they hoped that the nationally televised program would provide new leads to help wrap up the Ricci investigation.

As production began for the documentary, tragedy hit the family in another form. On December 18, Wayne Owens, my sister Cynthia's father-in-law, died unexpectedly of a heart attack while walking on a beach in Tel Aviv, Israel. Wayne, who helped launch the Center for Middle East Peace and Economic Cooperation, had been in Israel on a peace mission and decided to take a walk before his flight home. Wayne was an environmentally progressive former four-term Democratic congressman from a conservative, Republican state—something of a paradox in Utah, which spoke volumes about what people thought of him as a person. The entire Owens family had become a part of ours with their son Doug's marriage to Cynthia. Wayne had inspired us all during the search for Elizabeth. He had worked tirelessly in the search center and defended our family vigorously after the *Salt Lake Tribune* started speculating that the kidnapper might be a family member. Doug flew to New York City and escorted his father's body to Salt Lake City. At the cemetery, after the funeral, Doug said to me, "Maybe Dad can give us some help from the other side."

On the Emmanuel front, Ed became more and more anxious for the search to go public. Ed still wasn't sure whether Ricci had been involved in the kidnapping—maybe he had even been involved somehow with Emmanuel. What Ed *was* sure of was that his ten-year-old daughter said that it wasn't Ricci in her room that night. He also knew that the strange preacher Mary Katherine identified needed to be found.

Lois, on the other hand, had made her own peace with Ricci's guilt. She was content to agree with the police that the investigation should focus on him. She believed the various experts' assertions as to why it had to have been Ricci. In many ways it was important she had that comfort; it freed her from the incapacitating grief of constantly worrying about what could be happening to Elizabeth. She had resolved not to let the monster who had taken her baby destroy the lives of the rest of her children.

Both Lois and Ed wanted what was best for the case, but they saw the Emmanuel lead differently. It didn't help ease the tension when all of Ed's brothers and sisters also wanted to go public with Emmanuel.

Another strong advocate for going public was our family public relations representative, Chris Thomas. He was constantly studying the case and looking at different scenarios and possibilities. Chris even dared go where the rest of us wouldn't—the chat rooms on the Internet, where absurd theories about possible Smart family involvement and other misinformation circulated around the clock. One night, I was on the phone with Chris while he was working on a Lexis-Nexus search on his computer, linking the words "Emmanuel," "preacher," and "abuse" in the search engine. Several articles came on his screen about a case involving a Catholic priest in San Diego who in 1993 allegedly raped a fourteen-year-old girl following the funeral of her grandfather. The priest's name was Emmanuel Omemaga and he was thirty-five years old when he was charged with thirty-nine counts of sexual misconduct. The Catholic Church, Chris learned, had transferred Omemaga to a parish in Lakeside, California (in hindsight, an eerie coincidence), and then he had disappeared. There was still a warrant out for his arrest. Could this be the person we were looking for? I called the photo librarian for the *San Diego Union-Tribune*, Renee Shea. She located a mug shot of Omemaga and e-mailed it to me along with several articles. I forwarded the material to Ed, who looked at the photo and determined it wasn't our Emmanuel.

In his position as family media liaison, it was not uncommon for Chris Thomas to hear about developments in the case before anyone in the family. In early December, while on a trip to New York City with Ed and Lois to tape interviews with *The Early Show* and *The View* (to run on the six-month anniversary of the kidnapping), Chris was the first to hear about a lead involving the death of a forty-seven-year-old man named David Fuller. Authorities in Little Rock, Arkansas, had found Fuller's dead body after what appeared to be a self-inflicted gunshot wound. Lying next to Fuller's body was the lifeless body of a thirteen-year-old girl, Kacie Rene Woody. Apparently Fuller had shot the girl before he shot himself. It turned out that the two had corresponded through an Internet chat room and Fuller, who lived in California, had flown to Arkansas, rented a van, abducted and abused Kacie, and then, for unknown reasons, ended both their lives.

Law enforcement traced Fuller's credit card history and discovered he had traveled through Las Vegas the previous June 4, the night before Elizabeth was kidnapped. It wasn't inconceivable, police theorized, that he could have made it to Salt Lake City, 450 miles away, and abducted Elizabeth in the early morning hours of June 5. There was no disputing that Fuller fit the pedophile profile. Adding to the suspicion was the fact that Fuller's family lived in Salt Lake City and he had attended high school at Olympus High School at the same time as Elizabeth's mother—and, to further the coincidence, Cory Lyman.

The media in Salt Lake story picked up the story, and Chris fielded several phone calls from reporters while he was in Manhattan.

In subsequent checking, law enforcement was unable to make any connection between David Fuller and Elizabeth Smart, and the lead, like so many before it, evaporated.

Two weeks after the Fuller incident, Chris again accompanied Ed and Lois to New York to tape interviews that would run during year-end specials for *The Paula Zahn Show* and *The John Walsh Show*. On that trip, Chris helped set up a meeting between Ed and Lois and John Walsh, who had become their trusted friend. Along with many of us in the extended family, Chris felt that a vote of confidence from Walsh about going public with the Emmanuel lead would help persuade Lois, in spite of what the police were saying.

Chris gave Walsh a heads-up that Ed and Lois had something confidential they needed to talk to him about, strictly off the record and off the air. When Ed and Lois told Walsh about the second handyman, Walsh pushed hard for them to go public with the news. Walsh told Ed and Lois his views about how police bureaucracy makes it difficult to solve cases; he informed them that his track record rivaled that of any law enforcement organization. He detailed several cases that had gone unsolved for years until he went public with them on his show; those cases were solved within weeks. The power of television was formidable. Walsh had been a crusader and victim's advocate long before he became a television star; he was so passionate about the importance of going public that in the limo ride back to the hotel, Lois seemed open to the idea.

Walsh had additional advice for Ed when the men talked privately. "Your daughter is probably dead," Walsh told Ed. "But take care of your marriage. Don't lose that." Walsh had personally experienced excruciating damage to his own marriage after his son's kidnapping and murder. He understood firsthand the collateral damage from a kidnapping case.

Before Ed and Lois left New York, they promised their friend that they would think about what he had told them, and they would let him know when they wanted him to break the story.

Walsh agreed to wait for their call. But when just days later, on Monday, December 23, he appeared as a guest on CNN's *Larry King Live*, he couldn't help himself. To Larry King's oh-by-the-way question as to whether he had any fresh insight into the progress of the Elizabeth Smart investigation, Walsh looked into the camera and said, "Their young daughter has now said that she believes that Ricci wasn't the guy in there that night, that it may have been another guy that did some work on their roof, an itinerant guy that worked at a homeless shelter, and he may be a suspect, and I don't want to give away a lot of breaking information here, but *America's Most Wanted* is going to take a look at the Smart case...."

After the show, Walsh was contacted by the SLCPD and asked not to release the Emmanuel sketch because it would jeopardize the case against Richard Ricci. When other media contacted the SLCPD, investigators downplayed the roofer lead. The *48 Hours* producers, who were wrapping up the production of their documentary, pressured Ed to keep the Emmanuel lead quiet until their story, which focused on Ricci, had a chance to run. For her part Lois was upset that Walsh had broken the story before she and Ed had given him permission. Although the rest of us were surprised at what Walsh did, we were also privately pleased that it happened. Ed told me he was relieved the story was finally out, even if, as Chris Thomas pointed out, the day before Christmas Eve might qualify as the worst possible time to break the news.

The only place the story got any legs at all was, predictably, on CNN, and it wasn't positive. In a broadcast of *The Paula Zahn Show* not long after Walsh's announcement, Marc Klaas appeared with CNN anchor Leon Harris. Apparently still miffed from our summer dealings, Klaas took the opportunity to disparage the Emmanuel lead, the Smart family, and me in particular.

Klaas: And now apparently they're looking at a roofer. And I'm just really concerned that there are some real class distinctions in this case that upset me very much because I don't necessarily ...

Harris: What do you mean by that?

Klaas: Well, what I mean by that is that they've gone after four separate guys that were either itinerant, homeless, drug addicts, or in some other way socially impaired. And it just seems to me that they're trying to draw distinctions that don't really exist. I don't think that any of these guys had anything to do with it. In fact, I think that one is probably going to find the answer to this case a lot closer to home than one would want.

Harris: Well, you mean that means someone in the family, then?

Klaas: Well, you know, the problem is that whoever took that young girl had a voice that was identified or at least it was recognized by the sister Mary Katherine. So it was somebody that obviously she had been around before. It was somebody that knew their way around the house, somebody that apparently cut the screen from the inside. They refused to let Jeanne Boylan in for weeks and weeks and weeks. There were something like a dozen friends and family in the house before law enforcement ever got there. One of the brothers said that it was in many ways a beautiful story, that he didn't think that the kidnapper was a bad person, and that he had his own issues or law enforcement had their own issues with his polygraph.

Harris: Yes.

Klaas: So, you know, given all of this pile of circumstantial information, it seems to me that instead of pointing at roofers or pointing at
handymen or pointing at drug addicts, they should possibly be looking
in other directions.

Klaas's speculation notwithstanding, most details about Emmanuel the
homeless handyman remained known only to a few people in law enforcement and the family. The police were so tight-lipped that even Mayor Rocky
Anderson didn't get a heads-up. The mayor didn't find out about Emmanuel
until he went to a dinner during the holidays and happened to sit next to
Kathy Wilson. For more than two months, the police hadn't given the lead
enough credibility to bother to inform their own mayor.

On Saturday, December 21, the extended Smart family got together to celebrate my parents' fiftieth wedding anniversary. Despite the difficult emotional journey we had been on, we were determined to make it a joyous and
memorable occasion. We gathered at the Homestead Resort in Midway, Utah.
There were thirty-eight of us there. Only Elizabeth and twenty-year-old
Chris Smart, Jr., who was still on his LDS mission, were not present. We all
tried to focus on the joy we have as a family. All of us piled in two Clydes-
dale-drawn wagons and journeyed over the snow-covered hills surrounded
by steam from the area's many hot springs. After the ride we took photos of
each family by the horses, trying to ignore the heartache while snapping
images of Ed and Lois's incomplete family. We gathered in one of the large
conference rooms for dinner after the teenage girls gave the gathering a
fashion show of dresses Mom had worn fifty years earlier.

Angela, her son Mitch, and I put together an hour-long DVD with narrative, hundreds of photos, and video documenting the lives of both Mom
and Dad—their courtship, marriage, and present. Toward the end we had a
small segment talking about the ordeal of the last year, with three or four
photos of Elizabeth that accompanied the following narrative:

When the unimaginable happened and Elizabeth was kidnapped, June
fifth, all of our lives changed. Although we haven't found her yet, the

nation has watched a strong, loving family who has done everything in their power to find her. She has touched the hearts of millions and because her story has caused a higher awareness for missing children, many lives have been saved, and continue to be saved. We learn more about ourselves in difficult times than in good times. We have learned that love, family, faith, and community are all that really matter. Knowing that is a gift that we have all been given. We continue to pray and search for Elizabeth as she, no doubt, does for us.

We all felt the pain in our hearts as we acknowledged our missing child, granddaughter, cousin, and niece. The show finished with a video of happy times we had spent together.

After the holidays, the focus shifted to the *48 Hours* broadcast, which was scheduled to air on Saturday night, January 11, 2003, and which both family and law enforcement hoped would help revive the case. To heighten interest, Mayor Anderson and the SLCPD held a press conference the day before the broadcast to announce it was adding another $20,000 to the city's long-standing reward of $25,000. The police made it clear that the money wasn't only for evidence identifying the kidnapper, but also for information leading to the discovery of Elizabeth's body. The $250,000 private reward put up by family and friends also still stood, as did the two $3,000 tips-for-cash offers—a grand total of $301,000 in reward money. Before the press conference, Ed sat down with the mayor and explained in detail the importance of the Emmanuel lead. Ed told the mayor he wanted to go public with the information during the press conference, along with the added news that Mary Katherine had always maintained that it wasn't Ricci in her room. There was another meeting between Chief Dinse, Anderson, Ed, and Lois. Although it had been nearly three months since the search for Emmanuel began, the chief said, "Give us a chance to find Emmanuel before making it public and scaring him off." Ed, Lois, and Rocky were told that the police would vigorously pursue the lead.

The CBS documentary was expertly produced. It captured the anguish Ed, Lois, and their children had been going through since June, but as far as investigative journalism, it was little more than a rehash of the unofficial indictment of Richard Ricci. When Ed and Lois were asked, as a key part of the documentary, if they thought Ricci was involved, they did not hesitate to answer that, yes, they believed he was somehow involved. In their account of the night of the kidnapping, Ed and Lois revealed for the first time in public that Mary Katherine had heard the man say something about taking Elizabeth for ransom. CBS laid out Cory Lyman's case for him. The task force commander told viewers that he believed the kidnapping was an inside job, committed by someone who knew the house well, who possibly had access to a key, and who used the cut window screen as a ruse— all the same old details that pointed straight at Ricci.

With television cameras rolling, Lyman took Jane Clayson to Ed's house and showed her the window from the outside. Pointing to the window, Lyman said, "When somebody goes through a point of entry, especially one that's going to be a pretty narrow area to go through, they leave traces behind, pieces of clothing, they brush dust and dirt off the window panes, they scuff the walls where they climb up with their shoes. There's a number of indicators that they'll leave behind that say they went through there. They weren't here."

Those of us familiar with the crime scene could only watch in disbelief. We knew there didn't need to be any telltale scuff marks because the intruder could have stood on the hose bib or the back of the propped-up chair to reach the window. And although Lyman knew the screen had been cut from the outside, he did not clarify that point, nor did he mention the palm print on the window frame that had not been identified or eliminated.

Angela Ricci was interviewed for the program and defended her late husband, insisting yet again that he was next to her the entire night of the kidnapping and that he'd had nothing to do with the crime. But it was old news and it rang hollow—the network's token nod to giving equal time. There was no mention of the Emmanuel development, not even in the closing wrap-up. CBS knowingly sat on the case's newest and potentially biggest lead, a fact that surprised even Lyman.

On the local television news that followed the show, Chief Dinse told viewers that he kept a "Pray for Me" button with Elizabeth's picture on his desk and he looked at it every day and would keep it there until she was found. He also said that the mention of ransom was something he hadn't heard before. That puzzled us. In our family, it was common knowledge that when Elizabeth asked the kidnapper, "Why are you taking me?" Mary Katherine heard him say "for hostage or ransom." Mary Katherine later asked her dad what "hostage" meant. We had discussed this with Fennerty several times. We couldn't understand why Chief Dinse didn't know about it.

No new leads resulted from the documentary. Soon after, Lyman let us know that he had accepted an offer to become the new police chief in Ketchum, Idaho, and would be leaving the SLCPD before the end of January.

There was a good deal of optimism in the family that the new task force commander, Lieutenant Jim Jensen, would be more amenable to going public with the Emmanuel lead. But to our dismay, Jensen stuck to Lyman's and Chief Dinse's opinion that it was best to look for the street preacher on the quiet.

If we wanted to go public with the Emmanuel lead, it was clear that we would have to defy the authorities and release the information independently as a family. We didn't want to do that because we didn't want to risk alienating the people who were best equipped to solve the case. But we decided we really had no choice if we hoped to see any progress on the lead.

To go forward without the police meant we had to have complete family solidarity—and that meant making sure Lois was comfortable with the decision. Lyman's departure helped. Until he left for Idaho, Lyman had stayed in constant contact with Lois and Ed; he'd become a trusted friend to both of them. His conviction that Ricci was the kidnapper had rubbed off on them.

David had a frank discussion with Lois toward the end of January when he accompanied Ed and Lois on another trip to the National Center for Missing and Exploited Children (NCMEC) in Alexandria, Virginia. The center was hosting a focus group on the Team Adam Project—a gathering of parents and family members of missing children along with law enforcement personnel from around the country. The concept behind Team Adam was to organize a program that would enable the NCMEC to quickly put someone on site whenever a kidnapping took place. That person would then act as a liaison between family and law enforcement. David was there because of the computer search program he wanted to assemble as part of the project.

One meeting included the Smart family contingent, along with other families that had dealt with the horrors of missing or murdered children, and various law enforcement officers, including Lyman, who was in his final days with the SLCPD. One of the subjects was how law enforcement might gracefully bow out of an investigation, a subject that David thought alarmed Lois. After the meeting, Lois asked David why he thought Lyman's opinion that Ricci kidnapped Elizabeth was incorrect. Lyman had considerably more experience in law enforcement than Mick Fennerty, who was the leader of the opposing viewpoint. So did Don Bell, for that matter. Why didn't we side with Lyman, Bell, and Chief Dinse? David first took Lois through the list of reasons that pointed away from, not toward, Ricci; but he began to make real headway when he told Lois that there were others in law enforcement, besides Fennerty, who didn't think it was Ricci. Lois had not heard that before.

David went on to tell Lois about an experience he and my brother Chris had the week before at the FBI office in Salt Lake City, when Fennerty conducted an impromptu poll for Dave and Chris's benefit. He turned to his coworker, Sonja Sorenson, who had worked extensively on the case, and asked, "Of all the people we've investigated in this case, who do you believe *didn't do it?*"

Sonja answered, "Richard Ricci."

Mick then asked the same question of an SLCPD officer who had overheard the conversation. The policeman had the same answer, "Richard Ricci." He asked one more agent in the office the question and received the same reply. Finally, while leaving the office, they ran into one more SLCPD cop. When Fennerty asked his question the officer seemed frustrated at being put on the spot. He said he couldn't answer the question because he might get in trouble.

"In that case, you just answered the question," said David. The point of the story, as David explained to Lois, was that while the public perception was that virtually everyone in law enforcement thought Ricci was the kidnapper, the behind-the-scenes sentiments were somewhat different.

During the last week of January 2003, I went to Kristianna Circle specifically to talk with Lois. My discussion focused on the fingerprints taken at the crime scene, the palm print from the window, and the matching prints from the bedpost in Elizabeth's bedroom and the backdoor handle. While none had yet been identified, Ricci's prints definitely did not match. Aside from Mary Katherine's recollections, the prints, never revealed to the public, remained the most important clue in the case. "One of those prints is the guy who took Elizabeth, and it is not Ricci," I said. "We need to find out who it is. We need to find Emmanuel and see if it's him."

I lobbied Lois hard using other points that led away from Ricci, many of which Lois had never heard before. One was a tip about an attorney in Cedar City who said he had a client who could exonerate Ricci. Fennerty had told us that this could turn out to be the most important lead in the case. If this mystery person could clear Ricci, it may be because he or she knew who actually did the kidnapping. According to the tip, the person had reportedly had some contact with the family. A friend helped me locate client lists from this attorney's criminal docket and I turned them over to the FBI. The only relative David or I could think it might possibly be was Doug Owens's sister, Sarah, who had once lived in Cedar City. Sarah had a doctorate in psychology. She had come to Salt Lake City from her home in New Mexico as soon as she heard about the kidnapping and had helped the family and many volunteers deal with the psychological trauma of the situation. She had since returned to New Mexico. Fennerty and Detective Scharman flew there to meet with her to check on the Cedar City lead only to find she had no idea what they were talking about. Still, there was apparently someone out there besides Ricci's wife, Angela, who could provide evidence to clear Ricci.

After I'd gone through all my points, Lois finally said, "Let's do it."

The date was Friday, January 31.

Coordinating everything with Chris Thomas, we decided to hold a press conference at which Ed and Lois would deliver two announcements: One was that the family was offering a new $10,000 reward to anyone who could provide information to exonerate Ricci of the kidnapping. The other, more important item was the Emmanuel lead.

We scheduled the press conference for the morning of Monday, February 3. That gave us the weekend to alert the various media outlets. We arranged to hold the press briefing at Shriners Hospital in the same boardroom that eight months earlier had served as Search Central. It seemed like an appropriate place to launch yet another search.

Unlike the June press conferences that had attracted close to a hundred members of the media, this one drew only a handful of reporters. The lack of official police endorsement didn't help. Still, all the major local newspapers and television stations showed up. Although we had the photocopy of Dalene Nielson's sketch of Emmanuel, we decided not to use it because it was police property. We hoped, however, that by reporting that a sketch existed, SLCPD would feel enough pressure to release it themselves. Apparently, just knowing about Ed's copy was enough to motivate the police to release their sketch. Just before the press conference, Ed's cell phone rang with the caller ID showing it was someone from the police department. "I'm so sick of those guys trying to talk me out of this," he said as he turned off the phone. As we were walking into the room to start the press conference, David's cell phone rang. Detective Jay Rhodes was on the line, asking if there was anything the department could do. "Yes," Dave said, "bring the sketch." Rhodes said to hold tight and he would have someone bring it up immediately. About halfway through the media briefing, Detective Fred Louis appeared with the sketch. Our press conference put the police in a strange position. While they did not fully endorse going public with the Emmanuel lead, they still couldn't afford to come off as unsupportive of our family's need to solve the case.

Ed and Lois opened the press conference by announcing the new $10,000 reward for anyone who could exonerate Richard Ricci. The Cedar City lead wasn't specifically mentioned, but we hoped this would bring out the person we'd heard about who could clear Ricci. Then they spelled out their history with Emmanuel, all five hours of it. Lois told how she met the man on the downtown streets and invited him to call her husband for work. She described him as well-mannered and nice and said she had been impressed with how clean he was for a homeless man. She remembered that he was clean-shaven and wore Levi's and a work shirt. "He looked like he could work," she said.

Ed said Emmanuel was a soft-spoken man. He mentioned that while they had sat next to each other fixing the roof they had talked a little about the Bible but not much else. Ed and Lois said they hadn't seen the man since that day, and they had no idea where he lived. He had told them that he traveled with his sister teaching the gospel, and that they were staying at the time at a house in the Salt Lake City area. Both Ed and Lois stressed that they had no idea why this person would have kidnapped Elizabeth—if he indeed had anything to do with it—but that it was important to find and question him because of what Mary Katherine said about him.

The story about Mary Katherine's sudden recall four months after Elizabeth's abduction was also aired publicly for the first time. Ed and Lois were careful to say only that their daughter thought Emmanuel "might be" the kidnapper.

It was a lot to absorb in just a few minutes, especially in a case that had produced very little in the way of new breaks and hard news in the eight months since Elizabeth had been taken. Other than the name he gave them, "Emmanuel," no one knew where he came from, where he lived, or who his family was.

The media had many questions, some of them not particularly pleasant. For months, Ed and Lois had come under attack for hiring a felon such as Ricci to work on their house. Some felt that Ed and Lois had brought the situation on themselves by allowing strangers to hang around their children without any kind of background checks. Now the Smarts had admitted to pulling a person straight off the street and then bringing him to their home. Was this a habit of theirs? Why did they do it? When it came to handymen like Ricci, their hiring practices weren't any different from others in the area, and their handout to Emmanuel was exactly that—a gesture of kindness to someone who asked for help and appeared to be in need. But in the frustration at not finding Elizabeth, the media's attitude had become that the careless Smarts almost deserved what they got. Because of that mood, we worried that the importance of the Emmanuel lead might be missed—a worry that was borne out when the lead angle from the press conference for most of the media was the reward to exonerate Ricci. The Emmanuel story took second billing.

The *Deseret News*, which was able to include the story in its metro edition the same day, ran a headline that read: "Smarts offer reward to exonerate Ricci." The first half of the article was about the new Ricci reward, followed by the Emmanuel information and a small copy of the police sketch. The story ran at the bottom of page two of the local section. That night's television newscasts followed a similar tack, airing the story later in the broadcast and giving equal time to the Ricci reward and the Emmanuel lead. Tuesday morning's *Salt Lake Tribune* ran the story on the front page of the local section and didn't even use the sketch.

Ed had been in touch with caseworker Charles Pickett at NCMEC to inform him of the new development. Pickett had long been supportive of going public about Emmanuel, and when Mick Fennerty called him to let him know the sketch was now public, he was able to display it on the NCMEC Web site along with the other information on the Smart kidnapping.

Nationally, the story went out over the newswires, but there was no real buzz. In the days following the press conference not a single national media organization came to Salt Lake City to follow up on the story.

The police response was similarly apathetic. Yes, they verified they had been looking for Emmanuel since October, and, yes, they wanted to talk to him. But there was no particular urgency. "He's significant, but no more significant than fifty other people who worked on that house," said Detective Fred Louis as he talked to reporters after delivering the sketch to the press conference. "We want to find him, we want to talk to him, and we want to clear him."

30

He was drunk when they found him, but not disorderly. Dressed only in foul-smelling long underwear, Brian David Mitchell was awakened from an alcohol-induced stupor by San Diego county sheriff's deputies, who ordered him to get on his feet and off the floor of a classroom in the preschool wing of the Lakeside Presbyterian Church.

In the early hours of the morning, on February 12, 2003, Mitchell had pried open one of the classroom's windows, crawled through, and, after taking off his soaked clothes, passed out on the floor. After a winter of negligible rainfall, the skies had opened the day before, and throughout the day and night more rain fell in San Diego County than in the previous two months combined. Nearly three-quarters of an inch was recorded at Lindbergh Field, San Diego's international airport. The California Highway Patrol responded to nearly two hundred highway crashes, including two with fatalities, in San Diego County. At midnight, the National Weather Service posted a flash flood watch for mountain and desert areas.

Although the temperature was warm—the low for the night was fifty-five degrees—the combination of rain and alcohol effectively prevented Mitchell from making his way back through town to the camp he shared with Wanda and Elizabeth. It was long after midnight when he made his detour into the church's preschool. He might have awakened later in the morning to a room full of startled four-year-olds if not for a woman who lived near the church who saw Mitchell jimmying open the window. She called the sheriff.

Mitchell told the deputies his name was Michael Jenson and gave his birth date as October 17, 1954. The graveyard shift deputies handcuffed him, hauled him off the church grounds, and took him to the police station in nearby Santee to finish their paperwork. After that, Mitchell was transported twenty miles to the San Diego County Central Jail at 1173 Front Street in downtown San Diego. There, he was housed with about a thousand other inmates and charged with misdemeanor vandalism and burglary. The jailers fingerprinted him and ran his prints through the National Crime Information Center (NCIC), a routine procedure, and discovered the man's legal name was Brian David Mitchell and his birth date was October 18, 1953.

No one knew why the man who broke into the church was using an assumed name, but no one was surprised either. Jails are full of people with aliases. In the Central Jail, a male-only facility that services every law enforcement jurisdiction in the southern half of San Diego County and books anywhere from one hundred to two hundred males a day, each person charged with a crime is officially referred to by his systems number, not his name *du jour.* When Mitchell's NCIC "rap sheet" revealed no outstanding warrants (the shoplifting warrant in Salt Lake City, a misdemeanor, would not have made it onto the national database), he was locked in a housing unit and given an arraignment date. With the President's Day weekend approaching, cases were backed up. Mitchell wouldn't go to court until the following Tuesday, February 18, after spending six nights and seven days in jail

Late in the day on February 18, Mitchell was finally escorted to the Central Jail's Video Arraignment Court on the fourth floor, where he got in the back of a long line of people charged with misdemeanors. He was provided a court-appointed attorney, David Lamb from the San Diego Legal Defender's Association. Before appearing via closed-circuit television in front of California Superior Court Judge Charles Ervin, who was located in the San Diego County Courthouse a block away on Broadway, Mitchell and Lamb discussed the case for about twenty minutes. "It was not an unusual case," remembered Lamb. "He's a homeless man who's maybe a little bit unstable. That's not out of the ordinary in San Diego, or, I would suspect, anywhere. All he did was break into a church to help his family. That's what he said. I don't recall him mentioning any aliases, but it wouldn't have made a bit of difference if he had. It wouldn't have been relevant to the case. He was really a pleasant, pathetic guy. He showed no signs of aggression or violence. He seemed very peaceful, friendly, and remorseful in my dealings with him. We talked about his case and the best way to proceed. I did most of the talking. We had a judge who wasn't known for being easy; he's fair but he's tough."

It was a busy day in arraignment court, with more than a hundred cases on the docket. Lamb represented around a dozen clients that afternoon. Normally, the attorney hesitated having clients address the judge directly, out of fear they would hurt their chances. If they did address the judge, he could press a mute button at his fingertips if he thought they were jeopardizing their case.

But when Mitchell addressed Judge Ervin, his attorney had no compulsion to press the mute button.

"Nothing he said sounded inappropriate," remembered Lamb. "There wasn't anything that made me think that as his lawyer I should stop him."

Clad in blue jail-issue clothing, with his long hair combed and parted in the middle, and answering to "Michael Jenson," Brian David Mitchell's day in court began just before 6:00 P.M.

Mitchell pled guilty to the charge of misdemeanor vandalism, after which the judge accepted the plea and dismissed the burglary charge. Judge Ervin then asked, "Mr. Jenson, where are you going to be living when you get out of custody?"

"Sir," said Mitchell, his high-pitched voice meek and submissive, his piercing eyes downcast, "I don't know that yet. My wife and my daughter are staying with some friends presently in Lakeside, and I'll be there, too. We're staying with some friends in the Lord Jesus Christ. I'm a minister for the Lord and..."

Sensing that his client wasn't catching the judge's nuance that he wanted assurance that the defendant had somewhere to live when he left custody, Lamb turned to Mitchell and asked, "Where are you living, Mr. Jenson, do you have a place you'll be staying?"

"With these friends, yes," said Mitchell.

"Very well," said Lamb.

Judge Ervin then asked Mitchell, "On the day that you broke into the church, where were you living?"

"With these friends."

"All right," said the judge. "I'm going to release you from custody and put you on a grant of probation. Now, you just told me you're a minister for Jesus Christ, and I appreciate that. But if you're going into the Presbyterian Church or any of those churches out there in Lakeside for the purpose of ministering and they don't want you on the property, or if you don't have permission to be on the property, that's going to be a violation of the charge of burglary that I'm sure Mr. Lamb is going to discuss with you momentarily. Also, if you're going into those churches and you're breaking the window and you're going in there because you don't have a place to live, that likewise could be a violation of the law. Do you understand that?"

"I do, your honor. That was the worst night and the worst week of my whole life. For the first time in twenty-two years I got drunk that night and the whole night was just a nightmare and this week in jail has been like Jonah gettin' swallowed by the whale. It's turned me right around and I know I need to do what the Lord wants me to do with my life and I'm deeply sorry, and nothing like that's going to happen again, I can assure you."

The judge set the term of Mitchell's probation at three years and fined him $250 payable to the state and $100 payable to the Lakeside Presbyterian Church for damages. He was told that the state fine was satisfied by Mitchell's jail stay, while the payment to the church was to be paid during the probation term. The judge explained to Mitchell that the violation of any laws, other than parking infractions, would terminate his probation.

"Do you understand the terms and conditions of your probation, Mr. Jenson?" asked Judge Ervin.

"Yes I do, your honor," said Mitchell.

"And do you accept them?"

"Yes I do, your honor."

"Good luck."

The entire proceeding lasted four minutes. Mitchell shook David Lamb's hand and was again a free man. Because he was indigent, before they turned him loose, the jailers gave him a token for bus fare back to Lakeside.

■   ■   ■

There were no further recriminations awaiting Mitchell in Lakeside. Without ever meeting him, Pastor Bob Mentze of the Lakeside Presbyterian Church forgave him his trespass. "It wasn't the first time that's happened—a person who had too much to drink looking for a warm place to sleep it off," said the pastor. "They said he vandalized the place, but there was nothing broken but the window. And he was all alone. He just needed someplace to go."

But if the pastor's charity was heartwarmingly Christian, and if the police had set him free, life in Lakeside was nonetheless on the decline for Mitchell. It wasn't just the week in jail and the fine he now owed; those were just the latest in a succession of problems. On a strictly economic level, Lakeside was no Salt Lake City. There simply wasn't the volume of pedestrian traffic to produce a steady stream of panhandling revenue. On a good day of begging in Utah, Mitchell had once confided to his lymphologist mentor Sam West, he might bring in two hundred dollars. But in Lakeside, particularly in the winter with few tourists around, there were never any paydays even close to that. The heaviest traffic days were Sundays, when steady streams of cars would pass on Wildcat Canyon Road below Mitchell's hillside camp, filled with people headed either to or from the Barona Valley Resort & Casino. Rarely were any of them inclined to part with more of their money. Sometimes Mitchell would take Wanda and Elizabeth into San Diego so he could panhandle there, but that meant expenses getting to and from downtown.

The preaching wasn't going well either. During December and January, Mitchell made some religious pamphlets that he passed out around town, all to no avail. He also preached on street corners as he begged. The reception was tepid at best.

To make matters worse, in early February the county fired Roy Miranda and Judy Gaspers as caretakers at Cactus County Park. It seemed there was an escalating problem with drug trafficking in the park and surrounding area, and the sheriff's department thought Miranda and Gaspers, despite their protests of innocence, might somehow be involved. Police had discovered a lot of marijuana growing in the vicinity. The authorities didn't charge Miranda and Gaspers with any crime, but they did tell them to find somewhere else to live. The decision rendered the couple homeless. It also left Mitchell's camps without a buffer at the edge of the park. Helicopters began flying randomly over the area, with heat sensors to help scope out drug operations. Sometimes they swooped directly over Mitchell's camps.

After nearly five months, there were plenty of reasons to leave Lakeside. Wanda added another one when she told Mitchell that while he had been in the San Diego jail, she'd had a vision that they were to pack up and depart. Wanda had her purported revelation while she prayed desperately, nearly continuously, during Mitchell's unexplained absence, at a secluded altar she and Mitchell had built in the river bottoms and named "Golgotha." Wanda claimed that she was visited at the altar by, among others, heavenly angels, her late father, and Johann Sebastian Bach.

When Wanda wasn't praying during her husband's unexplained absence, she barked at Elizabeth to stay put, be quiet, and keep out of sight in their rain-soaked camp. Without Mitchell, she was more wary than ever of being found by the authorities. When they ran out of rations, Wanda did not go for more. When Mitchell finally did return, triumphant that he had been delivered yet again out of man's jail, he found Wanda on the verge of hysteria. Both Wanda and Elizabeth were muddy, fatigued, and near starvation.

Almost immediately, Brian and Wanda began making preparations to leave. For two people who had never spent as much as a year in one spot since they were teenagers, it would be nothing new. In seventeen years of marriage to each other, their lives had involved constant migration, and the hard earth was their mattress for more than half of it. Behind them, scattered like debris in the desert, lay broken homes and promises, abandoned and battered children and dreams, and shattered attempts at normalcy. In their self-adopted personae as prophet and prophetess, they had granted each other amnesty from the past, immunity from the present, and ignorance of the future, managing to evolve in the process from tax-dodgers to kidnappers, all the while clinging to a reality as tenuous as the crumbling California sand on which they slept.

It was getting warmer with every sunrise, and the days were growing longer. Once March arrived, Mitchell, Wanda, and the girl they called Augustine would leave California—and they would go back home.

31

Tom Holbrook had an impression. Then he forgot about it. It came to him while he was watching television Sunday evening, February 2, 2003. Holbrook didn't normally watch television on Sunday—a more devout Latter-day Saint would be hard to find—but there was a movie on that night he thought looked wholesome. During a commercial break, an ad for the 10:00 news announced a press conference that the Smart family would hold the next day. Holbrook had a feeling—an "impression," as he would later describe it—that he should make sure he found out what was going on.

Keeping up with the Smart kidnapping had become second nature to Holbrook over the past eight months. By coincidence, he had seen Elizabeth Smart at her grandfather's viewing three days before she was kidnapped. Holbrook's family owned and operated the Holbrook Mortuary in Millcreek, the location of Myron Francom's viewing on Sunday night, June 2, 2002. Holbrook's day job was with the LDS Church—for twenty years, he had worked as a senior design engineer in the audiovisual department—but he helped out with the family business when he could. For the Francom viewing, he had mostly stayed in the mortuary office, but he made his periodic rounds through the foyer and viewing room to make sure everything was OK. Before the viewing started, a member of the mortuary staff introduced him to Ed and Lois Smart. While Holbrook hadn't met Elizabeth directly, he had watched as she and Mary Katherine brought their harps into the mortuary, and later heard them play their music.

He would have thought no more about it had it not been for Elizabeth's abduction three days later. To Holbrook, the kidnapping was personal. Elizabeth seemed so sweet, so young and innocent. Every night since the abduction, as the Holbrooks—Lisa, Tom, and their ten children—knelt together for family prayer at their home in South Jordan, they prayed for peace, health, safety, strength—and Elizabeth Smart.

In the last week of January, to combat a mild case of sleep apnea, Holbrook had undergone surgery to remove his tonsils, repair a deviated septum, and trim the turbinate bones at the back of his throat. He had been recuperating at home, but on Sunday, February 2, he thought he felt well enough to go to church. It proved too much for him, and on Monday he stayed in bed and forgot all about the Smarts' press conference.

By Wednesday, still at home but feeling much better, Holbrook again remembered the press conference and was about to see if he could find a story about it on his computer when he got distracted and moved on to something else. The next day, he returned to work at the LDS headquarters in downtown Salt Lake City, and set to making a dent in all the work that had piled up in his absence. It wasn't until the end of Friday that he again thought about the press conference. By now, the urgency to investigate the news was gone. If what the Smarts had to announce had any major significance, Holbrook reasoned, he'd have probably heard about it by now. But he still wanted to know what the news was, so in the few minutes before he needed to catch the bus home, he clicked onto the Internet site of the *Deseret News*. He soon found the story, written by staff writers Pat Reavy and Jennifer Dobner. It began with the news that the Smarts were offering $10,000 to anyone who could exonerate Richard Ricci—nothing new there. But as he read on, he learned, in the second half of the article, of yet another handyman the Smarts were looking for:

> Also Monday, the Smarts released a police composite sketch of a transient who worked in the Smart house for just five hours.
>
> Lois Smart, Elizabeth's mother, said she met the man about a year ago while crossing the street between two downtown malls where he was panhandling. She gave him $5 and asked if he needed work. The following day, the worker, who used the name "Emmanuel," came to the family's house to work on the roof and pull some weeds.

"I was sitting there at my computer and I started to almost physically shake in my chair," Holbrook remembered. "It hit me like a ton of bricks. I knew the person they were describing was Lisa's brother."

It was nearly 5:00 P.M. Holbrook printed out the article, stuffed it in his briefcase, and hurried to catch his bus.

An hour later he walked into his home, found his wife in the kitchen, opened his briefcase, and said, "Lisa, you've got to read this." Holbrook watched as Lisa began reading. When she got to the second half of the article, she left the kitchen and walked down the hall into the bedroom to finish. Holbrook, who said nothing as Lisa read, followed her. When she was finished, Lisa looked up.

"Do you think this is Brian?" she asked.

"I do," said Holbrook.

Lisa paused. "Well," she said, "I think it is, too."

Through the night, the Holbrooks discussed the article and what to do about it. The man it described—a street preacher who went by the name of Emmanuel—certainly described Brian David Mitchell, although Mitchell spelled his version of the name *Immanuel*. Mitchell did odd jobs when he needed money, as did the man who'd worked at the Smarts' house. The sketch that accompanied the text did not look like Mitchell, but the Holbrooks passed that off as an artist's attempt at drawing someone's likeness from memory. "Regardless of the sketch," Holbrook later claimed, "we thought it was Brian."

The question was what to do about it. Should they call the police? Should they get involved? They talked about the sensitive family issues involving Brian. They didn't want to bring unnecessary pain and humiliation to their family, or to Brian himself. They were sure they would be criticized by some in the family if they went to the authorities. While it was true that Mitchell dressed in robes and claimed to be a prophet, nothing in his past behavior suggested he was capable of kidnapping. Working at the Smart home for a day didn't mean he had anything to do with Elizabeth's abduction. The only criminal history in Brian's past anyone in the family knew about was related to his abuse of drugs—and those problems predated his current phase as a religious zealot by decades.

Brian's sister and brother-in-law had a difficult decision on their hands, one made more painful because they already felt some resentment from family members because of their actions the previous spring. Not only had they helped Irene Mitchell get the protective order against Brian and Wanda that banned them from her property, but the Holbrooks had also assisted the stake president in serving the papers that resulted in Brian and Wanda's excommunication from the LDS Church. Since those episodes, Brian had contacted no one in the family. If he found out the authorities wanted to question him, he was likely to go so far underground that his family might never see him again. Brian and Wanda were known to live in warmer areas in the south in the wintertime. With this development, they might just stay there.

But the more they talked the more the Holbrooks concluded that the right thing to do was to call the authorities. The police needed to clear this up, and the Smarts deserved closure. The Holbrooks felt they had a moral obligation. After praying for guidance—prayer was a part of every decision in their lives—they got up off their knees and decided they needed to call the police.

"We felt Brian was definitely the person they were looking for, and he needed to be questioned," said Tom Holbrook. "Our hope was that he had nothing to do with Elizabeth. Our feeling was, here's a case where they're trying to find a needle in a haystack and he's just another piece of hay to be eliminated, so they can find the needle."

Early the next morning, Holbrook was scheduled to work at the mortuary. It was agreed that when he returned, he and his wife would call the police together. But Lisa was anxious to get it over with; after all, Brian Mitchell was *her* brother. So she summoned her courage and phoned before her husband got home.

When the dispatcher at police headquarters answered, Lisa came straight to the point.

"I think I know who it is you're looking for in the Elizabeth Smart investigation," she said.

"Why would you think that?"

"Because I think it's my brother."

"And why would you think that?"

"Because he goes by the name of Immanuel and he's been panhandling for years; he just fits the description. His real name is Brian David Mitchell."

As the dispatcher asked Lisa a series of questions about her brother, he plugged the name and the birth date she gave him—October 18, 1953—into the police database. Almost immediately the shoplifting citation Mitchell had received the previous September 27 appeared on his screen. The officer read the incident report to Lisa.

"That's him," Lisa said. "That is definitely my brother."

She made a point to tell the officer that while her brother typically dressed in robes and had long hair and a beard, as described in the shoplifting report, when he worked for the Smarts he would have had short hair and regular clothes. That was not long after the September 11 attacks, she explained, and Mitchell had dressed normally for a while after that to avoid looking like Osama bin Laden or some other terrorist.

The dispatcher took down her name and phone number and said he would have someone working on the Elizabeth Smart investigation get back to her. When Lisa Mitchell Holbrook hung up the phone, her hand was trembling.

About two hours later, just before Holbrook returned home, Detective Cordon Parks called Lisa from police headquarters. Lisa repeated what she had already told the dispatcher and assured Parks that his search, at least for Emmanuel's identity, was over.

The Holbrooks went to sleep that Saturday night fully expecting a series of police interrogations to begin right away. But to their surprise, their phone did not ring. The police did follow up with a call to Lisa's mother, Irene Mitchell. But Irene was only able to tell them that, like everyone else in the family, she hadn't seen or heard from her son or his wife since police had escorted them off her property almost ten months ago.

After hearing from the police, Irene phoned Lisa, upset by any suggestion that Brian could be involved with the Elizabeth Smart kidnapping. She was sure he couldn't possibly do such a thing. Other members of the

Mitchell family felt the same way. But Lisa told her mother she wasn't so sure. "At least entertain the idea that he could be taking polygamous wives," she said.

As the week wore on, and there were no stories in the newspapers or on television about Brian's connection to the Smarts, the Mitchell family relaxed a bit. They figured that the police were taking care of the matter discreetly and quietly.

And they were right. The police were taking care of the matter discreetly and quietly—and without any sense of urgency. Lisa Holbrook's information stayed below the radar along with all the other information on Emmanuel.

Detective Parks did contact the security department at Albertson's and collected the Polaroid photograph store security had taken the previous September. But when Parks prepared a poster with the photograph and Mitchell's vital statistics and hung it on the second floor of the station house, Parks's superiors took it down. They told Parks he was allowed to hang the poster only in the detectives' area, far from where the rank-and-file officers could see it. They also told him to remake the poster and change the heading "Wanted" to "Wanted for Questioning," despite the fact there was an outstanding warrant for Mitchell on the shoplifting charge.

No one in the family or, for that matter, the FBI, was let in on Emmanuel's true identity. It wasn't until Thursday—six days after Lisa Holbrook's call to the SLCPD—that Fennerty learned the news, and even then it wasn't because of an official communiqué between the SLCPD and the FBI, but because of a conversation he had with Cordon Parks, during which Parks casually dropped the information, "We found out who Emmanuel is."

In contrast to the police's lethargy, Fennerty jumped on the detective's news. He quickly found out that not only had Emmanuel been identified, but the police also had a photograph of Brian David Mitchell in their files. He borrowed the Polaroid from Parks and scanned the image on his computer, making two copies, one with the full frame of Mitchell as he sat on the supermarket floor, the other a shot of his face.

Fennerty called David and asked him to run variations of "Brian," "David" and "Mitchell" through the Elizabeth Smart Search Center database. He didn't tell David why, but clearly something was up, and David called me to talk about it. After talking to David that evening, I went to Fennerty's office.

"Tom," Fennerty said as soon as I sat down, "we know who Emmanuel is."

He told me what he knew about Mitchell and said that the information had come from a sister who had called the SLCPD. It was a simple bit of information, a name and a birth date, but the news nearly overwhelmed me.

The press conference worked! We had a real name to go with the person Mary Katherine said was the man who took Elizabeth! What was almost as shocking was when Fennerty showed me the photo of the bearded, robed man sitting on the floor of a grocery store. I recognized him as the Jesus Man, the guy my sister Angela had said gave her the "heebie-jeebies" outside Kinko's the day after Elizabeth was kidnapped—the same man I had summarily dismissed as a suspect. It didn't mean the case was solved, but after so many disappointments and dead ends this was the biggest break yet.

Fennerty read my mind as well as my expectations. "Now, let's not jump to any conclusions," he cautioned. "Don't put all your eggs in one basket, like so many did with Richard Ricci. But let's find him."

Fennerty was aware that the SLCPD's intent was to keep the information quiet and continue trying to find Emmanuel/Mitchell on their own. But he felt strongly that it was now crucial to mount a public search.

Mick explained to me that the reason he created the two images from the Polaroid snapshot was so that they could be sent to *America's Most Wanted*. He wanted to capitalize on the FBI's close working relationship with John Walsh's television program and, if possible, he wanted to do so by Saturday night's show. He'd already arranged with the media agent of the FBI's Salt Lake City office, George Dougherty, to send the photos and Mitchell's vital statistics to FBI headquarters in Washington, D.C., where the person who worked on a regular basis with *America's Most Wanted* could get things moving. Dougherty didn't ask if Fennerty had permission to send the information and Fennerty didn't let on one way or the other. Dougherty did ask if Fennerty thought Mitchell was the kidnapper. "I don't know," Fennerty replied, "but I think it is important to get him in here so we can find out."

The next morning, unaware that Mitchell's photo and identity were now in the hands of *America's Most Wanted* and about to go public, law enforcement finally showed Ed the Polaroid of Emmanuel and asked him if it was the handyman. Ed studied the photograph carefully. Since the man who worked on his roof had not had a beard and long hair, he had to visualize those changes. Still a little gun-shy at once having thought the truck driver identified by LDS security might be Emmanuel, Ed said he wasn't positive, but he thought it was. When police showed the photo to thirteen-year-old Andrew Smart, he said, "It really, really, really looks like him."

As we had hoped, the deep, authoritative voice of John Walsh, host of *America's Most Wanted*, informed television viewers across the country on Saturday night, February 15, that the "handyman roofer" who worked at the Smarts' house and called himself Emmanuel was in fact forty-nine-year-old Brian David Mitchell, a five-foot-eight Caucasian male who walked the streets wearing robes and a beard as shown in the photos. The show broadcast the images Fennerty had scanned of the robed shoplifter and Dalene Nielson's sketch of a clean-shaven Emmanuel. Walsh passed on information that Mitchell and his wife were known to go to warmer climates for the winter, possibly Florida, Texas, or Arizona. Walsh could add few details beyond what Fennerty had prepared for him, but he reprised the Elizabeth Smart kidnapping story and explained Mary Katherine's epiphany about Emmanuel and stressed the importance of finding this man so the police could talk to him. Anyone who had any information should immediately call 1-800-CRIME-TV.

Among the millions watching *America's Most Wanted* that night, none were more shocked than two people in Salt Lake City. One was Derrick Thompson, Wanda Mitchell's son. The other was Debbie Mitchell (formerly Debbie Woodridge), Brian Mitchell's second wife.

Derrick hadn't seen Brian or Wanda in nearly a year—since the scene the two had caused at Glenn Corbett's funeral the previous April. He reached for the phone and called the toll-free number. When he got a busy signal, he called his brother, Mark, who hadn't seen the show, and filled him in on what happened. Then Derrick called the SLCPD, who took his telephone number and, since it was late Saturday night, said they would call him back. The news so unnerved Derrick, the third oldest of Wanda's children, that he went out that night and searched Salt Lake City's homeless shelters to see if he could find Mitchell.

Mark, too, had a difficult time getting through to 1-800-CRIME-TV, so he telephoned the FBI in Salt Lake City. He was transferred to none other than Mick Fennerty, who, after the broadcast, was helping work the phones at the Elizabeth Smart Hotline, hoping for tips. Mark explained to Fennerty Mitchell's religious fanaticism and told him of the so-called revelation Mitchell had written and passed out to members of the family. He told Fennerty where he could find Brian's mother, Irene, and late that night SLCPD officers Cordon Parks and Bill Silver visited Irene Mitchell's home to talk to her and get a copy of Mitchell's religious manuscript. Outside Irene Mitchell's home, Parks and Silver telephoned Fennerty, who by now was searching downtown homeless shelters himself. They read him parts of *The Book of Immanuel David Isaiah.*

Debbie Mitchell's reaction was different than Derrick Thompson's, but it was no less dramatic. The woman who once spent nearly five years in a tumultuous marriage with Mitchell could barely catch her breath when his image came on the television screen. She was at home, watching television alone. By now her three older daughters were out of the house, and Joey, almost twenty-one, was in Paraguay on an LDS mission. Only twenty-year-old Sarah was still living at home, and she was out for the evening.

"I just happened to watch *America's Most Wanted* that night," remembered Debbie, "and when that face came on TV I thought, 'Oh, that looks like Brian. His eyes look like Brian's.' I was typing an e-mail to my son so I was doing two things at once, and then they said, 'We've got a name to go with the face,' and they said it was Brian David Mitchell and I just started hyperventilating. I was hysterical. I didn't know what to do."

The first person she thought to call, once she composed herself, was her LDS bishop, Darrell Newbold. When Newbold picked up the phone he thought someone was harassing him and almost hung up. "All I could hear was heavy breathing," Newbold said. "I thought it was a sexual call."

But Debbie found her voice and finally said, "It's him! It's Brian!"

"Who is Brian?" asked Newbold.

"He kidnapped Elizabeth Smart!" said Debbie.

After calming Debbie down and learning more details, Newbold suggested that she call the police. Debbie was scared, she told her bishop, who had never met Brian. She explained that she hadn't had any contact with Sarah and Joey's father in eighteen years and it was traumatizing for her to think of having any association with him again in any way. After speaking with the bishop, Debbie called her middle daughter, Becky, who expressed the same feeling; she didn't want Brian David Mitchell to again touch any of their lives.

But Debbie and Becky agreed that Mitchell was fully capable of stealing a young girl. "I remember thinking that I would not be surprised if he was a kidnapper," Debbie said. "I lived with him. I could see him manipulating, tormenting, molesting, and raping."

Recognizing that it was something she had to do, Debbie summoned her courage and called the police. She told the dispatcher that the man identified on *America's Most Wanted* as a person wanted in connection with the Elizabeth Smart investigation had sexually abused her children, abused her physically, and was an evil, dishonest man.

When she was finished, the dispatcher said that someone would call her the next day. On Sunday, February 16, Debbie stayed near her phone. When she hadn't heard from the police by Sunday afternoon she again called Newbold for advice; he suggested she call the police again. This time Debbie talked to a detective who responded to her unflattering description of her ex-husband with what she felt was a condescending attitude.

"He treated me like I was nothing but a bitter ex-wife," remembered Debbie, who also remembered that the detective told her that Richard Ricci was the top suspect. "Ma'am, we have our man," he said before hanging up.

Derrick Thompson sensed a similar lack of enthusiasm from the police department when they failed to call him back. But *America's Most Wanted* did return his call, and when the producers heard his story they quickly made plans for a trip to Salt Lake City to meet with Derrick, Mark, and two of their sisters, Rhonda and LouRee, all of whom agreed to an on-air interview and to allow the *America's Most Wanted* crew to follow and film them as they searched the streets of Salt Lake City for their stepfather.

By Monday, after they had been brushed off by the SLCPD, both Debbie Mitchell and the Thompson siblings decided to contact the Smart family directly. With Bishop Newbold's help, Debbie located the Elizabeth Smart Search Center on the Internet and got in touch with David by e-mail. Meanwhile, Kate Levier, Derrick Thompson's girlfriend at the time and a person I had worked with previously in the photography business, contacted me.

Kate told me, "Tom, we have all these photos of Mitchell and the police don't seem to care."

I thanked her, and told her, "I care, and I'm sure there is someone in the FBI who will also." As it turned out, Fennerty was already in the process of getting the photos from Mark Thompson, who also sent them to me. When I opened the images on my computer, I immediately forwarded the image of a clean-shaven Mitchell to Ed and stayed on the line as he opened the attachment. I heard him gasp as he exclaimed, "That's him, Tom! That's Emmanuel!"

We quickly began learning more about Brian David Mitchell. Little of it was complimentary. Debbie Mitchell talked to David for more than two hours. Unlike the police, David listened intently as Debbie told him about the mice Brian put in her oven to terrorize her, and about how he would sometimes wake her and the kids by shouting in their faces. She said all five of her children had gone through hell because of Mitchell. She laid out a sordid history of sexual abuse suspicions and charges. She talked of inappropriate nude photos Mitchell kept of his older children. Her kids, she said, had gone to the Children's Center, the Division of Family Services, and a number of therapists and doctors with problems that stemmed from their father's abuse. Beyond the one official abuse charge filed with the state in 1985, she said she had documented everything in a diary. She explained to David how she successfully ended Mitchell's visitations with Sarah and Joey by tape recording, at the suggestion of social services, the screaming protests of the young children when their father came to pick them up. She said no one in her household had seen Mitchell or any of his family in eighteen years. "I wanted to avoid any contact with a child molester—or anyone supporting a child molester," she said.

As disturbing as Debbie's narrative was, one thing she said gave David a ray of hope. "Brian is a molester, but he is not a killer," she said. "If Brian took Elizabeth, then she would still be alive."

Derrick Thompson wasn't any more flattering when it came to discussing Mitchell. He openly admitted to the press that he despised the man who married his mother. He said he had briefly spent some time with Brian and Wanda after they were married in 1985 and that his brother, Mark, and sister, LouRee, who were both younger than him, lived with them for a few months. He said LouRee, as she would later affirm on *America's Most Wanted*, felt that Mitchell was "always touching me inappropriately" and she "felt like he was always watching me." His unwelcome advances, his incessant preaching, and his insistence that he was a prophet drove the kids from their mother's house. Parroting what Debbie Mitchell had said to David, Derrick also spoke of "inappropriate nude photos" of Brian's oldest kids that he said his aunt discovered in Brian and Wanda's trailer.

"For seventeen years he's given us the creeps," said Derrick. "He's turned our mom against us. She was never much of a mom, but maybe with a little help and medication she could have been. From the get-go, this guy's been a creep and he's just slowly, progressively gotten worse. We'd like to find him because our mother's involved and because the Smarts need closure. If he's innocent and there's nothing wrong, then what's wrong with the police questioning him? But we think he very well could have done something like this. It's just a horrible thing and we want to make sure that if he's guilty, he's caught, and if he's not, then the police can move on to other suspects."

At the FBI offices, Fennerty ran a national fingerprint check on Mitchell to see if he had any criminal history. He found that Mitchell had a rap sheet from his arrests many years ago, and his fingerprints were on file. Fennerty got Mitchell's prints from the Criminal Justice Information Center in West Virginia and compared them with those taken at Ed's house the day of the crime. Although the forensics experts weren't able to compare the palm print, they could compare the fingerprints, and they proved negative. The prints on the back door and in the bedroom were definitely not Mitchell's. The news devastated Fennerty. The crime scene prints seemed to be the only real pieces of potential physical evidence attached to the crime. They did not belong to Ricci, to anyone in Ed and Lois's family, or to any other potential suspects in the long lineup over the past eight-plus months. They had been the biggest factor in keeping the investigation alive, and everyone who knew about them knew how important they could be when it came to securing a conviction. But whoever they belonged to, it wasn't Brian David Mitchell.

I still felt strongly about Mitchell and I told Fennerty so. The fact that he didn't leave his fingerprints did not prove he was not there. "Mick, this is the guy," I said, stressing what I called "the religious wacko theory." I pointed out that the white robe and cone-shaped hat Mitchell wore matched Mary Katherine's description of a kidnapper wearing light-colored clothing and a hat she had difficulty describing. And if the motive was some twisted religious vision, it explained why there had never been a ransom demand.

For me, the need to find Mitchell shot beyond urgent on Thursday, February 20, following a flurry of additional information that came at me almost all at once.

I was at work, talking to several coworkers in the photo department about Emmanuel. Any number of people at the newspaper were familiar with the Salt Lake City street fixture. Sharon Johnson, the head of the promotions department, remembered seeing the Jesus Man often at the malls across the street. She recalled a time, shortly after the September 11 terrorist attacks, when she was surprised to see him without a beard and wearing short hair.

As Sharon was talking, Heidi Perry, the newspaper's chief paginator, walked by. "Wait a minute!" Heidi said. "That guy in the robes, the Jesus guy? He was here. Last summer, I caught him inside the building trying to pull down the Elizabeth Smart poster off the front window."

Heidi said she'd stopped the Jesus Man and asked him what he was doing.

"They already caught the guy," the man told her. "I read it in the *Tribune*."

"I don't think so. You keep that up there," said Heidi and a verbal confrontation began. He started to scare her so she ran upstairs to the City Desk for help. When she returned, she said the man was gone and the poster was still there.

After hearing Heidi's story, Laura Seitz, a staff photographer, added an encounter of her own. "My husband has seen that guy in the robes a bunch of times in the mountains," she said. Laura explained that her husband, Zack Bagley, who was working on his doctorate at the University of Utah, liked to ride his mountain bike to school. He would leave their home and ride into the foothills and onto the Bonneville Shoreline Trail, which skirted the mountains behind Ed's home, and then to the university. He'd told Laura about seeing the Jesus-looking character more than once during these rides.

Laura called Zack and he provided more details over the phone. He said he hadn't seen the man at all during the past summer, but the summer before he had seen him a couple of times on the trail, and once, when he was riding several miles back in a remote area of Dry Creek Canyon, he ran across him at a camp. Zack said he'd also seen a woman with him.

Stunned at the information that Mitchell had a camp in one of the canyons behind Ed's house, I got the GPS coordinates from Zack and called David and Chris. We decided we couldn't wait and arranged to meet immediately for a search at the mouth of Dry Creek Canyon. As I drove to meet my brothers, I had a feeling that finally, after all these months, we were onto something that made sense.

It was late in the afternoon when we started into the canyon. We didn't have much daylight left, but we hiked until after dark. The coordinates Zack gave us were in the North Fork of Dry Creek Canyon. We searched along the faint trails and undergrowth for several miles and found one camp but no evidence of Mitchell or Elizabeth.

After our search, David and Chris stopped by Ed and Lois's house to talk about what we had found out and where we'd been. (It was Sierra's twenty-second birthday and I went to have dinner with my family at a downtown restaurant.)

Like me, David was becoming excited about the Mitchell development. When Lois asked, "Do you really think it could be him? Is he as bad as Richard Ricci?" David launched into a recitation of his conversation with Debbie Mitchell and her allegations of her ex-husband's sexual abuse. Chris could see the horror filling Lois's eyes; he nudged David, waving him off before he could go into more detail. David ended the discussion with, "Ricci's MO doesn't fit; he was a robber. Mitchell's MO does fit; he's a pedophile!"

Before going to dinner, I called Fennerty at the FBI office and told him about Zack Bagley's sightings and our little investigative venture into the mountains. Early the next morning, Fennerty called to tell me that Detective Bill Silver was going up in a police helicopter to search the canyon. Because there was only light snow on the ground and the leaves were off the trees, the chances were good that Silver might spot something from the air. He asked me to call Silver and give him Zack's GPS coordinates, which I did. It was the first and only time I ever talked to Detective Silver. Fennerty had repeatedly told us how hard Silver and Parks had been working for the family.

After I gave him the coordinates I told Silver, "I'm sure you might have heard about our frustrations with the police, but I want you and Parks to know how much we appreciate what you are doing. Our frustration is not with you."

"Thanks," the detective said, "That means a lot."

The helicopter search later that day revealed a campsite that the police thought might belong to Mitchell, although they found nothing definitive that could be connected to Elizabeth.

Suddenly, for those of us in the family, information about Brian Mitchell, the Jesus Man, was coming from all directions. It seemed that every time the conversation came up, someone remembered having seen him. Friday night, my daughter was at a party at her sorority house at the University of Utah when two of her friends, who each worked at a different Souper!Salad! restaurant in the valley, said, "We know that guy. He comes into Souper!Salad! all the time. He's always wearing his gear." Amanda asked her friends for the locations of the restaurants and the names and phone numbers of the managers. She was about to call me on her cell phone, but stopped when she realized it was 1:00 A.M. She waited until the next morning to call me.

I took down the information and went to work making fliers with photos of Brian and Wanda, their physical descriptions, and instructions for anyone who saw them to call 911. The next day, Sunday, February 23, Heidi and I took the fliers and made the rounds of the valley's three Souper!Salad! locations. Heidi and I remembered sitting at the booth next to the Jesus Man and his woman companion two years earlier when we'd eaten dinner one evening at the Brickyard restaurant. At each Souper!Salad! we posted the fliers and talked to workers and managers.

The most helpful person was the manager of the Midvale store, Lindsey Dawson, who said that on several occasions she had talked to the man and woman and, while she did not know their names, she did know something about their diet and their preaching. Lindsey added the detail that the last time they came in a third person was with them, another woman, and both of the women were covered in veils, which was new. In the past, she could always see the woman's face. I asked Lindsey how close she was to the women. She said at one point she was standing right next to both of them, she could have reached out and touched them. When I asked how long ago that was, Lindsey answered, "A long time ago, sometime last summer." My mind and heart were racing, but I didn't go further with my questions.

The next day, I got a message from Lindsey, asking me to please call.

"Tom," she said when I phoned her, "I've been wanting to talk to you. I didn't want to overreact when we were talking, but I've been thinking about it, and it wasn't two women that I saw. It was a woman and a girl."

"Do you think the girl could have been Elizabeth?" I asked.

Her answer dropped me to my knees.

"Yes," she said.

"My God," I cried, "she's alive!"

32

Despite all the revelations about Emmanuel, the police investigators remained largely unimpressed. It was almost as if no one had come forward with accusations of sexual abuse and bizarre, antisocial behavior, let alone the eyewitness's positive identification. Debbie Mitchell was shrugged off as the quintessential disgruntled ex-wife, and Wanda's grown sons and daughters as stepchildren holding a grudge against their stepfather. Debbie lamented to David that the situation made all the tortured memories of eighteen years ago come rushing back. "No one wanted to believe me back then either," she said.

The Thompsons saw the SLCPD's indifference firsthand when the *America's Most Wanted* crew came to film them as they went from homeless shelter to homeless shelter looking for Mitchell.

"While we were out looking, a police car pulled up and the officers got out and asked what we were doing," remembered Derrick. "We said, 'Well, your job, basically.' It took them a minute for it to even click what we were talking about. One of them finally said, 'Oh yeah, it was on TV,' and then they drove off. It just didn't seem like they were that interested." The problem, of course, was that most of the officers on the street still hadn't received any information.

Detective Don Bell, who hadn't been assigned to the Elizabeth Smart investigation in more than five months, but periodically consulted on the case, was quoted in the February 18 edition of the *Deseret News* as saying, "My personal opinion is Ricci is number one and there isn't even a close second. There have been hundreds of these [potential suspects]. They just haven't reached this level to reach the press. I don't know of anything that would elevate him [Emmanuel] above the many, many others." The story, written by reporter Pat Reavy, reported that Bell "has a hard time believing someone who was at the house for only five hours could remember the lay-out well enough to come back six months later and abduct the teen."

I was at the newspaper office and read Bell's quotes as soon as Reavy's story came off the press about 1:30 P.M. It disturbed me so much that I went straight to Mayor Rocky Anderson's office. When I walked into his reception area I saw that he too was upset; he'd already read the article on the Internet. "I know why you're here," he said.

Anderson assured me that he was already in the process of writing a memo to Chief Dinse asking why Bell was commenting, unauthorized, on the case. In particular he wanted to know why Bell was publicly dismissing a potential suspect that Dinse himself had assured the mayor the police were doing everything possible to track down.

The police's public attempt to discredit the Emmanuel lead did not stop with Bell's quotes in the *Deseret News*. Through the media grapevine, I learned that the police were telling reporters off the record that the Emmanuel lead was just something the Smart family was doing to try to attract more publicity for the case. "We just don't want them to embarrass themselves," one officer told a television reporter who had asked for background on the lead. Mindy Sink, a reporter for the *New York Times*, called me after talking to the SLCPD public information officer, Dwayne Baird, and asked, "Just what is going on between you guys and the police?"

The *New York Times* quoted Baird as saying that Ed and Lois "hired homeless people on many occasions, and we've had to track down more than fifty of these guys. He's just one of those people, that's all." To local reporters, Baird said, "We want to talk to him, he's a person of interest. But we're not willing to put him up as a suspect because we're not sure of his involvement, if any. He's one of dozens of people, mostly homeless, who worked on that home for Ed and Lois Smart. They hired a lot of those kinds of people. I don't mean a handful, I mean dozens and dozens. We're just not willing to say this is the guy." Baird, who failed to differentiate between homeless charity cases who worked on Ed's house, of whom there were very few, and dozens of qualified subcontractors, further downplayed the possibility that Mitchell could be the kidnapper by adding, "Within about four hours [of the kidnapping] there was an immense search-and-rescue operation in the foothills with helicopters, horses, and ATVs. The likelihood that this guy on foot would have been able to scoop her up and take her somewhere up there and not be detected is pretty remote. Ricci is still our guy, because of the overwhelming circumstantial evidence in the case pointing to him."

Lieutenant Jim Jensen, Lyman's replacement as task force commander, took on the air of a beleaguered general instead of someone with an important new lead. "There were fifty-eight people who worked at the house that we've been able to identify so far," Jensen said. "He is only one of two we haven't been able to locate and talk to. We're actively looking for him but I want to add the cautionary note that we've got nothing to tie him directly to anything."

Jensen said there were more than two hundred sightings called into police departments all over the United States after the February 15 airing of America's Most Wanted. "Every skinny guy with a beard got fingered," said Jensen. "We interviewed a person late last night, a jail inmate, who said he'd seen him [Emmanuel] hanging around in central city. If he'd been around in central city in robes, you and I would have seen him by now."

"By no means is this the only thing on our plates right now. We've eliminated hundreds of people who have some reason to be suspect. How could we complete the case if we have somebody that comes to our attention if we don't either eliminate them as a suspect or show that they did it? You know, Brian Mitchell is one of those people. It does have some added interest when we've been told that Mary Katherine says it could have been him. Something piqued her attention about that. It could be so simple that she's trying to help her family, her mom and dad, who are in terrible straits over this whole thing, because she's a young impressionable girl. I'm not saying that is what happened. She has said something and we take that very seriously. We need to talk to this guy."

I talked to Mick Fennerty and asked him if he thought it would do any good to have a personal talk with Chief Dinse about Emmanuel. Fennerty just looked at me and shook his head. "Chief Dinse isn't going to believe it wasn't Richard Ricci," he said, "until Elizabeth walks up and tells him so."

This situation between the police and the Smart family was a familiar scenario—we were tugging in opposite directions. To the family, the importance of the information on Mitchell was clear. Our frustration was always close to the breaking point. At dinner one night, I went on about the depressing stalemate with the police while my daughter was listening. I guess I laid it on pretty heavy because that night she went back to her dorm room at the university and sobbed. Amanda and her roommate lived on the floor above many of the school's football players. One of them, Lynzell Jackson, heard Amanda crying and asked why she was upset. "Because the police suck," Amanda sobbed. Then she filled him in on the SLCPD's lackluster search for Emmanuel.

"We're going to go out and find Emmanuel ourselves," was Jackson's response. "Oh, don't you worry," he told Amanda, "If the police can't do their job, the football team can."

"I printed out like ten posters and gave them to the football players," said Amanda. "These are big boys. The next day, they went around downtown Salt Lake and the shelters, searching."

I got a call early in the week of February 23 from Fennerty. He said he needed to have a Circle of Trust meeting. The Circle of Trust was what we called our family visits with Fennerty, where we all shared information about the case with the understanding that no one's trust would be compromised. Fennerty said he had something important to tell us and asked to meet with all the siblings, except Ed. He had to be out of town briefly, so we scheduled a time to meet on Thursday afternoon, February 27, at the FBI office.

By the time Thursday afternoon rolled around, I was drained and distraught as I joined Cynthia, David, and Chris in Fennerty's office, braced for the worst. Angela was out of town and couldn't make the meeting. When we were all sitting down, Fennerty gave us the news: he was being taken off the case.

We had known for some time that the FBI was planning on transferring him to Washington, D.C,. to work as a supervisor at the Crimes Against Children unit, but we'd understood that wasn't going to happen until the middle of April. His departure date hadn't changed, Fennerty said, but he was being taken off the Elizabeth Smart case immediately. He told us how hard it was for him to leave the investigation, that he couldn't remember investing more energy and emotional commitment in any case in his career, but he also gave a glowing recommendation for his replacement, Kevin Fryslie, and said the change was necessary so there would be a smooth transition.

"You're not going to have the same interaction with Fryslie as you have with me. You can't sit and theorize with him, but he is a man of action and I'm confident he'll do a good job for you," Fennerty told us.

We had known for some time that Fennerty had been raising some hackles within both the FBI and the SLCPD because of his against-the-grain views on the Smart investigation, especially his insistence that Ricci wasn't the kidnapper. What we did not know—and what Fennerty declined to tell us during our Circle of Trust meeting—was that he was being taken off the case for getting Mitchell's photo and information to *America's Most Wanted*. By publicizing the identity of Emmanuel, something the SLCPD and his FBI superiors were against, he had finally annoyed enough people who mattered. As we would find out soon enough, he was ordered not to have any more contact with the family. He was to participate on the case only on a limited basis.

Fennerty did an excellent job giving us the company line, explaining how important it was for him to have time to get ready for the move back east. We believed him about this as we had believed him all along. I really thought Agent Fryslie was going to be a good handoff and that Fennerty simply needed two months to get ready for his move to Washington.

That didn't make the transfer any less devastating for us. If not for Fennerty, it was depressing even to think about what might have happened to the investigation or how we, as an extended family, would have been able to keep our sanity. Cory Lyman was close to Ed and Lois and was their go-to guy when they had questions, but Lyman viewed the case much differently than Fennerty; he rigidly believed Ricci was the kidnapper. Ed would share his information from the police and we would share our information from the FBI. Fennerty and Ed were the lifelines that kept us informed, and, with Lyman gone, Ed was getting very little information. It was Fennerty who had listened to us. He had been willing to push for an investigation that went beyond Richard Ricci.

Before I excused myself to pick up Ed for a dinner meeting we had scheduled that night with the mayor, David and I shared with Fennerty the latest that we'd learned about Mitchell. I told him about Mitchell's religious fanaticism and suggested that might be the motive. Fennerty just shook his head and said, "Sex, sex, sex. Tom, it's all about sex." I told him about the sightings at the Souper!Salad! of Mitchell and two women and said, "Mick, I think she could be alive."

"Don't even go there, there's no chance," he answered quickly. I could tell he thought we were getting too worked up. When David told him about Debbie Mitchell's charges that Mitchell molested the children, he put his cop face on. "That's great, I'm glad you have that information," he said. "But it doesn't matter because we don't have him. We don't have Brian. Let's get him." He told us he didn't necessarily think Mitchell was the kidnapper but he thought it was the best lead we had, and Mitchell was a much more likely suspect than Ricci had been. He kept cautioning us not to make the same mistake others had made throughout the investigation: don't rush to judgment, don't get tunnel vision, and don't rely too much on circumstantial evidence.

As I was walking out, Fennerty explained that the reason he hadn't wanted Ed at the meeting was out of concern that the news of his transfer might upset Ed. He asked us to tell Ed if we thought the timing was right; otherwise he would talk to him personally the next day.

I picked up Ed at his house and we met the mayor at a restaurant near the University of Utah campus. Anderson, who apparently knew the place well, ushered us to a table in the back where we could talk more privately. We had asked to see the mayor so we again could voice our concerns about the police and see if there wasn't something he could do to get them moving on the case. It seemed to us that the SLCPD was so locked into their Ricci theory that other strong leads were being ignored or outright dismissed. And now the police were discrediting the family's attempts to further the Emmanuel lead.

We went through the list of reasons why the investigation needed to pursue Mitchell aggressively and why we felt the police were part of the reason that wasn't happening. I gave the mayor a memo Chris Thomas had written regarding comments from sources in the media about how the police were dismissing the Emmanuel lead:

Tom—

Here is the information you requested. Please tread lightly, we do not want to hurt any of our relationships with the local media, especially *America's Most Wanted*. If something can be done internally to fix this, it would really be appreciated.

Rick Segall, reporter for *America's Most Wanted*, said that the SLCPD told him that they didn't give Emmanuel much credence because he didn't fit the profile of the investigation. SLCPD said they would go on camera, but asked Segall not to make this "into a national manhunt." While interviewing the SLCPD, Segall said he got frustrated and turned the camera off and told the spokesperson that he was coming off as if the police did not care. The spokesperson was a little more cooperative when the camera was turned back on, but Segall told me this week that after reviewing the tapes that there is nothing that AMW could use from the police interview. He further expounded, "Someone is going to have to tie Emmanuel up, put a bow on his head and deliver him to the SLCPD before they are going to find and question him."

Please be careful not to hurt relations between AMW and SLCPD. Segall has been very careful not to burn bridges despite the fact that he has lamented on the phone for hours about his disappointment with the SLCPD's lack of interest in this lead. He said that 90+ percent of police departments are incredibly cooperative in this type of situation and that he is absolutely baffled as to why they are acting in this manner.

I do not want to give names of my local contacts unless it is absolutely necessary. One in particular informed me that SLCPD has told him Emmanuel is of little interest and is something the family is using to bring attention and publicity back to the case. This also has been mentioned in conversations from local reporters as well as Segall. This particular local reporter has asked me numerous times if the family thinks the police are trying to cover something up. Another local reporter told me that SLCPD has assured Emmanuel's family that SLCPD believes he had no involvement with Elizabeth's abduction and that it is again a publicity stunt by the family.

Please let me know if you need anything further.

Chris

Mayor Anderson gasped out loud several times as he read the note. Then Ed and I reviewed for him the reasons why Emmanuel was our top suspect. As we talked, the mayor found a scrap of paper and began to write. When we were finished, he had a list of nine points that he promised he would bring to Chief Dinse's attention immediately.

"Rocky," I said, "what's going on in this investigation makes the Salt Lake City Police Department look like the Keystone Kops compared to the Boulder Police Department [which notoriously botched the JonBenet Ramsey investigation]. The buck has to stop somewhere."

"I know," said Anderson. "And it stops right here."

After the mayor left, Ed and I stood on the sidewalk outside the restaurant and continued to talk. I told my brother what I had learned from my visits to the Souper!Salad! restaurants, including Lindsey Dawson's assertion that Mitchell and two others had come into her restaurant.

"Ed," I said, "she said one of them was a girl."

We stood silent for a moment as traffic moved by on 13th East, and that thought hung in the air. I hesitated and then I told Ed what Fennerty had warned me against just hours earlier. "Ed, I think she's alive."

Ed had a faraway look in his eyes. "Tom," he said finally, "whatever you do, please don't repeat that to Lois. It might put her over the edge."

■ ■ ■

The evening's developments prompted me to tell Ed about the meeting that day with Fennerty.

"Who else was there?" he demanded.

I said, "Well, Chris and David and Cynthia."

"Why wasn't I there? Why wasn't I involved?" Ed shouted. He was furious. "Just give me one good reason why he wouldn't talk to me? If anyone should be there, I should!"

I agreed with him.

"I am so damn sick and tired of this," Ed fumed. Then he reached over, ripped the cell phone out of my hands, and called Fennerty. When Fennerty answered, Ed went into a tirade that lasted about thirty seconds. "Thanks a lot. I am so sick and tired of being left out. This is what I have been through this entire time. I am Elizabeth's father! I should know these things first!" He hit the end-call button before Fennerty could reply, and then stormed up to his door.

Once he was inside his house, Ed called David and Chris and chewed them out, too. Later that night, Ed called each of us back and apologized for overreacting. Each of us told him the apology was unnecessary.

The next day, the last day of February, the mayor made good on his promise. He prepared a memo that listed each of the nine points we had discussed at the restaurant, along with a demand for an explanation as to why these leads weren't being given attention:

To: Chief Rick Dinse
From: Rocky Anderson
Date: February 28, 2003
Re: Elizabeth Smart Investigation

Although I have tried to stay out of the Elizabeth Smart investigation as much as possible, leaving it for the Police Department to do its job, I have felt it appropriate to intervene on occasion to follow up on matters that have, in my view, negatively impacted members of the Smart family or the investigation.

I wrote to you about leaks of information (or simply rumors) from members of the Police Department. In response, you issued a directive about communications that are made by members of the Department. I have also had significant concerns about the failure of the officers who initially responded to secure the crime area, about the manner in which information was issued to the media, and the misinformation that seems to now be part of the commonly accepted account of events (e.g. the as-yet uncorrected "factual" account that several people were swarming throughout the Smart home when the police first arrived).

I have been especially concerned with the public commitment of the investigators to the Richard Ricci theory. The following outlines the major areas of my concern:

1. The only eyewitness, Mary Katherine Smart, has maintained from the beginning that she did not think Richard Ricci was the abductor.

2. There is no physical evidence tying Richard Ricci to the abduction.

3. Richard Ricci has no past history of sexual abuse or abductions.

4. Mary Katherine independently suggested the abductor may have been "Emmanuel."

5. Emmanuel was somewhat familiar with the Smart home.

6. Emmanuel has a history of child sexual abuse.

7. Emmanuel was seen nearby, at a Kinko's on 1st South, near the University of Utah, on the afternoon Elizabeth was abducted.

8. Emmanuel was known to camp out near the Shoreline Trail, above the Smart home.

9. Perhaps most telling, Emmanuel apparently has left the area since information about his possible involvement was disclosed.

I am at a loss as to why the Police Department did not aggressively pursue the Emmanuel angle and why it (and you) discouraged Ed Smart from disclosing the possibility of Emmanuel being involved...it now seems clear that there is far more to indicate that Emmanuel was involved than the slim evidence pointing at Ricci. We should be aggressively pursuing the possibility that Emmanuel was involved in Elizabeth's abduction.... Our police may very well be going off in entirely the wrong direction, committing themselves to the wrong theory, disregarding or not obtaining evidence that does not fit their theory, and undermining the chances of solving this tragic crime.

The Mayor closed his memo with this plea: "Why is the Police Department, through its investigators and public information officer, downplaying the possibility that Emmanuel was involved? I have one foremost interest here: To bring Elizabeth's abductor to justice and to provide the family with answers. We must make certain that egos and commitments to erroneous theories do not get in the way of a resolution of this matter."

The night of Mayor Anderson's memo, Scott McKane of KSTU, the local Fox affiliate, aired a news report about Mitchell sightings in the downtown area the previous summer. McKane interviewed a number of downtown residents who insisted that Mitchell stayed for a few nights at an apartment building sometime during the late summer or fall, possibly even as late as December.

The next night, Saturday, March 1, *America's Most Wanted* aired a follow-up program on Emmanuel/Mitchell, featuring the interviews with Derrick, Mark, Rhonda, and LouRee. Wanda's sons and daughters told viewers nationwide about their mother's fragile mental condition and the odd, transient life she'd lived since she married Mitchell. They left no doubt that they believed Mitchell could have kidnapped Elizabeth Smart.

This time, additional photos that Wanda's family had provided accompanied the police photo of Mitchell in his robes. Included were older photos of a clean-shaven Brian Mitchell and a smiling, unveiled Wanda. The pictures of Mitchell were displayed side by side in a kind of before-and-after comparison. Again, viewers with information were urged to call 1-800-CRIME-TV.

One Salt Lake City viewer who watched *America's Most Wanted* with particular interest was Daniel Trotta. It was Trotta's apartment complex the people who had been interviewed on the KSTU broadcast Friday night had been talking about. Trotta tried to telephone the police after *America's Most Wanted* but could not get through. He walked to the police station and asked to talk to someone there, but it was after hours. Finally, he used the phone in the police lobby, called 911, and told them that a person he believed to be Elizabeth Smart had spent several nights in his apartment the previous year, along with Mitchell and Wanda. Since it was a weekend, he was told someone would get back in touch with him during the week. Trotta, who had lost his job at Wild Oats Market, sat in his apartment and waited. The police did not call back for several days.

Someone else who had lived in close proximity to Mitchell called the police. Karl West, son of Mitchell mentor C. Samuel West, phoned the SLCPD and told them that Mitchell and Wanda had stayed at the Wests' family home in Orem and he could provide the police with details. As with Daniel Trotta, Karl West was promised a return call from the police. It never came.

The mayor's memo resulted in a Monday, March 3, meeting at Ed's house. Ed, David, the two new point people for law enforcement (Jim Jensen of SLCPD and Kevin Fryslie of the FBI), and I met in an effort to make sure all possible ground was being covered on the Mitchell front. As we talked, it became obvious we knew far more than law enforcement.

When the discussion turned to Ricci, Jensen defended, as always, the police's case against him. He cited the 1983 pharmacy burglary when Ricci shot and wounded SLCPD officer Michael Hill.

I said, "I thought Ricci had been shot at first." When Jensen denied this, my blood started to boil. By coincidence, I had shot photos of that particular crime scene for the *Deseret News*. I remembered the incident well, including the fact that the burglar, Ricci, shot at the officer after two shots had been fired at him first. I had taken a photo of Officer Hill with a small piece of lead pellet in his scalp and four or five in his hand. Firing when he was fired upon didn't justify Ricci's actions—either in robbing the pharmacy or returning the gunfire—but it didn't make him a cold-blooded killer either.

Then Jensen said that they hadn't been able to document a credible sighting of Mitchell since the first part of October. I stood up at that point and started pacing the floor. I was seriously debating whether to walk out. It seemed too convenient, linking that time frame to the one of Mary Katherine's epiphany. Later, it would turn out that Jensen was absolutely correct. But there had been people on the television news who reported Mitchell and Wanda had been seen downtown as recently as December, and the police knew nothing of those reports. When David pressed Jensen about the downtown apartment where Mitchell supposedly spent some time, he said, "What apartment?" We told him about the KSTU report, and his response was, "Well, you know you can't trust everything you see or hear in the media."

Ed asked about whether law enforcement's profile of the kidnapper had changed over the course of the investigation, to which he received a non-committal response. On that note, the meeting ended in a cloud of disappointment for all concerned. The next day I e-mailed Fryslie and Jensen a copy of the twenty-year-old *Deseret News* article that reported Ricci having been shot at before returning fire. I also included information about the various Souper! Salad! sightings Heidi and I had chronicled, as well as the news that one of the restaurant's managers, Lindsey Dawson, said she had seen Mitchell with two veiled women. I included the contact information for all of these leads. I received an e-mail from Fryslie acknowledging he'd received my e-mail and one from Jensen stating that he couldn't open my attachment. That was the last time I communicated with either of them. Later I would learn that neither the police nor the FBI ever checked on the Souper!Salad! leads.

Walking out of Ed's home, it was as if nine months of searching had melted away and we were back where we had started. The urgency and the sense of panic had returned.

I knew what was fueling my mania. It was my belief that Elizabeth was alive. While that feeling had never really left me, it had been dulled by the long months of searching. Now the unmistakable impulse that she was alive and needed to be rescued took precedence over everything else. We weren't looking for a body; we were looking for a living, breathing girl. That's why I became Detective Tom again. All the old habits returned. I became so absorbed in the search that I forgot to eat, I ignored and neglected everything unrelated to the search, and I stopped sleeping except when I took a sleeping pill.

I caught a bad head cold and on Tuesday, March 4, I called in sick to work, which gave me an excuse to wrap myself in the case all day at home. I sat in front of my computer, calling up document after document related to the case's history. I looked up transcripts of press conferences and national media interviews and all the local newspaper stories of the past nine months. I printed these out, and as the stack of papers grew on my desk, I tried to make sense of all that had happened in the investigation. I was specifically trying to find information that would exonerate Ricci so the police would become fully engaged in finding Mitchell. If I could put together a report that I could lay on Police Chief Dinse's desk that removed all possibility that Ricci was the kidnapper, maybe *then* the case would be able to move forward.

I was willing to do whatever it took. I called Michael Janofsky at the *New York Times* bureau in Denver, thinking the *Times* might be interested in what I was working on. Janofsky wasn't there, but Mindy Sink, who answered the phone, asked what she could do to help. I told her there was a big twist to the story, but as she began to push for details, I realized I wasn't ready to try to explain why I believed the police were not being forthright about the evidence regarding Ricci. I said I'd call back when I had more. Sink said, "Whenever you're ready to talk to us, we will listen."

I called Sierra, who was now working full-time at Intrepid with Chris Thomas, and asked her to do a LexisNexus search for some transcripts I needed. She told me she'd been talking to her mom and she was worried about me. I assured her that she was going to be very proud of me when this was all over.

"Dad," she said, as she began to cry, "I'm already proud of you." Then she added something I'll never forget. "It's not what you've lost," she said, "it's what you have."

Heidi wanted me to get some medication, not for my cold but for my hyperactive, obsessive behavior. To help Heidi feel better (I had lost hope for me), I agreed, so we went to the office of Dr. Barkley Bigelow, who's also a good friend, and he prescribed an anti-anxiety drug. As we were driving home along Highland Drive, we witnessed a traffic accident in the lane next to ours. A van rammed into a Mercedes that had stopped for a red light, and the Mercedes then hit the car in front of it. No one seemed to be seriously hurt, but there was quite a bit of damage to the vehicles, so we pulled into a nearby gas station in case anyone might need an eyewitness (no one had to tell a Smart the importance of an eyewitness). I stayed in the car as Heidi got out to talk. I watched a man arrive with another man who seemed affiliated with the woman who caused the accident. I knew I'd seen one of the men before, although I wasn't sure where. I thought he might have had something to do with the kidnapping investigation and maybe he was a cop. They rushed the woman, who apparently had overdosed on something, to the hospital and later the familiar man returned. At this point my curiosity got the best of me, and I got out of the car and approached the man, who spoke before I did.

"You're a Smart, aren't you?" he asked. I said I was and then he said, "Perhaps it's fortuitous that we meet. I'm Richard Townsend, director of the state crime lab."

After telling me that he and his family had been praying and searching for Elizabeth ever since she'd gone missing, the lab chief said, "You know Tom, I'm not sure your family has been dealt with fairly. I don't understand why some people have said some of the things they have."

Townsend spoke specifically about the cut window screen at the crime scene and the condition of the Jeep the police had taken from Neth Moul's garage. The crime lab was well aware, he told me, that the screen had been cut from both sides, which had never been made public. Townsend affirmed that the side cuts were done from the outside and the bottom incision was cut at least partially from the inside, just as I had been informed early in the investigation. As for the Jeep, Townsend said there was no evidence found of mud or much dirt of any kind. Even if Neth Moul had washed the vehicle down, as he said he had, there would have been particles of mud or dirt on the chassis. But it was exceptionally clean. He also told me that the state lab had processed more than 88,000 prints trying to match the ones from Ed's house.

"If there's anything you need to know about the window or the car, you can come down with your brothers and I'll be glad to go over it with you," Townsend said.

It's hard for me to describe my reaction to meeting the head of the crime lab completely by accident that afternoon. As with several other things that happened during the search for Elizabeth, it seemed it was no coincidence at all. I came away with even more energy to overhaul the investigation. The trip to the doctor had given me just the prescription I needed.

The next day, I called Townsend and we talked some more.

"You said you would answer some questions about the car and stuff," I began.

"Sure," he said.

"I understand that the car was basically clean."

"It was, especially considering with a trip up to wherever it went five hundred miles and five hundred miles back, it was very clean. The seats were especially clean, the front seats. It was clear that they had seat covers on them."

"There were front seat covers?"

"Yes, front seat covers … the back seats didn't have any cover and they were filthy."

"How about as far as it being off-road?"

"Nope. I could not find dirt anywhere. It is very problematic, even at best. A big deal was made by the media about being able to compare soil samples and that is pretty much hogwash. Even if it had a lot of dirt, which it didn't, we would have had a very, very difficult time; that would have offered no probative value. Always remember that word, *probative*. That is a big word in my world because so much is not probative that we get in. A lot of the evidence that we got in right after the mad rush, after Elizabeth was kidnapped, was just nonprobative. We processed everything from blankets to knives to camping accessories to all kinds of stuff. Not one ounce of that was related to Elizabeth or you Smarts."

"Could you say, fairly positively, that the car hadn't been off-road?

"Certainly. By the time I saw it, absolutely…because when I processed it, it was clean. No dirt. There was no dirt on the undercarriage. I got on an automobile mechanic's roller and looked and there was no dirt under the car."

"And you would have given your report to the investigating officers fairly quickly?"

"Oh yeah, it was within the week."

My mind flooded with memories of the numerous remote searches the police had directed us to because Ricci's Jeep was supposed to have been off-road. But I had other questions on my mind. I asked about the window screen.

"There are different reports about whether the screen was cut on the inside or the outside," I said.

"It was cut on both," said Townsend. "The cut on the right side, a downward cut on the long part of the screen, was cut on the outside. Then, whoever cut the screen reached from the inside and drew the knife back toward him along the bottom. Does that make sense to you?"

"Yes."

"Just like you have an Exacto knife and on the outside you cut down, then once that's cut, it allows you to stick your hand in and draw the knife back toward you at a right angle."

"So he went down the right side, then he stuck his hand inside and cut toward the right, and then wasn't there a cut on the left side, too?" I asked.

"Maybe. I can't remember, but I can find out."

The director of the state crime lab then felt it important to give me a professional disclaimer. "I want you to understand something, Tom," he said. "I like you and I like your family and I have prayed a lot for Elizabeth, but one thing that you have to keep in mind is that I cannot, in my professional position, be pitted against the Salt Lake City Police Department or the FBI. The crime lab deals in facts. I'll share the facts as I know them with you and let you draw your own conclusions. But it would not be professional of me to get in any sort of a compromising position. So if I feel like I am getting boxed in, I'll probably back off a little bit. I know you folks are frustrated. I know you feel like you haven't been dealt with straight up. I don't understand the motivation behind that, if indeed that is true, because there is no reason why you shouldn't have been. There is just too much at stake here for anybody to be trying to pull the wool over anybody's eyes.... As you well know, we have spent tens of hundreds, if not thousands, of hours on your niece's case and we don't intend on letting up. Every single shred of physical evidence that comes to the crime lab will be dealt with as though the crime occurred yesterday, you have my word on that."

Townsend said he would go to the Utah public safety commissioner for clearance in working with the family. I suggested that perhaps it might be better if I talked to the governor, Mike Leavitt, whom I had gotten to know over the years and who had helped considerably in allocating resources and manpower to the kidnapping investigation. "I don't ever want to back you into anything," I said.

"If you want to talk to the governor, Robert Flowers is the commissioner and they see each other several times a week, and I'm sure the governor will most likely defer to the commissioner," said Townsend. "I will just sit down with Commissioner Flowers and tell him that I have made your acquaintance under these circumstances. What he is going to ask me is if it is going to compromise anything, and my response to that is going to be no. I mean, what is there to be compromised at this point? I'd be more than happy to lay out every single thing we have done. There needn't be any secrets."

No one had seen or heard from Brent Cook since the kindly old gentleman had tapped me on the shoulder on June 8 at Shriners Hospital, announced that he was a friend of Ira's, and handed me the note that in many ways had shaped the attitude of the family ever since. The elderly man's suggestion—that Elizabeth was in the hands of someone who had not killed her and might be persuaded to let her go if we appealed to his good side—took on added importance with the discovery of Mitchell's identity.

I found Brent Cook's address and phone number. He lived in the Salt Lake Valley and was home when I called. The only time we had ever talked were those few seconds on June 8. I told him that our family had never stopped thinking about his advice over the past nine months. I asked him when it was he had worked with Ira in the Salt Lake Temple, and he said he'd worked in the temple just the past two years. This was a shock because Ira had been dead about twenty years. Brent wasn't even certain of the name, maybe it was Ezra Sharp, he said. Finally we realized the Smart relative he knew from working in the temple was Howard Sharp, my mother's brother and a counselor in the current temple presidency.

"Howard is very close to us," I said. "But you're a friend of Ira's—that is what you said to me."

"Well, I meant whoever is in the temple presidency," said Cook.

"That is very interesting, because the fact that you said you were a friend of Ira's was very significant to us. . . . Ira is Howard's father."

"Wow."

"What I am interested in right now is that the person we are looking for fits the description of the type of man you suggested we would be looking for in your note. There have been some sightings of this person with someone we think is Elizabeth."

"Really?" Cook asked. "You mean she's alive? I hope and pray so."

"I know that would be nothing short of a miracle if that were the case," I told him.

"Well, we all pray for a miracle," he replied.

"I just wanted to thank you for what you did. Strangely enough, it was what you said and wrote and that you said you were a friend of Ira's, whether you meant to or not—it was very important."

"Sometimes those things are spiritual.... We are going to solve this thing."

"I pray so," I said. "I think we are getting close, but we'll see."

I hung up and let what I'd just heard sink in.

By Saturday, I was able to have a phone conversation with Tom Holbrook. While the police had kept Lisa Holbrook's identity from the media, privately we were aware that it was Lisa, along with her husband, Tom, who had tipped off law enforcement about her brother, Brian Mitchell. Holbrook told me the details of how he and Lisa came to call the police, which was a gratifying endorsement of our decision to go public at the February 3 press conference. He explained about the fragile Mitchell family dynamics and told me that after the *America's Most Wanted* broadcast, he and Lisa had borne the brunt of some intense family criticism. In a media interview, Mitchell's father, Shirl, said Lisa had "thrown us to the wolves." In an attempt to soften feelings, Lisa had called Detective Parks after the television show and asked if her initial report of February 8 could be kept confidential.

From the tone in his voice and the way he talked about his brother-in-law, it was obvious Tom Holbrook was a man of integrity. He took great care not to bash Mitchell, while at the same time describing a person with serious problems.

"He's very smart, very intelligent, and he can be very well behaved and well mannered," Holbrook said. "But he is just crazy enough that there is a possibility he could be involved. We feel like we did the right thing in calling the authorities, but we have some family members that are madder than heck at us. Their approach is that there is no way that Brian could have had anything to do with it and we have dragged him into something high profile totally needlessly.

"I would be surprised if he did have anything to do with it," Tom added, "but unlike many of the other family members who are very upset, I'm not ruling it out."

I hadn't seen the religious book Mitchell had written, but I told Holbrook I had the impression the police thought it was "so much mumbo jumbo." When I asked him about it, Holbrook responded, "I think the document is very relevant because it describes how mentally unstable he is." Then he added, "One thing that Lisa and I talked about is that if he does have something to do with it, we are of the opinion that there is a really good chance she is still alive. He is a religious zealot and very fanatical in his religious beliefs, but I don't think he is malicious. So if it was him it was probably in the name of this religious thing that he is doing and would have to be something to do with plural marriage or some way to build and support this religious thing, which would indicate that she might be alive, and you know, possibly heavily brainwashed."

The familiar shiver went through me as Holbrook talked about the possibility of Elizabeth being alive. It increased when he told me about an incident that happened earlier in the week. Holbrook was commuting home one evening on the bus and was talking on his cell phone about his brother-in-law's possible connection to the kidnapping of Elizabeth Smart. As he talked, a female passenger who overheard his conversation interrupted him to tell him that she had seen the robe-wearing preacher a few months earlier at the downtown library, and that two women were with him wearing robes and veils.

Tom said he had no way of knowing if the man at the library was Mitchell, but he thought it was important to pass the information along.

"We kind of wonder why we aren't being asked these questions by the police," Holbrook said before we ended our conversation. "They haven't asked a lot of questions about Brian. We would be happy to talk to any of the investigating people, FBI or police. We would be fully cooperative. All we want to do is find Elizabeth. If it turns out Brian had nothing to do with it, at least this might be, finally, an opportunity for him to get some professional help, because he is in desperate need of it."

After additional conversations with Richard Townsend, who helped provide details about the size of the cuts along the edges of the screen (thirty-eight inches along the right side, fifteen inches across the bottom, and thirty inches down the left side), countless hours on the phone reviewing information with David and other family members, more late-night research, and more sleep deprivation, I was more convinced than ever that we needed to do something to get law enforcement off its treadmill.

Hundreds of calls to *America's Most Wanted* and to the SLCPD had generated some action. One tip reported a possible Mitchell sighting in Florida that was promising enough to send Rick Segall of *America's Most Wanted* and the FBI to check it out. By Monday, March 10, SLCPD investigators finally showed up at Daniel Trotta's basement apartment to look for evidence and fingerprints that would verify Mitchell, Wanda, and Elizabeth had indeed spent time there.

I wanted to show patience and let law enforcement do its job, but it seemed we were at a point where we didn't have much to lose by pushing for action. Proving that Ricci *didn't* do it still seemed an important priority to get the search for Mitchell going on full power. To that end, I drafted a letter for Ed to Chief Dinse saying that we were prepared to hold another family press conference, independent of the police, where we would distribute hundreds of fliers with information on Mitchell. In essence, we would organize our own manhunt. There was no doubt in my mind that if we released information about the two veiled women to the press, things would start rolling in a big way. The plan was to forward a copy of the letter to the governor, outlining what we had learned from the state crime lab that could cast serious doubt about Ricci as the kidnapper.

A third part of our plan was to re-energize the media. In spite of the exposure from *America's Most Wanted*, the media had not jumped on the Brian David Mitchell story. The police's indifferent attitude appeared to be contagious. There were a few reports here and there. Locally, Scott McKane at KSTU continued to work the story hard, and there were others who filed periodic updates. The *Deseret News* published two strong opinion columns by Lee Benson that questioned the police's apparent lethargy in pursuing Mitchell, and stressed the importance of finding and questioning him. But there was no widespread coverage. It wasn't until I called Kevin Cantera at the *Salt Lake Tribune* that I found a reporter willing to stir things up.

The irony was, I hadn't called Cantera to do a story. I had called wearing my investigative hat to see if I could sort out who was telling the truth about the screen. In the article Cantera had written in the *Tribune* on November 14, he had reported that the then task force commander, Cory Lyman, said the screen at Ed's house was cut from the inside, suggesting an inside job. But when Ed confronted Lyman about that, Lyman said he was misquoted and that he was going to call the *Tribune* and ask for a correction. We had never seen a correction, and I wanted to know if Lyman had ever asked for one.

"You know, he called me and we talked about it," said Cantera. "But he never asked for a correction and I didn't, I mean, as we talked I think we both agreed that it was accurate." (Lyman later was adamant that he did, in fact, ask for a correction, but did not check the newspaper to see if it had run. Lyman said he was besieged the next day about going on the record about the screen and claimed he told the media that Cantera had misquoted him. He did not, however, set the record straight with the other media, but told the *Deseret News* that "whether or not it was cut from the inside wasn't germane").

Cantera vigorously defended the theory that he and Michael Vigh had been reporting for the past eight months. "The way I kind of understood it," he said, "is that whoever was in there, they cut that screen from the inside and had alternate access to the home. I mean in the Ricci scenario they think he had a key. He got into the house and then either on his way upstairs or on his way out of the home he makes that cut to, you know, supposedly throw people off."

"Right," I answered. "And what I'm saying is you're dead-ass wrong."

"How can you be so sure?"

"Because I probably have better sources than you do."

"You probably do. I wouldn't be surprised."

I explained to Cantera what had been explained to me: that just because the screen was cut from the inside didn't mean that *all* of the screen was cut from the inside, nor did it mean that the person cutting the screen needed to be standing inside to make the cuts. Then I asked, "Now, knowing what you reported, would you think that's a true statement, that that's what Cory told you?"

"If there is more detail I'd like to get an investigator to tell me that it was cut from the inside but that doesn't mean the person was inside," said Cantera. "Because, yeah, that is definitely a very important point to make. But no one made that point to me before just now."

I proceeded to get a few things off my chest with the reporter who had made life so difficult for my family. I told him how far off some of his speculations had been, but I was willing to give him the benefit of the doubt that I believed he had sources, however faulty. After a time, we discussed the Emmanuel lead.

"Does it bother your family that the police are putting this guy on such low priority?" Cantera asked.

"Well, we do believe the police are vested in Ricci. They are overvested in Ricci," I answered.

"Is there some feeling though—I mean, we are getting the feeling that police aren't very interested in finding this guy."

"It's Maslov's law," I told Cantera.

"Pardon me?"

"It's Maslov's law: the first, most important principle need is self-preservation."

"Huh?"

"Cover your ass."

"That's what the police are doing, do you think?" Cantera sounded intrigued.

"You don't want me to say that," I answered.

"No, you don't want a pissing match with the police."

"No, we need the police. Good Lord, we want them."

"But you also want to light a fire under their ass," Cantera said. "If I wrote a story and put in that the family feels Emmanuel is the biggest lead right now, I mean, is that good, and is the family good with that?"

"Yes. Sit down and talk with Ed. Ed will tell you that."

"I'll get Ed and we'll try to figure this one out," Cantera promised.

"Yes. And call Chris Thomas. Tell him we talked. I told him I was going to call you. But Kevin?"

"Yes."

"Emmanuel is the most important lead in this investigation, period."

"All right, I'm going to try to get that in there."

"OK. Bye." And with that, I hung up.

It was my understanding that Cantera's story would run in the next morning's *Tribune*. Cantera was going to write a story *not* pointing a finger at the family, but at the police. The reporter who had caused us so much trouble would be writing about our speculations for a change, and this time there would be no unnamed sources. I told him he could use my name all he wanted.

After talking to Cantera, I called my sister Angela, who was in Hawaii, and told her about the article that would run in the morning paper. As it happened, Angela had just watched a special on A&E about polygamy.

"I think she's with Brian David Mitchell," Angela told me. "I think he's got her, and I think it's got something to do with polygamy." But she added a caution. "Be careful, Tom," she said. "Don't get too close to the edge. Everything you're saying is right, it makes sense, but what if you never find him? Don't allow looking for him to put you in a padded cell."

That night Heidi and I had dinner with a friend, photographer Larry Rubenstein, and his wife, Jan, who were in Utah for a ski vacation. Larry works for the Reuters wire service. As we talked about what was happening in the kidnapping case, I told Larry about my conversation earlier in the day with Kevin Cantera.

"You need to check out his article in the morning *Trib*," I said. "Tomorrow, it's really going to hit the fan."

33

On Wednesday, March 12, 2003, 281 days—exactly nine months and one week—since Elizabeth Smart had been kidnapped from her bed, the *Salt Lake Tribune* published its story, "Smarts Frustrated with Police Progress."

Under Kevin Cantera and Michael Vigh's dual byline, and accompanied by a photo of Brian David Mitchell, the *Tribune* article on the front page of the local section laid open the contention between the Smarts and law enforcement that had been simmering for so long.

> Two divergent theories about who kidnapped Elizabeth Smart—one advanced by detectives and the other formulated by the girl's family— have led the missing teenager's family to openly criticize police for the first time. Since the June 5 abduction, the Smart family has been careful not to fault Salt Lake City police investigators trying to crack the case. But now Tom Smart, Elizabeth's uncle, says police are dragging their feet in the pursuit of a homeless drifter fingered by the crime's lone witness, Elizabeth's sister, ten-year-old Mary Katherine Smart, in October. To that point, she had not mentioned vagabond preacher Brian David Mitchell, who worked odd jobs for the Smarts for five hours in November 2001.
>
> "They should have caught this guy by now," said Tom Smart, who has often spoken on behalf of the family. "But the police are too vested in (their top suspect Richard) Ricci.... It's a way to cover your ass."

So there it was. For the first time in 281 days, the family publicly criticized law enforcement.

I say "family" but, in fairness, it was me. I was the one who had given Cantera what I knew were inflammatory quotes. Ed was quoted later in the article, which tempered my bluntness a bit. He said he hoped the police weren't "downsizing the chance to find Elizabeth. We can't afford to make assumptions.... When the only eyewitness says it could be [Mitchell], that is important."

But he did not accuse the police of trying to cover their asses, as I had, even though I had asked Cantera (and he had agreed) not to use that specific phrase.

The timing of the story didn't help David much. The day before, Detective Bill Silver had asked him to come to the police station Wednesday morning for a talk. When David arrived at police headquarters around 9:00 A.M., the *Tribune* had already made the rounds. "When I entered the elevator with Silver he told me I might get a few bad looks because of the article in that morning's paper," David recalled.

Detective Parks greeted David and Silver and all three went to an interview room, where the detectives placed a tape recorder on the table. They proceeded to ask David about a diary the detectives said they had heard Elizabeth kept. Did he know about the diary? When did he see it? What did it say? He told them that he had seen a diary of Elizabeth's the first week of the kidnapping when he had gone to Elizabeth's room to find a yearbook picture of one of her schoolmates. As far as he knew, it was nothing more than a teenage girl's journal.

The detectives said that they had not seen the diary and thought it might hold some clues. They made it clear, however, that they weren't looking at the diary because of Brian David Mitchell; they told David not to discuss their meeting with anyone, particularly the media. Silver also articulated the resentment the police were feeling over the fact that the Smarts had released the sketch of Emmanuel to the media without authorization. David responded that the police had supplied the sketch. Silver refused to believe him until Parks interceded. "Yes, the police did supply the sketch," Parks said, "but only because if we hadn't, we would have been crucified by the media."

David suggested to the detectives that if the family hadn't come out publicly with the Emmanuel lead the police still wouldn't know who they were looking for, or what he looked like. Parks countered by saying he hoped the public information wouldn't scare Mitchell underground.

The detectives complained to David that the family's fixation on Emmanuel/Mitchell was undermining the department's continuing investigation of Ricci. They specifically blamed the Mitchell lead for stalling talks with Ricci's widow, Angela. Parks stated that the Smarts, by making comments in the newspaper about Mary Katherine's contention that she didn't think it was Ricci in the room that night, had blown months of work the police had done in gaining Angela's trust.

The detectives' insinuations agitated David, but he didn't want to alienate them further. "I told them how much the family appreciated all their hard work and that the article in that morning's paper was pointed higher up the ladder, not at them," David said. "Everything cooled down and then Silver took me to the elevator and walked me out. We left on somewhat good terms."

Overall, the family wasn't too pleased with the *Tribune* story. They feared that it could cost us the cooperation of law enforcement. Early in the morning, moments after the *Tribune* article began to circulate, Ed and Chris Thomas started fielding calls from the media. Soon Ed was on the phone with me. Although he understood how I felt and agreed with what I had said, he was worried about the fallout.

I put a positive spin on the situation. I pointed out that we had the mayor on our side, we had the sympathy of the head of the state crime lab, and I was confident we would soon have the support of the governor. I was prepared to keep the heat on. I felt the next step was to go public with some of the SLCPD's problematic crime-scene myths. After that, we could release the Souper!Salad! report of Mitchell and Wanda having been in the company of a young girl.

I e-mailed a draft of the letter I wanted to send Governor Leavitt and Chief Dinse to my lawyer brother-in-law, Doug Owens, for proofing. Then I went to work at the paper. I shot three photo assignments that morning while trading phone calls with Chris Thomas and Ed. Chris told me he had already scheduled two television interviews for 2:00 P.M. that day in front of the Federal Heights wardhouse to discuss the *Tribune* article.

At about the same time I was shooting my photo assignments, a nineteen-year-old man in neighboring Utah County named Ryan Johnson took a detour on his way back to work to drop off the three passengers in his car.

Johnson had been taking a midmorning break at a McDonald's in Springville, about sixty miles south of Salt Lake City. As he was getting his food, a bearded man in grimy clothes had struck up a conversation with him. The man told Johnson he was a preacher coming from San Diego; he was traveling with his family to Salt Lake City to spread a new gospel. With the man were an older woman and a teenage girl. When Johnson was ready to return to work, he asked the man if he could give him and the women a ride to a nearby bus stop. The man accepted his offer. Brian David Mitchell got into Ryan Johnson's front seat, while into the back climbed Wanda Barzee Mitchell and Elizabeth Ann Smart.

They had packed up and left Lakeside, California, shortly after the first of March. Librarians at the Lakeside branch of the San Diego County Library System remembered the three of them coming in and asking to look at an atlas of Arizona. The Lakeside Library is on Vine Street at the edge of Lindo Lake Park, but Dusty Harrington, the branch manager, had no idea the man, woman, and young girl who walked in wearing "the dirtiest street clothes I've ever seen" were the robed people who for the past four months had been regulars in the park. "We just thought they were a homeless family and my first thought was, 'Why isn't that kid in school?'" the librarian recalled.

As the three sat at a table across from the librarian's station, Dusty studied the girl, who was wearing jeans, a T-shirt, a large windbreaker, and a pair of oversized dark glasses. The older woman had hold of the girl's wrist, Dusty noticed, as the man studied the map the librarians had found for him. After a short while they left without a word.

The map proved unnecessary. The Mitchells and Elizabeth retraced their path of the previous fall. They turned north out of Lakeside, making their way through California toward Nevada. Three rock-climbers reported loading the trio into their car during a rainstorm on Tuesday, March 4, near Escondido, about forty miles northwest of Lakeside. Mitchell introduced himself as Peter and told the rock-climbers that he and his wife and daughter were headed to Las Vegas. A week later, on the afternoon of Tuesday, March 11, police officers in North Las Vegas reported talking to three transients near the I-15 freeway—the main route to Utah. The police listed the transients' names as Peter and Juliette Marshall and their daughter Augustine. Although the three had no identification, police did not detain them or charge them with any criminal activity. As was the case with police throughout the country, the North Las Vegas police had not received notice from the Salt Lake City Police Department or the FBI to be on the lookout for the Mitchells and their captive.

In Escondido and Las Vegas, the three were reported wearing their robes, and the women were veiled. But by the time Ryan Johnson loaded them into his car at the Springville McDonald's on Wednesday morning, the "Marshalls" were dressed as Dusty Harrington had seen them two weeks earlier at the Lakeside Library—in dirty jeans, sweatshirts, and T-shirts, with jackets tied around their waists. Mitchell wore a wide-brimmed brown hat with flowers on top. Elizabeth wore sunglasses, a reddish gray wig, and a T-shirt tied veil-like around her hair. They were carrying tarps, packs, and plastic milk jugs filled with water.

As Ryan Johnson drove, he kept looking in the rearview mirror at the younger girl. Her eyes seemed to be trying to say something, he would recall later, but she didn't speak at all until she got out of the car and a loose door handle and panel came off in her hand. "I'm sorry," she said, and again Johnson had an impulse to talk to her, but did not. As he drove away, the troubling sensation would not let up. After driving the short distance to the Champion Safe Company where he worked, Johnson decided to report the strange family to the Provo police. In his haste, he looked up the phone number for the Provo Police Retirement System instead of the Provo Police Department. When no one answered his phone call, he gave up and started work.

The bearded man had told Johnson they were trying to get to Salt Lake City. Johnson had given Mitchell all the quarters in his ashtray, about five dollars' worth, and then dropped the threesome at a bus stop near the Springville-Provo border. From there, they made their way across Provo to the Utah Transit Authority bus stop adjacent to the campus of Utah Valley

State College near the I-15 freeway in Orem, about ten miles farther north and less than forty miles from Salt Lake City.

A UVSC student, Ryan Blake, arrived at the bus stop about 11:00 A.M. The mangy-looking threesome was already there, waiting for a northbound bus. About ten people were at the bus stop, including a recently returned LDS missionary who engaged Mitchell in a religious discussion that quickly became heated.

"They started yelling back and forth about God and everything," remembered Blake. "Then the returned missionary looked over at the girl and said, 'Why does your daughter have blond hair sticking out under her wig?' and the guy yelled, 'Don't ask me a question like that!' and really started flipping out. The returned missionary apologized and said he didn't mean anything by it. Neither of the women said anything. The guy tried to change the subject and finally took the women and stormed off, leaving the bus stop area entirely." But they soon returned, and when the Salt Lake bus pulled up, they climbed aboard.

They arrived in the Salt Lake Valley around noon. They got off the bus in the south suburb of Sandy, alighting into a business district crowded with car dealerships, strip malls, restaurants, gas stations, and the South Towne Shopping Centre. They first walked into a Wal-Mart, where, several clerks and customers remembered, the three looked at sleeping bags and tarps in the sporting goods section, and used the restrooms.

Back outside, they walked north on State Street, the main highway, in the direction of the Sandy light rail terminal and, beyond that, Salt Lake City. They passed a bus stop at 10200 South. They were 102 blocks now from the Salt Lake Temple and no more than twenty miles from Elizabeth's front door.

As the strange little group walked alongside the busy street carrying their tarps and packs, two couples in separate cars noticed them. Rudy and Nancy Montoya had just left the Kinko's at 10291 South, where Rudy, who was looking for a new job, was copying resumes. At the same time, Alvin and Anita Dickerson were driving toward the Kinko's. Almost simultaneously, the Montoyas and the Dickersons came to the conclusion that the bearded man on the sidewalk was Emmanuel, the person they had seen on *America's Most Wanted*.

Nancy Montoya pointed out the homeless people to her husband, who said, "I think that's Emmanuel. Call 911." Nancy picked up her cell phone and made the call. At 12:51 she spoke to a Sandy police dispatcher, explaining, "I think I see that Emmanuel they're looking for."

While Nancy was giving dispatch the details, Anita Dickerson's call came through. Anita had actually dialed 911 earlier than Nancy, after Alvin pulled their car over by the Kinko's and Anita got out so she could get a closer look at the bearded man coming toward her on the sidewalk. But the 911 operator had first patched Anita's call through to the Salt Lake City Police Department, who rerouted it to Sandy Police Department.

Officer Karen Jones, a member of the Sandy City Police Department for two years, was closest to the scene. Within two minutes of the call from dispatch, she pulled her squad car near the three people as they crossed in front of a cemetery on the east side of State Street. She blocked the far right lane of northbound traffic on the busy street as she stopped her car, got out, and motioned for the three to stop walking. The five-foot-two officer was in uniform and had a gun on her hip. Her first question was directed toward the bearded man as the women lingered behind. "What's your name, sir?" she asked. The man answered that he was Peter Marshall and he was traveling with his wife, Juliette, and their daughter Augustine. They were messengers of God, he said, free of all worldly possessions—including any identification. The women with him said nothing. When Jones asked the girl for her name directly, Elizabeth confirmed that she was the couple's daughter, "Augustine Ann Marshall."

While this interrogation was taking place, Officer Troy Rasmussen arrived. He stepped out of his patrol car to join Jones. "That looks like Elizabeth Smart," was one of the first things Rasmussen said. Jones, continuing to focus her attention on the man, since he was the subject of the 911 report, glanced in the girl's direction. "Yes, it does," she agreed as she left Rasmussen with the three detainees and returned to her patrol car to check with dispatch on the names and birth dates she had been given. At this point, she also had dispatch call the Salt Lake City Police Department and inform them of the developing situation.

Dispatcher Marty Reese ran the data Jones gave her through the department computer and came up with no matches. Jones returned to Mitchell and said, "None of the information you have given me checks out. You people don't exist."

"It is because we move around a lot and we have given everything away," said Mitchell, who then asked the officers if they recognized the Lord Jesus as their savior.

About this time, Officer Bill O'Neal, who had noticed the commotion while running radar farther down the street, arrived on his motorcycle. The girl looked familiar to O'Neal. "I know you. How do I know you?" he said as he got off his bike. The girl did not answer.

Rasmussen walked over to O'Neal. "Bill," he said, pointing at the bearded man, "I think this is Brian Mitchell, and that," he said, motioning toward the girl, "I think that is Elizabeth Smart." He said this out of earshot from the three.

A light went on for O'Neal, who had also watched the *America's Most Wanted* episode about Brian David Mitchell. "That's how I know them. Yeah," O'Neal said to Rasmussen.

In spite of Jones informing the transients that their identities did not compute, they refused to budge from their story that they were the Marshall family, missionaries for the Lord. Elizabeth became defensive when O'Neal, Jones, and Rasmussen asked her why she was wearing a reddish-gray wig.

"Lots of girls my age have red hair," she said.

"What's your age?" asked O'Neal.

"Eighteen."

"What's your birth date."

She hesitated before answering, "November 4, 1984."

"You sure about that?" said O'Neal. "What's your social?"

"You're insulting me," Elizabeth answered.

By now, a fourth officer, Sergeant Victor Quezada, who had been informed of the developing situation by Reese, had arrived on the scene. Quezada, Jones, and Rasmussen led Elizabeth about forty feet away to the middle of a dry cement pond on the cemetery grounds, separating her from the adults. O'Neal stayed with Mitchell and Wanda and peppered them with questions.

Mitchell told O'Neal that they had lived for eighteen years in Miami, Florida. But when O'Neal, who was raised in Jacksonville, Florida, asked for specific addresses, zip codes, and area codes in the Miami area, Mitchell could only guess at answers.

"That's not right," said O'Neal.

"How do you know?" asked Mitchell.

"Because I grew up there," answered O'Neal, and he saw a worried look cross the man's face.

"I work for God," said Mitchell.

"I don't care who you work for," said O'Neal. "Answer my questions. Give me an area code."

Two more motorcycle officers, Ray Howe and Brandon Colton, pulled up. O'Neal asked Howe to make a run to the police station, only a half-mile away, and pick up a flier with Elizabeth Smart's face on it.

About this time, SLCPD detectives Cordon Parks and Bill Silver arrived from Salt Lake City. The Smart investigation veterans stepped out of their car and onto the sidewalk and took in the scene of the shabbily dressed transients surrounded by uniformed officers. Parks walked over to where Elizabeth was standing and, as Jones had earlier, asked her name.

"Augustine Marshall," Elizabeth replied.

Parks sized up the young woman in front of him. In his view, she was too tall, too heavy, and her cheekbones were too wide to be Elizabeth Smart. But they had to be sure, and Parks knew who to call to find out whether this was Elizabeth. The detective moved to the side of the crowd and called Ed Smart's cell phone. He knew the number by heart. Lois answered and Parks asked for Ed. When Ed came on the line, Parks told him to get in his car and drive to the Sandy Police Station right away. Parks provided no further details but asked Ed not to say anything to anyone. He did not tell Ed about the transient girl because he did not believe she was Elizabeth. The SLCPD detective didn't want another false alarm to turn the situation into a media circus.

Isolated from Mitchell and Wanda, a worried-looking Elizabeth continued with her evasive replies to the Sandy officers. "I know who you think I am. You think I'm that girl who ran away, but I'm not," she said as Rasmussen asked her to remove the dark glasses she was wearing. When she said she couldn't because she had recently had eye surgery in San Diego, he asked her for the name of the doctor and hospital. She had no answer. Then O'Neal came over and asked her for her zip code in Miami. She first said she couldn't remember, and then made a stab at it with a six-digit number instead of the standard five.

The Sandy officers assured Elizabeth that she didn't have to be afraid. They told her that the entire state had never stopped looking for her, that her family was worried sick and would be elated to see her, and that she wasn't in any trouble; all anyone wanted to do was help her. They told her that she was safe and that they could protect her.

Still, the frightened girl tried to maintain her story. The cable attached to her mind connected her to her captors even as she stood surrounded by uniformed police officers with guns and handcuffs at their sides and a fleet of patrol cars and motorcycles blocking traffic on the street. The skinny, bearded man with the crazed eyes and his sun-baked, stooped-over wife were forty feet away, but their grip on the young girl's psyche remained. For nine months and a week, they had manipulated her impressionable mind, filling it with crazy notions that the entire world was evil except them. Her parents, her brothers and sister, her grandparents, her country, her community, her church—all were evil. They had taken a girl without guile, a child who was by nature and upbringing anxious to please, and used her lack of rebelliousness, her goodness, to achieve their own twisted purposes. Her identity had been trampled along with her virtue. She was poorly fed, clothed in bizarre costumes, deprived of privacy, not allowed to bathe, and forced to sleep outside in the cold. All the while, her captors terrorized her, using holy scripture as a weapon, as they systematically stole her innocence.

But one thing they could not steal was the truth. And as the police officers persisted with their assurances and their questions, the lies became all too obvious. As Elizabeth's mental battle played out, her chest heaved so much that officers Rasmussen and O'Neal feared the girl's heart would leap right out of her body. Officer Jones saw tears welling up in the frightened eyes behind the dark glasses as Officer Howe arrived with the flier from the station and placed it next to the girl's face.

She was heavier now—her weight had ballooned from the carbohydrate-heavy diet of the homeless—and her cheeks were ruddy from exposure. But there was no mistaking the eyes.

"Just tell us you're Elizabeth Smart," pleaded Sergeant Quezada.

"Are you Elizabeth?" asked Officer O'Neal.

Through her tears, the first strands of the mind cable unraveled as Elizabeth quietly answered the police in the language of her oppressors, "If thou sayeth."

Quezada looked at O'Neal and asked, "What did she say?"

Bending nearer, O'Neal asked the girl again, "Are you Elizabeth?"

Again she answered, "If thou sayeth."

Quezada looked at O'Neal and said, "We'll take that as a yes."

As police handcuffed Mitchell, Wanda, and Elizabeth, in accordance with standard police procedure, and ushered them into three separate police cars for the two-minute drive to the Sandy police station, Ed was already on his way.

He had jumped into his car immediately, anxious to know what the trip might bring. Obviously something had happened. His best guess was that police were going to ask him to identify something that had to do with Mitchell. Maybe they had even found Mitchell himself. Or maybe it had something to do with the *Tribune* article, although he couldn't imagine why the Sandy police would be involved.

Ed and I had planned to meet within the hour at the Federal Heights wardhouse for the television interviews. In the meantime, I had driven to the Intrepid offices in South Salt Lake to meet with Chris Thomas and my daughter Sierra to discuss how we would address the media.

While he was driving, Ed called me on his cell phone. "Tom," he said, "Parks called and told me to get to the Sandy police station immediately, but he didn't tell me why. What's going on?"

"I don't know," I said, "but we'll find out."

I passed the cell phone to Chris Thomas, who had a contact in the Sandy Police Department. Chris called his contact. The news was more than either of us could have hoped for: "We have a transient girl down here we think might be Elizabeth Smart."

I immediately called Ed back. "Ed," I said, "I think you're going to see your daughter."

To this day I can't explain why I was confident enough to tell Ed something that would have been utterly devastating if it had not been true. But I *knew* it was Elizabeth in Sandy. I didn't break down in tears at the news. I didn't freak out. Chris Thomas was also very composed as we both put our arms out and hugged and said, "Thank God! It is over."

Sierra, however, did freak out. "Dad, you can't say that," she said, beginning to cry. "You can't get everyone's hopes up. You don't know. Please don't go there."

But I *had* gone there, and there was no turning back. Almost immediately, my cell phone rang again. This time it was Amanda. "Dad," she said, "is there any truth that Elizabeth is in Sandy alive?" It turned out Chris Thomas wasn't the only person with a contact in Sandy. Amanda had a friend who was in a class at the university when three female students shouted, "They found Elizabeth Smart and she's alive!" It turned out that one of the students had an uncle who was a Sandy policeman, and he had called his family with the news. They in turn reached the niece on her cell phone at the university. Amanda's friend ran out of the class and called Amanda, who called me. Word was spreading fast.

"There may be some truth to it, but I can't talk right now, I'll call you right back," I said, and hung up. By this time Chris had called back his contact in Sandy and he was looking at Sierra and me with huge eyes. While he was still on the phone, he started nodding his head up and down very fast. What he was hearing was that Ed had arrived at the police station and had identified the transient girl sitting in the police station as his daughter. Sierra began sobbing uncontrollably after hearing the news, and I went to her and held her.

We tuned the radio to KSL and the news was soon on the air. One minute they were previewing a news report about that morning's *Tribune* story, plugging my quote that the police were too vested in Richard Ricci; the next minute they were interrupting with breaking news that Elizabeth Smart had been found alive.

My phone rang again. Ed was back on the line, calling from the police station. He was in tears. "It's her. I have her here. Tom, thank you, I love you.

It's a miracle." He could barely speak but he kept repeating, "I love you."

After racing to Sandy, despite what he had heard from me, Ed had walked into the police station wary and anxious. After nine months, he was not ready to trust anything but his own eyes. Officer O'Neal met him at the front door and informed him that, per police procedures, he was not allowed to tell Ed anything other than the fact that he needed to identify someone. O'Neal escorted Ed down a hall to the door of one of the station's interview rooms.

Inside the room, Elizabeth was sitting on a couch, next to Officer Jones, who looked up and moved off to the side when she saw Ed come through the door.

Elizabeth had changed since he had last seen her. She was in ragged clothes, she was taller, heavier, and her blond hair, free now of the wig, was in pigtails.

Ed ran to Elizabeth and they embraced; then, trembling with emotion, he released her and leaned back so he could gaze at her. "Is it really you?" he said through tear-filled eyes.

And Elizabeth replied, "Yes, Dad."

34

Mick Fennerty was on an airplane from Salt Lake City to Washington, D.C., and he'd shut his cell phone off during the flight. When he turned the phone back on after landing at Washington's Reagan Airport, there were fifteen messages waiting for him, all of them from Salt Lake City. He started listening to his messages and one of the first was from Juan Becerra of the FBI, who told him, "We found Elizabeth Smart. She's in Sandy."

At first Fennerty thought it might be a joke. To make sure, he called the Sandy police, where he got a confirmation that Elizabeth Smart was alive and safe and the two people she'd been found with, Brian David Mitchell and his wife, Wanda Barzee Mitchell, were in custody.

Suddenly, Fennerty's legs didn't work very well. Overwhelmed by the news, he dropped to the concourse floor. After a moment, the FBI agent he was traveling with helped him to a chair, where he buried his head in his arms and cried.

After he composed himself, Fennerty called my cell phone. I was still at Intrepid with Chris and Sierra. I'd just hung up from talking to Ed.

"Tom, did you hear?"

"I heard."

"My God, Tom, you were right. I can't believe it. I can't believe it. You were right." There was a pause, and then he added, "If you don't believe in God now, what do you want?"

About the same time I was talking to Fennerty, Lieutenant Jim Jensen called Lois at her home and told her to come straight to the Salt Lake City Police Station as soon as possible. He told her that Ed was on his way there from Sandy with Elizabeth. Jensen had no idea that no one had yet contacted Lois with the news.

Shaking uncontrollably as she hung up the phone, Lois asked Charles, who had just received his driving permit, to drive her to the downtown station. On the way, despite what Jensen had told her, Charles kept telling his mother not to get her hopes up. This had happened a number of times before, only to end with disappointment. But then Lois's cell phone rang. It was Ed. He told her he had Elizabeth in his arms and they were on their way to the Salt Lake police station.

"I love you! I love you!" Lois shouted to her daughter over the static-filled cell line. Lois and Charles arrived at the station before Ed and Elizabeth, and while Lois went to the sixth floor to wait for her daughter, she sent Charles to pick up the rest of Elizabeth's siblings from their schools.

Chris Thomas and I started calling family as fast as we could. My first call was to my dad. He was in Palm Springs, where he and my mother were spending a few weeks at their condominium.

"Dad," I said. "Elizabeth's alive and she's well." I wanted to get the "well" part in as quickly as possible. My dad told me later that it was the happiest moment of his life. It was definitely the most rewarding phone call I had ever made. Dad immediately called Ed, who told him that, yes, it was true; Elizabeth was safe.

Dad then went to the nearby condominium of Scott and Jean Calder, close friends from Arlington Hills who were spending spring break in the desert. Scott was home while Jean had gone with my mother and the Calders' fifteen-year-old daughter, Elizabeth, one of Elizabeth Smart's best friends, to watch a tennis tournament at the Indian Wells Arena. As Dad was talking to Scott, Jean happened to call home between games of a set. Scott quickly told his wife the news. Mom was sitting next to Jean at the time. She watched as her friend turned pale, said, "You better tell Dorotha," and handed Mom the cell phone.

Scott said, "Dorotha, I just talked to Charles and he had just finished talking to Ed, who told him that he had Elizabeth in his arms." At that point, the tennis match resumed and everyone had to be quiet. "I wanted to scream right then and tell everyone in that stadium that Elizabeth Smart was found and she was alive," said my mother, who somehow managed to stay quiet until the end of the game. Then she, Jean, and Elizabeth made a hasty exit. They were so overwhelmed by the news that they couldn't find where they'd parked the car. A volunteer had to drive them up and down the rows in the parking lot until they finally located it.

A short while later, the news was broadcast to the crowd at the tennis tournament. By that time, crews from Palm Springs television stations were already interviewing my parents outside their condominium. Mom and Dad gave a short interview, but as soon as they could, they got in their car and headed for Salt Lake City. Their hasty dash through the desert was a reenactment of their rush home from Ticaboo nine months earlier. But there was one huge difference: this road trip was born out of joy.

They stopped for gas and snacks at Twenty Nine Palms, a small California desert town fifty miles from Palm Springs. As she laid the snacks on the counter inside the store, my mother, bursting with the news, said to the clerk, "I'm Elizabeth Smart's grandmother and I just got the most wonderful news. She has been found and she is alive." The clerk nodded his head toward the back room, where the sound of a television could be heard. "I know," he said, "My mother called to tell me and I've been watching it on TV." Then he pushed her money back toward her. "No charge," he said. "It's on the house, and congratulations."

After I reached my dad I called Heidi. She was at work at the University of Utah Medical Center, where she was assisting on a procedure in the gastrointestinal lab. When they said she was in a procedure, I told them I had kind of an emergency. I didn't want to alarm her, so I added, "It's good news, so don't shock her." I had never called her at work before—she is usually unavailable—so they knew it was important. They hurried and brought Heidi to the phone, where about ten doctors, nurses, and staff surrounded her. When she got the news she broke down in tears, which alarmed everyone. But through her tears she gave them all a thumbs-up. Then she ran to the parking lot—and realized I had the car. She was on her way to Amanda's dorm on foot when Amanda picked her up.

David and his wife, Julie, were shopping less than two miles from the

Sandy police station when David got the call from Chris Thomas. "At first I thought Chris was joking around with me, but then he said in a stern voice, 'David, I'm serious, they found a homeless girl they think might be Elizabeth.' Then I heard shouting in the background and he said it was definitely Elizabeth and Ed was on his way to meet her. I just felt like raising my hands and screaming for joy. After all this time it finally had happened. No more searching or wondering. I ran through the store to find Julie. When I reached her and told her she just broke down in tears. Julie and I went running out of the store with all these people staring at us. We drove straight to the kids' elementary school to get them out of class. We didn't want to tell the kids what had happened until we went home and got our oldest son, Kole. When we got home, it was already on the news and Kole said, "Did you hear?" I asked him to be quiet until we could tell the other kids together, so we all piled in the van and I said 'Your mother and I have something very special to tell you,' and then we said, 'Elizabeth has been found and she's alive.' The kids just started cheering and Cessilee just broke down. Of all the kids, Elizabeth's disappearance had been hardest on Cessilee. She sobbed uncontrollably. The kids wanted to know if Elizabeth was OK. We said it sounded like she was healthy."

Chris and I had decided Cynthia and Doug's house, located near the middle of the valley, would be a good spot for the family to meet. After I'd finished talking to Heidi, I called Cynthia to tell her the news. Then I added that she could expect a large crowd there very soon.

"I was on the phone in the house," remembered Cynthia, "and I had a beep that I had another call. I looked at the caller ID and it said 'Tom Smart' and I thought, 'Oh, I'll call him later.' Then my cell phone rang next to me and it said 'Tom Smart.' I thought, 'Tom really wants to talk to me,' so I finished my call and I phoned right back. It was just before car pool and I was holding three-year-old Emmeline. I just started crying and screaming and she was looking at me and she said, 'Mom, what's wrong?' I knew she'd understand when I told her Elizabeth had been found, but I was so full of emotion I couldn't let it out. When I finally did tell her, she said, 'Mom, you're supposed to be happy.'"

Cynthia called her husband, Doug, who was in court, and left a message on his cell phone. By the time Doug got home, David and Julie and their family were there, along with Heidi and Amanda, waiting for the rest of us. Plans had changed by that time, however.

Already, news media from around the country were converging on Salt Lake City. The city had called a press conference in front of the police station for 5:00 P.M. I got a call from Mayor Rocky Anderson inviting the Smart family to participate at that press conference, but we decided instead to hold our own press conference, separate from the police, on the lawn in front of the Federal Heights wardhouse. It only seemed fitting. The place that for so long had been the center of the public search would now be the center of the public celebration.

I called Cynthia's house and asked everyone to meet at Federal Heights. As Doug and Cynthia and their family started on their way, Cynthia remembered the weathered copy of the "I will save thy children" verses from Isaiah that had been hanging above her bathroom sink since June. She asked Doug to turn the car around and they went back to the house to get the paper so Cynthia could read the scripture at the press conference.

My brother Chris was in the Phoenix airport when his wife, Ingrid, reached him with the news. He had just gotten off an America West flight and was on his way to a business meeting when he turned his cell phone back on. I'd called Ingrid about forty-five minutes earlier when I couldn't reach Chris. On the flight to Phoenix, Chris had stuffed Elizabeth Smart kidnapped fliers in the airplane's seat pockets, a nine-month-long habit.

"I got off the airplane and checked my voice mail," remembered Chris, "and Ingrid was saying, 'You won't believe it—they found Elizabeth.' She started out very calm, then she just started talking faster and faster and finally she said, 'Oh yeah, she's alive.' I was in the walkway in the airport right next to the security place and I just stopped when I heard 'She's alive.' I kept repeating, 'Oh my gosh, oh my gosh,' and the security guard came over and told me to please go to another area. I went down a little farther and I just wanted to confirm it so I called David. 'It's true, I'm on my way to a family meeting,' he told me. 'She's with Ed right now.' Then I was just inundated on my cell phone with all these TV shows and radio shows wanting a comment. I told them I was thrilled to death but I had to get back home.

America West was so great. I went back to the counter and said, 'Look, I'm Chris Smart, I'm Elizabeth's uncle, they just found her, I have to get home.' The next flight to Salt Lake City was in forty minutes and it was booked, but they got me on it. One of the people in first class heard about what was going on and gave me his seat. When I landed at the airport my friend Joel Van Orden, who had taken part in dozens of searches, picked me up. I'd never made it to Federal Heights so fast. We got there just as the press conference was starting."

Among Ed's siblings, only Angela wasn't able to make it home that day. Angela, Zeke, and their family were three time zones, two thousand miles, and one ocean away, at Kaanapali Beach on Maui, Hawaii. "The first phone call I got was from Cynthia," remembered Angela. "She was bawling and she said, 'Angela, have you heard?' The first thing I thought was Mom and Dad are dead. We'd been trying to preserve our parents, with Dad's heart problems and Mom's high blood pressure. There were times when they really questioned if they wanted to live any more anyway. They said they'd rather cash it in and then they'd know what happened with Elizabeth. So when Cynthia said, 'Did you hear what happened?' and she's bawling on the phone, that's the first thing that went through my mind. Then she said, 'They've found Elizabeth' and I thought, 'Oh my gosh!' It was such a relief that they found Elizabeth, whether she was dead or what. Then I heard Cynthia say 'She's alive' and it was 'Whoaaaaah.' The news was unbelievable."

Angela's family had flown to Hawaii on frequent-flier tickets and it was March, the height of the tourist season, so the airlines were crowded and spare seats were scarce. Hawaiian Airlines found a seat for Angela that day, but Zeke and the five kids were going to have to wait for a day and a half to fly home. "But Tori was so funny," Angela remembered. "She just said to me, 'I have to go home, I have to see Elizabeth.' I said, 'Tori, they are only letting one person on the plane and it's going to be me.' She said, 'I'll pay for the ticket myself. I have a thousand dollars in the bank. I'll pay for it myself. I have to go back, Mom.' So we called and they got her on the flight, and she didn't have to pay for it. They accepted her air-mile ticket. Both Hawaiian Air and Delta Airlines were very helpful in getting us back."

In my immediate family, only Nicole was out of town, and so she was the last one to find out the news. She had gone to San Diego for spring break with several friends. "We were actually on our way home and we stopped at an In-N-Out Burger," she remembered. "I had like five or six calls on my cell phone but I wasn't answering because it was out-of-state and too expensive. But I listened to my messages and both Mom and Amanda frantically said to call back because they needed to tell me something. I first called my dad and he didn't answer so I called Mom and Amanda, who were together. Mom said, 'We found Elizabeth.' I couldn't believe it. The first thing I asked was 'Is it a body?' When I heard she was alive I just broke down and everyone in In-N-Out Burger didn't know what was going on. We left and came straight home."

People all over the country responded to the news with euphoria. In Ketchum, Idaho, the resort town's new chief of police was in the middle of a meeting in the city offices when he received a message from the SLCPD that Elizabeth had been found, alive. The man, who for so long had headed the kidnapping investigation, adjourned the meeting and went to his office alone, in shock. "I closed the door and just sat there and shook," he said. "I was surprised how hard the news hit me."

In Salt Lake City, someone passed a note to Jay Rhodes, one of the first officers to help us the day of the kidnapping. Rhodes was with about a hundred other police officers attending the annual meeting of the Police Mutual Aid Association. There was some commotion at the beginning of the meeting, and Rhodes suddenly left the room. No one knew the reason, but at the end of the meeting, Rhodes came back and announced to the group that Elizabeth Smart was alive and home. As soon as the words left his mouth, the officers and others in the room spontaneously rose to their feet and started applauding. Many hugged each other and some shed tears, including Jay Rhodes, a good, caring cop who later told me, "I know there has been some bad press out there concerning the police department. But when you look at individual effort and take all the politics out of it, there were many, many individuals who went way above the call of duty to try to make sure that a little fourteen-year-old girl came home alive. In my twenty years at the police department it is the most complex case I have ever seen. I don't think Utah, in its history, has ever had a case like that. In a lot of ways, many of us will never be the same."

In Lakeside, California, Roy Miranda and Judy Gaspers got the word shortly after they watched a helicopter swoop low over Cactus County Park and the adjacent hillside where Mitchell, Wanda, and Elizabeth had camped less than two weeks earlier. Sheriff Gus Kurupas and his partner Jim Seal pulled up in their squad car and told Miranda and Gaspers that they had just received word that the kidnapped girl, Elizabeth Smart, had been living in Lakeside.

"Where was she?" Miranda asked.

"Right there," said Kurupa, motioning to the hillside. "That's where they camped. They were those people in the robes."

Roy and Judy exchanged astonished glances. "Them's the ones that did it?" they asked in disbelief.

When Angela Ricci heard the news on television in her trailer in Kearns, she received it with both joy and heartache. Elizabeth's rescue brought an end to the pain of the Smart family and finally removed the cloud over her husband's memory—but it came much too late to save Richard Ricci's life. "I've always felt she was alive. That may be my motherly instincts, but I've always felt that," Angela told reporters. "I believe that finding her should clear Rick completely. I just want to make sure he's completely cleared." Then Ricci's widow added, "It will always be sad for me because I lost the love of my life."

Debbie Mitchell and her twenty-one-year-old son, Joey, were on a flight returning from Paraguay, where Debbie had traveled to pick up Joey at the end of his two-year LDS mission. Before Debbie and Joey could make it to their home in Sugarhouse, where friends and neighbors had hung ribbons and balloons in the driveway welcoming "Elder Mitchell" home, there were already media trucks and reporters camped at their front door, waiting to talk to Brian David Mitchell's ex-wife. Sensing the unfortunate timing, Darrell Newbold, the Mitchell's bishop, found a house where Debbie and Joey, who hadn't seen his father since the age of two, could stay that night. Joey's homecoming celebration was moved to the Nibley Park wardhouse, out of the sight of the media.

■　　■　　■

Some have said that Elizabeth Smart had more support and more prayers offered on her behalf than any girl in history. I'm in no position to say if that's true, but I wouldn't disagree, especially after witnessing the amazing reaction to the news of her rescue. Almost immediately, telegrams, cards, and flowers began pouring in. It was as if the world stopped, for a brief moment, to acknowledge something good. In a way, it seemed that Elizabeth Smart had been stolen from everyone, and when she came back, the whole world got her back. The Utah Jazz were in Florida, warming up for a NBA game that night against the Orlando Magic. The Jazz players asked for a portable TV to be brought onto the floor, where they stopped shooting baskets and crowded around the set. The news fired up Karl Malone, the Jazz's star forward, so much so that he credited the forty points he scored that night to the news of Elizabeth's return.

The scene at the Federal Heights wardhouse was reminiscent of the search at its height. Satellite trucks with their cables and dishes were already lining the street as huge crowds of media and the general public arrived. But the somber, resolute faces of summer were now replaced by bright smiles, high fives, cheers, hugs, and laughter.

We moved as a family to the high council room at the west end of the building, once the scene of strategy meetings and heavy hearts. Members of the Smart and Francom families were joined by dedicated volunteers who had become our adopted family. When the room was full, we shut the door and knelt around the table and thanked God that Elizabeth was back.

By that time, at the end of an unbelievably happy yet excruciating day, Elizabeth was already at home. There had been a few tense moments before she got there. Earlier, at the Salt Lake City police station, investigators had told Ed that before Elizabeth could go home they first had to interview her. Ed and Lois went into a room with Chief Dinse, Mayor Anderson, FBI agent Chip Burrus, Chris Thomas, and others, while investigators took Elizabeth into a separate room. There they began interviewing her about the nine-month ordeal. While this was happening, Chris talked to John Walsh on the telephone. When Walsh heard what was going on at the police station, he asked to speak to Ed. "Get her out of there," Walsh told Ed. "She doesn't have to go through that right now." Walsh knew that Elizabeth was entitled to, among other things, a victims' rights advocate, and an appropriate amount of time to acclimatize and reunite with her family before she was interviewed.

Despite the triumph of Elizabeth's return, Ed felt he had once again been manipulated by the police. That, added to the fact that they were now trampling on his daughter's rights, sent him over the edge. At the very least, Elizabeth's interview should have taken place at the Children's Justice Center in a much more private environment. As it was, information about Elizabeth's ordeal was already leaking out into the crowded room of officers. Ed became so angry he started to shake the table. He demanded that investigators terminate the interview with his daughter. Some people were afraid he was going to start throwing chairs. The message was clear: Ed's daughter was finally back, and he was going to protect her.

Finally, Mayor Anderson told investigators to stop the interview, clear some of the people out of the area, and let Elizabeth have some time with her family. The police brought Elizabeth to the area where her brothers and sister were waiting. Elizabeth held her youngest brother, William, in her arms, as she teased Andrew about getting straight A's on his report card. They prayed together as a family and thanked God for Elizabeth's safe return.

After things calmed down, with Ed's permission, Elizabeth finished the interview. And although it is not standard procedure to let parents watch such interviews, investigators allowed Ed and Lois to observe. As Ed and Lois listened to the details of their daughter's captivity, all hope that Elizabeth had been in the hands of confused but caring people was dashed. After leaving the police station, Elizabeth underwent a check-up at a local medical center before finally being allowed to go home.

Meanwhile, on the lawn outside the Federal Heights wardhouse, the celebration continued. We each took our turn at the microphone, stepping forward to thank the thousands upon thousands who had supported the search for Elizabeth. Our common theme was "We believe in miracles." When it was Cynthia's turn, she held up the weathered scripture from Isaiah and said, "I would also like to publicly thank the Lord, God Almighty."

After the press conference, beleaguered police spokesman Dwayne Baird, who had come to monitor the activity, walked up to David and congratulated him, and told him that he hoped the family wouldn't hold a grudge against him. He said he couldn't do or say anything throughout the investigation without approval. "I was just doing what I was told to do. I was just doing my job."

At about 9:00 P.M., David, Chris, Cynthia, and I broke away from the celebration and drove up the hill to Ed's house. Chris Thomas had told us about Ed's outrage at the police station, and we thought he might need our support. All the window shades were down, but as we approached Ed's house, we heard laughter and piano music. Ed answered the door.

It was the first time any of the rest of us had gotten to see Elizabeth. She came up and hugged me and the first words she said were, "You know, Uncle Tom, I haven't been on a horse for nine months."

"Well, we'll get you out on one soon," I said. She was very shy and I'm sure she was still in shock—we all were. But the most heartwarming thing was that hug. She hugged all of us, and for a young girl who had been through such hell to be able to be so loving—the feeling was indescribable.

As we stood in the living room, Ed pointed to a button that one of us was wearing. "See your face on that button," he said to Elizabeth, and then he pointed to all of us. "You have no idea what they've done to find you. They've been looking for you for nine months. They never stopped."

David pointed to a shelf filled with eleven thick binders. He said, "Do you see all those white binders? They contain thousands of e-mails from all around the world containing prayers for your safe return."

"You mean all of those are for me?!" asked an astonished Elizabeth.

Lois put her arm around her daughter and said, "Yes, just for you."

As I stood there gazing at Elizabeth, I believed that despite all she'd been through, she was going to be fine. Elizabeth had come home.

It was well after midnight when Mom and Dad drove up Virginia Street. They had made record time from Palm Springs, but it was still late and the homecoming celebration had long since subsided. They considered going directly to Ed's home, but when they looked up Kristianna Circle all they saw were glaring lights and a small army of media, so they drove to their house. Although we had asked the police to let Ed's family have their first night without being surrounded by cameras, the street wasn't cleared until Mayor Anderson ordered it the next morning.

Despite the unnatural commotion outside the house, on her first night back, Elizabeth immersed herself in the life she had been away from for so long. Surrounded by her family, she watched her favorite movie, *The Trouble with Angels*, and made a stab at playing the harp for the first time in nine months—joking, after playing a few off notes, "Well, it's been nine months."

Finally, after countless hugs and kisses, and a long soak in a bubble bath, Elizabeth kissed her parents goodnight and walked down the hall to her bedroom to sleep. Ed and Lois told her she didn't have to go there; she could sleep anywhere in the house she wished. She could stay and sleep in their room if she liked. But she insisted she wanted to be in her own room, that she would be fine there.

In the same spot where her ordeal began, it ended. As Elizabeth crawled into the queen-size bed beside Mary Katherine, she held onto her sister's hand, and the two girls drifted off to sleep.

Epilogue

The day after began early. Most of the family, including Mom and Dad, met at 4:00 A.M. on Thursday, March 13, 2003, at Shriners Hospital to tape interviews for the various network television news shows.

We planned a family press conference at the ward house for later that morning, and we received word that law enforcement wanted to meet with us beforehand. Between the Francom family, the Smart family, and law enforcement, there were about forty people in the room. Cory Lyman had driven down from Ketchum, Idaho, during the night to make the meeting. Before the meeting started, he came up to David and me and apologized for some of his mistakes, but he added, "I have never been so happy to be wrong." FBI Special Agent in Charge Chip Burrus and his assistant, Dan Roberts, also came to congratulate the family.

When the meeting began, Chief Dinse went into detail about why Richard Ricci had been such a strong suspect. It was painful to watch him try to justify what had happened. Cynthia asked why the police hadn't sent out an all-points bulletin to find Brian David Mitchell. The response—incorrect as it turned out—was that police *had* sent out an APB.

David had perhaps the most pertinent question. "Did Mitchell have anything to do with the Wright break-in?"

"Yes," answered the police chief, which brought an audible gasp from Steven Wright, who had been asking that question—and not getting any answers—for months. The meeting could easily have turned into an indictment of law enforcement, but it became clear that it was a time for healing and celebration, not recriminations.

At the press conference that followed, Ed publicly thanked everyone for contributing to Elizabeth's safe return. "She's alive!" he said. "It's a miracle!" As part of his gratitude, he added a phrase only insiders would understand: "Thank you, Mick Fennerty!"

Chief Dinse then took the microphone and finally verified publicly that the screen was cut mostly from the outside; he said that the police now believed Mitchell had entered the house through the cut screen. The chief also stated that Ricci was exonerated as a suspect.

The media wanted information about how Elizabeth was doing, and they requested photos of her. The only photos that had been taken the day before showed her in braids and rags as she left the police station. The media was anxious to see pictures of her reunited with her family. There was absolutely no possibility of allowing an outsider to shoot photos of the family, but I realized that without releasing something, Elizabeth might be stalked by photographers trying to get an exclusive. And, too, I really felt the world should see a happy, beautiful girl safely at home with her family, not one in transient clothes and dirty braids.

After the press conference, with Lois and Ed's permission, I took photographs of Elizabeth and her family at their home, with all the photographer's royalties earmarked for the National Center for Missing and Exploited Children. We allowed newspapers, wire services, and television networks one-time-use rights to the photos the day they were released; after that anyone using the photos paid a fee to Getty Images. There were no exclusives, and no tabloids were allowed to use the photos.

While we were doing the photo shoot, the doorbell rang. It was Mom and Dad coming to greet Elizabeth for the first time. For me, the most memorable photo I have ever taken was Dad holding Elizabeth gently and welcoming her home.

The photos ran on the front page of most major newspapers. Publications continued to use the photos of Elizabeth's homecoming in the months that followed. As a result, more than $60,000 went to the NCMEC in the first nine months.

■　　■　　■

The afternoon after Elizabeth's return, I was at the *Deseret News* when my dad called. He seemed upset.

"Tom," he said, "I am worried that the tabloids are going to be coming out with all this information about Elizabeth being Mitchell's wife."

I said, "Dad, you don't have to worry about that, it is on the front page of today's *Deseret News*." In front of me sat the afternoon paper, which was just about to hit the streets. The headline that ran across the width of the front page read, "Elizabeth was his 'wife'." The headline seemed a bit of yellow journalism—a girl kidnapped and sexually assaulted isn't someone's wife, regardless of the delusional thoughts the kidnapper might have had. But the story under the headline was a solid piece of journalism, written by Elaine Jarvik and James Thalman, which extensively quoted Vicki Cottrell, who, besides being a good friend of Wanda's, was also the head of the Utah chapter of the National Association for the Mentally Ill. The story reported that Wanda had told Vicki during a jailhouse visit that, among other delusions, her husband believed Elizabeth was his plural wife. The article added, "The couple was instructed through revelation to take young wives, Cottrell reported, because as you get older you get set in your ways."

The *Deseret News* story helped communicate Cottrell's belief that, despite the terrible crimes of which the Mitchells were accused, Wanda had once been a very different person. In Cottrell's opinion, Wanda needed professional help. I told Dad that the plural marriage angle was painful, but apparently it was true, and if it was inevitable that it was going to be public knowledge, the legitimate press was the best place to break it—before the tabloids got hold of it and twisted it around.

That evening, Mayor Anderson organized a celebration in Liberty Park for the community that had invested so much in the search for Elizabeth. Lois did not want to leave Elizabeth alone, and Elizabeth was of course not ready for a public appearance so soon. Everyone felt it would be too overwhelming for her just as she was settling back into her former life. Mom and Dad stayed at home with Elizabeth during the celebration. A reunion photograph and a personal message blown up into a six-foot poster stood in for Elizabeth. She wrote, "I am the luckiest girl in the world! Thank you for your love and prayers. It's a wish come true!! I'm home! I love you all—Elizabeth Smart."

John Walsh flew into town for the celebration. Walsh would meet with the family the following day to give some much-needed direction in getting a victim's advocate for Elizabeth to ensure the protection of her best interests during the legal proceedings to come.

The celebration in the park—the same venue where there had been a prayer vigil for Elizabeth the previous June—was a reunion with hundreds of volunteers who had helped in the search. Lois was radiant when she expressed to the crowd that she was the "luckiest mother in the world" and thanked everyone for their long months of prayers and support.

Three days after her return, I took Elizabeth out for the horseback ride I'd promised her. Dad, Mom, Mary Katherine, Elizabeth, and I drove to a pasture outside the town of Oakley, where we keep the horses for the winter, and saddled up Moscow, Sky, Ranger, and Star. Dad and Mary Katherine rode on ahead and I stayed back and said to Elizabeth, as she trotted along on Moscow, "You know, we missed you and we are so happy you are home."

She smiled at me, reached across to my horse and grabbed my hand. "Thank you," she said. "I am so happy to be back." She kept a firm grip on my hand as I worked to hold back my tears.

Not long after her return, Elizabeth volunteered to take her parents, her siblings, and her uncle Chris to the two Dry Creek Canyon campsites where Mitchell had held her captive. They hiked along the trail in the bottom of the canyon, but she explained that Mitchell had taken her straight over the tops of the mountains the morning of June 5, and that it was already light before they reached the top. She showed them the shoe tree at the bottom of the Dry Creek trail where Mitchell had them hang their hiking boots and exchange them for sandals for their walks into the city. She showed them the lower campsite where they stayed in August and September, the apple trees, and the spring where they got water. At the steep hillside campsite at the end of the canyon she showed them the cable marks on the trees where the steel cord had held her captive. When Lois asked Elizabeth how she felt as she gazed upon the place that had once imprisoned her, she threw her hands in the air and said, "Triumphant!"

Since her return I've noticed a toughness in Elizabeth, a resolve to move beyond the nightmare she experienced. Theorists lined up to explain what happened to her and why she behaved the way she did toward her captors, including showing concern for their fate for a brief time following their arrest. More than anything, people wanted to know why Elizabeth didn't simply make a run for it when she was in public and had the chance. The name Patty Hearst came up often, as Elizabeth's ordeal was compared to that of the publishing heiress who was kidnapped in 1974 by a militant socialist group called the Symbionese Liberation Army that held her captive for more than a year. Patty Hearst was bound, gagged, raped, and kept in a closet for fifty-seven days at the start of her captivity. Later, before she was captured by the FBI, she was caught on camera helping the group rob a bank in San Francisco.

In an appearance on *Larry King Live* after Elizabeth was found, Patty Hearst, now a married mother with daughters of her own, explained to Larry King, "Because you have been so abused and so robbed of your free will, you come to a point where you believe any lie your abductor has told you. You don't feel safe. You think that either you will be killed, or if you reach out to get help, you believe that your family will be killed.... You have absorbed this new identity that they've given you. You're just surviving." And Patty Hearst had been a nineteen-year-old college student, engaged to be married, when she was abducted—not a fourteen-year-old eighth-grader.

What I observed following Elizabeth's return was a person who had done what she felt she had to do, not only to survive, but also to protect her family. Given her circumstances, her captors' irrationality, and her adolescent frame of reference, she steadfastly refused, throughout her ordeal, to take any risks that would jeopardize her life or the lives of her siblings and parents. Her loyalty and dedication to her family made her a pliable victim.

In early May 2003, nearly two months had passed since Elizabeth's return. Her accused abductors, Brian David Mitchell and Wanda Barzee (for a reason even Wanda's family couldn't decipher, Wanda identified herself to police by her maiden name instead of her married name), were behind bars, each with court-appointed counsel paid for by the state, and bail set at ten million dollars apiece.

After reviewing Elizabeth's interview with police investigators, the Salt Lake county attorney filed six felony charges against both Mitchell and Barzee, including first-degree felony kidnapping, two counts of first-degree felony aggravated sexual assault, two counts of first-degree felony aggravated burglary, and second-degree felony attempted aggravated kidnapping.

Mitchell went on a fast and refused to talk to his lawyer, prompting the first of what would become a long string of mental-competency evaluations. Wanda initially accepted visits from various members of her family, and from her longtime family friend, Vicki Cottrell, but she became outraged when they suggested she was anything other than God's chosen prophetess. She wrote off her family, and her own string of competency evaluations began.

The state court judge presiding over the case placed a gag order on everyone associated with the legal process, and Mitchell and Wanda weren't talking anyway. Wanda's family's hoped that her separation from her husband might help her see the need to treat her mental illness. But this hope disappeared after Vicki Cottrell urged Wanda to seek professional help. In response, Wanda wrote a letter to her mother, whom she addressed simply as "Dora" in her trademark calligraphy:

> For me to be in receipt of a letter from Vicki Cottrell has been the culminating factor for me to write this letter. It is to sever any further communication with you and whosoever else in the family who is lifted up in the pride of their hearts and self-righteousness and selfish ambition, etc.—and who call good evil and evil good and who put light for darkness and darkness for light. It is for your continued willfull rebellion and fighting against the Lord's true servants—being that Immanuel David Isaiah (ne Brian David Mitchell) is in TRUTH and in FACT the Righteous Right Hand of the Lord, Jesus Christ; and I, Hephzibah Eladah Isaiah (ne Wanda Eileen Barzee), is in TRUTH and in FACT the Mother of Zion, and the Kingdom of God upon the earth and the New Jerusalem. Who so hath an ear, let him hear!

In late summer of 2003 a grand jury indicted Barzee and Mitchell, which eliminated the need for a preliminary hearing. News of the grand jury was kept secret for close to a year when the district attorney's office announced the proceedings, a stark contrast to the grand jury convened for Richard Ricci, which had dozens of media staking out the courthouse.

After more than a year of motions and judicial delays concerning competency and media access, in the summer of 2004, officials twice found Wanda Barzee incompetent to stand trial. However, Third District Judge Judith Atherton said that there was "substantial probability she may become competent in the foreseeable future." On August 30, 2004, Brian David Mitchell was deemed competent to stand trial and three days later a trial date was set for early 2005.

The comprehensive Child Protection Act of 2003, which included the Amber Alert, passed soon after Elizabeth's return, along with other legislation protecting children. Senator Orrin Hatch told me that it might be the most important legislation on behalf of children ever passed. He stressed that he didn't think it would have happened without the public awareness that followed Elizabeth's kidnapping.

Like Elizabeth, I tried my best to return to a normal life. After months of neglect and the recession of 2002, my Winterton Farms development needed plenty of attention—but not nearly as much as my family did. My monomaniacal nature had taken its toll at home. The irony was that while the search for Elizabeth had made me appreciate and love my amazing wife and daughters more than ever, it also caused me to neglect them. I resolved to make up for lost time and let go of the obsession that had ruled my life for nearly a year.

But hard as I tried, I couldn't let the case go completely because of one nagging problem: the leaks kept happening.

Almost immediately after her return on March 12, information from Elizabeth's supposedly confidential police interviews began to appear in media reports. More stories from "inside the investigation" followed, citing the usual "unnamed law enforcement sources." A report published by both the *Salt*

Lake Tribune and the *National Enquirer* detailed a police trip to process Mitchell's camp in Dry Creek Canyon. The police's work was meant to be off-limits to the media, but stories and photographs followed anyway. Soon thereafter it came to light that the police had processed the wrong abandoned campsite.

Tired of the unauthorized release of sensitive material and the distortions and innuendo that were so often a part of it, Ed, David, and I contacted Randy Dryer, a Salt Lake City attorney with a solid reputation in First Amendment law. With Elizabeth safely home, we no longer had to worry that our actions would take the focus off finding her. We wanted to stop the leaks, and we wanted to clear our names.

At the top of our list of grievances was the story that ran in the *National Enquirer* the previous July 2, which alleged that Ed, David, and I were involved in a "gay sex ring." The story mentioned a "horrifying journal" that supposedly substantiated the claim. Our attorney conducted his own investigation, which concluded that there was no "horrifying journal" and that much of the scandalous information could easily have been verified as untrue.

Our attorney made it clear to the *National Enquirer* that its inaccurate story had caused great pain and suffering and that, in our opinion, it had displayed a reckless disregard for the truth. The publication agreed to an out-of-court settlement. The settlement included a monetary payment, a published apology that admitted the tabloid's errors, and a release of all nonconfidential sources who contributed to the story; that is, the people who fed them the wrong information in the first place.

Those sources turned out to be none other than Kevin Cantera and Michael Vigh, the lead reporters on the Smart kidnapping for the *Salt Lake Tribune*. We learned that in exchange for $10,000 each, Cantera and Vigh had sold information from what they represented were their law enforcement sources to Utah-based *National Enquirer* correspondent Alan Butterfield. Our attorney also discovered that in order to find out the identity of the sources Cantera and Vigh had used, he would have to talk to them.

The issue might have remained a private negotiation between the two reporters and Randy Dryer if not for a curious chain of events. After Dryer contacted Cantera and Vigh and asked for their sources, the reporters went to *Salt Lake Tribune* editor James E. ("Jay") Shelledy and, after confessing their clandestine dealings with the *National Enquirer*, tried to resign. Shelledy, however, talked the reporters out of resigning—he told them he would take them off the Smart case and place them on probation for free-lancing without authorization—and then, in his weekly "Letter from the Editor" the following Sunday, he broke the story, including his decision not to fire the reporters for their actions. He described Cantera and Vigh's collaboration with the *National Enquirer* as "akin to drinking water out of a toilet bowl...dumb, distasteful and, when observed, embarrassing, but neither illegal nor unethical."

Not only did the *National Enquirer* take exception to Shelledy's remarks, threatening to sue if a public apology was not forthcoming, but so did forty-three of the *Salt Lake Tribune's* journalists, who published a signed statement decrying the ethics of their colleagues.

In the ensuing fallout, the *Enquirer* got its apology from the *Salt Lake Tribune*, Cantera and Vigh were fired, and Shelledy resigned.

In a taped interview under subpoena, Cantera and Vigh cited their reported sources within the SLCPD, the FBI, the Utah Department of Public Safety, and the Secret Service—and information these sources reportedly gave them. The vast majority of the information was ludicrous and extremely painful to even listen to, but one or two items contained some details that obviously came from confidential information deep inside the investigation—information that should never have been leaked. But once it had been leaked, it got seriously distorted. It was obvious that Cantera and Vigh weren't the only people culpable. In the interview, both reporters extended apologies to the family. Shelledy never did apologize; that duty was left to *Salt Lake Tribune* publisher Dean Singleton, who later met with members of our family and apologized for the actions of his paper. Subsequent internal investigations by these departments named as sources did not result in any official censures or reprimands, and not one of Cantera and Vigh's unnamed sources was ever publicly identified. But the important thing was that the leaks stopped.

■   ■   ■

Gradually, the headlines began to disappear. The $250,000 in reward money was split eight ways—four shares went to the Montoyas and Dickersons and four to persons or groups wishing to remain anonymous. (The terms of the city's additional $45,000 reward stipulated that it could only be distributed following convictions.)

The ironies of this story are plentiful. Many of the leads that pushed us toward the person we called Emmanuel turned out to be red herrings. The light-colored clothing, the strange hat, and the fingerprints, for example, weren't the keys to solving the crime that we had thought they were. Mitchell, it turned out, wore a dark ski cap and normal clothing during the abduction (probably similar to the jeans and shirt he wore while working on the roof with Ed)—even though Mary Katherine's description of a kidnapper in light-colored clothing and an odd hat corresponded to the robes and biblical-style hat Mitchell regularly wore on the streets.

As for the fingerprints in the bedroom and on the back door at Ed's house, and the palm print on the window frame, all remain unidentified. However, those prints, along with Mary Katherine's statements, provided the primary impetus to keep investigating.

The reports that Elizabeth was taken at 2:00 A.M. also appear to be inaccurate, as we now know that much of Elizabeth's forced journey with Mitchell that morning took place in daylight. Still, the kidnapping, if not the getaway, would have taken place before sunrise, and since the moon didn't rise over the Wasatch mountains until daylight on June 5, and a tree blocked the streetlight from the girls' bedroom window, the only light during the kidnapping would have been the ambient light from the city. Given that fact, it is no wonder some of Mary Katherine's descriptions weren't entirely accurate. Color and shades of clothing are only possible to discern relative to the available light. She thought she saw a gun instead of a knife, and the "wrinkles" she described on the side of Mitchell's face were probably his beard. But what Mary Katherine nailed perfectly—the abductor's height and vaguely familiar voice and manner—provided the combination that first produced a generally accurate physical description, and later summoned her miraculous recollection. She doesn't like being called the hero, but without her resolve and amazing powers of recall, the investigation could never have steered toward Mitchell.

Many of the events that I thought were part of a law enforcement conspiracy to frame Richard Ricci also turned out to be just bizarre coincidences. When Chief Dinse announced on June 11 that "We are going to get you" and that "It is possible we have already talked to, or will soon talk to, the suspect responsible for this crime," he was saying what the profilers were telling him to say, not speaking directly about Ricci, who we now know didn't become a prime potential suspect until the day he was arrested, June 14. And the fact that law enforcement called a press conference to alert the media to the exact type and color of hat that Mary Katherine saw the day after arresting Ricci, and then finding that type and color of hat in Ricci's father-in-law's house soon after, seemed suspicious, if not conspiratorial, but apparently all these things were random as well.

Harder to digest is that the police raised the approximate height of the suspect after bringing the six-foot Ricci into custody, and that we were not told as a family that Ricci's DNA was never found on the father-in-law's hat. Neither were we told about the forensics on Ricci's Jeep, which showed no evidence of being splattered with mud. For law enforcement to send the family and many volunteers searching for hundreds of miles in the mountains and deserts on false information is inexcusable. It is doubtful that Ricci ever took the Jeep in the first place.

As for the story of the screen being cut from the inside, one reason law enforcement gave for being quiet on that theory was because they did not want to give away information about evidence at the crime scene. But the misinformation that repeatedly made its way into the media was disguised as fact. The pain that caused the family was enormous.

Perhaps the greatest irony in this saga has to do with my grandmother, the late Lois Cannon Sharp, Ira's wife. Loisie, as we called her, had a habit of hiring high school girls who needed work to help her around the house. Often these girls would also come help open the Weber cabin, the favorite family gathering place, and become a part of the extended family. In 1963, Loisie had hired a young girl from South High School. The girl's name was Wanda Barzee. Fate is the author of the most bizarre.

In August 2003, Angela Ricci filed a lawsuit against the Utah Department of Corrections and the Salt Lake City Police Department. In September 2004, the State of Utah settled the case for a sum of $150,000. The State acknowledged no wrongdoing. The case against the SLCPD is still pending as of the publication of this book.

On July 8, 2003, almost four months after Elizabeth's return, my daughter Sierra married her longtime boyfriend, Chase Campbell. We held the marriage ceremony and reception at Red Butte Gardens, a nature preserve at the entrance to Red Butte Canyon, which adjoins the University of Utah campus and sits next to the Bonneville Shoreline Trail. Elizabeth played her harp as part of the ceremony, a promise she'd made to Sierra long before the kidnapping. As I watched Elizabeth's fingers fly across the strings, I couldn't help reflect on the miracle that allowed Elizabeth to keep that promise.

At the reception I looked around and saw many of the friends and family who had dropped everything thirteen months earlier and started searching. My parents and all my brothers and sisters were there. All of us still intact, amazingly enough, still united, and more aware than ever of the worth and importance of not just the family as a whole, but every individual in it.

As a family, we have a form of post-traumatic stress syndrome, even after a satisfying outcome, which is a challenge to overcome. But with time, life is slowly returning to normal, something even more precious than before. Offering the greatest testament that such a transformation can occur is the person who went through the most—Elizabeth. Not only did she return, but she is really back—a loving teenager with a healthy sense of humor and an inner strength that gives her the ability to cope with each new challenge.